SEX &
SEXUALITY
IN MODERN
SOUTHERN
CULTURE

SEX &
SEXUALITY
IN MODERN
SOUTHERN
CULTURE

x x x

EDITED BY TRENT BROWN

Louisiana State University Press
Baton Rouge

Published by Louisiana State University Press
Copyright © 2017 by Louisiana State University Press
All rights reserved
Manufactured in the United States of America
First printing

DESIGNER: Michelle A. Neustrom
TYPEFACE: Cassia
PRINTER AND BINDER: Sheridan, Inc.

LIBRARY OF CONGRESS CATALOGING-IN-PUBLICATION DATA

Names: Brown, Trent, 1965– editor.
Title: Sex and sexuality in modern southern culture / edited by Trent Brown.
Description: Baton Rouge : Louisiana State University Press, [2017] | Includes index.
Identifiers: LCCN 2017008825 | ISBN 978-0-8071-6762-5 (cloth : alk. paper) | ISBN 978-0-
    8071-6763-2 (pdf) | ISBN 978-0-8071-6764-9 (epub)
Subjects: LCSH: Sex customs—Southern States. | Sex role—Southern States. | Southern
    States—Social conditions. | Southern States—Race relations.
Classification: LCC HQ18.U5 S46 2017 | DDC 392.6—dc23
LC record available at https://lccn.loc.gov/2017008825

CONTENTS

CONTENTS

ACKNOWLEDGMENTS

I want to thank the contributors to this volume, both for their excellent essays and for their patience as this book took shape. My other major debt, which it is a great pleasure to acknowledge, is to the staff of the Louisiana State University Press. Rand Dotson was especially encouraging at all stages of this project. Thanks as well to MaryKatherine Callaway, Jennifer Keegan, Lee Sioles, and all the others at the Press who make it an indispensable resource for those who study the South. I am grateful to have had this chance to work with them again. Thanks also to Joanne Allen for copyediting the manuscript.

Linda Sands and Amra Mehanovic, at Missouri S&T, provided a great deal of help as I prepared this book for publication. In the profession, I appreciate the good wishes and encouragement of Ronald Granieri and Mitzi Walker Jones. Thanks again, as ever, to my friend Vance Poole.

My family continues to be a rich source of love and support. My wife, Jennifer, encourages me, indulges my interests, and takes care of the important things. She does more for me than I deserve and more than I can ever repay. My children, Jack and Ellie, so far have seen little from their father's writing other than the listing of their names in a few books. My thanks to them here hardly seems much of a recompense for the time that my research and writing have cost, I'm afraid.

Finally, I wish to acknowledge my friend and high-school history teacher Donald Paterson, who expressed interest in this book in its earliest stages. Don's love and guidance over many years meant a great deal to me. I regret that his death has taken from me the opportunity better to express my thanks to him.

SEX &
SEXUALITY
IN MODERN
SOUTHERN
CULTURE

Introduction

On Studying Sex in the American South

TRENT BROWN

Stop that dope smokin'!

Stop that masturbation!

Take the lord into your heart and stop that fornication.

—DRIVE-BY TRUCKERS, "Too Much Sex (Too Little Jesus),"

    Alabama Ass Whuppin' (Soul Dump Music, 1999)

I have a regrowable hymen. I stay virgin tight.

—ARKANSAS WOMAN'S LISTING on a sex-jobs website,

    www.sexyjobs.com

In one of his less-celebrated short stories, "Black Music," William Faulkner writes of an artist—an architect's draughtsman—who wishes to be a faun, or a "farn," as he puts it. His client's wife (Mrs. Carleton Van Dyming, nee Mathilda Lumpkin of Poughkeepsie) fails to grasp the significance of his vision. "I saw," she reports, "a man bent over and hopping on one leg, who to my horror I realized to be in the act of removing his trousers."[1] The would-be faun later protests: "I aint as evil to God as I guess I look to a lot of folks" (818). While Faulkner's story is not set in the South, it does seem to reflect something of the mixture of misunderstanding and occasional punishment that has attended sexual expression in the American South. It suggests too the fact that southern vocabularies of sex and sexualities have drawn upon deep, old, and often chaotic stories of order, propriety, and self-expression. One of the central concerns of this collection of essays—and indeed one of its core arguments—is the variety of manifestations and embodiments of sex and sexualities one finds in the American South. The period under consideration roughly comprises the years from the middle of the twentieth century to the present, when the South, like the rest of the nation, experienced World War II, the civil rights movement, the women's rights movement, the gay and lesbian rights movement, and other bracing social and economic changes. The essays here demonstrate that there is no central theme to southern sexual history, any more than there is a central theme to southern history generally. That is far from saying, however, that there are not central themes, concerns, and common areas of inquiry apparent in these essays. So while there is no "southern" way of sex, there are indeed histories of its expressions and embodiments that merit further and continuing study by scholars of American history and of the South.

As one might expect, race plays a significant part in this story. Essays in this collection examine topics such as interracial sex in the civil rights movement, the Blaxploitation film *Mandingo,* and black sexuality in the comedy of Steve Harvey. Perhaps more than any other shaping body of thought and system of power, race has informed the ways that southerners have reflected about and acted upon their sexual desires and interests as long as there has been an American South. To take an example earlier than this collection considers, for instance, the laws of seventeenth-century Virginia early on manifested a concern with policing the sexual conduct of black and white men and women by defining the relationship of the children of enslaved women. Much of the sexual history of the South indeed has been inscribed in the formal legal record, from definitions of miscegenation to regulations surrounding heterosexual interracial marriage to current battles over the decriminalization of gay and (historically a matter of lesser concern) lesbian sex and the clash of federalism versus states' rights in the definition of marriage and the rights of religious organizations to enforce their beliefs in employment and business practices.[2] As the recitation of these areas of conflict makes clear, not all of the legal history of southern sexuality has to do with race, a reductionist formulation that tends to obscure as much as it reveals. But race is often surely present—overtly or implicitly—as rhetoric or as a shaping discourse in the struggles over legality and propriety that the reader will see in these essays.

Much of the history of the South has been concerned with the making and maintenance of notions of orderly and disorderly conduct and boundaries, racial as well as sexual, the latter history one that has increasingly engaged historians in the last few decades.[3] The history of race is so obvious and so tenacious in the South that one might be tempted to ask which of the two— race or sex—is more important in understanding the region's history. That question seems to me to miss or to risk conceptualizing the problem in the wrong way. First, after Foucault, it is hard not to start with the observation that both sex and race in the South are fundamentally about power.[4] Foucault continues to be quite suggestive in this southern application, mainly to underline the fact that sex and sexuality have a complex but recoverable history in the South, one that has involved discourses, institutions and other policing, including self-policing, and representations that replicate and disseminate ideas of proper and improper conduct. Essays here on venereal-disease control and prostitution explicitly demonstrate the state working to control women's bodies. But the statement that sex is about power in the South is merely a starting point; it is practically as obvious and as necessary to explore as the statement that race in the South is about power. Certainly it is. This collection reveals, I hope, that sex and sexuality in the recent American South have a vital history involving powers of many kinds that one must trace in order to make sense of the region's peoples.

Following Foucault, too, one must resist the temptation to tell the story of sex in the South as one of a movement from silence to speech or from repression to openness. Speech and openness—political, sexual, or otherwise—in any case have functions other than liberation, in the recent South as well as in the history of Europe. An essay here on Christian girl culture and sexuality reveals the complex interplay of rhetorics of sex, propriety, and liberation in the recent South. A necessary further caution is to avoid speaking of the history of sex in the South merely as the history of a construct. Since the 1980s, the history of race in the South has profited as well as suffered from treating it as a construct, as if, as too simplified a use of the term suggests to some, it therefore were not real. If anything, sex in the region has been treated as even more real than race, in the sense of its being fundamental, biologically determined, and essential to the broader social order.

Sex in the American South, however, is not solely a matter of legal history. The sexualized South, an important component of what Deborah Barker and Kathryn McKee term the "southern imaginary," has enjoyed a long, productive space in American representations of the South.[5] Some of the earliest examples of these representations, mainly textual, posit the South as a land of sexual license. One thinks here of abolitionist rhetoric that represented the South as a vast brothel, either literal or metaphorical, in which white men could indulge their passions and then escape the consequences of parentage by selling their offspring.

These voyeuristic, quasi-pornographic descriptions of the South served a variety of ends and exist in a variety of valences. The notion of the South as a brothel existed in American political rhetoric from anti–Thomas Jefferson attacks through Charles Sumner's denunciation of South Carolina. By the nineteenth century, the brothel itself was an ancient image that had served a variety of narratives of order and disorder, both cultural and political. In the nineteenth century it was deeply imbued with Orientalist fantasies ranging from Mozart's *Abduction from the Seraglio* (1782) through Victorian travel narratives. Representations of the seraglio, or brothel, like other American and European depictions of women in sex slavery, invite vicarious participation of various sorts, to put it delicately, and do not serve simply as a critique of a repressive regime.[6] This image proved so useful and marketable that not only the American South was represented in such a fashion. In the broader American tradition, the most widely circulated seraglio narrative was *The Awful Disclosures of Maria Monk* (1836), at once a critique of Catholic despotism and a titillating view into a community of sexually available women. Do these older images have much to do with the recent South? Some of the essays here, such as Richard Hourigan's study of the marketing of sex and men's leisure in the South, indeed show the lingering American fascination with representations of lands and places of male sexual privilege. One might point as well to a long tradition of representations of the South as a land of sexual freedom or access. As Anthony Stanonis has shown in his study of tourism in the coastal South, this image of hot times in the South reveals an interplay of outsiders' expectations and local businesses' desire to give the customer what he wants.[7]

Thus, there is a long and complex history of representations of sex in the American South, which always occur within the broader context of Western sexual discourses. For most of the nineteenth and twentieth centuries, these textual representations of a sexualized South, whether on the stage or in fiction, art, journalism, or film, were produced mainly by white Americans and marketed to and consumed by them. Very often these texts engaged in and constructed larger arguments about the health of the southern body politic, as well as southern bodies generally. Abolitionist accounts, as I have suggested, overtly stressed the depravity of the region; *Uncle Tom's Cabin* (1852) and *Incidents in the Life of a Slave Girl* (1861) are but two examples of a large literature that saw the corruption of enslaved bodies and those of slave owners as well as evidence of the threats that southern sexual license posed to the larger body politic. These narratives of sexual danger almost always drew upon a large set of nineteenth-century English texts that allowed the threatened domestic order to function not only as a political commentary but also as a source of vicarious titillation. Consider, for example, the figure of Eliza in Stowe's *Uncle Tom's Cabin.* Her staged representations, which almost always showed her racialized as white, allowed an audience to enjoy both the thrill of the chase and the thrill, as well understood by any avid consumer of several generations of horror films, of the pursued.[8] As these examples suggest, the history of representations of sexuality in the South is hard to separate from histories of gender in the South, a point that many of the essays in this collection serve to make clear. Discussions of mastery and submission always engage and shape broader discussions of gender and sexuality. Overtly sexual tales of sadism and masochism and brothels are examples that sometimes obscure the degree to which southern sex—without such consciously outré trappings—has been enacted upon a gendered and racialized field.

Sexual propriety, access, and order in the American South have long been understood within broader notions of social class as well as race, and those understandings of race should not obscure the lines and divisions of power and hierarchy within which sex occurred. An obvious example is privileged white men's decisions about the people with whom they could have sex, whether or not that sex could be widely acknowledged, and the ability of other institutions, such as law and the church, to limit or discipline sexual transgressions. There is ample testimony that white men of all social classes viewed black women—enslaved or not—as somehow free of the kinds of sanctions that might have policed other kinds of sexual behavior. For instance, sex with black women, when discovered, did not consistently risk the legal and even capital punishment that might visit white men who took sexual satisfaction from animals, other men, or white women who had the ability to resist or resented the forcible taking of their bodies. The law did recognize the need to ensure that the progeny of white men and enslaved black women remained under the ownership of a white master, but this is only the most obvious example of the South's legal insistence that sex between white men and black women was in a fundamental way different from other kinds of sex. The image of the sexually disordered or simply sexually uncivilized black person outside the moral (and sometimes state) law thus has a long history in the South and in America.

White men of rank and privilege (a privilege often measured often against the price of a woman's labor) enjoyed literal physical access to the bodies of women other than their wives. Joseph Crespino's study of Strom Thurmond demonstrates this point in a southern context.[9] Other Western cultures, especially in England, recognized that servants within the home represented a temptation to men and, somewhat secondarily, a moral and physical threat to the women themselves. An excellent example of the intertwining of race, class, and religion with southern sex can be found, as can so many other revealing matters, in William Byrd's *Secret Diary*. Byrd (1674–1744) is not a representative figure, of course, in his wealth, power, or excellence of expression. But it is not difficult to imagine the scenarios that Byrd describes being played out in many southern households of varying degrees of wealth. Byrd, for instance, relates a series of sexual adventures, ranging in location from England to the Tidewater and involving women from his wife through white servants, black slaves, and white women of presumably equal rank to his own. It is easy to scold or condemn Byrd for his sexual profligacies (six women in nine days in London) and for what cannot be called other than his preying upon those women without the power to resist him. But within Byrd's writing are other insights into sex and masculinity in the eighteenth-century South. For Byrd and his wife did seem to enjoy a sexually companionable marriage, at least in his telling. He "rogeres" his wife in moments of tenderness—after lying late together in bed in the morning—and also after fights, when they had sex "by way of reconciliation." Byrd also records instances in which he "took refuge in uncleanness," for which he prayed forgiveness, as he did occasionally for other acts and thoughts that he privately regretted as sexual transgressions. Byrd's contemporaries and later Americans would have understood his regret over masturbation, to take one example, as a feeling of guilt over incontinence or intemperance, and it is that understanding of intemperance that throws a good deal of light on southern sexuality. Thus, sex in the American South clearly has a history of anxiety and shame as well as one of pleasure and privilege.[10]

One of the most critical of these histories of sexual anxiety has centered upon notions of intemperance. Intemperance has been conceived in American history and in southern history as fundamentally a loss of power or control over oneself. It is vital here not to read the matter of temperance and control only through a nineteenth-century evangelical lens, the claims of which Byrd, to take one prominent southern man, would have no doubt rejected had he known of them. But there is no mistaking that nineteenth- and twentieth-century southerners were powerfully immersed within a landscape in which essential matters were understood through an evangelical Protestant lens, sex being a primary one of these matters. But in Byrd's case, questions of temperance and control were understood through conduct ideals that white southern men of Byrd's class believed were derived from sources almost as authoritative as scripture. One of those conduct ideals was a sense of honor and mastery inflected through their understanding of models of Roman republican virtue and manhood. That ideal certainly persisted alongside and occasionally in tension with later Christian evangelical notions of conduct and mastery.

As many scholars, including Edmund Morgan and Stephanie McCurry, have noted, white southern men's fear of loss of mastery—of their sexual urges or other aspects of their bodies—seemed such a present issue because of the literal presence of men and women who, in theory at least, possessed neither mastery nor even volition.[11] Thus, nineteenth-century evangelical Protestant concerns about temperance, control, and indeed purity resonated deeply with a white southern culture that already prized such virtues as self-evident goods. Well into the twentieth century, when white southerners imagined or represented chaos, disorder, or loss of control, their cautionary tales often took the form of narratives of sexuality, especially black sexuality, freed of civilized or civilizing restraints.[12] A common thread thus runs through such cultural scares as prohibition, the overthrow of Reconstruction, worries about black soldiers, the menace of the civil rights movement, and the polluting effects of Elvis Presley and other rock-and-roll artists of the 1950s.[13]

Many astute observers of southern culture, including Joel Williamson, have rightly understood that all these narratives of what Williamson calls "the black beast rapist" were animated by more than a literal fear of black insurrection and pillaging.[14] Indeed, Freudian notions of projection come so easily to mind here that it is tempting to dismiss them as too obvious and worn an explanation. But what if such an explanation is seriously entertained? What if the white South—at least the dominant cultural voices—were acting upon an impulse, however unconscious, that the policing of sex and the definition of orderly and disorderly sex were matters that pertained not only to black bodies but to their own as well? Some southerners have indeed clearly embraced Freudian explanations of southern sex and violence. Lillian Smith, in *Killers of the Dream* (1949), notes James Cobb, was convinced that "male sexual anxiety lay at the heart of the white man's impulse to lynch and torture black men."[15] It seems to me unproductive here to ask whether white southerners thought about or had sex more or less often than other Americans. Demographic figures suggest that the latter was not the case, at least when accounted in numbers of offspring. But what can be examined are the things that white southerners said and did about sex and sexuality. Such an examination need not yield confirmation of Freudian answers, but certainly should demonstrate the misdirections, vicarious uses, and conscious and unconscious deployment of sexual figures and types for reasons other than individual desire or procreation.

What then of the desires of white southern males, particularly heterosexual ones? For the large majority of white southern men, their race and gender did not provide them—some antislavery narratives notwithstanding—access to a brothel of women, degraded or otherwise, no matter how much nineteenth-century antislavery rhetoric emphasized the sexual improprieties of the institution and the moral depravity of the region. It is important not to view white southern men monolithically as willing creators of a system designed to check women's sexuality except in ways that satisfied one impulse or another of theirs. White southern men lived in a culture in which the obvious levers of definitional power simply were not apparent or accessible to all of them, nor is there convincing evidence that very many believed that they were somehow sexually privileged or deserving creatures. Far from it. Indeed, many men who recorded their thoughts reacted with the same anxiety as did William Byrd over the connection between sexual expression and incontinence, and not simply in a spermatically economic nineteenth-century view of the wasted energy in private of semiprivate vice, with its broader moral and social consequences.[16]

Well into the twentieth century, many white southern men were schooled in an ideal of manhood and masculinity that did not include the sexual libertine as a component. As in the antebellum period, the black man in later decades was often deployed as an example of manhood not fully realized by the failure to attain a civilized government of the passions. For instance, in Judge Tom Brady's *Black Monday* (1955), the manifesto of the Citizens' Council, the black man is asserted to be basically uncivilized.[17] Brady displays many familiar stereotypes associated by whites with black men. They are capable of "abysmal vulgarity" (47), along with less alarming childlike lack of restraints. They are precociously sexualized, which was of course long a critique of integrated public-school education. And the black man has a large brood of acknowledged and unacknowledged children, for which the patriarchal, long-suffering white southern man must occasionally provide (48).

A less sinister view of black sexual mores is presented in William Alexander Percy's *Lanterns on the Levee: Recollections of a Planter's Son* (1941). Benjamin Wise has recently shown us just how queer a text Percy's memoir is and just how Percy was able and unable to live the life of what Wise calls a southern sexual freethinker.[18] Rumor in the Mississippi Delta long suggested Will Percy's sexual taste for black men, although many who listened to such stories might have been inclined to view Percy's habit as a curious weakness instead of a fundamental degeneracy. Neither view seems to have occurred to Percy, for whom men were a lifelong sexual desire, whatever their race. Still, the mannerly Percy does give the impression that black men were more given not only to sexual license but also to vulgar talk about it, a habit that Will Percy for a variety of reasons would have abhorred.

Finally, one can always detect among some white southern men a grudging admiration or jealousy for the license or primitivism or escape from responsibility that allegedly characterized the black male experience, sexual and otherwise. Men long before Norman Mailer brooded over the alleged freedom enjoyed by black men. "The Negro," fantasized Mailer, "could rarely afford the sophisticated inhibitions of civilization, and so he kept for his survival the art of the primitive, he lived in the enormous present, he subsisted for his Saturday night kicks, relinquishing the pleasures of the mind for the more obligatory pleasures of the body."[19] "Just be a nigger for one Saturday night," ran the tired old southern saw, "and you'll never want to be a white man again." Of course such a remark reveals more than jealousy, including as it does an implicit view of Darktown as a place where white men can go to indulge all their carnalities. More ominous still is the essentially built-in excuse for exposing their desires (and other things) to black women, who must be used to all that, the remark suggests.

Much of this talk of white manhood, restraint, and mastery was built upon the figure of the Southern Lady. The Southern Lady is a well-examined but still central figure here, freighted as she is with so many larger southern matters beyond the sexual, such as ideas about other broader and imbricated issues of order and power.[20] But the Southern Lady, whatever her other attributes, was always represented as sexually chaste, a conversation feature or fiction or rationalization that persisted well into the twentieth century and beyond. Wherever southern white womanhood has been upon display, whether in beauty pageants or college campuses, broader southern culture and many white southern women have insisted that such women were or at least should appear to be sexually chaste before marriage and indeed not to present a sexual self, discuss the act or the desire for it, or otherwise acknowledge it outside the guidelines of proper courtship and marriage. Again, one should note that the Southern

9

Lady is fictive, not descriptive, but certainly real in the sense that she dominated a certain strand of sexual discourse.

Why this insistence that southern ladies should be innocent of sexual practices and sexual desire? The South was of course part of a long Western tradition that saw female sexuality as potentially disruptive and threatening—in some ways as potentially threatening as the sexual desire of black men (or white men). Certainly one common assertion about the South holds that old-fashioned or retrograde or repressive notions about women and sexuality persisted longer there than they did in other parts of the country. Within the civil rights movement, to take one example, the apparently greater freedom of northern white women to express sexual desire or to disregard regional customs caused no little concern to movement organizers, who initially expressed grave reservations about sending white women into the field in the Mississippi Delta, where they would necessarily come into proximity with black male bodies. There is disagreement among volunteers themselves about how much interracial sex occurred in the South in the 1960s, but the fact that the practice is so differently remembered speaks to its obvious transgressiveness, to black and white southerners alike.[21] White southerners were of course quick to imagine that the civil rights movement had a good deal to do with sex, as well as atheism, communism, Yankeeism, and other self-evident evils. Freedom Houses were reviled for their alleged interracial sleeping arrangements, and white women workers were subjected to coarse insults about their sexual desire for black men.

One can cite other examples as well of white southern insistence upon the appearance of chastity in the Southern Lady. Colleges in the region were slower to abandon *in loco parentis* paternalism toward women, with single-sex dormitories, close regulation of male visitors to those dorms, and deans of women to monitor and enforce regulations other than strictly academic ones.[22] Southern social sororities long considered rushees' "reputation" in their hometown, with rumors of sexual license at the top of the list of concerns. Southern college newspapers also appear to have been later than other schools to adopt the ubiquitous 1990s sex-advice columns, with letters and columns advising sexual experimentation among women sometimes drawing disgusted responses.[23] Beyond the campus, where the majority of southern women lived, there were also many other signs that they lived and indeed participated in building a culture that could be said to impose limits on their sexual expression. The cultural power of evangelical Christianity is evident here too, as public schools avoided or greatly neutered the teaching of sex education, with no apparent concern that ignorance of contraceptive technology might account for the region's high rate of unmarried teen pregnancy.

There is much more to white women's sex and sexuality in the South than the stereotype of the Southern Lady. Not all white women were southern ladies, either according to definitional stereotypes or representations or in the ways they lived their lives. Before nineteenth-century anxieties about black men's sexuality and black freedom and civil rights created the perceived need to protect white southern womanhood (and white men's prerogatives) from black men, the South recognized that white women practiced sex in a variety of ways, including across the color line. Seventeenth-century laws in Virginia and the rest of the Chesapeake recognized that white women and black men could have sex that was certainly not uniformly recognized as forced or co-erced by black men. In the early years of the Virginia colony, there were certainly some interracial marriages between black men and white indentured servants. The question of mixed-race progeny and the law was forced by Virginia's decision to, or need to, turn servitude into a racial caste system, with children of African mothers following the legal status of them, typically into slavery. By the eighteenth century, interracial marriage was outlawed in Virginia, as it would remain until late in the twentieth century. But what of the offspring of white mothers and black fathers? The Virginia decision that children follow their mother meant that these children would be free, and the relatively small but significant number of free blacks in Virginia by the time of the American Revolution largely descended from these unions of black men and white women.

What of white women's sexuality that did not produce troubling mixed-race children? As the example of William Byrd suggests, white southern men recognized some white women as sexualized or sexually available. Southern court records from the eighteenth and nineteenth centuries testify to the presence of prostitution in the South. Regardless of the circumstances that led white women to that trade, the fact of prostitution did at least present to white southern communities the fact of white southern women as sexualized beings, albeit ones that were by definition beyond the pale of respectability and of claims to southern ladyhood. The testimony and personal accounts of these public, sexualized white women in their own voices is rare to the point of near nonexistence, except perhaps in court testimony or, rarer still, in diaries and correspondence. Not until the twentieth century did southern women of whatever race or racial mixture leave much written public testimony to the ways in which their sexuality and sexual practices mattered to them.

From early southern days, however, and in contrast to the chaste Southern Lady, people wrote about and otherwise represented overtly sexualized southern women. Such representations tell us much about intersections of race, gender, sexuality, and social class in the American South. These sexualized women—slatterns, whores, or disorderly women—were asserted to stand outside respectability, if not always outside the law.[24] Again, little testimony exists to tell us what these sexual women thought of themselves and their sexuality. Social class presented obstacles as formidable as those of race in this regard. However, not all sexualized women were thought degraded in terms of social class. Certain kinds of sexuality, such as maternity within marriage, were publicly lauded. But sex for its own sake or sex for pleasure or any public expression of sexual activity—all were carefully or perilously embedded within larger discourses of family, the private and the home, and a medical establishment that spoke as if white women's bodies were not their own to enjoy on anything like the same terms as men were at least tacitly and in the right ways allowed to do.[25]

Broad representations of sex in the twentieth-century South tended to fall into one of two broad categories. The first assumes that southern sex is characterized by limits and constraints; the other, that it is not. The South is sexually repressed, or it is libertine. But is it? Even these representations (to say nothing of southern bodies themselves) seem more complex than a presumption that in one stereotype the South is characterized only by sexual limits, while in the other stereotype the region's bodies are as heated and sultry as the climate. Accounts that foreground religion, to take one southern cultural form, can just as often be characterized as heightening rather than inhibiting southern sexual pleasure. And not all these accounts score the South for hypocrisy. Suzi Parker, for instance, subtitles her popular examination of southern sex *Unbuckling the Bible Belt* and genuinely delights in finding active and various expressions of sex and sexualities in the region. Parker takes the presence of sex and evangelical religion as a fact of life rather than as evidence of an apparent contradiction. But she does seem to presume an irony, at least, in the presence of plenty of churchgoing and plenty of sexual interest and activity. Parker leads her volume with the autobiographical note that "the first time a boy told me that he wanted to fuck me, I was sitting on a pew in the First Baptist Church in Russellville, Arkansas."[26]

Of course there are many other examples from the mid-twentieth century and beyond of southern women writing openly and searchingly about matters of sex and sexuality. While W. J. Cash may have asserted that "the old sentimentality and Puritanism" haunted some white southern women with a "longing for the old role of vestal virgin," a number of others simply did not long for such a role, as haunted as they might have been by the models and practices in which they had been schooled. Writers as different as Lillian Smith, Florence King, and Dorothy Allison bear testimony to the variety of women who spoke with a frankness about the ways in which sex and the broader culture informed their experiences.[27]

In the American imagination, then, the South has been represented as both sexually open and sexually closed, as sometimes outwardly chaste and inwardly sultry, and as simply sexually demonstrative and open. Even more than representations of other aspects of southern culture, those involving sex and sexualities have had difficulty moving beyond views of the South as somehow inherently pathological, either because of its broader views of race and religion or simply because of inherent vice, depravity, and a sexuality that revels in the shocking and the disgusting. It is not difficult to see the instrumental value of the sexually depraved South for southerners and non-southerners alike. Indeed, so useful has been this vision of a South either benighted by race and religion or un-uplifted by education and sanitation that one does not need to turn to a vocabulary of repression or projection to find this kind of sexual South on parade.

The South's production of and representation in fictional texts, both high and low, has been so prolific and so influential that images of the South from these texts are often the first that come to mind.[28] Although he does not rank chronologically first in his fictional explorations of southern sex and sexualities, one could do much worse than to start with Tennessee Williams and his very useful division of southerners into those of high and those of low degree.[29] Williams reminds us that the white southern fetishization of the primitive does not play itself out only along racial lines but partakes too of sex across the social-class line. Blanche and Stanley of *A Streetcar Named Desire* are so well known that they may sometimes suggest to casual readers that the two figures represent conclusively Williams's assessment and judgment of southern sexual mores. But in the larger body of Williams's work, as well as in his own peripatetic and priapic life, sex and desire need not fall into Blanche's repression and consequent explosion and destruction or Stanley's naturalness, which leads into real brutality and violence toward both Blanche and Stella. No, many of Williams's characters, especially those who transgress fundamental markers of white Waspy southernness, find real freedom and liberation—healing, even—in a frank, honest embrace of physical sexuality. On the other hand, Williams could also express the chaos and destructiveness of the erotic.

In considering southern writers such as Williams, it bears repeating that the South that he uses as the setting of his best work is Williams's own land, not to be taken literally as a description of the southern mores of Louisiana or Mississippi, as much as his figures might have spoken to and indeed created impressions of the South that his New York audiences were certainly prepared to believe. His work is an imagined South, as vast a creation in some ways as Yoknapatawpha and just as influential, especially to a popular audience, through, in part, the successful film adaptations (usually neuterings) of Williams's plays. With a few very important exceptions, Williams's sexual South is violent, with expressed desire or sexual activity often bringing destruction to oneself or to others, as with Blanche's young husband, or characters variously literally or figuratively cannibalized, as in *Night of the Iguana* or *Suddenly, Last Summer.* In considering the southern settings of these two plays, it is perhaps enough to say that Williams was ahead of the scholarly curve in mapping a global South. But there is certainly also an important strand in Williams that treats violent sex or violence stemming from sex not as evidence of the dysfunctional fruits of American or southern puritanism or hypocrisy but rather as evidence of a taste for sexual violence against women that it is difficult not to see as misogynistic. There is Blanche, of course, but also the example of *27 Wagons Full of Cotton,* in which rape seems to be rape in a grimly literal sense, whether or not it is somehow figured as New South or new men versus old ones or not. There are no useful or intriguing Dionysian analogues that can quite carry those rapes into the figurative in ways that many of Williams's other scenes can be read.

Williams should not be singled out here, for many other representors of the South have given audiences tastes of southern bodies, particularly women's bodies, which are there for the taking and the using. For much of the twentieth century, these white southern female bodies freely to be had were largely working-class ones—or, more true to the southern setting, hillbilly, redneck, or white trash ones. For every bit of lip service that southern politicians, certainly through the Emmett Till lynching, paid to the homogeneity and sanctity of the white female body, imaginative works certainly did draw a line between those whose white southern female bodies could be ogled, touched, or even vicariously penetrated and those whose respectability seemed largely to foreclose that possibility. The degenerate southern white female body has enjoyed a long run, from Erskine Caldwell through John Faulkner through Larry Brown, to take only a few examples drawn from the ranks of the region's novelists. In film, the figure enjoyed a vivid Indian summer in various hicksploitation films of the 1970s, such as *Gator Bait,* in which a woman is murdered with a shotgun blast to the vagina.

That garish, awful violence, to be found in a variety of 1970s exploitation films, certainly says both a lot and a little about the South. If nothing else, it reinforces the sense many southerners have had that any act of degeneracy set in the American South will be viewed by some observers as documentary. One can only imagine the disappointment of some people to learn that the Trans-Mississippi Amateur is not a film but instead a golf tournament dating from 1901 played on the Gulf Coast. But the South cannot protest too loudly if some people associate the region with sexual freaks, as southern writers have indeed purveyed some of those images. Faulkner's Oxford neighbors certainly thought so, but interestingly enough, the figure that most drew their ire was not the city druggist's clerk swindling Dewey Dell Bundren, or Ike Snopes besmirching the family name by stock diddling, but rather the gangster Popeye raping the Ole Miss "coed" Temple Drake with a corn cob, which Faulkner had the indelicacy to point out became bloody.

Representations of the sexual South also display the same sort of duality or Janus-faced quality that one finds in representations of the region's broader health. Some, for instance, find the South's code of manners, to take one example, to be charming, honorable, and a survival of better days that the rest of the nation has abandoned. At the same time, others see these manners as stultifying, retrograde, or the enablers or signs of a broad culture of discrimination based on race, gender, and social class that, whether or not it is representative of broader American trends, is deeply ill. So it is with white southerners and sexuality. There has been, especially in the twentieth century, a long tradition of portraying sexualized white womanhood that is not obviously to be read as degraded or as evidence of sickness. At the same time, of course, many of these representations that see white women as sexualized may be sexist or certainly

wink at, leer at, or objectify white women's bodies or use them as an erotic fan-
tasyland, often partaking of the same kind of enjoyment of the primitive that
marks many white male fantasies about access to dark-skinned women.

To take two examples from many options, consider two southern Daisys:
Yoakum and Duke. The first is from the long-running comic strip "Lil' Abner,"
by Al Capp. The second is from the 1970s television series *Dukes of Hazzard*.
Both Daisys are highly attractive, although the cartoon Daisy sports an exaggerated pair of breasts. Both are customarily attired, with little concession for
weather or seasons, in cut-off shorts, to which the latter of the Daisys gave her
name in broader popular culture. Both are sexually alluring but not seemingly
sexually active. Indeed, for years the plot of the comic strip featured attempts
by Daisy to lure Lil' Abner to the marriage altar by hook or by crook. When
she finally did in the 1950s, the event made the cover of *Life* magazine. Both
Daisys could be viewed as nongrotesque sexualized women because the men
with whom they were featured were essentially nonsexualized boys. Hunky, to
be sure, and rubes of a sort, especially Lil' Abner, but by no means were Abner
and the Duke boys obviously sexually active. But of course one cannot say that
images or impressions of degenerate southern white women did not suggest
other, less conventionally authorized ways to read those and other nonsexualized characters, as a host of Mexican pornographic comics (Tijuana Bibles)
and other obscene renderings make clear.[30]

Representations of the South have also long traded in representations of
white and black women who are not obviously sexualized and are chaste too.
Perhaps the most famous of these icons is the black mammy, present through
much of the century in Old South fantasy films and on packages of pancake
mix.[31] But such women can also be white; witness Mayberry's Aunt Bea. The
playful girl children of *Hee Haw*, like the boy children, partake of both the
image of white sexualized woman and that of nonsexualized but obviously
chaste woman. The question of the chastity or the lack of chastity of southern
sexual subjects points to a larger issue in writing about sex in the South and
about the South generally: that of tending or wishing to see the region in terms
of dualities—oppression and freedom; change and continuity; and of course
black and white. So much work by scholars of the South over the last half century has pointed to the limits of these schemas that it seems hardly necessary
to say so. "National perceptions of the South," writes Karen Cox, "were, undeniably, often oversimplified."[32] And it is also quite clear that southern representations and southern subjects alike show many, many exceptions to this

tendency to view the South and southerners as falling into one of two main categories. But it is at least worth considering the degree to which this desire for binaries has shaped not only representations of the sexual South but also the experiences of southern sexual subjects.

It is certainly the case that well into the twentieth century the South treated interracial sex as a practice that was shaped both by conceptions of dualities and by an awareness that these dualities were at a real, live level hardly natural. Marriage between blacks and whites was proscribed. Children at birth were assigned to one of two racial categories. Brothels as well as other public accommodations in some cities were racially segregated. White mobs could exact murderous retribution upon black men who allegedly revealed a desire for white women; certainly the Emmett Till slaying was not the last southern lynching predicated upon a black man's inappropriate desire for a white woman. At the same time, of course, not all brothels and prostitutes discriminated in terms of race, as Faulkner's Joe Christmas learns to his horror. White southern men long used rumor and supposition about black women as a pretext for exercising their lusts upon them, with varying degrees of coercion or violence involved. Southern churches and religious expression long continued to assert that sex and sexuality was either bad or good, depending upon the context and the participants. Ted Ownby has shown that southern evangelical churches had begun to lose their ability openly to discipline their members for sexual and other peccadillos by the end of the nineteenth century.[33] But as observers of the South have been well reminded over the last decades, the evangelical tradition that was at one time suspicious of the arm of the state later saw nothing improper in attempting to use not the church itself but rather the state as a tool to police their visions of proper and improper sexual conduct, with the post-1973 battles over abortion access being only one example.

Legal prohibitions against interracial sex and marriage are gone with the wind in the South, although a number of essays in this collection show just how tenacious the figure of interracial sex has been in regional culture and just how many arguments about propriety, order, and manners do have at root something to do with the region's lingering ghosts of what was publicly prohibited but often privately experienced. Other conflicts over sex and sexuality in the recent South are more overt and do not have to be limned for any hidden languages or the return of anything repressed. Gay and lesbian rights and sex education in public schools, to take two examples explored in the essays in this volume, continue to be highly contested fields.

Southern states have been creative leaders in attempting to limit access to abortion services, with many southern politicians frankly avowing their intention to shut down abortion providers entirely. Southern states were among the last to decriminalize consensual homosexual relations, even within the privacy of one's own home, as the 1996 Supreme Court decision of *Bower v. Hardwick* reminds us. Currently, the South seems determined to resist a national swell of legal and other opinion making marriage legally available to all citizens. Some states, including Mississippi, continue to maintain that gays and lesbians make unfit adoptive parents. And since the 1980s, at least, the region has been home to various organizations that wish to monitor and press the film and entertainment industries to refrain from portraying unacceptable forms of sexual content, especially in materials that may be available to minors. But none of these attempts should be taken to mean that the South is anti-sex in any simplistic or dualistic sense of the term. Indeed, defenders of any of these initiatives would maintain that it is not sex per se that is wrong, but rather sex that is not traditional or is presented in an inappropriate fashion. To repeat, nothing suggests that the South is or has been opposed to sex or sexual pleasure itself. But what has mattered and continues to matter is the fact that sex and sexualities shape and are shaped by a culture that has been—for both black and white southerners—an oppositional culture for significant parts of the twentieth and early twenty-first centuries, thus accounting in part for some perceptions that the region is puritanical or not sex-friendly.

The South has never been of one mind about sex and sexuality, of course, and it is inaccurate to see the region's peoples as making and experiencing sex only within clearly defined limits of propriety and impropriety. Or perhaps it is better to say that the region's peoples—black, white, and other races—have found the lure of the improper to be alluring. Southern music, folktales, and jokes have exhibited a variety of uninhibited expressions of sex, starting with jokes as old as English letters involving cuckolding or the use of sex to bring the haughty low or to point out the hypocrisy of southern saints such as preachers and church women. Music, especially the blues but also country and rock and roll, have featured frank and spirited defenses of sex as freedom, rebellion, or recreation, whether it violates social lines of respectability or not. And southerners and non-southerners alike have drawn upon the region's reputation for commonness and even depravity by making the region the site of countless stories about incest and bestiality, with again the works of William Faulkner featuring some of the most noted representations of the southern vices. But none of this play on or use of sex should be construed as an argument that sex in the South is singular or that there is a southern way of sex that departs in substantive ways from sex and sexualities in the rest of the United States. For sex is yet another southern cultural practice that has not existed in isolation from the rest of the United States but rather has been engaged in a complex counterpoint that has certainly given the South as much as the rest of the nation has taken from it.

Sex in the South has been both imagined and made and has involved physical bodies and places as much as it has occupied and created imagined ones. These physical places are made and used within a broader cultural context in which bodies and spaces are begotten and made by the imagination. Consider a list of iconic southern places that have been made and used in the production of sex and sexualities: backseats of cars; pickup trucks; pastures and fields and rivers and streams; antebellum mansions and tenant shacks; barns and even churches; and the southern woodlands themselves, where, as William Alexander Percy famously put it, the common (and trashy, in Percy's judgment) southern Anglo-Saxons retreated to fight and fornicate after their passions were aroused by religious revival services.

It is important here too not to overemphasize the degree to which southern sex has been experienced as either liberatory or enjoyably transgressive. Many of the most frank expressions of southern sex, such as the lyrics of the blues, tell of a physicality that exists within a culture of violence and repression, within which sex is seen not as an escape but as an expression of that violence, as Adam Gussow has noted in his examination of the southern blues subject.[34] For many southerners, especially women, sex was long associated with anxiety over the dangers of childbirth. It is certainly true as well to say that the intense religiosity of much of the South has made sex a site of guilt, and not a pleasurable guilt that comes with the satisfaction of pushing back against cultural constraints. Pace Freud, sometimes guilt is guilt, and it has certainly led to destructive or self-destructive expressions of sexuality in the South.

Sex in the South has always been political in the strict sense of its being a matter of the state. So sex remains a contested issue of electoral politics and public policy. As in other electorally conservative sections of the country, the southern states have witnessed abortion become a perennial issue of concern to "values voters," who seek to restrict it, as well as a smaller number of activists who insist on women's access to a guaranteed right. The provision and content of sex education in public schools has been another area of broad concern in the region, with most conservative voters insisting that the schools ought not to tempt young minds with amoral sexual instruction, as they see it. More recently, gay and lesbian marriage and the rights of transgendered people have become matters of great moment in southern churches and among politically active people in the region. In short, then, the South has trended conservative on most of the major issues of sex and sexuality that admit of contest in the political arena. At the same time, the region features some of the nation's highest rates of teen motherhood, unwed pregnancy and birth, and divorce. But should these gaps between legislative prescriptions and southern behavior be seen as evidence of hypocrisy? Or social control that replicates earlier patterns of discrimination along lines of race, class, and gender? Or of evidence that committed social activists have a disproportionate voice in southern legislatures, as they do in presidential election campaigns? No potential answers to the questions allow the story of sex and sexuality in the recent South to be cast neatly as a narrative of progress and liberation.

For one thing, it is abundantly clear that to many southerners of all races, openness and frankness about sex—whether in a biology classroom or in a movie theater—has not been a sign of progress. Quite the opposite, in fact, as a host of southern moral censors since the 1970s have argued. In these tellings, the South has succumbed to a broader American culture of immorality and degradation that can best be corrected by evangelical Christianity and vigorous political action. But there have always been southern as well as other American voices that see the signs of the time as signs of moral decline, and there probably always will be. As in other times of moral worry and outrage, the targets and monsters of these tales tell us much about the South. Tales of a white slave trade have been current, in one form or another, for nearly one hundred years. Some contemporary southerners worry about a global South that has brought an international trade in women and children for sexual purposes to the region. Fears of predatory homosexuals or pedophiles (sometimes southern narratives fail to draw a distinction here) have been a regular feature of southern discourse whenever gay and lesbian rights have become a national or a regional issue. Opposition to abortion is in no sense regionally specific or exclusive, except in the creativity of states such as Texas and Mississippi to find new ways to limit access to it. Most recently, Planned Parenthood has served as a convenient boogeyman and as a literal target for the ire of antiabortion activists in all areas of the country.

What of the oldest and most tenacious of the southern cast of sexual villains, the black beast rapist, as Joel Williamson called the figure? Fear of that creature and the lynchings sometimes justified as a means of repressing him were indeed one of the figures of southern sex that seemed to make the region different in not only degree but kind. Where has the creature gone? In one sense, of course, the black beast is no longer the star attraction that he was for so long in southern political discourse from Reconstruction through battles over public-school desegregation. The last period of clear, overt, and unapologetic deployment of the black beast in southern political and cultural discourse was from the mid-1950s through the mid-1960s, from the Brown decision through the Freedom Summer of 1964. Such was the case in Mississippi, at least. Mississippi was often the state where the language of racial difference and the violence that supported it were most overtly deployed. The Citizens' Council especially featured in its publications the specter of school integration leading to rape, interracial sex, and venereal disease. Such worries were expressed initially in Thomas Brady's *Black Monday* and continued in the pages of the council's periodical, *The Citizen,* which provided readers into the 1960s with news of violence and teen pregnancies that attended the racial integration of public schools in northern and midwestern cities, as well as Washington, DC.

During the voter-registration and other civil rights campaigns in the South in the early and mid-1960s, both activists and their critics were aware of the potentially volatile mixture of black male and white female activists. But sometimes the alleged threat of interracial sex was more overtly expressed, as in McComb, Mississippi, in 1964, when opponents of the voter-registration drive in that city alleged that black men intended a campaign of rape against white women. So, then, the black beast rapist figure crescendoed rather than diminished in the years just before the 1970s, by which time such stories seemed to have disappeared from the southern mainstream press and southern political discourse. However, it is certainly more accurate to say that the figure did not simply disappear but rather took other forms, some overtly sexual and southern, others not.

The disorderly black man fit well into broader American narratives about social breakdown and the need for law and order that figured so prominently in the rise of the conservative movement in the 1970s and 1980s. The best-known example here is the Willie Horton television advertisement featuring a literal black rapist that George H. W. Bush used against Michael Dukakis in the 1988 presidential campaign. Today, the figure of the disordered and disordering colored rapist has become a staple of anti-immigration politics, with rape and murder standing as a galvanizing figure to stir opposition to immigrants from areas south of the southern border of the United States. Walls, not lynching, are offered as the potential solution these days, along with a liberal application of the death penalty, delivered Texas-style.

So, then, to return to the question with which this essay began: is there a distinctive southern way of sex? Is there a distinctively southern history of sex and sexualities? The answer to the first question is relatively simple. There is not, nor has there been, a particular or unique southern way of sex. As long as there have been arguments about the South as a section or a region, the sexual folkways there seem not to have been of one sort, any more than those of other people anywhere else. Southerners have imagined and performed their sexualities, and continue to do so, in a variety of ways. But at the same time, there has been a history of sex and sexualities in the region that deserves continued examination. The fact that this history has been shaped by and has helped to shape the broader American notions of sex makes it all the more worthy of study. Particularly in the areas where race and sex elide and shape understandings of each other, the story of southern sexualities has been a fundamentally American story, albeit one that is less broadly examined than those of other institutions and practices shaped by racial discourses. This collection seeks above all to show that southern sex is not to be understood simply along some continuum of privacy versus public or "normal" versus depraved or as solely a function of southern poverty, wealth, or other economic or material factors. Sex in the South has been fluid, dynamic, and resilient, at times operating in very broad daylight and at other times less obviously present in other discourses and practices. It has not been static, primitive, or pure, whatever precisely those terms may mean in this context. But it has been, and continues to be, a living, shaping element that is fundamental to the lives of southern people.

NOTES

1. William Faulkner, "Black Music," in *Collected Stories of William Faulkner* (New York: Vintage, 1995), 799–821. See also Ann J. Abadie and Annette Trefzer, eds., *Faulkner's Sexualities* (Jackson: University Press of Mississippi, 2012).

2. See Catherine Clinton and Michele Gillespie, eds., *The Devil's Lane: Race and Sex in the Early South* (New York: Oxford University Press, 1997); Martha Hodes, ed., *Sex, Love, Race: Crossing Boundaries in North American History* (New York: New York University Press, 1999); Martha Hodes,

White Women, Black Men: Illicit Sex in the Nineteenth-Century South (New Haven, CT: Yale University Press, 1997); and Pippa Holloway, *Sexuality, Politics, and Social Control in Virginia, 1920–1945* (Chapel Hill: University of North Carolina Press, 2006).

3. One of the most productive fields of study has been that of the history of the queer South. See John Howard, *Men Like That: A Southern Queer History* (Chicago: University of Chicago Press, 1999); John Howard, ed., *Carryin' On in the Gay and Lesbian South* (New York: New York University Press, 1997); Brock Thompson, *The Un-Natural State: Arkansas and the Queer South* (Little Rock: University of Arkansas Press, 2010); E. Patrick Johnson, *Sweet Tea: Black Gay Men of the South* (Chapel Hill: University of North Carolina Press, 2008); and James T. Sears, *Lonely Hunters: An Oral History of Lesbian and Gay Southern Life, 1948–1968* (New York: Basic Books, 1997). On sexuality and the law in a national context, see Margot Canaday, *The Straight State: Sexuality and Citizenship in Twentieth-Century America* (Princeton, NJ: Princeton University Press, 2009).

4. The fundamental text here is Michel Foucault, *The History of Sexuality, Vol. One: An Introduction* (New York: Vintage, 1978), although his writings on sex and power are prolific and influential. On the use of Foucault by historians, see Jan Goldstein, ed., *Foucault and the Writing of History* (Cambridge, MA: Blackwell, 1994).

5. See Deborah E. Barker and Kathryn McKee, eds., *American Cinema and the Southern Imaginary* (Athens: University of Georgia Press, 2011). Barker and McKee write that "we can think of the southern imaginary as an amorphous and sometimes conflicting collection of images, ideas, attitudes, practices, linguistic accents, histories, and fantasies about a shifting geographic region and time" (2). For a broader study of southern identity and representations of the South, see James C. Cobb, *Away Down South: A History of Southern Identity* (New York: Oxford University Press, 2005).

6. On the broader history of Western imaginings of "the Orient" as a place of sexual fantasy, see Edward Said, *Orientalism* (New York: Vintage, 1979).

7. Anthony J. Stanonis, *Faith in Bikinis: Politics and Leisure in the Coastal South since the Civil War* (Athens: University of Georgia Press, 2014). Stanonis rightly notes that the access and freedom that many male tourists in the South expected also included the enjoyment of gambling and alcohol.

8. For illustrations of Eliza, see Patricia A. Turner, "The Rise and Fall of Eliza Harris: From Novel to Tom Shows to Quilts," accessed 4 October 2016, utc.iath.virginia.edu/interpret/exhibits/turner/turner.html.

9. Joseph Crespino, *Strom Thurmond's America* (New York: Hill & Wang, 2012). On Essie Mae Washington-Williams, Thurmond's African American daughter, see 306–11.

10. See James McWilliams, "Roger That," *Paris Review*, 13 May 2015, www.theparisreview.org/blog/2015/05/13/roger-that/; William Byrd, *The Secret Diary of William Byrd of Westover, 1709–1712*, ed. Louis B. Wright and Marion Tinling (Richmond, VA: Dietz, 1941), quotations from entries for 25 and 26 January and 29 October 1710; and Byrd, *William Byrd of Virginia: The London Diary (1717–1721) and Other Writings*, ed. Louis B. Wright and Marion Tinling (New York: Oxford University Press, 1958). For a critical study of Byrd, see Kenneth A. Lockridge, *The Diary, and Life, of William Byrd II of Virginia, 1674–1744* (Chapel Hill: University of North Carolina Press, 1987); on Byrd's sexual attitudes and practices, see 49, 104–5, 86, 67, 101, 148.

11. Edmund Morgan, *American Slavery, American Freedom: The Ordeal of Colonial Virginia* (New York: Norton, 1975); Stephanie McCurry, *Masters of Small Worlds: Yeoman Households, Gender Relations, and the Political Culture of the Antebellum South Carolina Low Country* (New York: Oxford University Press, 1995).

12. I have explored some of these themes in *One Homogeneous People: Narratives of White Southern Identity, 1890–1920* (Knoxville: University of Tennessee Press, 2010); see esp. "The Road to a Closed Society: Mississippi Politics and the Language of White Southern Identity," 1–40. See also K. Stephen Prince, *Stories of the South: Race and the Reconstruction of Southern Identity, 1865–1915* (Chapel Hill: University of North Carolina Press, 2014).

13. Joel Williamson notes that by the late 1950s, Colonel Tom Parker and Elvis Presley had worked hard to craft a less sexually threatening image of Elvis, one that did not seem "a menace to the morals of America." See Williamson, *Elvis Presley: A Southern Life* (New York: Oxford University Press, 2015), 51.

14. See Joel Williamson, *The Crucible of Race: Black-White Relations in the American South since Reconstruction* (New York: Oxford University Press, 1984).

15. Cobb, *Away Down South,* 195.

16. The classic study of cultural anxiety over wasted men's seed and energy is Ben Barker-Benfield, "The Spermatic Economy: A Nineteenth Century View of Sexuality," *Feminist Studies* 1, no. 1 (Summer 1972): 45–74.

17. Tom P. Brady, *Black Monday: Segregation or Amalgamation… America Has Its Choice* (Winona, MS: Association of Citizens' Councils, 1955).

18. William Alexander Percy, *Lanterns on the Levee: Recollections of a Planter's Son* (New York: Knopf, 1941); Benjamin E. Wise, *William Alexander Percy: The Curious Life of a Mississippi Planter and Sexual Freethinker* (Chapel Hill: University of North Carolina Press, 2012).

19. Norman Mailer, "The White Negro," *Dissent,* Fall 1957, www.dissentmagazine.org/online_articles/the-white-negro-fall-1957.

20. See Ann Firor Scott, *The Southern Lady: From Pedestal to Politics, 1830–1930* (1970; reprint, Charlottesville: University Press of Virginia, 1995); Glenda E. Gilmore, *Gender and Jim Crow: Women and the Politics of White Supremacy in North Carolina, 1896–1920* (New York: Oxford University Press, 1996); and Grace Elizabeth Hale, *Making Whiteness: The Culture of Segregation in the South, 1890–1940* (New York: Pantheon, 1998).

21. See Danielle L. McGuire, *At the Dark End of the Street: Black Women, Rape, and Resistance—A New History of the Civil Rights Movement from Rosa Parks to the Rise of Black Power* (New York: Knopf, 2010); and Faith S. Holsaert, Martha Prescod Norman Noonan, Judy Richardson, Betty Garman Robinson, Jean Smith Young, and Dorothy M. Zellner, eds., *Hands on the Freedom Plow: Personal Accounts by Women in SNCC* (Chapel Hill: University of North Carolina Press, 2010).

22. See Kelly Morrow, "Sex and the Student Body: Knowledge, Equality, and the Sexual Revolution, 1960–1973" (PhD diss., University of North Carolina, 2012).

23. On sorority rush on one southern campus, see Elizabeth Boyd, "Sister Act: Sorority Rush as Feminine Performance," *Southern Cultures* 5, no. 3 (Fall 1999): 54–73. On sex-advice columns in campus newspapers, see Daniel Reimold, *Sex and the University: Celebrity, Controversy, and a Student Journalism Revolution* (New Brunswick, NJ: Rutgers University Press, 2010).

24. See Kathleen M. Brown, *Good Wives, Nasty Wenches, and Anxious Patriarchs: Gender, Race, and Power in Colonial Virginia* (Chapel Hill: University of North Carolina Press, 1996).

25. See, e.g., Sally G. McMillen, *Motherhood in the Old South: Pregnancy, Childbirth, and Infant Rearing* (Baton Rouge: Louisiana State University Press, 1990).

26. Suzi Parker, *Sex in the South: Unbuckling the Bible Belt* (Boston: Justin, Charles, 2003), xi.

27. W. J. Cash, *The Mind of the South* (New York, 1941), 339. For a searching and understudied memoir that has much to say about sex and southern women, see Rosemary Daniell, *Fatal Flowers: On Sin, Sex, and Suicide in the Deep South* (Athens, GA: Hill Street, 1999).

28. For a superb study of same-sex desire in southern fiction, see Gary Richards, *Lovers and Beloveds: Sexual Otherness in Southern Fiction, 1936–1961* (Baton Rouge: Louisiana State University Press, 2007).

29. For a recent biography of Williams that sets his work within the context of his own tumultuous personal life, see John Lahr, *Tennessee Williams: Mad Pilgrimage of the Flesh* (New York: Norton, 2014).

30. There is of course a very long tradition of representations of white male southerners like Lil' Abner or the Duke Boys as highly sexualized. On the literal marketing of an image of the priapic white southern male, see Patrick Huber, "The Riddle of the Horny Hillbilly," in Anthony J. Stanonis, ed., *Dixie Emporium: Tourism, Folkways, and Consumer Culture in the American South* (Athens: University of Georgia Press, 2008), 69–86.

31. On Aunt Jemima, see M. M. Manring, *Slave in a Box: The Strange Career of Aunt Jemima* (Charlottesville: University of Virginia Press, 1998).

32. Karen L. Cox, *Dreaming of Dixie: How the South Was Created in American Popular Culture* (Chapel Hill: University of North Carolina Press, 2011), 7. See also Tara McPherson, *Reconstructing Dixie: Race, Gender, and Nostalgia in the Imagined South* (Durham, NC: Duke University Press, 2003); and Allison Graham, *Framing the South: Hollywood, Television, and Race during the Civil Rights Struggle* (Baltimore: Johns Hopkins University Press, 2003).

33. Ted Ownby, *Subduing Satan: Religion, Recreation, and Manhood in the Rural South, 1865–1920* (Chapel Hill: University of North Carolina Press, 1990).

34. Adam Gussow, *Seems Like Murder Here: Southern Violence and the Blues Tradition* (Chicago: University of Chicago Press, 2002).

1

Extraordinary Powers

Controlling Syphilis in Wartime Florida

CLAIRE STROM

Throughout American history, the prosecution of war has led to the infringement of individual liberties. From the Alien and Sedition Acts of 1798 to the suspension of habeas corpus during the Civil War to the Espionage Act of 1917, the federal government has regularly reduced civil liberties in times of national emergency. Traditionally, such legislation focused on potential spies, critics, and traitors who might undermine the war effort by leaking secrets to the enemy or reducing the patriotic fervor of citizens. During the twentieth century, however, an increased understanding of disease propagation made a new group the focus of such legislation—women. With a clearer grasp on the causes of venereal disease but without a quick, efficient cure, the federal government focused its actions on trying to contain infected women who interacted with the troops. This effort reached its zenith in Florida during World War II, when the discovery of high rates of venereal disease impelled the federal government to act in order to protect the armed forces from infection. It used coercion to gain local and state governmental cooperation in the form of legislation and enforcement. The government's efforts created an effective infrastructure for attacking venereal disease; however, its efforts focused narrowly on those citizens who had interactions with the military and not on the wider diseased population. This policy ensured an increase of infection rates at the end of the war.

World War I had brought the problems of armies and venereal disease into sharp focus around the world. Every nation involved in the war tried to address infection in some way. The French established official brothels, where women received regular medical examinations; the British made it illegal for infected women to have sex with soldiers, with the penalty being imprisonment and fines; the Germans issued prophylactics to their military and examined prostitutes for infection.[1]

In the United States, Secretary of War Newton Baker created the Commission on Training Camp Activities (CTCA), which provided alternate entertainment and preventive education to the troops, while working to suppress prostitution around camps. The CTCA then cooperated with local officials to close brothels, dance halls, and bars near camps. If the officials refused to comply, the armed services threatened to move the camps or prohibit troops from entering nearby cities. When these measures did not reduce the infection rate, the CTCA mounted a national campaign to address venereal disease, which included encouraging state legislatures to pass laws allowing the arrest of women suspected of harboring disease. Thirty-two states passed such laws, and some refused to allow the women out on bail pending testing and required hospitalization if infection was detected. This policy led to the practical problem of where to put the large numbers of women arrested, a problem that was not fully solved by war's end. The policy also received criticism—from feminists for its focus on women and from the courts for its abridgment of civil liberties. Despite these setbacks, from 1918 to 1920 more than eighteen thousand women were arrested and detained in federal facilities. Detention time varied from ten weeks to a year, during which time the women could receive no visitors. To deter escapes, the facilities had barbed wire and guards.[2]

While civil authorities focused on infected women, the US military penalized men infected with venereal diseases during World War I. Starting in 1912, men who had failed to use prophylactics and became infected risked court-martial and were not paid for the time they were out of work. The military rescinded these measures during World War II, presumably being more concerned about maintaining the maximum fighting force than about fully controlling venereal disease.[3]

The experiences of World War I made the armed forces much more attuned to the problems caused by venereal disease and the need to control its spread as the nation mobilized for World War II. Efforts during this war were eased by the passage of the National Venereal Control Act of 1938, which allocated money to states to develop disease-control measures. The military tested all draftees for venereal disease, as it had during the previous war, but unlike during World War I, men who tested positive were rejected from service. In 1942, however, the army reversed this policy in 1942, a decision that became less objectionable toward the end of the war with the advent of penicillin as a cure.[4]

World War II was an economic boom time for much of the United States. In Florida, the long coastline proved invaluable to the navy, which established bases to protect allied shipping in the Caribbean, the Gulf of Mexico, and the Atlantic. World War II also saw the dramatic expansion of the Army Air Forces. Florida provided a perfect location for air bases, with clear skies, lots of flat land, and warm weather. Consequently, by 1943 the state was home to approximately 170 military installations. The population also grew. More than a million military personnel moved to Florida during the war, and a similar growth occurred in the civilian population as people sought jobs in wartime factories and support services.[5]

The war moved people, mostly young men, around the country in unprecedented numbers, and in places where these men were stationed, life changed for local residents in many ways. Many military bases were located in areas that had been mainly rural, with sizable minority and lower-class populations. The influx of the military into these areas created jobs, which included providing recreation for the soldiers, sailors, and airmen. The arrival of a base in a town spawned bars, dance halls, and other centers of entertainment. For many young women living in and around a base, the war was a time of great excitement. This was especially true for working-class women—in Florida often African American—who had little or no money for recreation. Having spent most of their lives enduring the hardships of the Great Depression, these women doubtless enjoyed the arrival of enlisted men, the lure of nights on the town, and the possibility of some extra money or a few luxuries. For them, contracting venereal disease was probably a distant theoretical risk, especially when weighed against the fun and transient thrill of their wartime lives.

The influx of this huge number of young men into Florida posed a particular problem as the state already had the highest rate of deaths from venereal disease in the nation. Significant statistics on venereal disease only emerged at the outset of the war, as all selective-service registrants were tested; if they were infected, they were rejected from the military. These tests revealed that Florida had the third highest rate of syphilis among whites and the highest rate among African Americans in the nation. Indeed, 40 percent of blacks tested had syphilis—eight times as many as whites. Officials recognized that nationally rates of infection were highest in the southeastern states and that the highest rates "are found among the young, the ignorant, the uneducated, and the poor." However, even though the officials clearly articulated educational and economic causal factors, they never considered racial segregation part of the problem.[6]

Trailing the military into Florida were young women, both wives and sweethearts of servicemen and prostitutes seeking business. Generally speaking, officials focused only on the prostitutes, reflecting a clear bias in favor of the middle classes. Early government reports mentioned the "influx of commercialized prostitutes" and characterized the women as "the primary spreaders of venereal diseases, especially among the members of the armed forces." Prostitutes also moved around Florida in response to law enforcement's actions. Thus, in 1944 the military blamed this increased incidence of disease on "an increase in the number of prostitutes in Orlando who have arrived from Tampa, Florida, where a strenuous drive against prostitution is in progress."[7]

Despite the government's emphasis on prostitution, many women moved to Florida during the war for other reasons, a point that authorities often did not recognize. In Orlando, a number of women arrested on suspicion of having venereal disease had husbands or brothers in the military. While this does not mean that they were disease free, it does suggest that they might have had nonfinancial reasons for hanging out with servicemen. Indeed, some military wives spent a considerable amount of time in jail and may well have had a venereal disease. One such woman wrote to Governor Spessard Holland from prison in Sarasota. She refused to give her name, for fear of receiving more jail time. She wrote, "They say that they are locking up all that has ever been seen with a solder [sic] no some of us has a husband that is in the army and was stationed here at the air base and we came down here."[8]

Women also moved to Florida during the war to follow a profession other than prostitution. Marjorie Swanson, of Peoria, Illinois, was 32 years old when she was arrested in Orlando in October 1942, along with Dorothy Christensen, from Superior, Wisconsin, who was 35. Marjorie came from a working-class family. Her father was a caretaker in a cemetery, while her brother earned his living as a machine painter. In 1930 Marjorie was living at home and working as a filing clerk at a dry cleaner. Her friend, Dorothy, came from a large, fairly wealthy family; both of her parents were from Norway. By 1930 Dorothy had moved to Chicago, where she was training to be a nurse. It is thus possible that she and Marjorie were both nurses working with the military in Florida and had developed relationships with airmen through the course of their work. Rosalie Blair, arrested in December 1942 and hailing from Columbia, South Carolina, was also a nurse, which indicates that at least some of the women whose behavior was criminalized during the war were also directly involved in achieving victory over the Axis Powers.[9]

From the federal government's perspective, controlling women who might infect servicemen was paramount. And the main problem, in the eyes of the military, was getting cooperation from civilian law enforcement. In 1939 a combination of state, federal, and military authorities drew up an Eight Point Agreement that mandated venereal-disease diagnosis, treatment, and education. It also allowed for the reporting of infected persons, their isolation, and the repression of prostitution.[10]

Florida was ill equipped to launch a major drive against venereal disease, lacking the necessary personnel, funds, and infrastructure for such a campaign. State public health only started in Florida in 1935, when Social Security money became available. The state used the money to establish county health units, although by 1942 five counties still did not have a facility. The state did not create a Division of Venereal Disease Control until 1938, with the arrival of federal funds. This division was responsible for coordinating local efforts, distributing venereal-disease information and drugs, and collecting data. It had a segregated organizational structure to work with both the white and black citizens of the state. During the war, the division focused its work on areas around military bases. Thus, its priority was protecting military personnel stationed in the state from infection from civilians, rather than helping the state's population at large address the problems of syphilis and gonorrhea. This meant that the campaign reinforced a double standard that saw women's sexuality as dangerous and requiring control.[11]

At the beginning of the war, Florida had few laws to enable it to counter venereal disease. Prostitution was legal throughout the state, and brothels operated openly in some cities. Communities generally addressed nuisance streetwalkers through vagrancy laws. Venereal disease had been recognized as a public-health issue in 1919, and infected persons could be quarantined against their will, treated, and the case reported to the state. However, this could only be done if someone reported contracting a disease from a suspected individual.[12]

Throughout the early years of the war, attempts to contain venereal disease using these provisions met with opposition from a variety of sources, as women contested limits being placed on their sexuality and their ability to earn a living. In 1941 health officers had started to quarantine brothels housing infected prostitutes. This power was not clearly spelled out in any legislation, and so prostitutes in the Jacksonville area launched a vigorous defense of their livelihood. They took the state board of health to court. The court ruled that the state board had the authority to implement quarantine, and consequently its personnel "placard the premises where known cases of veneral [*sic*] disease existed." This did not quell opposition, however.[13]

Economics seem to have been the foundation of a case in Tallahassee. There in May 1942, at the insistence of Colonel Wuest, from Dale Mabry Army Air Base, Leon County health officers quarantined the Seminole Hotel. Allegedly, the manager of the hotel was renting out rooms and supplying women to servicemen. The owner of the hotel secured a writ of injunction against the health authorities. However, as all actions had been taken within the bounds of the new laws, the case seems to have been dismissed.[14]

Lawsuits also focused on the treatment of the confined women. In 1942 a circuit court ruled that a woman arrested on a vagrancy charge in Duval County (with Jacksonville as the county seat) could not be "held in jail simply because she has a venereal disease." This ruling threatened the effectiveness of the program. Treatment for venereal disease took seventy weeks, and authorities found it hard to ensure patients' compliance without detaining them for the duration. The following year, another case was taken to the Florida Supreme Court with a different conclusion. Pauline Varholy, an employee at the St. John's River Ship Building Company and wife of a soldier stationed in Mississippi, was arrested on drunk-and-disorderly charges. She was tested and found to have gonorrhea and so was held over for treatment. She petitioned for release under writ of habeas corpus. Her petition was denied, as the public-health threat trumped individual liberties, even though authorities were paying no attention to men spreading disease.[15]

This gendered understanding was reflected in the people arrested for harboring the disease. In Orlando during the war, the sheriff's office arrested 312 women on suspicion of having a venereal disease. During the same time period, 26 men were arrested (one of whom was named Eliza Stokes, suggesting some sort of clerical error). The small number of men detained also demonstrates the gendered reality of most sexual policing. The sheriff, the police, and the military all failed, from either a lack of manpower, a lack of funds, or a lack of imagination, to ask the girls who had infected them and then arrest those men. They also did not arrest or punish the infected airmen, even though this had been military policy before the war (and was reinstated as policy after the conflict). Instead, the authorities just treated the men's infections and presumably tried to keep them from having more sex until they were cured.[16]

The gendered nature of the arrests was mirrored in the press. In pages and pages of clippings in the state archives following the success of "Venereal Disease" and "Social Hygiene" months, headlines consistently blame women—"Nineteen Women Arrested in Raid on Little Savoy," "Sixty Prostitutes Arrested Here," "Teen-Aged Girls Passing on VD," "Most VD Women from Florida," "State Effectively Combats VD at Ocala Girls' Camp," "Infected Mothers Should Consider Child's Health," "Young Girls VD Menaces."[17]

Throughout the campaign no officials publicly questioned its equity, except Judge Ernest E. Mason. He declared that the prosecution of prostitution in Escambia County, with Pensacola as the county seat, was one-sided. He complained that arrested women ended up in jail, while military men were turned over to military authorities and rarely received any punishment. Mason wanted more "Sauce for the Gander," stating that "the women wouldn't be in the business if they didn't have the trade." Unfortunately, the judge was probably speaking out of frustration that Escambia County had to house arrested prostitutes and had lost significant income from legalized prostitution rather than out of some proto-feminism.[18]

Other opposition came from law enforcement. Arresting prostitutes on vagrancy charges was fine, but it was unclear what local officials were meant to do with the girls after they had served their nominal sentence. In March 1942, Sheriff Andreu, of Bradford County, southwest of Jacksonville, addressed this problem in a letter to the governor: "I have no place to put this class of women but I do jail them and keep them, at the expense of the county, until they get really homesick, then I take them to the county line in the opposite direction of the Camp [military base], and put them out with a thorough understanding that if they come back to Bradford County I will have the Judge send them to the County Prison Farm. Of course I am bluffing them, but it seems to help some."[19]

If the women who were arrested tested positive for venereal disease, the problem for local law enforcement increased. While the federal government and the armed forces were anxious to have women infected with disease identified and removed from the streets, sheriffs and police had to find somewhere to house arrestees while they were being treated. In 1939 the standard recommended treatment of syphilis patients was thirty weekly shots of arsenic into the arm, followed by forty weekly shots of a bismuth compound into the hip. For at least fifty-two weeks of the treatment, patients were to refrain from sexual intercourse for fear of infecting their partners. Unfortunately, symptoms of the disease could disappear early in the treatment, and officials did not trust most carriers to either continue the medical regime or abstain from sex. Thus, housing arrestees for treatment required a combined hospital and detention center.[20]

Congress could only legislate regarding prostitution by claiming a need to protect the military, and it did this with the May Act in 1941. Under the provisions of this act, prostitution around a military base was considered a federal crime, and the federal government could close down brothels and arrest women suspected of selling sexual services to military personnel, thus federally encoding the sexual double standard. Over the course of the war, the May Act was rarely invoked. Possibly to avoid a discussion about its legality, the May Act was most commonly used as a threat, with communities around bases being encouraged to clean up their red-light districts to avoid provoking federal intervention. Thus, in April 1942 the navy threatened to place the city of Miami under "military police supervision" if "civilian authorities failed to correct existing lewd conditions." Generally, as in the case of Miami, the threat was sufficient to ensure more diligent local policing of prostitutes, brothels, dance halls, and bars.[21]

The May Act gained Florida's attention. In 1942 Governor Holland wrote a circular letter to all law-enforcement personnel, asking them to "cooperate with the military and naval forces" and "redouble your efforts to stamp out prostitution." But there was still the problem of where to put the arrested women. As Sheriff Jon Scott, of Panama City, replied to the governor, "There is no detention place provided in Bay County, other than the jail, and the feebleness thereof of this Institution in providing a place for those that are picked up for treatment only a very small number can be taken care of." Similarly, the Orange County sheriff's office in Orlando had space for only seventeen women. Officials arrested them, tested them, treated them, and tried to move them on but were seriously limited by the space restrictions. They only arrested 38 people in 1942 and 44 in 1943, but 146 in 1944 once the housing problem had been successfully addressed.[22]

Thus, by 1942 two key problems had emerged in the governmental fight to control venereal disease in Florida: the lack of appropriate legislation and the lack of places to keep infected women. The former proved easier to solve than the latter. After quarantining brothels had been upheld in the courts, law-enforcement personnel continued to close down such establishments, so that by the end of 1942 none existed openly in the state. The next year, the state legislature passed a bevy of laws against prostitution. The laws were thorough, addressing prostitutes and pimps, as well as boardinghouses and restaurants that might promote solicitation. One omission in the legislation, however, was any penalty for the men who purchased sex.[23]

The second problem, what to do with infected women while they were being treated, was more difficult. Initially women who did not have their own doctor were treated at county clinics. By 1940 these were being funded by the federal government as well as the state in order to provide medical personnel to treat all the infected civilians. However, it was next to impossible to ensure that people completed the lengthy treatment without holding them for the duration, which strained city and county resources to their limits. In 1942, therefore, the Federal Works Agency awarded the state funds to operate three quarantine hospitals. To further speed the process, the army gave several Civilian Conservation Corps camps in Florida to the state to use for the hospitals, which were designated Rapid Treatment Centers.[24]

Many in law enforcement rejoiced at the decision to house infected women in camps. Sheriff Enzor, of Crestview, telegrammed the capital, "Have jail full of prostitutes please advise how long before camps are ready." But not everyone was so pleased. One camp was in the north of the state, at Wakulla, just sixteen miles south of Tallahassee; one was in the central part of the state in the Ocala National Forest; and the third was in Myakka State Park, seventeen miles east of Sarasota. While the first two camps caused no problems, the one outside Sarasota caused considerable conflict. When it was first proposed, state officials received letters from the Florida Forest and Park Service, the Sarasota Chamber of Commerce, and concerned local citizens. The state park service asked that no camps be located in state parks, because they had "been built for the public good" and "irrepairable [sic] damage would be done if an undesirable isolation camp were located within sight... of these public use areas." The Sarasota Chamber of Commerce likewise saw such a camp as a "deterrent to public traffic" to the park.[25]

The state initially seemed willing to consider other options, but it became clear that there were no other good options in the region. Additionally, since the army owned the camps, it could decide which ones were allocated for use as Rapid Treatment Centers. Protests continued, although somewhat muted, as no one wished to be dubbed unpatriotic. The state park service asked that the site be moved away from the main entrance to the park, but that proved too expensive. The park officials also contested the site based on the last will and testament of Bertha Palmer. Palmer had given the land to the state for the park "stipulating that it should be used as a State park... and for no other purpose."

The park service questioned the legality of using the land for other purposes, but seemingly to no avail. Finally, the city and the park service resigned themselves to the treatment center, believing that "if the 'Government' or 'Army' wanted the camp there badly enough, they would have it there, in spite of his [the mayor's] or the Chamber of Commerce's objections." For reasons that are unclear, however, the camp was never completed.[26]

When the Rapid Treatment Centers at Ocala and Wakulla became operational, doctors could employ new ways to cure syphilis. Most common initially was a recently developed ten-week treatment of arsenic. The toxicity of the arsenic was potentially dangerous and so could only be used on inpatients. The length of treatment meant that officials needed to devise something to do with the patients, and a work program was developed that helped offset the cost of the centers. Other new treatment methods were used. At the Rapid Treatment Centers some patients were given an intensive five-day treatment, while in the Duval County Hospital in Jacksonville some patients received one super shot of arsenic, after which their temperature was raised in a hot box. Not only were these methods dangerous but their success was less certain. They were only used on patients in the early stages of infection, and only on those patients who could be trusted to follow up with regular blood tests.[27]

The state adjusted its use of Rapid Treatment Centers to fit the need. Initially the centers at Ocala and Wakulla only treated women, while both men and women were treated in the Jacksonville facility. In 1943 scientists discovered that penicillin cured syphilis effectively and quickly. The drug was not available for use immediately, but by April 1944 the centers were using it, and treatment time was reduced to days. In April 1944 the center at Wakulla closed, but a new one opened in Pensacola, where there was more need. That center closed after only a year, leaving only the centers at Ocala and Jacksonville. In April 1946 a major fire destroyed the hospital in Ocala. Three months later, the Jacksonville center moved to the Ernest Hinds Hospital Ship, anchored in the St. John's River. The ship closed in the spring of 1947, but a new treatment center that treated both black and white men and women opened at the former naval air base in Melbourne, continuing operations into the 1950s.[28]

In 1943, therefore, with the opening of the centers and the passage of anti-prostitution legislation, arrests and detentions for venereal disease skyrocketed. Law-enforcement personnel were willing to arrest more women, knowing that there was somewhere to send them. Similarly, county health clinics did not need to treat all the patients themselves but just diagnose them, which vastly increased the number of people they could see. By the end of 1943, 1,077 patients had been released from the Rapid Treatment Centers. Without the centers, these women would have been incarcerated in regular jails or trusted to obtain treatment on their own. Thus, the centers relieved pressure on the key bottleneck in the medical and legal structure set up to address venereal disease.[29]

While the opening of the Rapid Treatment Centers eased the medical problem facing authorities, the new laws against prostitution did not help as much as some had predicted. Increasingly, authorities focused on another source of infection: "good-time girls." These young women, often in their teens or early twenties, became promiscuous because of "misguided patriotism." Or as the *Miami Herald* stated, perhaps less generously, "Non-commercial girls of the juke joint beer-guzzling category are largely responsible for the 100 percent increase in social diseases." Some authorities understood that "the nervous tension of war has promoted the clandestine meetings of juveniles in juke joints, concession stands, movies, bowling alleys, dance halls, and taverns" and that these meetings often led to sexual relations. The problem, as some saw it, lay with the parents, who should have been monitoring the girls' behavior rather than allowing them to "roam ... the streets at all hours of the night."[30]

The Rapid Treatment Centers allowed authorities the opportunity to profile patients, who were all women. The resulting profiles supported the idea that locals, rather than out-of-state prostitutes who were following the troops, were actually the heart of the problem. An analysis of women released from the Rapid Treatment Centers showed that 74.4 percent claimed their place of residence to be Florida, while 70.8 percent had been born in Florida, Alabama, or Georgia. Similarly, in the Orange County sheriff dockets, the resident addresses for 320 arrestees are somewhat legible. Of these, 73 percent were in Orlando, 86.9 percent in Orange County, and 92.8 percent in Florida.[31]

To reach good-time girls, the campaign's focus had to shift from the seedier sides of society to its mainstream. Consequently, Governor Spessard Holland declared January 1944 as "Venereal Disease Month" and February as "Social Hygiene Month," and the state embarked on a mammoth campaign to promote testing and treatment. Stamps and lapel pins abounded. Radio and TV stations offered talk shows and short skits about the perils of venereal diseases. Local clubs like the Jaycees, the Kiwanis, and the Rotary showed movies about venereal disease and sponsored testing campaigns. Billboards urged treatment. In Tampa the mayor announced a "Venereal Control Week" in February 1944, and a tent hospital and testing center was set up downtown. In other cities across the state, shop windows displayed photographs showing the effects of disease. Boy Scouts in Orlando distributed literature, and pamphlets accompanied utility bills and were dropped on rural communities from army bombers. This campaign, complete with images and text, offers insight into the gendered and class ideas that surrounded and drove the anti-venereal-disease campaign.[32]

Many of the pamphlets and newspaper advertisements were simply factual. With little illustration, they laid out the basic information about venereal diseases. Promoting the importance of medical authority, they stressed that home remedies and patent medicine were not effective against gonorrhea and syphilis, that all people were at risk of infection, and that a medical test was the only way to be certain whether infection was present. Along with being relatively cheap to produce, these materials highlighted the objective, scientific nature of the disease, placing the locus of power solidly with medical authorities.[33]

Another set of posters and pamphlets stressed patriotism, implying implicitly or otherwise that it was a citizen's duty to find out if he or she had venereal disease in order to protect the armed forces and help them win the war. Some of these used patriotic images, such as the eagle and stars, to convey their message, while others talked about being "strong" and "guarding" against disease. Other posters were more direct, with Uncle Sam demanding that VD be "stamped out." These underscored the reality of the campaign. Venereal disease had been of little concern to Floridians, despite the high incidence, until the military demanded that they pay attention and protect the armed forces in the state from infection.[34]

Throughout the campaign, despite rhetoric about civilian health and even despite a 1945 state law requiring premarital and prenatal testing, the focus remained fairly clearly on the military necessity. The military initially rejected infected draftees, who then returned to their communities. Few attempts were made to follow up with these men. The military reported their cases to the county health units, and the infected individuals were supposed to undergo treatment. However, authorities rarely followed through to ensure that the men did indeed submit for treatment. This became a problem in segregated Lake County, just north of Orlando, in early 1942. According to the lawyer J. W. Hunter, who wrote to complain to the governor, nearly eight hundred black men in the county had been rejected by the military because they were infected with a venereal disease. Of this number, only thirty-five had received treatment from the county health unit. The others, according to Hunter, had realized that "if they do not complete this treatment they can not be sent into the army. Therefore very few are going to take it, unless they have to do so. This is all wrong, because when one of these men is sent back, some healthy white man has to take his place in the army while the worthless, diseased negro is permitted to run at large and spread this disease." Hunter went on to point out that these "worthless, diseased negro[es]" were also "refusing to work knowing they are safe from Army service."[35]

No governmental authorities, neither federal nor state, addressed this pool of diseased young men. Indeed, men were seldom arrested for prostitution or on suspicion of having a venereal disease, and there is no evidence that law enforcement or doctors questioned arrested women about their partners or about how they had contracted the infection. During 1943 the military changed its policy, starting to take a "small percentage of selectees with syphilis" and treating them during limited duty. This would have reduced the number of infected men somewhat, but it did not address the greater problem caused by gendered medical treatment.[36]

Indeed, the profile of people who received treatment in the Florida venereal-disease campaign, albeit unwillingly, clearly reaffirms the overwhelming governmental concern to protect the military. Although African Americans suffered from syphilis at a rate eight times that of whites, they were treated at the Rapid Treatment Centers about half as often. This reflects the much lower number of blacks in the armed services. Of the 16 million Americans who served during World War II, fewer than 10 percent were African American. In the segregated South, white servicemen would have almost uniformly sought the services of white prostitutes or the company of white good-time girls. Thus, from a military perspective, the white women posed a much greater threat to the war effort than did the African Americans, even though the latter were much more likely to be infected. Additionally, although the test results indicated that Floridians of all ages suffered from infection, most of the women detained were in their late teens and early twenties, as were most servicemen.[37]

The consequences of this narrow focus were inevitable. At the war's end, with the removal of federal funding and federal pressure, the problem of venereal disease rebounded. By 1946, sixteen Florida counties lacked a county health facility, presumably because of postwar funding cuts. At the same time, as less effort was invested to address venereal disease and people moved back home, the untapped male reservoir of infection started to spread illness once more. From 1945 to 1946 the number of primary and secondary syphilis cases diagnosed in the state increased by 43 percent. Additionally, the campaign against prostitution, so reluctantly embarked upon by many in local law enforcement, faded, and "there is every reason to believe that those who control the prostitution racket have already developed plans to renew their activities."[38]

Ultimately the campaign against venereal disease in Florida clearly demonstrates the federal government's willingness to adopt and enforce extraordinary powers during a time of crisis. Additionally, it reflected and reinforced a sexual double standard, according to which women were expected to be pure, while men's sexuality was harder to contain and mirrored their fighting fitness. To reduce infection among servicemen, the government arrested and detained women without trial, threatened to take over communities abutting military installments, and poured money and resources into the state. Whether these measures actually reduced the incidence of venereal disease remains unclear. The number of civilians being treated in Florida reached a high in 1943 and then started to fall. This might reflect a reduction in the number of infected people, or it might demonstrate that once the military had access to penicillin and a quick cure for servicemen, they were less worried about addressing the source of disease. Regardless, the focus of the campaign on young white women addressed the military imperative while neglecting the wider public-health concerns of the civilians in the state.[39]

NOTES

1. Susan R. Grayzel, *Women and the First World War* (London: Pearson Education, 2002), 71–73.

2. Allan Brandt, *No Magic Bullet: A Social History of Venereal Disease in the United States since 1880* (New York: Oxford University Press, 1985), 52–95.

3. Edward F. Witsell to Inspector General and commanding generals of armed forces, 12 June 1946, Box 141.280-2/141.281-2, Air Force Regional History Agency, Montgomery, Alabama (hereafter AFRHA).

4. Brandt, *No Magic Bullet,* 77–78, 143–44, 169–70; State Board of Health, *Florida Health Notes* 33 (February 1941): 21–22.

5. David J. Coles, "Keeping the Home Fires Burning: Florida's World War II Experience," in Florida Department of Veteran Affairs, "Florida's World War II Memorial," accessed 4 October 2010, www.floridavets.org/wwii/history.asp; Kevin M. McCarthy, *Aviation in Florida* (Sarasota: Pineapple Press, 2003), 27; Lewis N. Wynne, Tracy J. Revels, Dawn Truax, James A. Schnur, Paul S. George, Robert D. Billinger Jr., Carolyn J. Barnes, James R. McGovern, and William D. Miller, eds., *Florida*

at War (Saint Leo, FL: Saint Leo College Press, 1993), 4–6; Joseph Freitus and Anne Freitus, *Florida: The War Years, 1938–1945* (Niceville, FL: Wind Canyon, 1998), 2–4.

6. Florida State Board of Health, *Forty-Third Annual Report of the Florida State Board of Health for the Year Ending December 31, 1942* (Jacksonville: Florida State Board of Health, 1943), 46–48, 51–52, 54; Florida State Board of Health, *Forty-Fourth Annual Report of the Florida State Board of Health for the Year Ending December 31, 1943* (Jacksonville: Florida State Board of Health, 1945), 181; State Board of Health, *Florida Health Notes* 34 (February 1942): 19.

7. Florida State Board of Health, *Forty-Third Annual Report,* 54; "Historical Data: Squadron M—902nd AAF Base Unit, AAF Tactical Center, Orlando, Florida," June–December 1944, Box 287.17-7/287.17-9, AFRHA.

8. On specific arrestees, see Sheriff dockets, Orange County History Center, Orlando (hereafter OCHC). The relationship of arrestees to military personnel was worked out using ancestry.com. Letter to Governor Holland, 22 August 1942, File 3, Box 52, Series 406, RG 102, Florida State Archives, Tallahassee (hereafter FSA).

9. Information on Marjorie Swanson and Dorothy Christensen from federal census records accessed through ancestry.com.

10. *Official Statutes of Florida, 1983* (Tallahassee: State of Florida, 1983), chap. 796; State Board of Health, *Florida Health Notes* 35 (September 1943): 156–60; James R. McGovern, "'Sporting Life on the Line': Prostitution in Progressive Era Pensacola," *Florida Historical Quarterly* 54, no. 2 (January 1975): 132, 133.

11. State Board of Health, *Florida Health Notes* 33 (November 1941): 155; Florida State Board of Health, *Forty-Third Annual Report,* 57; Florida State Board of Health, *Thirty-Ninth Annual Report of the Florida State Board of Health for the Year Ending December 31, 1938* (Jacksonville: Florida State Board of Health, 1940), 8–9; Florida State Board of Health, *Forty-First Annual Report of the Florida State Board of Health for the Year Ending December 31, 1940* (Jacksonville: Florida State Board of Health, 1941), 15–17; State Board of Health, "Florida Syphilis Control Program Sets Remarkable Record During Past Year," *Florida Health Notes* 31 (February 1939): 21.

12. For arrests on vagrancy laws, see "Report on Tallahassee Quarantine of Hotel Seminole," File 2, Box 52, Series 406, RG 102, FSA; *General Acts and Resolutions Adopted by the Legislature of Florida* (Tallahassee: Appleyard, 1919), chap. 7829 (no. 47), 92–94; G. S. Osincup to Holland, 9 March 1942, File 2, Box 52, Series 406, RG 102, FSA.

13. Florida State Board of Health, *Forty-Second Annual Report of the Florida State Board of Health for the Year Ending December 31, 1941* (Jacksonville: Florida State Board of Health, 1942), 9; Osincup, undated letter, and Osincup to Holland, 6 March 1942, File 2, Box 52, Series 406, RG 102, FSA.

14. "Report on Tallahassee Quarantine of Hotel Seminole"; W. H. Pickett to Herbert Bryans, 25 May 1942, File 2, Box 52, Series 406, RG 102, FSA.

15. "Court Rules Venereal Disease not Jail Crime," *Tampa Tribune,* 24 December 1942; *Pauline Varholy v. Rex Sweat,* 15 So. 2d 267, 153 Fla. 571 (Fl 1943).

16. Figures for number of arrests come from the Sheriff dockets, OCHC; and Witsell to Inspector General and commanding generals of armed forces, 12 June 1946.

17. *Tampa Morning Tribune,* 9 February, 1 March 1944; *Tallahassee Democrat,* 11 January 1944; *Pensacola News,* 26 January 1944; *Tampa Daily Times,* 15 January 1944; *Panama City News Herald,* 14 January 1944; *Tampa Morning Tribune,* 11 January 1944.

18. *Tampa Morning Tribune,* 9 February, 1 March 1944; *Tallahassee Democrat,* 11 January 1944;

Pensacola News, 26 January 1944; *Tampa Daily Times,* 15 January 1944; *Panama City News Herald,* 14 January 1944; *Tampa Morning Tribune,* 11 January 1944; *Pensacola Public Record,* 29 January 1944.

19. A. O. Andreu to Holland, 26 March 1942, File 2, Box 52, Series 406, RG 102, FSA.

20. State Board of Health, "Syphilis Can be Cured," *Florida Health Notes* 31 (February 1939): 29; State Board of Health, "Rapid Treatment Centers," ibid. 36 (February 1944): 41. For more information on the treatments used for venereal disease, see J. Parascandola, "Quarantining Women: Venereal Disease Rapid Treatment Centers in World War II America," *Bulletin of the History of Medicine* 83, no. 3 (Fall 2009): 441–44.

21. Marilyn E. Hegarty, *Victory Girls, Khaki-Wackies, and Patriotutes: The Regulation of Female Sexuality during World War II* (New York: New York University Press, 2008), 14, 32–34, 37–39, 92–96; "Miami Threatened with MP Control Due to Prostitutes," *Orlando Sentinel,* 25 April 1942.

22. Circular letter from Holland, 24 March 1942, File 3; John Scott to Holland, 15 April 1942, File 2; and Sheriff Black to Holland, 13 August 1942, File 2, Box 52, Series 406, RG 102, FSA; Sheriff dockets, OCHC.

23. Florida State Board of Health, *Forty-First Annual Report,* 16; State Board of Health, *Florida Health Notes* 35 (February 1943): 33; ibid. 35 (September 1943): 156–60.

24. Florida State Board of Health, *Forty-Third Annual Report,* 64.

25. Isle Enzor to W. T. Fowder [Sowder], 22 August 1942; "Holland Tells Reason County Picked for Camp," newspaper clipping, late 1942; H. J. Malsberger to Florida State Board of Health, 12 August 1942; and J. V. Lawrence to Holland, 13 August 1942, File 3, Box 52, Series 406, RG 102, FSA.

26. Executive Secretary to Malsberger, 14 August 1942; Henry Hanson to Holland, 1 August 1942; memo to Dr. Ed Annis, 27 October 1942; Malsberger to Hanson, 6 October 1942; Wilson Sowder to R. L. Shipp, 30 October 1942; Malsberger to Tom Watson, 18 December 1942; and Wilson Sowder to Ralph Davis, 21 December 1942, File 3, Box 52, Series 406, RG 102, FSA; Florida State Board of Health, *Forty-Fourth Annual Report,* 193.

27. Florida State Board of Health, *Forty-Fourth Annual Report,* 193; Florida State Board of Health, *Forty-Fifth Annual Report of the Florida State Board of Health for the Year ending December 31, 1944* (Jacksonville: Florida State Board of Health, 1946), 79.

28. Florida State Board of Health, *Forty-Fifth Annual Report,* 75–76; Florida State Board of Health, *Forty-Sixth Annual Report of the Florida State Board of Health for the Year ending December 31, 1945* (Jacksonville: Florida State Board of Health, 1946), 5, 6; State Board of Health, *Florida Health Notes* 39 (February 1947): 39; ibid. 39 (August 1947): 190; ibid. 40 (January 1948): 26–41; Florida State Board of Health, *Annual Report State Board of Health, 1950* (Jacksonville: State Board of Health, n.d.), 96.

29. Sheriff dockets, OCHC; Florida State Board of Health, *Forty-Fifth Annual Report,* 81; Florida State Board of Health, *Forty-Fourth Annual Report,* 194.

30. R. F. Sondag, "Parents Blamed for Delinquency in Girls," *Florida Health Notes* 35 (September 1943): 147–48; *Miami Herald,* 25 February 25, 1944; Dawn Truax, "Social Protection and Victory Girls in World War II Tampa," in Wynne et al., *Florida at War,* 33–35.

31. State Board of Health, "Rapid Treatment Centers," 38.

32. Information on the campaign can be found in the newspaper clippings in Series 1410, RG 894, FSA. See, e.g., *West Orange News,* 31 December 1943; "Tent to Shelter VD Test Clinic," *Tampa Daily Times,* 4 February 1944; "Ravages of Syphilis Shown by Pictures in Window Display," *Ocala Star,* 23 January 1944; "Pamphlets by Plane," *Tampa Daily Times,* 21 January 1944.

33. Information on the campaign can be found in the newspaper clippings in Series 1410, RG 894, FSA.

34. Ibid.

35. Florida State Board of Health, *Forty-Sixth Annual Report,* 6; State Board of Health, *Florida Health Notes* 33 (July 1941): 92; J. W. Hunter to Holland, 29 January 1942, File 3, Box 52, Series 406, RG 102, FSA.

36. State Board of Health, *Florida Health Notes* 36 (February 1944): 28.

37. "WWII History Resources," www.intheirwords.org/wwii_history_resources/statistics; "African Americans in WWII: Fighting for a Double Victory," www.nationalww2museum.org/learn /education/for-students/ww2-history/at-a-glance/african-americans-in-ww2.html; Florida State Board of Health, *Forty-Sixth Annual Report,* 194–95; Sheriff dockets, OCHC.

38. State Board of Health, *Florida Health Notes* 39 (January 1947): 12; ibid. 39 (February 1947): 39, 37.

39. Florida State Board of Health, *Forty-Fifth Annual Report,* 78.

2

"America's Wickedest City"

The Sexual Black Market in Phenix City, Alabama

STEPHANIE M. CHALIFOUX

I n 1953, Sheila received a distressful phone call from her mother, Earline. Jailed in Phenix City, Earline asked her daughter to travel from Atlanta, Georgia, to Alabama to post her bail.[1] Phenix City police had arrested Earline for public intoxication. Sheila believed her visit in the city would be brief. Instead, she found herself embroiled in a vice market that included gambling and a lucrative sex trade. Sheila's involvement in the sex trade ranged from that of participant as a B-girl when she accompanied her mother to work in the town's numerous bars and as an observer who documented the market's inner workings in her diary. By the end of June 1954, Phenix City's corrupt illegal market would crumble when vice leaders assassinated a state politician in an attempt to ward off a cleanup campaign. Sheila's observations would prove crucial to the prosecution, who pursued charges against those involved, and to understanding the dynamics of the sexual black market. Much has been written about the events in Phenix City, including several scholarly works that address the assassination, and Hollywood capitalized on the country's fascination with the wicked city in a film loosely based on the occurrences in 1954.[2] The sexual black market remains mostly hidden in the narrative; there is only a cursory nod to some of the town's kitschy characters.

However, the sex trade in Phenix City was more than an aside to the assassination; indeed, it was rather substantial, revealing the limits of the influence of a modern postwar United States on the southern economy, society, and culture. The South's changing economic landscape, which benefited from federal projects during the Cold War, helped to bolster once small cities into thriving hubs in the industrial war complex. Phenix City, though, failed to reap the rewards in ways other than the consumer sex economy driven by soldiers stationed at nearby Fort Benning. The vice market provided Phenix City, with a population of just over twenty thousand and a stagnant local economy, a foundation for economic solvency. The market operations were profitable, complex, and sordid, reflecting in many ways the modern sex trade that existed in America's bar culture, which was predicated on male control and targeted toward the local male clientele. The city's sexual market employed more than three hundred women, some of whom worked as prostitutes and B-girls, while others were "country girl amateurs who heard that Phenix City was an easy place to make a living out of loving."[3] In addition to the resulting profits the vice trade generated, its existence, complexity, and size exposed the fallacious notions of the region's, and perhaps the nation's, assumed sexual conservativeness. The events in Phenix City in the 1950s shed light not just on the South but on the national sexual market as it transitioned away from brothels and fixed locations. After the cleanup in June 1954, many women in the market embarked on a regional sex-work migration as a means to circumvent law enforcement and the increasing crackdown on sexual vice in the era. The vice market in Phenix City reflected the changes in the southern sexual market. As the leaders in the sex trade exploited women's sexual labor to create a thriving black-market economy, the women who worked in it negotiated ways to profit from their sexuality and their wit.

The vice market in Phenix City had existed in some form since the city's inception in the 1800s but was bolstered by the establishment of Fort Benning, an army base located ten miles away in Columbus, Georgia, in 1918.[4] Fort Benning housed thousands of troops, many of whom flocked to Phenix City to enjoy the liquor, gambling, and prostitutes the city offered. When the city faced bankruptcy during the Great Depression, it began to rely on legal alcohol sales and fines for illegal sales. Additionally, the city licensed gambling, leveling a hefty penalty on those operating without a permit. The fees and fines from gambling and alcohol sales provided the city with a significant source of income, amounting to $228,000 annually by 1945.[5]

The troops at Fort Benning who visited the city contributed to Phenix City's vice proceeds. During World War II, more than six hundred thousand troops trained at Fort Benning; at one point, the number of troops on site reached nearly one hundred thousand.[6] Many of those men traveled across the Georgia state border to drink and play in Phenix City. Military officials at Fort Benning complained about the staggering number of venereal-disease cases among servicemen, which they believed originated from contact with prostitutes in Phenix City. In 1941, Secretary of War Henry Stimson deemed the town the "wickedest city in America," and General George Patton, commander of the

Third Army, stationed at Fort Benning, threatened to flatten the city with tanks.[7] By 1942, venereal infections at Fort Benning were the highest in the Fourth Service Command, which included military facilities in the states of Alabama, Florida, Georgia, Mississippi, North Carolina, and South Carolina.[8] Officials placed the city off limits, but they soon realized the futility of their actions when they discovered that troops continued to visit the city. Military representatives met with Phenix City officials and pressured them to close down the vice market to eliminate what that believed was the origin of infectious contact. The army implied that if the city would not control its vice problem, federal officials would intercede, and Phenix City obliged.[9] In 1942, the American Social Hygiene Association (ASHA), an organization designed to "promote health and public morality" by educating the nation about venereal disease, surveyed Phenix City's vice market and concluded that commercialized prostitution had in fact disappeared after 1942.[10] However, the ASHA lamented that as the war ended, "gambling and drink rustling has been resumed" and "local underworld characters maintain that pros[titution] will be reestablished."[11]

ASHA predictions proved accurate in the postwar years: vice operations returned and were stronger and more ubiquitous than in the past. A number of factors combined to transform the city's vice trade into a highly organized operation. The end of the war and the use of penicillin to treat venereal disease reduced the need to police the sexual dalliances of servicemen. And while military brass placed the city off limits on numerous occasions, citing concerns about the fleecing of soldiers, troops continued to travel across the Dillingham and Fourteenth Street bridges, which connected the two cities. About 80 percent of the soldiers spent at least some of their earnings on gaming, alcohol, and sex.[12] As early as 1945, the ASHA warned that "liquor and gambling interests are waxing rich from Ft. Benning soldiers' spending."[13] Some estimated that the combined income from the vice racket was $100 million annually, and the profits lined not just the pockets of the racketeers but the city coffers as well. Municipal tax revenue collection in 1952 had grown to almost $650,000, half of which came from the vice market.[14] Vice leaders' soaring profits gave them significant power and influence over every facet of the town. Leaders donated to local education and charity drives, attended Sunday church services, and in some cases served as local politicians and law enforcement.

The sizable vice trade in Phenix City operated out of approximately forty establishments and reflected changes in the postwar sex trade. Brothel prostitution, while still in operation in the United States, had undergone eradication campaigns during the war and given way to a bar culture in which sex workers operated. Almost all the commercial sexual activity in the city took place in bars or taverns or in facilities located on their property. The move to a bar culture had broad implications for the city's sexual black market and the women who worked in it. The owners of taverns and bars were the key operators of vice rings.[15] Through bar ownership, these men controlled the market itself.[16] In Phenix City, the shift from brothels to bars as the primary locations for the sexual market relegated women almost exclusively to the role of laborers rather than procurers or operators. With the exception of a handful of women, all of the vice-business proprietors were men, and the primary role for women in Phenix City's vice trade was that of sexual service laborer.

Because of its many facets, its organization, and its sheer size, the market attracted a diverse contingent of women. Sex workers in Phenix City fell between the ages of 16 and 40. Some were married, others were separated from husbands either by military enlistment or personal choice, and many were single.[17] Most women had roots in the South, but others had traveled to Phenix City from all regions of the country, including the industrial Midwest and the West Coast. They shared two characteristics: they belonged to the working class, and they were white. African American women worked in the city's gaming trade, but their commercial sex activities took place mostly in Columbus, Georgia.[18] The lack of substantive information collected on black women in the sexual markets around Fort Benning reflects the biases of those who shut down the market and the system of racial segregation in the South, which permeated neighborhoods, schools, and even the sexual market.

The records from the cleanup indicate that sex workers in Phenix City participated in a vibrant and dynamic vice trade structured around elaborate confidence games and sexual allusion. Gambling occurred within many of the city's establishments, and in some respects there was no clear distinction between Phenix City's gaming operations and the sexual market. Women often coaxed men to make wagers in rigged games, conned men out of money with tales of financial woes, and intimated that sexual intercourse might be theirs for the price of a few cocktails. Prostitution, typically defined as the exchange of sexual intercourse or other sexual acts, including fellatio or manual stimulation, for money did occur and sometimes overlapped with the cons.

In Phenix City, B-girls, or drink solicitors, played a significant role in the sex trade. B-drinking was a ubiquitous practice, sanctioned by law enforcement, who issued women permits to operate.[19] B-girls used their charm and sexuality to entice men to buy them drinks and then profited from each cocktail purchased. The success of a B-girl's efforts was predicated on the implication that sexual intercourse or some form of sexual intimacy was possible in exchange for purchase of the alcoholic beverages. The more flirtatious and the more available a woman appeared, the more drinks the patron bought. In one popular drinking establishment, Boone's Café, the bartender, Henry, coached women, including his daughter Johnnie, on the practice of B-drinking. Married 18-year-old Johnnie did not divulge her specific techniques, but in other cities, B-girls sat on patrons' laps, engaged in kissing, and sometimes "permitted pawing."[20] B-girl performances, no matter the location, shared a similar goal, which was to persuade men to buy them drinks. Unbeknownst to the purchaser, the drinks bought for B-girls were often liquor free, although some cocktails contained a small amount of alcohol so as not to arouse suspicion.

Phenix City B-girls earned eighteen dollars a week, as well as a percentage, typically 50 percent, of the cost of each drink, which was fifty cents. Bartenders kept the earnings of B-girls separate from the bar's other profits. At Boone's, Henry placed the money in a cigar box near the cash register, and he noted the number of drinks each B-girl consumed by placing a mark next to her name on a sheet of paper.[21] Some women kept the straw from each drink to ensure that the bar owner paid them fairly.[22] One B-girl told investigators that she might consume as many as 115 B-drinks in a single evening.[23]

Although B-drinking might prove lucrative for businesses and the women they employed, some owners encouraged women to use more deceitful means to make money. Ernest and Glenn Youngblood, considered two of the most powerful vice operators in town, owned several drinking establishments that employed B-girls. The Youngbloods instructed B-girls to arrange bogus "dates" for sexual intercourse with their customers. Carolyn, a 36-year-old B-girl from Columbus, told investigators that the brothers had told her to charge twenty dollars per date. Male patrons paid in advance, and the women would agree to meet them at a local motel. However, the arrangement was a ruse to earn more money, and often the B-girls did not show up. If a patron went back to the bar and demanded that his money be returned, the bartender would claim ignorance of the scam.[24] B-girls expressed no remorse for the con, nor did they state that they felt forced to engage in the deceptive practices. The women received a share of the money from the dates they arranged, the percentage varying from establishment to establishment. Although some B-girls did engage in prostitution, for many the objective was to solicit as many cocktails as a patron would buy or arrange dates, and when a man exhausted his night's finances, the B-girl moved on to another patron.

The perceived sexual availability of B-girls in Phenix City also played a role in the gambling racket. Bar owners relied on women to entice men to participate in gaming. One woman explained a scam called "putting the hat on." Game operators instructed B-girls to bring male patrons to the establishment's back rooms under the pretense of sex. When the pair entered the room, they would find it occupied with men playing cards. Once the patron was in the back room, one player would ask him to sit in for a round while the player took a phone call. The dealer fixed the game so that the patron would win and feel confident to play again, but with his own money, the goal of the scam.[25] If the patron refused to play or expressed disinterest, the woman was to take him back to the bar and "feed him more whiskey."[26] As with the other cons perpetuated by B-girls, they earned a percentage of the patron's losses to the house.

Vivian, a B-girl at Boone's Café, described another con called the "pawn racket." A B-girl would concoct a story about her financial woes that supposedly had resulted in her pawning a valuable item, such as her watch. She would persuade the patron to give her five to ten dollars to get the watch out of pawn. Vivian explained, "We girls were told by Mr. Boone to give our watches to the bar tender, then get some soldier to pay them out of pawn for us. If they paid . . . we would get one-half."[27] The women found that they could earn more money by employing the gender stereotype of the damsel in distress, and the racket leaders capitalized on the willingness of the patrons to play along with these gender scripts.

By far the most duplicitous means of earning money involved "rolling" patrons. This was the practice of stealing a patron's wallet, watch, or other possession after the individual became intoxicated and lost consciousness. A B-girl named Johnnie told investigators that the proprietor at Boone's Café had warned her to make certain that "the customer was passed out before I took any money off him to be sure there wasn't any trouble."[28] The practice sometimes involved a more nefarious component. In Phenix City, rolling might involve drugging a patron's drink with knockout drops.[29] Typically the bartender or the proprietor would administer the drops and the B-girl would wait for the drug to render the patron unconscious. The B-girl would then go through the patron's pockets in search of valuables, such as watches, rings, and cigarette lighters, as well as cash.[30] Bartenders took care to note the items or money the women earned from B-drinking, rolling, and the various rackets they executed. Some owners encouraged conning patrons more than others did. The Youngblood brothers instructed a B-girl named Arlene to get money from patients "anyway she could," including rolling. However, Arlene was warned that there would be negative consequences if she did not share the bounty she acquired.[31] Women turned over whatever they took from patrons and received half of the amount back at the end of the evening. Some women made a substantial amount of money from rolling patrons; according to Sheila, a woman could earn as much as $150 a night.[32]

Women sometimes learned techniques for rolling from other B-girls. Investigators considered Earline, Sheila's mother, a "known roll artist."[33] It is likely that Earline taught her daughter the intricacies of the B-girl trade. Sheila's entry into the sex trade as a B-girl demonstrates the limited options for daughters of sex workers. Women in the sexual market faced castigation, social opprobrium, and financial instability, all limiting their ability to foster a different path for their daughters. In some cases, mothers encouraged or forced their children into the market in order to exploit their labor or out of despair. In the case of Sheila, Earline's alcoholism and arrests led the young woman to the city, and lack of opportunity and her mother's reputation combined to limit her choices. Although it is impossible to know whether Sheila characterized herself as a victim of the trade or of her mother's lifestyle, her entrance into the sexual market was not an uncommon occurrence.[34]

Sheila admitted to investigators that she worked as a B-girl but denied that she engaged in prostitution. B-drinking and prostitution were not mutually exclusive, however. Shelia told investigators that most of the women she worked with could be "bought" for twenty dollars.[35] The specifics of filling dates with customers differed depending on the establishment. In some bars, women filled dates in back rooms or in trailers located on the property. Women who worked in establishments that lacked on-site facilities for intimate encounters filled dates at local motels. One restaurant and bar, Cliff's Fish Camp, was likely the closest there was to a brothel in Phenix City. Cliff's, operated by Cliff Entrekin, had six rooms upstairs and twelve stalls with booths on the first floor where women conducted business.[36] Prostitutes at Cliff's arranged their own dates, and clients paid the fee in advance to the women, who turned the money over to the bartender prior to filling the date. The bartenders recorded the number of dates each woman filled. Approximately five sex workers entertained between thirty and forty customers an evening, but the number of women workers increased to an average of eleven when Fort Benning soldiers received their monthly paycheck.[37] Troops told ASHA observers, "On paydays the joints are so crowded we got to stand in line."[38]

Cliff's was located six miles outside the city. The men who patronized the establishment often arrived by taxi. Drivers played a crucial role in the sexual market in Phenix City by ferrying male passengers to the bars. Business proprietors depended on taxi drivers and solicited their services. The owner of Cliff's hosted a fish dinner for cab operators at which he offered to pay drivers two dollars for each patron they taxied to his place.[39] Other bar owners, eager to capitalize on the profit potential, devised comparable business relationships with local cab drivers. Rudene Smith, one of only three women proprietors out of dozens of bar owners, hosted a dinner for cab drivers at which she coordinated a similar arrangement for one of her bars, the 431 Club.[40] In a 1951 observation of commercial vice activities in Phenix City, the ASHA confirmed that ten drivers had volunteered to "act as go-betweens" for three brothels.[41]

Cab operators played an important role as go-betweens in the commercial sex industry in large urban locations such as New York and Chicago.[42] They provided information to customers looking for prostitutes and developed valuable business partnerships with sex workers or operators of sex-work rings. The ASHA had long complained about the role of cab drivers in informing prospective patrons of the locations of brothels, bars, or hotels where sex workers operated.

The money paid to the cab drivers made earning a living tougher for sex workers. At Cliff's, 27-year-old Virginia charged $12 a date but made only $8 for her efforts—Entrekin kept $2, and the cab driver received $2.[43] Arlene, who worked for the Youngbloods, stated that she only made $4 after the brothers and the cab drivers took their share.[44] Yet, during one of the many trials that occurred after the cleanup, two women who worked at Cliff's claimed to have earned as much as $600 a week, and one speculated that some women earned as much as $800. The income stemmed from their combined labor as B-girls and prostitutes.[45] The trials overwhelmingly showed that most women did not earn $600 a week and that those who did only netted $350 after they split the earnings with the establishment's proprietor.[46] However, the wages were better than what women earned in one of the most common forms of labor in the South, factory work. On average, factory work in the United States paid women $1.50 an hour. In the South, earnings were less, with some estimates as low as 55¢ an hour.[47] While sexual labor was not consistent and was in many ways an unreliable form of income for women, it paid more than other jobs available to working-class women.

Women's reasons for entering sex work varied. While access to better wages influenced some, a number of women recounted coercive tactics that had led them into the sexual market. Profiting from the labor of sex workers was a lucrative venture in Phenix City, which makes the unscrupulous means sometimes involved in procuring prostitutes unsurprising. Several women recounted stories about police harassment, detainment, and sexual abuse. In January 1952, 32-year-old Earline originally went to Phenix City with three friends in search of work. All four women were arrested the night they arrived in town.[48] Earline told investigators that Ernest Youngblood had offered to secure her release if she agreed to work in one of his establishments. Earline declined his proposal. She and the other women spent three days in the Phenix City jail before the police released them. The three friends left town, but Earline remained in Phenix City. She searched for legitimate work but had no success and eventually agreed to work as a B-girl for Youngblood.[49] During her years in Phenix City, Earline was arrested quite often on alcohol-related charges.[50] The fines and fees proved costly, and Earline borrowed money from the Youngbloods to cover the expense. She found herself in a cycle of debt to the men, making it nearly impossible to leave their employment even if she so desired.

No other women mentioned being in perpetual debt to vice leaders, but Earline's circumstances reveal the role local police played in assisting vice leaders to procure sex workers. The story of 19-year-old Virginia substantiates the corrupt methods used to coerce some women. The assistant chief of police, Buddy Jowers, detained Virginia, along with her friend Anna, after a traffic stop in February 1954. Jowers did not charge the women with any violation, but he threatened to fine them fifty dollars and perform a strip search. The women did not have the funds and refused to consent to the search. Virginia told investigators that Jowers and another individual (presumably an officer) had suggested that the women could be released if they would "go back into a cell with them for an hour." Both women rejected the offer. Shortly thereafter, while detained in a cell, the women were visited by the Youngblood brothers, who offered to get the women out of jail, buy them clothes, and find them a place to live if they agreed to work as prostitutes. The Youngbloods explained that each woman would earn eight dollars for every date she filled (four dollars less than the actual price of twelve dollars for each date). The women refused but noted that a woman sharing their cell agreed to the proposal and the police released her. After several hours in the cell, another officer took pity on the women and allowed them to leave. Anna left Phenix City, but Virginia stayed, and when she could not find other work, she turned to prostitution.[51]

Police employed their powers as official authorities to coerce women into the sex trade, and women rarely defied police or vice leaders' dictates. However, one incident reveals the perils for women who did. A B-girl named Louise disclosed a violent confrontation during which she challenged the authority of a vice leader. One evening at the Haytag, police emptied the bar after a brawl involving Fort Benning soldiers. Louise asked Glen Youngblood whether her friend Judy, another B-girl, could end her shift early since the bar had no patrons. Youngblood warned Judy that if she left, she would forfeit her evening's pay. In front of employees and law enforcement, Louise accused him of swindling Judy out of her earnings. Youngblood angrily left and went to another of his establishments. Shortly thereafter, he sent for Louise. When she arrived, Youngblood told her he wanted to "kick [her] ass" and proceeded to slap Louise with considerable force. She fell through the front door and landed outside on the sidewalk. Youngblood followed her back to the Haytag, calling her a bitch, after which Louise threatened him with a broken bottle. A police officer who witnessed the attack on Louise arrested her on public drunkenness. She paid an $11.50 fine and asked the judge if she could swear out a warrant for Youngblood's physical assault against her. The judge advised her to reconsider retaliating and warned that "Glen had ways to get even with her."[52] While Louise's experience indicates that violence occurred, state investigators uncovered no other episodes. However, these incidents were likely unreported to local police and may not have been of particular interest to investigators, who focused on solving other crimes and breaking up the gambling racket.

While violence was not commonly employed to maintain control over sex workers, leaders in the vice industry subjected women to workplace regulations and expected women to abide by the rules. When the National Guard raided Cliff's Fish Camp during the 1954 cleanup, they found a written set of rules that dictated the women's shift hours, which began at eight o'clock in the evening and ended at three in the morning, and a code of behavior that prohibited becoming or arriving intoxicated at work. Accompanying each rule was a fine for violating the restrictions. The proprietor docked $12.50 from women's earnings for arriving late or inebriated, as well as for not showing up for a shift.[53] Many considered Cliff's a respectable establishment; therefore, it was not surprising that the rules expressly forbade rolling patrons.[54] Women also were not allowed to leave before the end of their shift without incurring a monetary penalty. Other proprietors instituted similar rules, but fines and restrictions varied.

The regulations Cliff's and other establishments implemented served to control women's behavior and therefore their sexual labor. The efforts to do so reveal the paradox in conventional examinations of women's sexuality in the 1950s, which focus on ideas of sexual containment, predicated on beliefs about men as breadwinners and women as caretakers of the home. Society expected women to make sure that sexual behavior was appropriate, confining it to marriage or to relationships expected to lead to marriage.[55] Rather than upholding a virtuous sexuality, one that included engaging in sex only in the marital bedroom to fortify the strength and respectability of the nation during the Cold War, sex workers in Phenix City were subjected to rules that exploited their sexuality to ensure its profitability.

In the black market in Phenix City, women's sexuality was lucrative and therefore placed them in positions as breadwinners, though their earnings benefited the men who ran the market far more than the women laborers. Creating an alternative code of behavior in the sexual marketplace served to contain women's sexual labor in a physical location in order to maximize profits. Restrictions on shift times, alcohol consumption, and leaving during a shift differed from the social-sexual rules for many women in the 1950s. Middle-class women faced social condemnation for operating outside pre-scribed sexual roles, but Phenix City's market created its own sexual ethos, encouraging women's sexual engagements outside the home and assigning a monetary punishment for those who traversed the lines of the ethos. Both sexual laborers and middle-class women who stepped outside the prescribed roles threatened male power by challenging the sexual rules governing their communities. When Louise argued with the bar owner about why her friend Judy could not end her shift early, she threatened the male-dominated power structure by questioning the rules. Women outside the sexual market too challenged the system of prescribed gender roles and often defied the rules. However, just as middle-class women in the 1950s pushed the boundaries of containment, so too did the women in the sexual black market.

While women lacked control over the operation and their hours of work and endured a regulatory structure that restricted their behavior, they exerted some control over their physical movements. Women found a means to withhold their sexual labor or at least exercise more power over its use through mobility. Many of the sex workers in Phenix City migrated between establishments, working at an average of four places in five years, sometimes returning to one place several times. Arlene worked at seven different bars after moving to Phenix City in 1949. Lola, who entered the sex trade in Phenix City in 1950, worked at eleven places from the time of her arrival to the 1954 cleanup.[56]

While mobility was a characteristic of prostitution in the postwar era, it was also evident earlier in the twentieth century. Geographical movement provided women with some control over their sexual commerce. While neither Lola nor Arlene noted why she left one establishment for another, Earline left because of an argument with other employees, and Carolyn quit temporarily when her husband returned from overseas.[57] One woman, Mary Lois, resigned when a bartender at the Blue Bonnet pressured her to prostitute. Instead, she found work as a B-girl at another establishment.[58] In other sexual markets women packed up and moved if the business dwindled or if local authorities cracked down on the trade.[59] Quitting was an act of resistance and adaptation and ultimately a way to exert power over one's sexual labor.

The leaders of Phenix City's sexual black market were almost exclusively men, but two women proprietors demonstrate the influence some women achieved in the male-dominated vice world. Beechie Howard, often referred to as Ma Beechie, owned a popular striptease bar in the city that opened in 1937.[60] Sixty-four years old at the time of the cleanup, Howard had five adult children and at least two former husbands. Her business, Beechie's, was successful, even attracting college men from nearby Auburn University. At Beechie's, patrons watched strip shows while prostitutes and B-girls plied their trade. Several women in the sexual market who were interviewed by investigators had worked for Howard at one point. Her age and bespectacled face made her a frequent subject in local newspapers.[61] After the cleanup Howard faced only gambling charges, despite evidence that she had employed prostitutes.[62]

Another woman, Rudene Smith, operated an extensive prostitution ring in town. While investigators believed that Entrekin, the Youngbloods, and another man were the major operators, journalists who followed the events believed Smith was in charge.[63] Smith rose through the ranks of the vice market in part through her male siblings, who played a significant role in the gambling racket, but also due to her business acumen. Smith began as a bartender at the Blue Bonnet in the late 1930s, earning just seven dollars a week. She gained a reputation for recruiting sex workers for the club and opened her own establishment in 1949.[64] By the time of the cleanup in 1954, Smith had financial interests in three Phenix City establishments: the 431 Club, the Silver Dollar, and the Silver Slipper. The 431 Club was part of a larger property that contained a private residence, four tourist cabins, and the Circle Motel. Despite her property and club ownerships, Smith claimed that she earned very little money and denied any involvement in prostitution. Investigators disagreed and believed that she employed B-girls and prostitutes at the establishments she operated; they also concluded that the Circle Motel served as the headquarters for her prostitution ring.[65] Two Birmingham, Alabama, journalists who later wrote a book about the events noted that 39-year-old Smith became one of the only women in the sexual market to hold a position of power and authority.[66] Her financial gains and her role in the trade undermined her protestations of innocence. Many sex workers implicated her and claimed they had worked at Smith's establishments. Her property ownership and her family connections suggest that Smith was indeed an influential woman in the black market.

Smith's and Howard's establishments drew numerous male clients. The men who patronized the vice district in the city were mostly soldiers from Fort Benning, although some were locals seeking the companionship of women in the industry. Journalists at the time referred to these customers as "suckers in the clip joints."[67] However, the men were not unaware of the operations of the sex trade, and while blame cannot be placed on the victims of Phenix City's vice circuit, it would be remiss not to explore how such an impressive fraud could be perpetrated against the soldiers and other male patrons. Even before the cleanup, Fort Benning officials placed twenty-nine establishments off limits due to fleecing of soldiers and violence perpetrated against them.[68] Some establishments found clever and easy ways to skirt the off-limits designation, sometimes by simply changing their name, as the Youngblood brothers did when they renamed the Maytag the Haytag.[69] While the name change may have fooled some military authorities, the location of the bar did not change, and troops continued to visit the establishment.

The practice of fleecing patrons, particularly those in the military, elicited few complaints from soldiers to police, but some men did complain to bartenders about B-girls and the fraudulent gaming. Complaints typically fell on deaf ears and sometimes resulted in violence. In one case, a scammed soldier waited until a bar closed to try to get his money back from a B-girl who had reneged on a date. A bartender pistol-whipped the serviceman, and military police placed the bar, the Hi-Lo, off limits.[70] In other cases, owners and bartenders reported "rolled" patrons as intoxicated to police.[71] Authorities would arrest the patron and charge him with an excessive fee or bond. According to Sheila, police would sometimes tow the cars of the "drunk" soldiers they arrested and then charge exorbitant fees to return them. The prices were so high that some troops could not afford to pay and had to relinquish their vehicles. Friends and family of the officers or the vice leaders would keep the cars.[72]

Even though base officials warned soldiers of the perils of spending an evening in Phenix City, they continued to visit the city and seek the company of B-girls or the gaming table. Soldiers and other male patrons engaged, sometimes willingly, in a complex relationship with B-girls that involved the hope of sexual intimacy for one and the chance of monetary gain for the other. In 1966, the sociologist Sherri Cavan studied public drinking spaces in the United States and in particular examined the B-drinking practice. She found that the motivation for men in these exchanges was the "purchase of sociability," and the act carried no negative stigma.[73] While some men may not have known that the encounter was a commercial one, most understood the sport. The possibility of intimate sexual contact or perhaps the desire for mere heterosocial relations itself outweighed soldiers' concerns about being fleeced. B-girls too understood this intricate interaction, albeit in a different light. One B-girl told a reporter from a jail cell that in her line of work "if anyone is stupid enough to let somebody do it [fleece] to them, there's always somebody stupid enough to do it."[74] A B-girl's economic success depended on this transaction, and for the men involved, perhaps the fleecing was worth the potential intimacy potential; it was a game in which both players understood the likely outcome.

The market ceased after the murder of Albert Patterson, the Democratic Party nominee for Alabama state attorney general. Patterson, a resident of Phenix City, campaigned on a promise to rid the city of vice, angering many of the operators and leaders in the city. On the evening of June 18, 1954, he was shot and killed as he walked from his law office to his car. Investigators, even before the state realized the extent of the involvement of public officials, quickly determined that the city had allowed the vice leaders to operate freely and with impunity. The governor of Alabama, Gordon Persons, declared martial law on July 22, 1954. National Guard troops entered the city and conducted raids on many of the city's vice establishments.[75] The Guard closed bars and gaming joints, and the state launched an investigation into the vice trade. Syndicate leaders threatened sex workers, who they feared might cooperate with investigators. One proprietor told his former employee Virginia that if she talked with the National Guard, she would "not get off with just a few bruises."[76] Of particular concern to some vice leaders was Sheila's diary. Sheila said that she had written notes "just to pass the time" while her mother worked. Her diary documented how the market worked, the practice of "rolling" patrons, and payoffs to local police. During the cleanup, Ernest Youngblood asked Sheila if she still had the diary. She replied that she did but that there was nothing to write about anymore. Youngblood warned her that it was "not healthy" for her to keep that diary. A fearful Sheila burned it that evening.[77]

While the National Guard closed down the city, investigators uncovered the scope of local authorities' involvement in the market (fig. 2.1). The Guard questioned dozens of sex workers and bar employees about what role city officials had played in the vice racket as they tried to solve Patterson's murder. What the Guard discovered was a complex, well-organized system of graft. The police had protected the market's existence by taking bribes to deter raids, and most

Fig. 2.1. Alabama National Guard in Phenix City, 1954. Courtesy Birmingham, Alabama, Public Library Archives.

businesses had paid the fee to high-ranking police officials, including Assistant Chief of Police Buddy Jowers, as well as the city's highest-ranking deputy, Albert Fuller. When asked if they had witnessed payoffs or bribes, numerous B-girls, prostitutes, and bartenders answered affirmatively and told of weekly bribe pick-ups, backroom meetings, and sealed envelopes. The B-girl Sheila told investigators that Fuller had visited a number of the bars where either she or Earline worked. According to employers at Cliff's, Entrekin had paid Fuller one-third of the earnings from prostitution at his place.[78] Investigators estimated that Fuller had earned approximately six thousand dollars a week from his vice protection racket.[79]

Fuller's financial interest in the vice market made him suspect to state investigators. The investigation also focused on two others, Archer Ferrell, the syndicate-friendly county solicitor general and the then state attorney general, Silas Coma Garrett III, both political enemies of Patterson. Investigators soon concluded that Garrett and Ferrell, along with Fuller, had conspired to murder Albert Patterson. In March 1955 the state found Fuller guilty of murder and sentenced him to life in prison. Prosecutors charged Ferrell and Garrett as well; however, the court acquitted Ferrell, and Garrett, who suffered a mental breakdown, never faced trial.

Ironically, by assassinating Patterson, Fuller had quickened the demise of the market rather than protected it from ruin. The black market in Phenix City crumbled when the state descended on the town. Guards confiscated gaming machines and arrested vice peddlers and leaders, and the flow of money that had once seemed endless vanished. Physically displaced by the cleanup and facing economic hardship, many sex workers left town. Military officials estimated that as many as a thousand prostitutes and gamblers left Phenix City in the days and weeks after the murder.[80] Some women moved to other parts of Alabama after the cleanup, while others moved out of state. Three sex workers moved to New Orleans, and another to Florida. One was found in Chattanooga, Tennessee, where police arrested her for vagrancy. Others only traveled as far as Columbus, Georgia, where city authorities worked quickly to stave off the development of a sexual market on par with Phenix City's by arresting the migrating sex workers.

By far the greatest number of women who took flight migrated to Aiken, South Carolina, with estimates of more than one hundred individuals moving to the town.[81] Many of those involved in the Phenix City vice market opened drinking establishments in Aiken in an effort to replicate the lucrative vice trade once vibrant in their former city. Vice leaders and two-bit players made the journey as well. During the investigation, no one offered an explanation about why Aiken became the destination of choice, but the city's population had changed dramatically with the development of the Savannah River Plant, a nuclear-power facility that opened in 1953. The plant had attracted approximately forty thousand temporary workers and another six thousand permanent ones, many of whom were young men—a ready-made clientele for vice leaders and migrating sex workers.[82] Aiken was also forty miles from Camp Gordon, an army training facility outside Augusta, Georgia. Members of Phenix City's sexual black market were not the only individuals to recognize that there was a potentially profitable vice market in Aiken. The ASHA expressed concerns that the area's industrial development, combined with the increasing number of troops training nearby because of the growing US presence in Asia, would create a situation ripe for sexual vice. They issued a report on the Savannah River Area concluding that "the racketeers who thrive on the earnings of prostitution can hardly be expected to fail to see in the Armed Forces and in the heavy industrial concentrations . . . splendid sources of revenue."[83] The ASHA's observations proved insightful and true. City officials and police in Aiken moved quickly to purge the Phenix City vice element. In July, Aiken police raided the city's bars and arrested fifty-three people on charges stemming from operation of a nuisance, selling beer on Sunday, gambling, and prostitution.[84] The ASHA's and Aiken officials' suspicions were confirmed: many of those arrested had come from Phenix City.[85]

Among those discovered in Aiken were several bartenders, including Henry, the bar owner Rudene Smith, and numerous sex workers, such as Carolyn, Johnnie, Vivian, and Sheila. Several of those who migrated faced Mann Act charges for enticing women like Sheila and Johnnie to cross state lines for immoral purposes.[86] When the pair returned to Aiken at the behest of their parents and the demands of authorities, they told investigators that they had recognized many Phenix City vice-trade participants in Aiken. They also confirmed that vice leaders had set up operations in Aiken similar to those in Phenix City; each place employed B-girls and offered gambling, and one establishment had prostitution. A former Phenix City bartender operated one of the new places, the El Morocco, which, much like establishments in Phenix City, had trailers on site and rooms in the back where women filled dates. Alarmed by the discoveries and the speed with which the vice trade had established itself in Aiken, the governor of South Carolina enlisted the assistance of the

FBI, hoping that the FBI's presence might deter the criminal element from solidifying its network.[87]

The closing of Phenix City's vice district and the investigation that followed revealed more than the migration of women out of Phenix City; it uncovered a substantial prostitution circuit across the South. Phenix City was but one stop on a circuit that included New Orleans; Jacksonville, Miami, and Pensacola, Florida; Mobile, Alabama; Aiken, South Carolina; and Augusta and Savannah, Georgia. Each of the cities on the circuit was located near a military base or a defense site. Women who traveled the vice circuit ranged in age from 17 to 24, and many moved with their husbands and children. The highly structured circuit involved a system of telegrams detailing the travel arrangements of women, known only by numbers rather than names. The communications contained a set list of prices, including ten dollars for a ten-minute sexual liaison, and the financial arrangements for participating establishments. The circuit, although speculated to include several places in Phenix City, seemed to only involve Cliff's Fish Camp, which according to newspapers was known throughout the world by American soldiers.[88] Journalists estimated that as many as thirty-five sex workers in Phenix City participated in the circuit. Little else is known about the circuit or the women that participated in it, though its existence is not surprising. As cities closed red-light districts, vice migrations were more frequent, and circuits sprung up throughout the South, providing steady work for women seeking to earn a living and elude authorities.[89]

The sex-trade circuit could only evade law enforcement when it remained clandestine, however. The events in Phenix City drew attention to the sex trade, and although authorities struggled to break the regional circuit, it succeeded in nipping one of its strongest city members. A grand jury ultimately indicted a total of 141 individuals on 734 criminal counts, including gaming without a license, vagrancy, aiding and abetting prostitution, and bribery.[90] The number of women arrested for violations involving prostitution is difficult to determine, as records have been destroyed or have disappeared, but ultimately few women faced charges. Journalists noted that the low number of arrests stemmed from the state's reluctance to prosecute individual sex workers, instead focusing on the vice ring's leaders.[91] The lack of arrests, though, also indicates the societal belief about women's sexuality as vulnerable to exploitation and misuse. While legal authorities indicted and convicted women like Beechie Howard and Rudene Smith for their roles in the racket, each facing primarily gaming charges, women who toiled in the market as sex workers escaped conviction. The sex workers were complicit in the sex trade's operations, though, so they can hardly be described as passive participants. In the court system, however, these women often served only as witnesses.[92] Despite destroying her diary, Sheila's observations proved crucial; in her testimony about the daily operations of the sexual black market, she noted the role of proprietors and law enforcement.[93]

In the aftermath of the cleanup and the trials, Phenix City sought to rebuild its image. The city razed buildings in the vice district and passed a new ordinance taxing garbage and car registrations to generate legitimate revenue. In December 1954 it claimed that the city had undergone a "moral recovery."[94] In January 1955, Governor Persons ended martial law, returning the city to newly elected and newly appointed officials.[95] After the trials and the waning public interest, Phenix City seemed to recover from its years of vice. Perhaps the fitting bookend to the story was the National Civic League's presentation of the All American City award to Phenix City in 1955.

Phenix City, once deemed "America's Wickedest City," eradicated its vice market. Many of its former criminal element endured lengthy jail sentences, and with the absence of those who controlled the market, the women in the sex trade migrated to locations with less stringent law enforcement or left the sex trade altogether. During Phenix City's sexual-market heyday, women's economic and sexual independence ironically depended on the men who controlled the market and created the social codes of sexual behavior they expected women in the market to adhere to. While some were forced into the market, other women entered it willingly. And all were not merely passive recipients of the sexual market's rules and structure or even simply the victims of those who exploited their sexual labor. Instead, southern sex workers in Phenix City eagerly participated in the market's devious operations and used their wit and their sexual labor to earn money. Many exerted what little power they had through mobility and worked within the system to profit, albeit minimally compared with those who crafted it. The tactics and methods imposed by the leaders of the crime syndicate defined sexual commerce in a bar culture, but sex workers often engaged on their own terms and illustrated the broad scope of sex work in the 1950s. The women in Phenix City participated in a sexual black market that they had not designed and did not control, but they negotiated its rules, regulations, and social structure to earn a living.

NOTES

1. The reasons why sex workers participated in the Phenix City market are myriad. Some worked by choice or in response to force, coercion, or necessity. Why women labored in the sexual market is at times impossible to discern. Because of the complex nature of sex work and the multiple names and aliases some women used, I identify women in the sex trade by their first name, adding an initial for the last name if necessary to distinguish women with the same first name.

2. In 1955, Allied Artists Pictures released the historical drama *The Phenix City Story,* based on the events in 1954. The film featured footage from journalists, and a few Phenix City residents appeared in the film.

3. Paul W. Burton, "America's Wickedest City: They Had Hot Time in Phenix City Until Marshall Law Put a Damper on Vice," *Kingsport (TN) Times News,* 8 August 1954, 8.

4. Phenix City began as a trading post, underwent several name and boundary changes, and developed an early reputation for raucousness and alcohol. For more information, see Alan Grady, *When Good Men Do Nothing: The Assassination of Albert Patterson* (Tuscaloosa: University of Alabama Press, 2003); and Margaret Anne Barnes, *The Tragedy and the Triumph of Phenix City, Alabama* (Macon, GA: Mercer University Press, 1998).

5. Lauren Wiygul, "Phenix City," *Encyclopedia of Alabama,* accessed 2 May 2012, www.encyclopediaofalabama.org/face/Article.jsp?id=h-2133.

6. Sharyn Kane and Richard Keaton, *Fort Benning: The Land and the People* (Fort Benning, GA: US Army Infantry Center, Directorate of Public Works, Environmental Management Division, 1994), online at www.nps.gov/seac/benning-book/benning-index.htm.

7. Grady, *When Good Men Do Nothing,* 6; Barnes, *Tragedy and the Triumph,* iv; "Crime: The Odds Were Right," *Time,* 28 June 1954, 24.

8. "Report on Columbus, Georgia War Area Sept 30, 1944," 22, Records of the Office of Community War Services, Richard H. Lyle Regional Director, 1941–44, 1945, box SG0014434, Alabama Department of Public Health, Alabama Department of Archives and History, Montgomery.

9. Joe Groetgut, "Phenix City Does Efficient Job in Suppressing Vice," *Thomasville (GA) Times Enterprise,* 24 September 1942, 4.

10. Charles W. Eliot, "The American Social Hygiene Association," *Journal of Social Hygiene* 1, no. 1 (December 1914): 1–2; Phenix City, Alabama, survey index card (December 1939–November 1944), box 105, Legal and Protective Surveys, American Social Hygiene Association (hereafter ASHA), Social Welfare History Archives, University of Minnesota, Minneapolis.

11. Phenix City, Alabama, survey index card (December 1939–November 1944), ASHA.

12. Edwin Strickland and Gene Worstman, *Phenix City* (Birmingham, AL: Vulcan, 1955), 199.

13. Phenix City, Alabama, survey index card (August 1945–November 1948), ASHA.

14. "Wave of Desperation Sweeps City After Crackdown," *Lake Charles (LA) American Press,* 25 June 1954, 1.

15. Timothy J. Gilfoyle, *City of Eros: New York City, Prostitution, and the Commercialization of Sex, 1790–1920* (New York: Norton, 1992), 310. Gilfoyle notes that the shift from brothels to a bar culture began to take place in the 1920s.

16. Exceptions, of course, existed in the predominantly male-owned bar culture. At least three women operated bars in Phenix City.

17. Burton, "America's Wickedest City," 8; Jack A. Warren Papers, Phenix City Investigation Papers, 1954, Department of Archives and Manuscripts, Birmingham Public Library (hereafter Warren Papers).

18. Records indicate that McCann's Place (a.k.a. Mack's Café), a gambling joint that catered to African Americans, employed black B-girls; however, the records contain only interviews with and information about white sex workers. "Report on Columbus Georgia War Area Sept 30, 1944," 22; McCann's Place index card, Warren Papers.

19. Earline statement, Warren Papers.

20. Ernest Lenn, "Widespread Use of B-girls in S.F. Gyp Bars Exposed," *San Francisco Examiner,* 22 January 1953, 1.

21. Henry statement, Warren Papers.

22. Virginia statement, Warren Papers.

23. "B-Girl Reveals Tricks of the Trade," *Fort Pierce (FL) News Tribune,* 29 August 1954, 2.

24. Carolyn statement, Warren Papers.

25. Sheila statement, Warren Papers.

26. Earline statement, Warren Papers.

27. Vivian statement, Warren Papers.

28. Johnnie statement, Warren Papers.

29. B-girls did not identify the drug used in the knockout drops. One B-girl said that the same drug was used as an abortifacient. Sheila statement, Warren Papers. The drug may have been chloral hydrate. See Herbert Asbury, *Gem of the Prairie: An Informal History of the Chicago Underworld* (New York: Knopf, 1940).

30. Sheila statement, Warren Papers.

31. Arlene statement, Warren Papers.

32. Sheila statement, Warren Papers.

33. Earline index card, Warren Papers.

34. Scant historical information exists accounting for the circumstances surrounding a sex worker's daughter's following her mother into the sex trade. However, Anne M. Butler provides an insightful examination of the subject in *Daughters of Joy, Sisters of Misery: Prostitutes in the American West, 1865–90* (Urbana and Chicago: University of Illinois Press, 1986).

35. Sheila statement, Warren Papers.

36. "Details of Prostitution Ring Found by Guardsmen," *Kingsport (TN) Times,* 24 September 1954, 6.

37. Ruth Faulkner index card, Warren Papers.

38. Phenix City survey index card (August 1950–July 1951), ASHA.

39. Robert Smith index card, Warren Papers.

40. Ibid.; John Henry Lisle Jr. statement, Warren Papers.

41. Phenix City survey index card (August 1950–July 1951), ASHA. The ASHA did not identify the three brothels.

42. The role of taxi drivers in procuring prostitutes for customers is explored briefly in Gilfoyle, *City of Eros;* and Kevin J. Mumford, *Interzones: Black/White Sex Districts in Chicago and New York in the Early Twentieth Century* (New York: Columbia University Press, 1997).

43. Virginia statement, Warren Papers.

44. Arlene statement, Warren Papers.

45. "Phenix City Vice Trial Jury Told of Prostitution Racket," *Lake Charles (LA) American Press,* 16 November 1954, 1.

46. "Phenix City Probe Finds Big Vice Ring," *Washington Post and Times Herald,* 25 September 1954, 3.

47. "Report on Columbus Georgia War Area Sept 30, 1944."

48. The charges were not listed, but police may have arrested the women on vagrancy charges, a relatively common charge for individuals who could not provide employment verification.

49. Earline statement, Warren Papers.

50. Sheila statement, Warren Papers.

51. Virginia statement, Warren Paper.

52. Louise statement, Warren Papers.

53. "Rules Told of 'Girls' at PC Camp," *Columbus (GA) Ledger,* 17 August 1954, 1.

54. Ruth Faulkner statement, Warren Papers.

55. The scholarship on postwar-era sexual containment is varied and nuanced. For a larger discussion, see Elaine Tyler May, *Homeward Bound: American Families in the Cold War Era* (New York: Basic Books, 1988); Beth Bailey, *Sex in the Heartland,* (Cambridge, MA: Harvard University Press, 1999); Lisa Lindquist Dorr, "The Perils of the Back Seat: Date Rape, Race and Gender in 1950s America," *Gender & History* 20, no. 1 (April 2008): 27–47; Joanne Meyerowitz, "The Liberal 1950s? Reinterpreting Postwar American Sexual Culture," in *Gender and the Long Postwar: The United States and the Two Germanys, 1945–1989,* ed. Karen Hagemann and Sonya Michel (Baltimore: John Hopkins University Press and Woodrow Wilson Center Press, 2014), 297–319.

56. Lola statement, Warren Papers.

57. Earline and Carolyn statements, Warren Papers.

58. Mary Lois index card, Warren Papers.

59. Amanda Littauer, *Bad Girls: Young Women, Sex, and Rebellion before the Sixties* (Chapel Hill: University of North Carolina Press, 2015), 29.

60. Strickland and Worstman, *Phenix City,* 32.

61. Investigator notes reveal few details on Beechie's, but the popularity of the establishment is noted in numerous fiction and nonfiction works. Howard's legacy, on the other hand, is difficult for a scholar to assess. Websites and monographs created by World War II veterans stationed at Fort Benning often describe Howard in affectionate and motherly terms, likely because of her appearance and age. See J. E. Kaufmann and H. W. Kaufmann, *G.I. Joe in France: From Normandy to Berchtesgaden* (Westport, CT: Greenwood, 2008); and "Welcome to Paratroopers of the 1950s," home. hiwaay.net/~magro/phenix.html.

62. Ibid., 47–51; "Outside Aid Eyed To Nab Missing 25," *Columbus (GA) Ledger,* 1 September 1954, 1.

63. Strickland and Worstman, *Phenix City,* 30. Strickland and Worstman believed that Smith was the largest prostitution operator in town.

64. Rudene Smith and Blue Bonnet index cards, Warren Papers; Barnes, *Tragedy and the Triumph,* 252.

65. Rudene Smith index card, Circle Motel index card, and Wyley Newton McWaters statement, Warren Papers.

66. Strickland and Worstman, *Phenix City,* 30.

67. Ibid., 199.

68. George McMillan, "Phenix City Discovering How Deep the Rot Ate," *Washington Post and Times Herald,* 7 August 1955, E1.

69. "State Draws Vice Picture from Ex-Cop by Ray Jenkins," *Columbus (GA) Ledger,* 2 February 1954, 1.

70. Tommy Thornton index card, Warren Papers.

71. Virginia statement, Warren Papers.

72. Sheila statement, Warren Papers.

73. Sherri Cavan, *Liquor License: An Ethnography of Bar Behavior* (Chicago: Aldine, 1966), 198–99.

74. "B-Girl Reveals Tricks of the Trade," 2.

75. "Troops take over Phenix City, Ala," *New York Times,* 22 July 1954, 34.

76. Virginia statement, Warren Papers.

77. Sheila statement, Warren Papers.

78. Ruth Faulkner statement and William Bryant Fuller statement, Warren Papers.

79. Grady, *When Good Men Do Nothing,* 37.

80. "Phenix City Vice Clean Up End Seen Near," *Washington Post and Times Herald,* 14 August 1954; "13 Nabbed in Vice Raid As City Keeps Guard Up," *Columbus (GA) Ledger,* 12 July 1954, 1.

81. "B-Girl Reveals Tricks of the Trade."

82. Kari Frederickson, *Cold War Dixie: Militarization and Modernization in the American South* (Athens: University of Georgia Press, 2013), 107.

83. "Proposed American Social Hygiene Services in the Savannah River Area (1952)," Military Correspondence, Savannah River Project, 1952, box 131, ASHA.

84. "Officials Probing White Slave Ring Said Interstate," *Anniston (AL) Star,* 17 August 1954, 1.

85. "Two State Probe Opens on Prostitution Racket," *Columbus (GA) Ledger,* 17 August 1954, 1.

86. Ibid.; "Federal Bureau of Investigation Reports December 1954," folder 12, box SG013721, Albert Patterson Case Files, Alabama Department of Archives and History, Montgomery.

87. "FBI Probes Phenix City Vice Spread," *Washington Post and Times Herald,* 18 August 1954, 3.

88. "Interstate Circuit Supplied Brothels," *Corpus Christi (TX) Times,* 24 September 1954, 14B.

89. Strickland and Worstman, *Phenix City,* 24; "Phenix City Probe Finds Big Vice Ring," 3.

90. Grady, *When Good Men do Nothing,* 163. Sources differ on the numbers. According to Margaret Barnes, there were 749 indictments for 152 persons. Barnes, *Tragedy and the Triumph,* 286.

91. Strickland and Worstman, *Phenix City,* 30.

92. "Guard Enters New Phase In Probe of Lotteries," *Columbus (GA) Ledger,* 24 August 1954, 1.

93. Barnes, *Tragedy and the Triumph,* 286; "Fuller Denies; Jury Awaits Charge by Ray Jenkins," *Columbus (GA) Ledger,* 16 November 1954, 1, 2.

94. "Anti-Vice Jury Quits," *New York Times,* 11 December 1954, 8; "PC Adopts Measures Taxing Garbage, Cars," *Columbus (GA) Ledger,* 28 December 1954, 1.

95. "Martial Rule to End," *New York Times,* 9 January 1955, 32.

3

"We Raised Them Up Never Even to Look at One"

SNCC, Local Organizing, and Interracial Intimacy, 1960–1963

FRANCESCA GAMBER

Jo was one of hundreds of northern white volunteers who spent the summer of 1964 in Mississippi supporting Freedom Summer, a massive voter-registration drive organized by the Council of Federated Organizations (COFO). Toward the end of the summer, Jo wrote home about a fight she'd had with a black male counterpart. The man had been playing a guitar that belonged to another white volunteer and responded with racial vitriol when the guitar's owner claimed it. Jo reacted by "ask[ing] the ranter why he didn't join the Muslims if he so badly hated the white man's guts." The pressures of sharing living and working space with strangers from different racial, ethnic, socioeconomic, and regional backgrounds during Freedom Summer in one of the nation's most violently segregationist states undoubtedly produced quotidian interpersonal conflicts such as this one. But as Freedom Summer came to an end, these disagreements reflected a discontent with interracial organizing that was taking hold in the Student Nonviolent Coordinating Committee (SNCC), which set much of the tone for COFO more broadly. "Summer volunteers are not SNCC . . . they are 'SNCC Freedom Corps,'" explained the minutes of a September 24 staff meeting of the Hattiesburg COFO office. The clarification was necessary because of concerns about "loss of black identity if summer people were part of SNCC proper."[1]

Undaunted by attempts to distance them from "SNCC proper," dozens of white Freedom Summer volunteers sought to remain on SNCC's staff. From 150 in 1963, the SNCC staff grew to more than 200, with another 250 permanent volunteers. In 1963, only six of SNCC's forty-one field-workers were white. After Freedom Summer, their representation grew to one-fifth of that staff.[2] Transitioning from a small, majority-black organization into a large and more clearly biracial one produced discomfort and sniping at the local level. During a November 1964 staff meeting at the COFO office in Jackson, workers' race, class, gender, and regional differences added extra venom to staff disagreements. One white woman criticized an African American staffer for "insist[ing] that people cannot do their job with your checking up on them." She cited as one example being required to show him the draft of a letter for his approval before mailing it. "Why do you insist I don't know things, Jesse?" she challenged. "I may not be from Mississippi and I may not be Negro, but I do know Freedom Schools and what they can do."[3]

SNCC's uncomfortable metamorphosis was complicated by the tension caused by the interracial romances that had emerged between black and white volunteers during Freedom Summer. Sustaining an interracial relationship after Freedom Summer could cause arguments between staffers debating SNCC's need to remain focused on the black community. "We've got to stop being Muslims during the day and integrationists at night," opined Doug Smith, who headed COFO's Fifth District, at a November 1964 staff meeting. A black woman in SNCC agreed that interracial staff tension "takes on a sex thing.... There's an unhealthy attitude in the Movement toward sex. The Negro girls feel neglected because the white girls get the attention. The white girls are misused. There are some hot discussions at staff meetings." In fact, concludes one Freedom Summer historian, "the 'sex thing' seems to have functioned as one of the most powerful pressures encouraging the expulsions of whites from SNCC."[4]

The historian Charles Eagles noted in 2000 that scholarship on the twentieth-century civil rights movement overlooks the frequency and consequences of interracial intimacy among activists.[5] Its youthful composition and its presence in a hostile South, however, have made SNCC a fruitful source for historians exploring this issue. Most of these scholars have interpreted interracial relationships in SNCC through the lens of the organization's shift from interracialism to separatist black nationalism, a transition that occurred in the aftermath of Freedom Summer's high-water mark of interracial cooperation and intimacy. SNCC attitudes toward interracial relationships do reflect its growing sense that the black freedom struggle would best be pursued without white assistance, but the story is more complicated than that.

SNCC activists were concerned about interracial romantic relationships between staff members or between staffers and local African Americans long before the influx of white volunteers during Freedom Summer. Though fears of white retaliation contributed to this concern, SNCC's origin as a southern-based movement led by African Americans was the stronger influence. Unlike the National Association for the Advancement of Colored

People (NAACP), which had been dominated by white activists in its first decade, SNCC was rooted in southern black communities from its beginnings. Its handful of white activists prior to Freedom Summer tended to be southern-born and generally allowed African Americans to take the organizational lead. The fact that some SNCC staffers began Freedom Summer prohibiting their volunteers from dating interracially flowed from the organization's originary blackness. From SNCC's founding in 1960, its organizers immersed themselves in the traditions and local leadership of rural black communities. In doing so, they confronted the legacy of a region in which white supremacy had been predicated on the sexual vulnerability of both black men and black women. Southern African Americans who staffed SNCC projects, as well as the residents with whom SNCC staffers lived and worked, carried family and sometimes personal memories that linked interracial intimacy with sexual exploitation and danger. In this way, SNCC workers encountered local constructions of interracial intimacy that problematized crossing the color line as risky, hurtful, and violent. The critical work of building trust between SNCC organizers and local people, perhaps even more than the imperative to minimize provoking white backlash, led to much of the organization's trepidation regarding interracial intimacy.

SNCC's oft-retold creation story begins at the Southwide Student Leadership Conference on Nonviolent Resistance to Segregation in April 1960. Held at Shaw University in Raleigh, North Carolina, the conference was the brainchild of the veteran civil rights activist Ella Baker and drew more than two hundred participants, who were inspired by the recent Greensboro sit-ins. Baker hoped the conference would allow student activists who were scattered across the South and affiliated with dozens of different universities, churches, and civil rights organizations to network with one another. More than that, Baker anticipated the establishment of an official student-run civil rights association that would avoid what she considered to be the mistakes made by the NAACP and the Southern Christian Leadership Conference (SCLC), two groups with which she had had years of experience. Baker guided the students as they formed the Student Nonviolent Coordinating Committee by the end of the conference, agreeing to serve as an adult facilitator. At Baker's urging, SNCC was founded on more egalitarian terms than most of its organizational forebears. It generally eschewed official titles and rigid hierarchies of leadership; it favored loose organizational affiliations to ease interassociational cooperation.[6]

SNCC's founders made specific efforts to reach out to white activists. In

January 1962, James Forman and Chuck McDew, SNCC's executive secretary and chairman, reported that the organization had hired a white field secretary, Robert Zellner, whose "function is to bring as many white students into the movement as he possibly can." The following year, SNCC enlisted Sandra "Casey" Hayden, a white Texan, to oversee its outreach to and fundraising among northern white students. But according to the African American SNCC activist Stokely Carmichael, "No 'white Americans' were ever on the SNCC staff.... Upon joining us, those comrades stopped being 'white' in most conventional American terms, except in the most superficial physical sense of the word." Carmichael attributed this shedding of whiteness to three factors involved in SNCC work: "working with blacks in complete equality; being on the receiving end of white racial hostility; *and* being immersed in the highest expressions of black culture while meeting the black community at its very best." Casey Hayden agreed, "We simply dropped race.... And we did love each other so much."[7] At this point in SNCC's history, color-consciousness, represented by the intentional outreach to white students and activists, figured as an essential means of creating a beloved community that would eventually be color-blind. That goal was enough to silence concerns that, as John Lewis, an African American SNCC member and future congressman, recalled, white people "might somehow be liabilities" as SNCC began voter registration and action projects in small towns in Mississippi and Georgia. Those reservations were "talk I wanted nothing to do with.... How could we ask others to look beyond race if we weren't able to do it ourselves?" Lewis asked.[8]

SNCC's most important departure from groups like the NAACP resided in its preference for grassroots organizing and immersion in local communities, where SNCC workers would defer to the experience of, and established authorities among, working-class and poor residents.[9] It was an organizing approach that in its emphasis on "native leadership" resembled the community-organizing model implemented by Saul Alinsky in Chicago's Back of the Yards neighborhood in the late 1930s. Like Alinsky, SNCC organizers emphasized the respectful observation of the traditions and values of the people with whom they worked. "The first stage in the building of a People's Organization is the understanding of the life of a community ... from the point of view of the collective habits, experiences, customs, controls, and values of the whole group," Alinsky advised in *Reveille for Radicals* (1969), his guidebook for community organizers. At the same time, he warned, "one should be constantly on guard ... against attacking local traditions."[10]

The care with which SNCC entered black communities in the Deep South was evident in the organization's first forays into the region. In the summer of 1961, SNCC dispatched Bob Moses to Mississippi purposely to acquaint the organization with existing local black leadership. In doing so, SNCC proceeded from a clear awareness that the struggle for racial equality in Mississippi long predated the civil rights movement of the 1960s. It worked to integrate itself into the traditions and priorities of a black freedom struggle that had been sustained at least since the late nineteenth century.[11] More than that, SNCC identified working with existing leadership as the way to create its own inroads in these communities, rather than reinventing the proverbial wheel. It also emphasized voter registration as its chief strategy, one that reinforced rather than challenged the strategy already pursued by black activists in the state. Moses arrived in Mississippi with introductions from Ella Baker, and he began meeting and talking with the leaders of the local NAACP branches. It was one of these local presidents, C. C. Bryant, of McComb, who agreed to host SNCC's first voter-registration initiative in the state. Moses was often accompanied to community meetings by Webb Owens, the membership chair of the McComb NAACP, who would be the one to both ask for and safeguard monetary donations. "Webb Owens was the key to the success of the fund-raising effort," notes the historian John Dittmer. "He was one of the most respected members of the community, and people trusted him with their money."[12]

Setting up shop in places like McComb, Mississippi, made SNCC's status as an interracial organization potentially treacherous. The segregationist South's historical tendency to link any campaign for integration with interracial sex was only inflamed by the sight of biracial groups of activists.[13] Even northerners associated SNCC members with sexual liberalism, an association SNCC inherited from a similar attribution associated with the Congress of Racial Equality (CORE). Barbara Jacobs Haber, a Jewish woman, was in college at Brandeis when she attended the 1960 conference at which SNCC was founded. She recalled finding the following limerick in her mail when she returned to campus: "There once was a coed in tights / who went in for big racial fights. / She said, I'm not a whore, / I just do it for CORE, / and color's the same without lights." Mark Naison was a sophomore at Columbia University when he got involved with the campus CORE chapter in 1963. "Some of my athlete friends implied that I had less than honorable motives for my civil rights activism," he said. "'We know you're in it for the girls,' they would say with a wink. 'We hear those CORE girls are really wild.'" Few northerners had difficulty transferring these assumptions to SNCC. "We[']re going to have a race of half breeds be-cause of the likes of a lot [of] pinkos like you," accused an anonymous writer from New York in an angry letter to the SNCC office in Atlanta. Even for sym-pathizers, being a part of SNCC carried a certain romantic connotation. In the fall of 1962, the white California journalist Jessica Mitford wrote approvingly to a friend that her daughter, Constancia "Dinky" Romilly, had taken a job at the SNCC office in New York. Dinky "has a job (of sorts) but mostly seems to have gone off with a Freedom Rider, who sounds heavenly," Mitford reported of Romilly's budding relationship with the black SNCC official Chuck McDew.[14]

Segregationist southerners needed no direct evidence of interracial ro-mances to respond to the new generation of direct-action protesters. The Flor-ida CORE protester Patricia Stephens reported after a March 1960 sit-in that "as a symbolic gesture of contempt," police who arrested protesters forced them to walk to the police station "in interracial pairs."[15] Although white activists were only a small proportion of SNCC workers prior to Freedom Summer, their presence marked them as racial traitors and generated special hostility. This was especially so in the case of white women, who had always borne the symbolic duty of perpetuating whiteness by reserving their bodies and repro-ductive capacities for white men.[16]

The phenomenon was not limited to rural deep southern backwaters. In the summer of 1960, Constance Curry and Bonnie Kilstein roomed together in Atlanta while working for separate civil rights organizations. That August, the *Augusta Courier* reported that Kilstein "has the habit of dating Negro men and she took communion at the Cathedral of St. Philip with one of her Negro boyfriends." The *Courier* also included Curry in a list of white women whose goal was "mixing the races." The following summer, a group of SNCC activists protesting in front of the courthouse in Monroe, North Carolina, heard white opponents scream at them, "Your mama is at home in bed with a nigger!" Dor-othy Burlage, who worked on a voter-registration project in Durham, North Carolina, in the summer of 1962, remembered going to lunch with a biracial group of friends when "some rough-looking white men started making threat-ening remarks about 'race-mixing.' . . . The men chased us out of the building and threw rocks at us." She and another worker got into a car and drove away, the driver "flooring the gas pedal." When the SNCC workers Mary King and Casey Hayden moved into an apartment in a black neighborhood in Atlanta in the summer of 1963, white locals "thought we were whores" and referred to them as "white pussy," King later wrote. The association with prostitution was a common one. The Mississippi Sovereignty Commission maintained a file on the German student Ursula Junk, whom one SNCC veteran remembered as a "famously chaste and devout young Catholic woman on the verge of taking sacred orders," that described Junk as a syphilitic prostitute.[17]

The Freedom Rides introduced SNCC activists to the reality that southern opposition would not stop at rumor and verbal harassment. Organized by CORE in 1961, the Freedom Rides deployed a biracial contingent of activists to travel throughout the Deep South to observe whether locals were obeying a recent Supreme Court decision mandating integrated transportation facilities. Departing from Washington, DC, that May, the Freedom Riders made their way south, en route to New Orleans.[18] As the buses pulled into Alabama, angry mobs stormed the buses and physically attacked the Riders; in Anniston, a bus was set on fire. Shaken by the violence, CORE began making arrangements to cancel the remainder of the Freedom Rides when SNCC activists came forward to replace the injured.[19] When the Riders reached Montgomery, a mob savagely beat the white activist James Zwerg, whom they called a "nigger-loving son of a bitch." At Jackson, Mississippi, local authorities arrested the Riders for disturbing the peace and imprisoned them for sixty days at the state's notorious Parchman prison.

The sexualized way in which southern white segregationists perceived the challenge of the Freedom Riders became clear in the treatment the jailed activists received. Female inmates, recalled James Farmer, were "given a vaginal search by a female guard using the same rubber-gloved finger, without washing between searches." Both Farmer and Carmichael remembered male Freedom Riders fearing that their imprisoned girlfriends would be raped. Prison officials also forced male inmates awaiting transportation to Parchman to stand naked while onlookers stared at them. "Holy Christ ... look a' that lil' nigger there! He got one like a hoss," exclaimed one, with "a touch of envy," Farmer wrote. "But look a' that one. . . . He ain't hardly got nuthin'," cried another.[20]

SNCC leaders were aware of the sympathy they could generate by exposing the severity of southern white violence, and they mobilized a sophisticated public relations apparatus to do so. The *Student Voice,* for example, described Freedom Riders "coughing and gasping for air" as they escaped from one of the buses, and the members of the mob that stormed the bus in Birmingham as "armed with lengths of lead pipe." The white CORE activist James Peck "had at least a dozen gashes on his scalp and neck." A report of a 1963 confrontation between SNCC workers and police officers in Americus, Georgia, noted that the activist Ralph Allen received such a beating that he needed "three stitches to close a wound above his eye." It also detailed the use of "guns, two-foot clubs, electric cattle prodders and black jacks" by police. Howard Zinn's 1964 book about SNCC inventoried the weapons used by police and white mobs against protesters, including high-powered fire hoses, dogs, pistols, and chains.[21]

SNCC publications made sure to note the ways in which white authorities even subjected women to these beatings. Zinn's book recorded instances in which police attacked pregnant women, causing a miscarriage in one instance. The sexual subtext of many of these attacks was seldom subtle. Bessie Turner, a teenager from Clarksdale, Mississippi, was arrested in January 1962 and forced to endure a flogging "between my legs." In a statement to the NAACP, another black Clarksdale resident, Odessa Brooks, described her stay in the city's jail after being arrested during a protest march: "Police officers were always violating our privacy by peeping in the cell saying 'man if we could get in there—nigger women have some good _____.'" Black women were particularly vulnerable to physical remonstrance, given southern white men's history of excluding them from the protections afforded to white women. When one woman informed a policeman, "I'm a woman! You don't hit a woman!," he replied, "You're a niggah and that's all you are!"[22]

While SNCC had an interest in broadcasting these instances to an indifferent public, it was loathe to provoke additional brutality by appearing to sanction interracial relationships between African Americans and its small number of white staffers. In 1962, the racial composition of a biracial contingent of volunteers bound for Albany, Georgia, who were spending the night in Atlanta aroused a neighbor's suspicions, and police were summoned. One volunteer remembered that Bill Hansen, a white staffer, hurried the women into another room, urging, "Get on some clothes, get on some clothes."[23] In the fall of 1961, newspapers were only too happy to circulate the story of an English-born woman and Freedom Ride veteran who, after being referred to a Dallas hotel by the regional NAACP office, was raped by a black man who was apparently unconnected to the movement. But the woman hastened to tell reporters, "This doesn't change my feelings about CORE or NAACP. It wasn't their fault. They kept us under strict supervision." Not wanting to appear responsible for putting a white woman in sexual danger, the southwestern regional office of the NAACP quickly issued its own press release denying that it had had anything to do with sending the woman to that particular hotel. "The leaders of the NAACP here are shocked and outraged at this whole unfortunate incident," averred the regional secretary, Clarence Laws, "and strongly resent any statements which falsely link the Association with it."[24]

The imperative for civil rights workers to distance themselves from interracial intimacy was not exclusive to heterosexual activists. In March 1962, police in Clarksdale, Mississippi, arrested Aaron Henry, a black pharmacist and president of the NAACP's Mississippi state conference. They alleged that Henry had given a ride to Sterling Lee Eilert, a white hitchhiker from Memphis. During the course of the trip, Henry supposedly had "asked him to find me a white woman," he wrote in his posthumously published autobiography. "[Eilert] said that when he had refused I had said he would have to serve as a substitute. Then, according to the boy's testimony, I reached over and grabbed his penis." Henry would serve six months in prison as a result of Eilert's charge. Although most of Henry's friends within the movement were aware that he was bisexual, the 1962 arrest was perceived as a political move. "I was convinced that they were trying to destroy my effectiveness in a movement in which most of the participants at the time were men. . . . No longer were bigoted officials satisfied with trying to brand us as communist. That charge, along with the claim that our goal was to put a Negro in every white woman's bed, had lost its punch," Henry astutely observed. In such cases, segregationists "picked a new charge—one detested equally by whites and Negroes—homosexuality."[25]

Black SNCC staffers did not hesitate to correct those white workers whose contravention of racial norms was done thoughtlessly or with intentional openness. During a frank 2004 discussion about sexuality in the civil rights movement on the website Crmvet.org, Willie Peacock related his recollection of one such incident that occurred in Mississippi in the early 1960s. Peacock claimed that Joan Trumpauer, the lone white woman volunteering with SNCC in the state at the time, would endanger black coworkers "by grabbing their hands and walking with them to infuriate the white man in a way. To possibly get the hell beat out of them." Pulled over by police while driving with two black men, Macarthur Cotton and Hollis Watkins, Trumpauer was forced to hide in the back of the car. "Enough of this. I'm sitting up," she declared. Cotton replied, "I'll choke you to death if you get up. If you raise your ass up." The white female volunteer who was oblivious to the explosiveness of her contact with black men was an object of ridicule well before she was joined by dozens of other white women during Freedom Summer in 1964. Peter deLissovoy, a white Harvard student participating in SNCC's Albany project, filed one such report with the *Harvard Crimson* in November 1963. His article poked fun at the image of a blonde-haired female movement volunteer, complete with inappropriately provocative long earrings, "bounc[ing] confidently and sensually over the red-clay Georgia road ... her face full and bright and her eyes flashing and darting as if she were caught up in a desperate search for someone to greet." She approaches a black man and corrects him when he starts calling her "ma'am": "And don't call me 'ma'am.'—I could be your daughter." The black man stammers, "OH NO MA'AM!—I mean yes, ma'am—I mean yes." Though the white volunteer congratulates herself "that she was identifying with the people and accepted and just like one of 'em," no one turns out at the courthouse to register to vote, as she had hoped.[26]

While police harassment certainly prompted SNCC's caution regarding interracial contact, the demands of everyday organizing work among disparate personalities also suggested the efficacy of avoiding the inevitable complications that flowed from these relationships. Dorothy Burlage, who led a voter-registration project in North Carolina in 1962, noted the problems caused by "competition for the same person ... that on occasion were articulated along racial lines." During one quarrel between two women over a common boyfriend, Burlage had to intervene because "one pulled a knife on the other. After helping them resolve their dispute peacefully, I felt more like a house mother than a civil rights worker." Many activists attributed these interracial romances to what Constance Curry called the "emotional maelstrom" experienced by white students involved in the black freedom struggle for the first time. "We were ready, black and white, to break all the taboos. SNCC men were handsome, they were brilliant, they were brave," explained Penny Patch, a white field organizer who joined SNCC in 1962 and dated a black man. Curry described a 1960 civil rights training session at which at least one white woman "fell in love with Chuck McDew. (This happened at all the seminars, and for most students it was the first time to be part of or witness to an interracial relationship)." Some white women found SNCC more accepting of their participation precisely because they avoided sleeping with its black men and did not become potential romantic rivals for black women or targets for southern white backlash. As Miriam Glickman recalled, after an unsuccessful attempt to join the SNCC staff in 1961, "I was finally accepted into SNCC in the summer of '63, because Chuck McDew came to Brandeis for a semester and I did not sleep with him." As Glickman's example suggests, not every white woman volunteer was eager for an interracial affair. Later that summer, while Glickman was working on a CORE project in Meridian, Mississippi, she found herself the subject of repeated sexual advances by a black staffer. "Every other time I ran into him, it took him just about 60 seconds to proposition me. And I found that extremely insulting," she asserted.[27]

Above all, however, its sensitivity to southern black communities disposed SNCC to approach interracial intimacy as a problem. Many SNCC staffers before Freedom Summer had been born and raised in Deep South black communities. They had grown up with an awareness of black women's vulnerability to white men. They would also have been familiar with—perhaps even witnessed themselves—the lynching of black men accused of raping white women.[28] This awareness stemmed in part from family histories. Fannie Lou Hamer, for instance, was the granddaughter of a slave named Liza Bramlett, who had been repeatedly victimized by her master; Hamer's family estimated that twenty of Bramlett's twenty-three children had been conceived as a result of rape. Charlayne Hunter-Gault, one of the first black students to integrate the University of Georgia, knew that her grandparents had sent her mother from South Carolina to Chicago to live with a relative because "some of the white men ... had their eyes on my mother, who was quite beautiful."[29]

All too often, however, exposure to the unwanted sexual advances of white men was a more recent and personal memory. Endesha Ida Mae Holland, who was recruited to the SNCC staff in Greenwood, Mississippi, by Bob Moses in 1962, had been raped by an elderly white employer in 1955 at the age of 11. The black Mississippians Joyce and Dorie Ladner were sisters who became involved in SNCC. When Dorie was about 12 years old, a white merchant had attempted to molest her when the girls went to his store for doughnuts. Dorie struck him with the bag of pastries. When she reported the incident to her mother, she replied, "You should have killed him. Don't ever let any white man touch you wrong." As children, southern-born SNCC staffers had been schooled by their parents, grandparents, and neighbors in the racial etiquette of life under Jim Crow, which Joyce Ladner likened to "walking a tightrope." Even black northerners who visited southern relatives during summer vacations were warned by their families about what not to do. Fourteen-year-old Emmet Till of Chicago had received these words of caution from his mother before traveling to his uncle's home in Mississippi in the summer of 1955. He was brutally murdered for allegedly making a pass at a white woman. Referring to them as members of the "Till generation," Ladner noted that SNCC staffers could cite the graphic pictures of his corpse printed in *Jet* magazine "as the key thing about their youth that was emblazoned in their minds."[30]

During Freedom Summer, northern white volunteers who encountered these stories learned that interracial intimacy was neither new nor uncomplicated in the Deep South. Sally Belfrage spent her summer living in Greenwood with the Amos family, who introduced her to the burden southern black men and boys bore as a result of the hysteria about white women's sexual purity. "We raised them up never even to look at one—they passes on the street, don't even look, that's the way down here," Mrs. Amos told Belfrage. But Freedom Summer volunteers could not miss the presence of light-skinned African Americans in these communities. Although white people "thinks the birds lays 'em," Mrs. Amos readily attributed these mulattoes to the sexual victimization of black women by the white men in whose homes they worked as maids and cooks. A white Harvard student wrote to his parents about attending a speech by a local preacher who asked, "If they don't believe in integration, how come they's so many half-white Negroes around?—somebody's been integrating for a long time." What Belfrage called "nighttime integration" was a phenomenon the summer workers witnessed with their own eyes; she recalled the "not infrequent sight of white men driving out of the Negro neighborhood at dawn."[31]

This historical sensibility, incubated for generations within southern black families, became part of SNCC's own organizing strategy. John Lewis remembered the pains taken to be "extremely sensitive about how we approached the local people" because many black southerners "had never been close to a white person in their lives. Some hands had never touched a white person's, and it was important to remember that when reaching out to shake those hands." SNCC prided itself on its activists' ability to ingratiate themselves with local communities, even residing in the homes of black families. For SNCC, that solidarity was a means of achieving longer-lasting civil rights victories than those engineered by more hierarchical organizations like the NAACP. SNCC workers replaced the Sunday-best respectable dress of SCLC activists with the blue jeans and overalls favored by rural black farmers. John Lewis occasionally scolded workers for taking advantage of the generosity of their hosts, including two staffers who stuck their host with "a $100.00 telephone bill." SNCC workers tried to avoid talking down to local people, drinking heavily, or engaging in obvious sexual promiscuity. Individual project directors also enforced stricter rules of behavior for white staffers, especially white women. According to Penny Patch, Charles Sherrod forbade the women working on his project from wearing pants, "because black people were unaccustomed to women wearing pants, especially blue jeans." Patch also claimed that Sherrod allowed black staffers "more freedom of movement. . . . to drink, relax, and have fun while white staff members remained at home or in the office."[32]

Respecting the sexual mores of a local community proved a particular challenge because, as the historian Charles Payne observes, SNCC staffers "were marketable items romantically." Young women often lingered around SNCC offices to flirt with the male activists. Most of these women's parents were upset by this, whether the object of their daughters' affections were white or black. In the case of black SNCC activists, local African Americans were often anxious that SNCC would only stir up strife with their white neighbors. One woman in Greenwood, Mississippi, forbade her daughters from becoming romantically involved with the black SNCC worker Sam Block for this reason. Nonetheless, young women found ways to socialize with the handsome, daring new arrivals to town in 1962 and 1963. "You had to be really acrobatic to keep those girls off you," Willie Peacock concluded. "And it was because they had never seen anybody face the Southern racist white-man power structure before. And that was the magnetism. They wanted to get close to you." A number of SNCC veterans recalled the eagerness of some local young women to become pregnant by civil rights workers and bear so-called Freedom Babies. "They were coming in like kamikaze pilots at us," Peacock quipped. SNCC removed at least one male staffer from his project in Mississippi after receiving complaints from several mothers about his sexual behavior.[33]

To the extent that SNCC accepted intraorganizational interracial relationships, it was most receptive to those between activists who had proven their fidelity to the black freedom struggle. John Lewis wrote approvingly of the romance between Paul LaPrad and Maxine Walker, a white man and a black woman, who "sat in at lunch counters together, were arrested together." The *Student Voice* reported the October 1963 wedding of Bill Hansen, a white field secretary, to a black field secretary named Ruthie Buffington. Hansen led SNCC's program in Arkansas, and the *Student Voice* carried articles about his frequent arrests; he even had his jaw and ribs broken in prison. The *New York Times* reported the wedding of the white SNCC worker John Perdew to a black woman named Amanda Bowen the following winter. But Perdew, a native of Colorado and a student at Harvard, was also a seasoned member of SNCC, having been "trampled on by police and beaten" in Americus, Georgia, in 1963 and jailed for four months there.[34]

In 1964, hundreds of northern white volunteers without Hansen's or Perdew's years of experience arrived in Mississippi to register black voters during

Freedom Summer. The influx of new volunteers who were neither black nor southern would have profound consequences for SNCC. Many historians—and movement veterans themselves—have chronicled the incidence of interracial relationships among volunteers, the violence they provoked from white southerners, and the internal conflicts they produced, especially between black women and white women.[35] Freedom Summer project directors sometimes issued explicit prohibitions of interracial dating among their workers. But these prohibitions, far from being reactions to the peculiarities of Freedom Summer, were in keeping with SNCC's existing approach to organizing rural black communities. While Freedom Summer staff expressed concern about the potential for white retaliation, much of their concern about interracial relationships that summer had to do with local reactions. SNCC had already spent several years in Mississippi incorporating itself into existing activist circles through careful and sensitive community organizing. While rural black Mississippians might not have assumed at that point that veteran SNCC staff would intentionally engage in behaviors that would provoke white backlash, they could not be so sure of the Freedom Summer volunteers.[36]

Cleveland Sellers, an African American worker at the Holly Springs project, remembered its director, Ivanhoe Donaldson, being "particularly emphatic about affairs between blacks and whites." Donaldson worried that interracial relationships, in addition to "provid[ing] local whites with the initiative they need to come in here and kill all of us," would cost civil rights workers "the support and respect of the people." Stokely Carmichael, who led the project in Greenwood, forbade relationships between white men and black women as especially offensive to local black people. But regarding relationships between black men and white women, "I don't know what our people's attitude will be," he explained. "We'll have to wait and see." Community attitudes could be more important than white hostility in determining how project directors approached interracial relationships. Although local people recognized qualitative and historical differences between these two different configurations of interracial relationships, they generally opposed both of them. Fannie Lou Hamer, for her part, was dismayed to see white women fraternizing with black men. She concluded in a conversation with another local activist, "If they can't obey the rules, call their mothers and tell them to send down their sons instead!"[37]

Understanding SNCC's approach to interracial intimacy as a function of its emphasis on local organizing responds to similar examinations under way in recent SNCC historiography. Several scholars have suggested that within SNCC's tradition of local organizing the shift to black nationalism was not such a radical transformation. Following the failure of the Mississippi Freedom Democratic Party (MFDP) to secure meaningful black representation at the 1964 Democratic National Convention in Atlantic City, SNCC leaders began searching for ways to turn black voter registration into black political agency in the Deep South. In 1965, Stokely Carmichael led the creation of the Lowndes County Freedom Organization (LCFO) in Alabama. The LCFO offered itself to voters as an all-black political party. The historian Hasan Kwame Jeffries describes its work at a moment of post–Freedom Summer organizational reflection as "a referendum for deciding if developing independent political parties ought to become SNCC's new organizing program." By the spring of 1966, positive local reactions to the LCFO had led SNCC to accept this model as its strategy for the second half of the 1960s. At a staff meeting in Kerhonksen, New York, in December 1967, SNCC leaders narrowly approved the dismissal of all the remaining white staffers in the organization. Jeffries and other recent historians have challenged the usual interpretation of SNCC's trajectory from "beloved community" to Freedom Summer to Lowndes County to Kerhonksen as a tragic one that attributes SNCC's demise to its adoption of the Black Power ethos. Instead, they connect the adoption of an overtly black nationalist mission to SNCC's origins in southern black communities and its tradition of local organizing. "SNCC's embrace of Black Power was not a break with the past, but rather a return to it," Jeffries argues.[38]

There is no denying that the turn to black nationalism and the forced departure of white activists from SNCC could have painful personal consequences. Many interracial relationships between movement volunteers became strained and snapped in its aftermath; others survived.[39] That not all interracial romances within SNCC shared the same fate encourages historians to refocus the lens through which they usually examine SNCC's activism. SNCC's caution regarding interracial intimacy well before the advent of Freedom Summer suggests that the relationships that had the greatest impact on SNCC's program in the Deep South were not those between black and white activists (though these were certainly important). Rather, it was the relationships between SNCC staffers and the local black residents with whom they lived and worked.

NOTES

1. Jo to John and Cleo, 12 August 1964, in *Letters from Mississippi,* ed. Elizabeth Sutherland (New York: New American Library, 1965), 185; Clayborne Carson, *In Struggle: SNCC and the Black Awakening of the 1960s* (Cambridge, MA: Harvard University Press, 1981), 133–37; Emily Stoper, *The Student Nonviolent Coordinating Committee: The Growth of Radicalism in a Civil Rights Organization* (Brooklyn: Carlson, 1989), 14–15; James Forman, *The Making of Black Revolutionaries* (1972; reprint, Washington, DC: Open Hand, 1985), 408–11; Belinda Robnett, "Women in the Student Non-violent Coordinating Committee: Ideology, Organizational Structure, and Leadership," in *Gender in the Civil Rights Movement,* ed. Peter J. Ling and Sharon Monteith (New York: Garland, 1999), 151; staff meeting minutes, Hattiesburg COFO, 24 September 1964, in *Student Nonviolent Coordinating Committee Papers, 1959–1972* (Sanford, NC: Microfilming Corporation of America, 1982), reel 3. On SNCC's dominance of COFO, see Len Holt, *The Summer That Didn't End: The Story of the Mississippi Civil Rights Project of 1964* (1965; reprint, New York: Da Capo, 1992), 33.

2. Forman, *Making of Black Revolutionaries,* 374, 420–21; Carson, *In Struggle,* 154–57; Charles M. Payne, *I've Got the Light of Freedom: The Organizing Tradition and the Mississippi Freedom Struggle* (Berkeley: University of California Press, 1995), 368–69; Winifred Breines, *The Trouble Between Us: An Uneasy History of White and Black Women in the Feminist Movement* (New York: Oxford University Press, 2006), 25; Kristin Anderson-Bricker, "'Triple Jeopardy': Black Women and the Growth of Feminist Consciousness in SNCC, 1964–1975," in *Still Lifting, Still Climbing: Contemporary African-American Women's Activism,* ed. Kimberly Springer (New York: New York University Press, 1999), 51–52.

3. Staff meeting minutes, Jackson COFO, 23 November 1964, Debbie Louis Collection on Civil Rights, Collection 1111, box 3, folder 4, Mississippi—COFO, 1964–1965, Department of Special Collections, Young Research Library, University of California, Los Angeles.

4. Fifth District meeting minutes, 25 November 1964, *Student Nonviolent Coordinating Committee Papers,* reel 3; black woman quoted in Paul Jacobs and Saul Landau, *The New Radicals: A Report with Documents* (New York: Random House, 1966), 145; Doug McAdam, *Freedom Summer* (New York: Oxford University Press, 1988), 124. For an alternative view of interracial liaisons as only "relatively minor distractions" during Freedom Summer, see Steve Estes, "Engendering Movement Memories: Remembering Race and Gender in the Mississippi Movement," in *The Civil Rights Movement in American Memory,* ed. Renee C. Romano and Leigh Raiford (Athens: University of Georgia Press, 2006), 297.

5. Charles W. Eagles, "Toward New Histories of the Civil Rights Era," *Journal of Southern History* 66, no. 4 (2000): 841.

6. On the founding of SNCC, see Stoper, *Student Nonviolent Coordinating Committee,* 6–7; Carson, *In Struggle,* 19–25; Barbara Ransby, *Ella Baker and the Black Freedom Movement: A Radical Democratic Vision* (Chapel Hill: University of North Carolina Press, 2003), 240–47, 273–74, 280–81; and Francis Schor, "Utopian Aspirations in the Black Freedom Movement: SNCC and the Struggle for Civil Rights, 1960–1965," *Utopian Studies* 15, no. 2 (2005): 173–89. For the organization's statement of purpose, see "Statement of Purpose," *Student Nonviolent Coordinating Committee Papers,* reel 1; and "Statement of Purpose," *Student Voice,* June 1960, in *The Student Voice, 1960–1965: Periodical of the Student Nonviolent Coordinating Committee,* ed. Clayborne Carson (Westport, CT: Meckler, 1990), 2.

7. James Forman and Charles F. McDew to Angela Taylor, 15 January 1962, *Student Nonviolent Coordinating Committee Papers,* reel 1; Wesley C. Hogan, *Many Minds, One Heart: SNCC's Dream for a New America* (Chapel Hill: University of North Carolina Press, 2007), 114–16; Stokely Carmichael, *Ready for Revolution: The Life and Struggles of Stokely Carmichael (Kwame Ture),* with Ekwueme Michael Thelwell (New York: Scribner, 2003), 307–8; Casey Hayden, preface to Mary King, *Freedom Song: A Personal Story of the 1960s Civil Rights Movement* (New York: William Morrow, 1987), 8. This is reminiscent of the historian John Stauffer's reference to the possession of a "black heart" by extraordinary white abolitionists like John Brown and Gerrit Smith; see John Stauffer, *The Black Hearts of Men: Radical Abolitionists and the Transformation of Race* (Cambridge, MA: Harvard University Press, 2002).

8. Stoper, *Student Nonviolent Coordinating Committee,* 9–13; John Lewis, *Walking with the Wind: A Memoir of the Movement,* with Michael D'Orso (San Diego: Harcourt Brace, 1998), 193.

9. Joe Street, "Spreading Ripples: SNCC and Social Capital in the Civil Rights Era South," *European Journal of American Culture* 30, no. 3 (2011): 197; Peter Ling, "SNCCs: Not One Committee, but Several," in *From Sit-Ins to SNCC: The Student Civil Rights Movement in the 1960s,* ed. Iwan Morgan and Philip Davies (Gainesville: University Press of Florida, 2012), 81–82, 93.

10. Saul Alinsky, *Reveille for Radicals* (New York: Vintage, 1969), 76–77. See also Robert Fisher, *Let the People Decide: Neighborhood Organizing in America* (New York: Twayne, 1994), 32–65. On the points of agreement and disagreement between Alinskyism and the New Left in general, see Jennifer Frost, *"An Interracial Movement of the Poor": Community Organizing and the New Left in the 1960s* (New York: New York University Press, 2001), 71–93.

11. In taking this chronologically long view of the black freedom struggle in Mississippi and indeed throughout the United States, I am in agreement with those historians who posit a "long Civil Rights Movement" that stretches from the 1930s to the 1980s. In fact, I have argued for a "very long Civil Rights Movement" that includes everyday slave resistance and would have its beginnings with the first Africans who arrived in North America in the seventeenth century. See Jacquelyn Dowd Hall, "The Long Civil Rights Movement and the Political Uses of the Past," *Journal of American History* 91, no. 4 (2005): 1233–63; and Francesca Gamber, "The Radical Heart: The Politics of Love in the Struggle for African-American Equality, 1833–2000" (PhD diss., Southern Illinois University at Carbondale, 2010). For a dissenting opinion on the "long Civil Rights Movement" concept, see Sundiata Keita Cha-Jua and Clarence Lang, "The 'Long' Movement as Vampire: Temporal and Spatial Fallacies in Recent Black Freedom Studies," *Journal of African American History* 92, no. 2 (2007): 265–88.

12. Street, "Spreading Ripples," 198; John Dittmer, *Local People: The Struggle for Civil Rights in Mississippi* (Urbana: University of Illinois Press, 1994), 102–5.

13. The charges that racial equality would bring "social equality" and that civil rights activists were really only interested in interracial sex were leveled against the abolitionists in the nineteenth century and the NAACP in the twentieth. See Gamber, "Radical Heart," chaps. 1 and 3.

14. Debra L. Schultz, *Going South: Jewish Women in the Civil Rights Movement* (New York: New York University Press, 2001), 31–32; Mark Naison, *White Boy: A Memoir* (Philadelphia: Temple University Press, 2002), 38, 46; "Anonymous," letter to SNCC, 12 February 1964, *Student Nonviolent Coordinating Committee Papers,* Subgroup A, Series IV: Executive Secretary Files, 1959–72, reel 6; Jessica Mitford to Peter Neville, 25 September 1962, in *Decca: The Letters of Jessica Mitford,* ed. Peter Y. Sussman (New York: Alfred A. Knopf, 2006), 295. Mitford's receptiveness to her daughter's involvement in an interracial relationship was a rare response for most northern and western families at this time;

when Mel Leventhal married the writer Alice Walker in 1967, his mother held a traditional Jewish funeral ceremony for him. See Evelyn C. White, *Alice Walker: A Life* (New York: Norton, 2003), 156.

15. Patricia Stephens, "Tallahassee: Through Jail to Freedom," in *Sit Ins: The Students Report*, ed. Jim Peck (New York: Congress of Racial Equality, 1960), unpaginated.

16. George Lewis, "'Complicated Hospitality': The Impact of the Sit-Ins on the Ideology of Southern Segregationists," in Morgan and Davies, *From Sit-Ins to SNCC*, 44–45. On the historical significance of the white female body to white supremacy, see Martha Hodes, *White Women, Black Men: Illicit Sex in the Nineteenth-Century South* (New Haven, CT: Yale University Press, 1997); and Catherine Clinton, "Bloody Terrain: Freedwomen, Sexuality, and Violence during Reconstruction," in *Half Sisters of History: Southern Women and the American Past*, ed. Catherine Clinton (Durham, NC: Duke University Press, 1994), 137–53.

17. Constance Curry, "Wild Geese to the Past," in Curry et al., *Deep in Our Hearts: Nine White Women in the Freedom Movement* (Athens: University of Georgia Press, 2000), 16, 20–21; Forman, *Making of Black Revolutionaries*, 188; Dorothy Dawson Burlage, "Truths of the Heart," in Curry et al., *Deep in Our Hearts*, 107–8, 110; King, *Freedom Song*, 75–76.

18. Raymond Arsenault, *Freedom Riders: 1961 and the Struggle for Racial Justice* (New York: Oxford University Press, 2006), 2, 28, 35, 89, 98–100, 133; August Meier and Elliott Rudwick, *CORE: A Study in the Civil Rights Movement, 1942–1968* (Urbana: University of Illinois Press, 1975), 135–36; Howard Zinn, *SNCC: The New Abolitionists* (1964; reprint, Cambridge, MA: South End, 2002), 41; Esta Seaton, "Courageous Ride Toward Freedom," *Phylon* 24, no. 1 (1963): 91–92.

19. Arsenault, *Freedom Riders*, 144–45, 165–66, 185; Meier and Rudwick, *CORE*, 137–42; Hogan, *Many Minds, One Heart*, 46–47; John Lewis, *Walking with the Wind*, 143; Carmichael, *Ready for Revolution*, 186.

20. Zinn, *SNCC*, 47; Hogan, Hogan, *Many Minds, One Heart*, 47–51; James Farmer, *Lay Bare the Heart: An Autobiography of the Civil Rights Movement* (Fort Worth: Texas Christian University Press, 1985), 9, 23–24; Carmichael, *Ready for Revolution*, 198. On Parchman prison, see David M. Oshinsky, *Worse Than Slavery: Parchman Farm and the Ordeal of Jim Crow Justice* (New York: Free Press, 1996).

21. "Freedom Ride, 1961," *Student Voice*, April–May 1961, unpaginated, in Carson, *Student Voice, 1960–1965*, 45; "In Americus, Georgia: Police Smash Demonstrators, Four Face Death Penalty," *Student Voice*, October 1963, 2, in ibid., 74, 76; Zinn, *SNCC*, 23–25. On SNCC's public-relations machinery, see Vanessa Murphree, *The Selling of Civil Rights: The Student Nonviolent Coordinating Committee and the Use of Public Relations* (New York: Routledge, 2006).

22. Zinn, *SNCC*, 80, 135, 138; affidavit of Odessa Brooks, *Student Nonviolent Coordinating Committee Papers*, reel 38; woman and policeman quoted in Cynthia Griggs Fleming, "Black Women Activists and the Student Nonviolent Coordinating Committee: The Case of Ruby Doris Smith Robinson," *Journal of Women's History* 4, no. 3 (1993): 73. See also Danielle L. McGuire, *At the Dark End of the Street: Black Women, Rape, and Resistance—A New History of the Civil Rights Movement from Rosa Parks to the Rise of Black Power* (New York: Knopf, 2010), 156–64.

23. Hogan, *Many Minds, One Heart*, 133; Penny Patch, "Sweet Tea at Shoney's," in Curry et al., *Deep in Our Hearts*, 141.

24. John Rutledge, "British Freedom Rider Says She Was Raped by Negro Man," in *Papers of the NAACP, Part 21: Relations with the Modern Civil Rights Movement, 1956–1965*, ed. John H. Bracey Jr. and August Meier (Bethesda, MD: University Publications of America, 1995), reel 12; "NAACP Denies Referral of Freedom Rider to Hotel," press release, 2 October 1961, ibid.

25. Aaron Henry, *Aaron Henry: The Fire Ever Burning,* with Constance Curry (Jackson: University Press of Mississippi, 2000), 116–28. See also John Howard, *Men Like That: A Southern Queer History* (Chicago: University of Chicago Press, 1999), 158–61.

26. "Women & Men in the Freedom Movement: A Discussion, June, August, & September 2004," accessed 25 June 2007, crmvet.org/disc/women1.htm; Peter deLissovoy, "Failure in Albany II: The White Minority," *Harvard Crimson,* 12 November 1963.

27. Burlage, "Truths of the Heart," 110; Curry, "Wild Geese to the Past," 17; Patch, "Sweet Tea at Shoney's," 155; "Women & Men in the Freedom Movement."

28. Accusations of rape were all too often merely the pretext for perpetrating extralegal violence against African Americans to quash an effort to exercise their newly acquired citizenship rights after emancipation. The nineteenth-century black reformer Ida B. Wells-Barnett famously referred to the rape justification of lynching as an "old thread-bare lie." See Ida B. Wells-Barnett, *"Southern Horrors" and Other Writings: The Anti-Lynching Campaign of Ida B. Wells, 1892–1900,* ed. Jacqueline Jones Royster (New York: Bedford/St. Martin's, 1997). The extensive scholarship on the use of lynching to curtail black political freedoms is summarized in the historiographical essay "Rape, Race, and Rhetoric" in Diane Miller Sommerville, *Rape and Race in the Nineteenth-Century South* (Chapel Hill: University of North Carolina Press, 2004), 223–59.

29. McGuire, *At the Dark End of the Street,* 156; Charlayne Hunter-Gault, *In My Place* (New York: Farrar Straus Giroux, 1992), 12.

30. "SNCC Women and the Stirrings of Feminism," in *A Circle of Trust: Remembering SNCC,* ed. Cheryl Lynn Greenberg (New Brunswick, NJ: Rutgers University Press, 1998), 140; McGuire, *At the Dark End of the Street,* 164–67; Joyce Ladner, "Standing Up for Our Beliefs," in *Hands on the Freedom Plow: Personal Accounts by Women in SNCC,* ed. Faith S. Holsaert, Martha Prescod Norman Noonan, Judy Richardson, Betty Garman Robinson, Jean Smith Young, and Dorothy M. Zellner (Urbana: University of Illinois Press, 2010), 217–18; Joyce Ladner quoted in Breines, *Trouble Between Us,* 42; Krystal D. Frazier, "Till They Come Back Home: Transregional Families and the Politicization of the Till Generation," in *Freedom Rights: New Perspectives on the Civil Rights Movement,* ed. Danielle L. McGuire and John Dittmer (Lexington: University Press of Kentucky, 2011), 137–61.

31. Sally Belfrage, *Freedom Summer* (1965; reprint, Charlottesville: University Press of Virginia, 1990), 45–46, 111; letter from Bill, 2 July 1964, in Sutherland, *Letters from Mississippi,* 158.

32. John Lewis, *Walking with the Wind,* 267; John Lewis, Six Month Report, 27 December 1963, 4, in *Student Nonviolent Coordinating Committee Papers,* reel 2; Patch, "Sweet Tea at Shoney's," 152–53; Payne, *I've Got the Light of Freedom,* 241, 306–7. On the politics of denim dress for both men and women, see Tanisha C. Ford, "SNCC Women, Denim, and the Politics of Dress," *Journal of Southern History* 79, no. 3 (2013): 625–45.

33. Payne, *I've Got the Light of Freedom,* 231–33, 251; Forman, *Making of Black Revolutionaries,* 287; Hogan, *Many Minds, One Heart,* 152; "Women & Men in the Freedom Movement."

34. John Lewis, *Walking with the Wind,* 273; "SNCC Wedding Stirs Arkansas Officials," *Student Voice,* 18 November 1963, 1–2, in Carson, *Student Voice, 1960–1965,* 81–82; Renee C. Romano, *Race Mixing: Black-White Marriage in Postwar America* (Cambridge, MA: Harvard University Press, 2003), 184; Brent Riffel, "In the Storm: William Hansen and the Student Nonviolent Coordinating Committee in Arkansas, 1962–1967," *Arkansas Historical Quarterly* 63, no. 4 (2004): 404–7; "White Civil Rights Worker to Wed Georgia Negro Girl," *New York Times,* 19 December 1964, 18; "In Americus, Georgia"; Zinn, *SNCC,* 185–86. For reports of Hansen's frequent arrests, see, e.g., "Little Rock Sit-Ins First in

Two Years," *Student Voice*, December 1962, 1, 4, in Carson, *Student Voice, 1960–1965*, 61, 64; "48 Jailed in Pine Bluff Sits-In," *Student Voice*, April 1963, 3, in ibid., 67; and "33 Jailed in Sit-Ins," *Student Voice*, 18 November 1963, 1, 3, in ibid., 81, 83.

35. See, e.g., "Women & Men in the Freedom Movement"; Chude Allen, "Ralph Featherstone," accessed 25 June 2007, www.crmvet.org/mem/feather.htm; Breines, *Trouble Between Us*, 41–43; Mary Aickin Rothschild, *A Case of Black and White: Northern Volunteers and the Southern Freedom Summers, 1964–1965* (Westport, CT: Greenwood, 1982); Sara Evans, *Personal Politics: The Roots of Women's Liberation in the Civil Rights Movement and the New Left* (New York: Vintage Books, 1980); Belinda Robnett, *How Long? How Long? African-American Women in the Struggle for Civil Rights* (New York: Oxford University Press, 1997); Cynthia Griggs Fleming, *Soon We Will Not Cry: The Liberation of Ruby Doris Smith Robinson* (Lanham, MD: Rowman & Littlefield, 1998); Romano, *Race Mixing*, 177–247; and Andrew B. Lewis, *The Shadows of Youth: The Remarkable Journey of the Civil Rights Generation* (New York: Hill & Wang, 2009), 159–61.

36. On the likely fears of rural black southerners about working with civil rights activists, see Belinda Robnett, "African-American Women in the Civil Rights Movement, 1954–1965: Gender, Leadership, and Micromobilization," *American Journal of Sociology* 101, no. 6 (1996): 1678–79.

37. Cleveland Sellers, *The River of No Return: The Autobiography of a Black Militant and the Life and Death of SNCC*, with Robert Terrell (1973; reprint, Jackson: University Press of Mississippi, 1990), 95–96; Stokely Carmichael, quoted in Belfrage, *Freedom Summer*, 42; Chana Kai Lee, *For Freedom's Sake: The Life of Fannie Lou Hamer* (Urbana: University of Illinois Press, 1999), 74–76; Dittmer, *Local People*, 263.

38. Hasan Kwame Jeffries, "SNCC, Black Power, and Independent Political Party Organizing in Alabama, 1964–1966," *Journal of African American History* 91, no. 2 (2006): 171–93. See also Street, "Spreading Ripples," 210. On the Kerhonksen decision, see Central Committee meeting, notes and decisions of May 1967, *Student Nonviolent Coordinating Committee Papers*, reel 3.

39. Memoirs by movement veterans or their children that link the breakup of interracial relationships to the pressures created by the turn to black nationalism include Amiri Baraka, *The Autobiography of LeRoi Jones* (New York: Freundlich Books, 1984), 200–201; Hettie Jones, *How I Became Hettie Jones* (New York: E. P. Dutton, 1990), 226; Naison, *White Boy*, 96; and Rebecca Walker, *Black, White, and Jewish: Autobiography of a Shifting Self* (New York: Riverhead Books, 2001), 60. For examples of interracial relationships that were sustained after the turn to black nationalism, see Forman, *Making of Black Revolutionaries*, xiv–xv; "Activist Who Succeeded Given Tribute in Capital," *New York Times*, 16 November 1972, 54; Burt Solomon, *The Washington Century: Three Families and the Shaping of the Nation's Capital* (New York: William Morrow, 2004), 123–26, 148–151, 180–82; and John Blake, *Children of the Movement: The Sons and Daughters of Martin Luther King Jr., Malcolm X, Elijah Muhammad, George Wallace, Andrew Young, Julian Bond, Stokely Carmichael, Bob Moses, James Chaney, Elaine Brown, and Others Reveal How the Civil Rights Movement Tested and Transformed Their Families* (Chicago: Lawrence Hill Books, 2004), 76–80.

4

Heat Wave

The Memphis Deep Throat *Trials and Sexual Politics in the 1970s*

WHITNEY STRUB

W hen hardcore pornography screened in mid-1970s Memphis, it was more likely to play in a courtroom than in a theater. Assistant US Attorney Larry Parrish had spent the first half of the decade pursuing smut with a ferocity unseen since the 1870s heyday of the notorious antivice crusader Anthony Comstock, and by 1976 his "Memphis Heat" had begun drawing national headlines. Busting porn distributors and theater owners was one thing, but when Parrish charged Harry Reems, the well-known male lead of the immensely successful *Deep Throat,* with criminal conspiracy to distribute obscene material, the Memphis Heat took symbolic importance as a key battle site in the culture wars of the sexual revolution and the emerging New Right.

As the first male porn star of note, Reems recognized that his persona "may conjure up visions of my lurking in dark bus terminals with reels of films jammed in my pockets." But "that's just not true," he contended in a mailing for the Harry Reems Legal Defense Fund sent across the nation in late 1976 and early 1977.[1] Facing five years' imprisonment and a ten-thousand-dollar fine, Reems wrote, "My case sets precedents that will change the artistic climate of the entire United States." It did not seem like an exaggeration at the time. When Reems had acted in the hardcore pornographic films *Deep Throat* and *The Devil in Miss Jones* nearly a half decade earlier in Florida and Pennsylvania, he certainly never dreamed he would one day face criminal charges in Tennessee.[2]

In the end, Reems's case had a negligible impact on the national artistic climate. Bogged down in a convoluted series of legal maneuvers, its arcane details perhaps made sense mostly to lawyers. Its paramount importance was instead in the broader cultural arena. Who would dictate American sexual mores—a genial porn actor who ambled his way through a series of cinematic sexual encounters or an ambitious federal prosecutor whose southern, evangelical perspectives might lead to the incarceration of a fornicating screen performer? The stakes went beyond the freedom of Harry Reems to include broader determinations of social citizenship and normative masculinity, revealing an incipient New Right chasing after an icon of the sexual revolution, in a significant foreshadowing of larger culture wars to come.

Larry Parrish won his case against Harry Reems, then lost it. Meanwhile, he won numerous other, less visible cases in his so-called Memphis Heat, a half decade–long crusade against smut in a Mid-South city that carried national implications, the most crucial of which had to do with the simple questions What is acceptable? and Who is to decide? Under the liberal Supreme Court of the 1960s, the answers were, effectively, anything with a claim to redeeming social value, and the nation as a whole. This legal regime nurtured the various elements of the sexual revolution, from contraceptive access and abortion, to gay and lesbian rights and visibility, to an increasingly graphic pornography market that extended from rural America to Times Square.

Parrish's answers were different, and operated as opening salvos in the coalescence of a Christian Right whose militant opposition to the new freedoms of the sexual revolution ultimately became a centerpiece of the modern Republican Party. To him, unregulated public representations of sex threatened to destabilize basic social relations like the family and "the work ethic." Parrish believed that the Constitution itself was "based on fundamental relationships" such as those, and he believed they needed to be defended through legal action.[3] The national press struggled to understand Parrish, a savvy, articulate public figure whose values seemed at odds with national, secular ones. And to an extent, that confusion has been passed on to the historiography of the origins of the modern conservative movement. Daniel Williams, for instance, emphasizes the southern origins of the Christian Right, while Kevin Kruse situates it in a broader religious nationalism harking back to the peak of the Cold War.[4] Prominent historians argue against a "myth of southern exceptionalism" that would isolate the South as uniquely backward-looking, yet the *idea* of a southern identity continues to carry currency both in the South and nationally. If the eminent southern historian James Cobb is correct in identifying a "national resurgence of political, social, and cultural conservatism that seemed to move the mainstream toward the South" in the 1970s, certainly the Memphis Heat marked that shift.[5]

To be sure, the South played an undeniably momentous role in forging modern conservatism. The political realignment of the once solidly Democratic region into the GOP's national base in the wake of the civil rights movement, as well as the southward gravitational shift on the national economy wrought by the emergence of the Sunbelt, testifies to the relevance of the region. The 1980 Republican platform would advocate a Christian Right agenda seemingly borrowed from the Southern Baptist Convention, which had swerved sharply toward social issues like abortion, gay rights, and pornography in the 1970s.[6]

Yet these markers of a regional politics ascendant coincided with broader national trends toward religiosity and sexual conservatism. In 1976, the year Reems was convicted in a Memphis courtroom, 50 million adults, amounting to one-third of the national population, identified themselves as born-again Christians, making evangelicals the largest religious denomination in the nation.[7] And though the Memphis Heat was narrativized as a reflection of southern sexual mores, it was also an expression of distinctly federal power—and a federal policy orientation set not by George Wallace, Orval Faubus, or Lester Maddox but rather by Richard Nixon.

What was understood nationally as the *Deep Throat* trial, then, in fact captured the confusion and complexity of an ascendant New Right, reliant on southern and Christian backing yet also amassing national support. The Memphis Heat, a cascading set of obscenity cases unevenly terraced as they bounced across the judicial system from a local court to the US Supreme Court and back again, appeared to many observers as a rearguard action against a sexual revolution whose advances had already been ratified by social consensus, a last gasp of old-fashioned puritan repressiveness allegedly swept away by the previous decade's social changes. In retrospect, however, Parrish's efforts against Reems and others look less like retrograde show trials and more like a precursor to the sexual politics of the Reagan era, in which the Christian Right launched a full-scale assault on the sexual revolution. As Harry Reems and Larry Parrish competed for legitimacy in the legal and cultural spheres, issues of sexual politics, evangelical religion, and the parameters of the public sphere were worked through in a legal setting that doubled as a political laboratory for the staging of a new regime of sexual regulation, one specifically informed by southern religiosity but tailored for national viability.

CULTURAL GYRATIONS

When hardcore pornography (defined by graphic imagery of unsimulated sex acts) first showed up on Memphis screens in mid-1971, the adult-theater operator Carl Carter had as little enthusiasm for it as the local authorities did. Since the assistant city attorney, Frierson Graves, had represented three adult theaters before making the unlikely transition to the other side of the law, Carter had been able to maintain an informal "bond" with Memphis legal enforcers. As long as he kept films "at a certain level of taste," criminal charges could be averted.[8] The softcore films Carter showed had grown more explicit since the nude frolicking of *The Stripping Wives* landed him in court in 1966 but still stopped short of graphic penetration shots. It wasn't Carter's Lamar Theater or other onetime movie palaces gone to seed as smuthouses, like the grand Airways Theatre, that led the charge into hardcore, but rather the four small storefront cinemas tucked into the rotting downtown infrastructure. The gyrating figures on their screens left nothing to the viewer's imagination.[9]

The arrival of hardcore offset Carter's delicate legal tightrope walk. He couldn't afford to ignore it: by the summer of 1971 his softcore fare was fading rapidly into obsolescence, as patrons showed a preference for the theaters that took full advantage of the freedoms newly afforded by the federal courts. Yet the limits of this legal freedom remained unclear, and testing them carried risk; by decade's end, Carter faced daunting prison sentences. If cultural mediators like Carter helped bring the sexual revolution to Memphis, they hardly did so without profound ambivalence.

This trepidation found its mirror reflection in the law enforcers who sought to contain what they perceived as the excesses of the sexual revolution at a time when their powers seemed on the wane. For much of the middle decades of the century, Memphis carried the dubious distinction of contending for recognition as America's most culturally repressive city. Though geographically in the Mid-South, it doubled as the northern tip and social center of the Mississippi delta, the "most southern place on earth."[10] With a board of censors headed by Lloyd Binford, widely known as "America's most notorious censor," Memphis barred everything from gunslinging westerns to overly bosomy Hollywood films. Most infamously, Binford suppressed all challenges to the racist color line, even those as innocuous as the interracial schoolyard antics of the 1947 children's film *Curley*. Though legal change had demolished the censor board's power by the mid-1960s, the ascent of the New Right mayor Henry Loeb to a second term in 1968 brought a resurgent moralism. Eager to displace the contentious politics of race, especially after his disastrous handling of the 1968 sanitation workers' strike, which culminated in the assassination of Martin Luther King Jr., Loeb latched onto moral crusades against smut as a rallying point for his nearly all-white voting base, who formed Memphis's contribution to what Richard Nixon famously labeled the national "silent majority."[11]

For a few years, Loeb exploited the smut issue masterfully, and he found the local press happy to indulge his cries; a *Press-Scimitar* reporter described the "most repulsive, shocking and unbelievable filth imaginable" available at the Adult Center in 1969—a warning and, perhaps, unintentional advertisement.[12] In an overheated editorial titled "Tidal Wave of Muck Rising to Hurricane Heights," the newspaper laid out the dizzying nexus of symbolic meaning in which pornography operated "as a political weapon," linking it to abortion, antiwar protesting, support for Castro, communism, drugs, and other social ills of the New Left and the sexual revolution. All these sinister forces, the paper contended, showed "open contempt for Christian ethics and the rejection of civilized moral standards," colluding to undermine social traditions.[13]

Such perspectives might make good politics and even coherent worldviews, but they translated awkwardly into the legal arena. The Supreme Court had steadily liberalized obscenity law since 1957, and by 1970 it was simply reversing without comment nearly every conviction that came its way. This left the lower federal courts to elucidate doctrine, and in general they read the high court's silence as permissiveness, thus creating the legal conditions that allowed hardcore to emerge.[14]

In Memphis this meant that a film like the graphic but still (barely) softcore *Starlet,* about a young woman's journey through the sordid underworld of the entertainment industry, could beat an obscenity charge in April 1970. It appealed to prurient interests, the criminal court judge Odell Horton ruled, and it was surely patently offensive—two traditional criteria of obscenity—but ultimately it was not utterly without redeeming social value, the third criterion needed for a conviction. Tawdry and salacious as it was, *Starlet* did show how young women seeking fame could be "physically and psychologically exploited for profit and how such persons live in bondage to unscrupulous film makers"—thus carrying some social value in its message even if it conveyed that theme with a "complete absence of any human warmth," the judge lamented.[15]

The result was an uneasy impasse. Loeb's successor as mayor, Wyeth Chandler, had none of his flair for political posturing, adhering instead to a bland agenda of Sunbelt-aspiring economic development upon his election in 1972. "Respectable conservatism," as Cobb notes, was a "vital part" of the Sunbelt business climate that Memphis desperately hoped to emulate; antismut zealotry hardly signaled a modern outlook anymore.[16] In addition, obscenity charges proved difficult sells to juries, even in a city of social conservatism and heightened religiosity. Prosecutors asked for only fines, not even jail time, in a 1972 case involving five softcore films, and an all-male jury still deadlocked 8–4 in favor of acquittal, resulting in a mistrial. By 1973, even the legal adviser to the Memphis Police Department called obscenity law "hogwash" in a newspaper article that described unofficial city policy as "leav[ing] adult theatres alone if they do not admit those below 18 years old."[17]

MEMPHIS HEAT RISING

By the early 1970s, then, Memphis possessed no unique claim to smut-busting nor even a clear local mandate for it. Indeed, the very page of the *Press-Scimitar* that reported the police's laissez-faire approach in 1973 also carried a story from the United Press International newswire about a New York City judge ruling the popular *Deep Throat* obscene.[18] Legal and cultural battles over pornography and obscenity were national in scope, if often local in contour. What became known as the Memphis Heat attempted to reshape this, as local prosecutors launched an all-out attack on smut that went well beyond the usual contestations over public sexuality. That the prosecutors were *federal* agents led to confusion over the nature of the Memphis Heat, which emanated out of larger national efforts by a militantly antiporn Nixon administration rather than the demonstrably ambivalent local authorities but played to the national audience as a reflection of conservative southern folkways.

President Richard Nixon's much-vaunted "Southern strategy" involved the repudiation of the black civil rights movement in (code)word and deed, cultivating an implicitly white "silent majority" from the ranks of the once-Democratic South and the white working and middle classes more broadly. Nixon signaled his sympathies through opposition to "forced busing" in schools and his abandonment of Great Society promises to inner cities in his "benign neglect" of urban poverty. The cues were well received in Memphis, where according to the historian David Tucker white Democrats were "an extinct species" by the end of the sixties.[19]

If the politics of race and inequality had proven inescapable in the turbulent 1960s of civil rights activism and urban unrest, Nixon sought to submerge those conflicts with a new moral politics that sidestepped overt white backlash sentiment. That nexus against which the *Press-Scimitar* had railed in 1969 typified Nixonian moralism—everything from long-haired antiwar types to drugs to the perceived excesses of the sexual revolution bled together in one "permissive society" that provided the president his nemesis. He paralleled at the national level precisely the attitudes Henry Loeb displayed as Memphis mayor— and won 84 percent of the evangelical Christian vote in 1972 by doing so.[20]

Pornography occupied a central role in Nixon's public displays of moralism. He bemoaned smut in the mails, he waxed apoplectic about a libertarian 1970 report by a leftover Johnson-appointed commission on obscenity and pornography, and he appointed Supreme Court justices he hoped would roll back the various liberalizations of the Warren Court. Before his departure under the shadow of Watergate, Attorney General John Mitchell pledged the Department of Justice to focus on obscenity cases. Within the administration it was understood as cynical political theater, but that perspective was not always shared at the various bureaucratic nodes of the federal apparatus.[21]

Thus the FBI, though at institutional loggerheads with the intrusive Nixon administration, shared its smut-fighting agenda. Director J. Edgar Hoover's interest in the issue stretched back nearly a half century, and he had linked pornography to everything from communism to cultural radicalism. The FBI had compiled a massive "Obscene File" over the decades and by 1973 already had a large dossier on *Deep Throat,* with planned action in the works against the film and its distributors in Milwaukee.[22]

Though the Milwaukee operation failed to get off the ground, it dovetailed nicely with events in Memphis. In fact, the first federal action in Memphis migrated down from Chicago, where FBI agents had attended screenings of *Lust Cycles* and *City Women.* Though viewed in Illinois, the films were seized five hundred miles to the south in Tennessee in May 1972.[23] Further cases quickly ensued. In September, the federal judge Robert McRae found several films obscene, including *School Girl,* a 1971 hardcore feature that had garnered positive reviews for its relatively nuanced portrayal of a female college student's sociological and personal exploration of the sexual revolution. Though best known for his liberal decisions regarding busing to desegregate local schools, McRae took a conservative approach to obscenity. The films "have some educational and therapeutic value, which might be used by a competent instructor in the educational system," he acknowledged; "however," he warned, "movie house education has some risk."[24]

These cases received minimal national attention, as did a November 1972 indictment involving the local theater operator Carl Carter. If the early cases had national fingerprints on them, the new one originated locally with the Memphis FBI branch. Thomas Turley Jr., the US attorney for western Tennessee, personified the ideal Nixonian justice official, gruff and no-nonsense in his law-and-order mentality.

When the national press began taking note of events in Memphis in early 1973, they appeared part of a nationally coordinated effort. Attorney General Richard Kleindienst, rather than Turley, announced a sweeping set of indictments, including fifteen persons and ten distribution companies, involving the shipping of *School Girl* from New Jersey to Memphis—a federal crime due to the border crossing and the earlier ruling by Judge McRae of the film's obscenity. The *Washington Post* called it "part of a national crackdown," and the *Des Moines Register* quoted unnamed Justice Department officials acknowledging a "national campaign" and linking the Memphis prosecutions to a New York case involving the film *Teenage Fantasies*.[25]

On one technical level, *all* obscenity prosecutions in 1972 were national, if only in the definition of obscenity applied. Such was the legal standard worked out over the course of fifteen frustrating years in the Supreme Court, where consensus on the issue had proved impossible to reach. This changed suddenly in 1973, as the messy ambiguity of obscenity doctrine resolved into a new conservative advantage, when all four of Nixon's appointees, including the new Chief Justice, Warren Burger, joined together with the Kennedy appointee Byron White in forging a new doctrine. *Miller v. California,* delivered in June 1973, announced the end of the national standard. "It is neither realistic nor constitutionally sound," the Chief Justice declared, "to read the First Amendment as requiring that the people of Maine or Mississippi accept public depiction of conduct found tolerable in Las Vegas, or New York City."[26] Though the national standard had always been a bit of rhetorical courtroom formality to begin with, *Miller* arrived at the precise moment when Memphis's own standards might take on powerful new impacts.

The *Press-Scimitar* film columnist Edwin Howard predicted that *Miller* would foretell the "gradual shutting down" of hardcore theaters in town, as well as more troubling efforts to hit at "borderline, X-rated," but not pornographic films like the acclaimed *Last Tango in Paris,* starring Marlon Brando.[27] At the same time, prosecutors viewed *Miller* as a "green light to combat smut," as the antiporn activist Charles Keating described it in a *Reader's Digest* article.[28] By October 1973 the Memphis Heat burned anew, with a new audacity. *The Devil in Miss Jones,* one of the more popular (and aesthetically ambitious) of the "porno chic" films that captured a mass audience that year, was impounded by the FBI in Memphis. Assistant US Attorney Parrish, coordinating the effort, broke new ground in his ten-person indictment. Named were not only the usual producers and distributors but also the director, Gerard Damiano, and the stars, Georgina Spelvin and Harry Reems (under their legal names, Chele Graham and Herbert Streicher).[29]

In Parrish's innovative legal schematics, Spelvin and Reems were part of a conspiracy to distribute obscene material. Neither took the case seriously at first: "Well, this is the 50th anniversary of the monkey trial in Tennessee, so I guess they had to do something," Spelvin noted sarcastically.[30] Civil libertarians expressed more concern. A spokesperson for the American Civil Liberties Union branch in Maine, where Spelvin had been performing in a theater troupe at the time of her indictment, worried about her being dragged to "the heart of the Bible Belt" and warned that "Memphis may become the standard for the whole country."[31]

Locally, the prosecutions found favor. "We wish Mr. Parrish and his associates success in their clean-up efforts," declared a September 1974 newspaper editorial. By that point, local officials claimed, there were no longer any hardcore films being screened in Memphis.[32] However, the new conspiracy charges had to await resolution of the earlier obscenity cases, which had been affected by the new *Miller* standards. Carl Carter, for instance, convicted by a jury in December 1973, had his conviction reversed on appeal; the newly conservative local *Miller* standards could not be applied to incidents that had transpired earlier, under the more liberal national standards.

Carter and his associate Donald Davis's retrial, beginning in September 1975, drew intense and detailed local news coverage. With eight of the thirty-six films in question scheduled to be screened at the trial, it promised riveting material. The reporter Kay Pittman Black called Memphis "the government's focal point in its legal battle to determine if interstate transportation laws may be used to stop the flow of such films throughout the nation," once more situating the Memphis Heat in a broader national context.[33] Thirty jurors were dismissed before the legal teams settled on a largely working-class jury of "moderates." A typical member, the security guard William Holley, had read the bestselling book *Everything You Ever Wanted to Know About Sex,* but the only film he had seen in the past eighteen months was the action movie *Billy Jack.*[34]

The trial delivered the promised spectacle, with nearly one hundred interested observers attending the courtroom screenings of such 16 mm films as *Miss Little's Dude Ranch* and *Three Into One.* Community sentiment was not all outrage; one "pretty young woman" brought her infant son, while a young man in a football T-shirt told a reporter that not only were the films not obscene but "in fact I'd like to star in one." Countering this view on the witness stand was the Utah psychiatrist Victor Cline, testifying for the prosecution that porn "could cause increases in rapes, sexual molestation of children and other sexual behavior that inflicts harm."[35]

When the jury sided with Cline, Carter received a three-year prison term and a ten-thousand-dollar fine. In handing down the sentence, Judge Bailey Brown felt the need to say that "I'm no prude," even noting that he had gotten "around a bit" in his forty-seven years of bachelorhood. Still, he added in a memorandum justifying the sentence, the films Carter screened "were almost completely without any plot and sexual acts were introduced almost from the beginning of the films and continued throughout." Prurient interest abounded, as "the camera was caused to zoom in on the genitals of the male and female partners." For that reason, a self-proclaimed moderate, modern judge could still see fit to hand down the most draconian punishment ever faced for obscenity in Memphis.[36]

Federal obscenity trials in Memphis proliferated as 1975 drew to a close. Allen Glen Bratcher, a Los Angeles mail distributor, managed to draw a mistrial in November, though not before prosecutor Larry Parrish and his witnesses told the jury that Bratcher's wares might "lead their viewers into 'abnormal sex habits' including group sex, infidelity, homosexuality, and bestiality."[37] In yet another case, involving members of Sherpix, the New York–based firm that distributed *School Girl,* Parrish secured three obscenity convictions in February 1976. Outside the hearing of the jury, Judge McRae dismissed the "bleeding heart defense" as "spurious." "You have people who came in here and said there was nothing wrong with cunnilingus, fellatio, and group sex," he exclaimed in dismay, shunning the sexual revolution's challenge to traditional mores.[38]

As to whether the prosecutions were local or national, there was no easy answer. Clearly, they joined in a larger federal project spearheaded by the Nixon administration; covering the "porno chic" moment in August 1973, *Playboy* identified ongoing federal action against smut in Chicago, Brooklyn, Buffalo, and Charlotte, North Carolina, in addition to Memphis. Threads in Memphis-based cases wove across the continent, from the upper Midwest to Portland, Oregon, where an FBI agent testified to having seen one of the films for which Carl Carter faced charges.[39] As the journalist Richard Rhodes also noted, offers of immunity (used repeatedly to protect witnesses) ran through the Justice Department in Washington, DC, suggesting some level of centralized coordination.[40]

Yet even Rhodes ultimately concluded that Parrish was leading the Memphis crusade, and not as a mere Nixon proxy. Indeed, unbeknownst to the public, the western Tennessee US attorney's office was at odds with the solicitor general, fighting for turf as the cases percolated up through the judicial system. When Carl Carter appealed to the Supreme Court, tensions over which body would represent the US government grew so fierce that the solicitor general—in correspondence that amused Court clerks described in private internal memoranda as "rather vituperative at times"—instructed the Court to disregard Parrish's legal briefs.[41]

Larry Parrish had shown himself an artful prosecutor, relying repeatedly on witnesses like Victor Cline, whose position on pornography and "sexual deviance" (which he defined broadly enough to include both rape and homosexuality) carried little weight in social-scientific circles but seemed compelling to jurors.[42] Yet the Memphis Heat still remained somewhat below the national-press radar, and while Parrish could win obscenity convictions, he had yet to succeed in his fresh effort to harness conspiracy charges to them; the Sherpix jury had granted his obscenity charges but had not convicted on the accompanying conspiracy counts. The enterprising young prosecutor's response was to think bigger. With his *Devil in Miss Jones* case held up in a protracted series of motions, he took aim at the central icon of sexual-revolution-inspired pornography, *Deep Throat*. Applying the same logic of a criminal conspiracy among all the persons involved in the film's production and distribution, Parrish set the stage for a landmark case, one that drew national attention not just as a legal showdown but as a contest between two models of masculinity in a decade marked by gender instability and anxiety.[43]

OBSCENITY AND THE MODERN MAN

In and of itself, prosecuting *Deep Throat* was nothing new. Convictions had been obtained against the film and its exhibitors in various districts across the nation, from New York City to nearby Little Rock.[44] Many aspects of the Memphis trial occurred as if by generic form of convention. The film's director, Gerard Damiano, granted immunity for his testimony, insisted that "the sexual aspect was also part of the plot" in the film, which he labeled "artistically in the sense of a comedy, a farce, possibly a social statement of our time."[45] Government witnesses linked the film's distribution to mafia violence, while well-credentialed experts offered differing views, with the defense witness Ted McIlvenna, a radical San Francisco–based minister teaching in Nashville at Vanderbilt, applauding *Deep Throat*'s therapeutic value and the Illinois political-science professor Lane Sunderland warning that "moral sensibilities may be dulled" by obscene films. Each side also brought in hometown experts from Memphis State University to reinforce those respective positions from a locally based perspective.[46]

As an obscenity case, the *Deep Throat* trial was important for its epic scale (Parrish brought seventy-six witnesses to the courtroom as the case dragged on for nine weeks) and also for its clear role as a barometer of social values in the wake of the *Miller* standards. The Supreme Court had returned the definition of obscenity to local standards—daunting enough to civil libertarians in state and local cases but more chilling by far in a federal case like this, which suggested that the government could forum-shop for a friendly prosecutorial climate for any film that crossed state lines. In this sense, Memphis became a symbol for provincial areas that sought to impose their own notions of morality on a national culture that had expanded freedoms dramatically in the past fifteen years.

But even above these concerns loomed the aspect of the case that drew the most attention: the indictment of Harry Reems on conspiracy charges. Thirteen individuals were named in the initial indictment, but twelve were clearly related to production and distribution of the film. Reems stood alone, not only in the case itself but in American legal history, as the only performer charged with criminal conspiracy to distribute obscene material. He had been initially hired as a set hand, then earned a mere hundred dollars a day for a few days of onscreen work, but "it doesn't matter if he swept the sidewalk," Parrish explained, "he's still in the conspiracy."[47] Damiano and Reems's costar

Linda Lovelace might also have been charged by similar logic but were instead granted immunity to testify for the government (though Lovelace went into hiding and never showed up).[48] Reems alone thus took on symbolic importance in the case. As the national press latched on to the sensational trial, Larry Parrish versus Harry Reems became the dominant narrative, which in turn played out as a story of New Right masculinity competing with the Sexual Revolution Man for cultural legitimacy.

Both men displayed awareness of performing on a national stage, and each played against the cultural stereotype that trailed him—Reems against the lecherous, predatory, porno sex pervert, Parrish against the Bible-thumping, antimodern fundamentalist that Georgina Spelvin had invoked with her comment about the Scopes Monkey Trial. Indeed, at times they almost seemed to converge on the same terrain, as Reems grew more lawyerlike and Parrish strove to display his modernism.

At stake in the cultural arena was which vision of masculinity would validate itself as normative. If the history of American masculinity was never less than vexed, the social upheavals of the 1960s had left it particularly destabilized. From the Beatles to Woodstock, increasingly long hair had taken symbolic significance as a rejection of Cold War masculine bodily comportment, with its militaristically erect posture and close-cropped heads. In Memphis, the reactionary police chief Frank Holloway had railed against "long-haired, foul-smelling hippies," and Mayor Loeb had openly despised them as well.[49] Yet if hairstyles seemed to draw political boundaries in the 1960s, by the next decade the counterculture had lost its monopoly. From the hardhats who attacked antiwar protestors in New York City in 1970 to reactionary white southern musical acts like Black Oak Arkansas and Lynyrd Skynyrd, long hair had lost its ability to situate a person at a glance.[50]

Sexuality too had come unmoored in cultural politics. While the media had reveled in the excesses of the counterculture's imagined free-love orgies, in reality premarital sex and cohabitation were commonplace by the seventies. While liberals remained discernibly more sympathetic to the inroads made by gay visibility, feminism, and abortion rights, sexual representation was not solely the province of underground arthouse theaters with their graphic if obtuse cinematic fare, but rather a central concern of the network television shows that millions of Americans watched and discussed on a nightly basis.[51] And while *Deep Throat* delighted in its fixation on oral sex, even the evangelical Christian authors Tim and Beverly LaHaye offered tentative affirmation of the act between married couples in their 1976 sex-advice bestseller *The Act of Marriage*.

These questions, of the presentation of the self at a time of confusing standards and proper sexuality at a time of purported revolution, informed the careful calibration of masculinity that Parrish and Reems undertook in their struggle. As the renegotiation of sexual mores transpired in the wake of the sexual revolution, they had to avoid the extreme poles of, respectively, Victorian prudery and hypersexual depravity if they were to curry favor with a public wary of both repression and licentiousness.

For Parrish, the task primarily meant distinguishing himself from the specters of Anthony Comstock. Comstock, the puritanical antivice crusader who had lent his name to the 1873 national obscenity law that undergirded all subsequent prosecutions, including that of Reems, had fallen out of favor with the onset of the twentieth century. As the new century endorsed what the historians John D'Emilio and Estelle Freedman term "sexual liberalism," essentially a social recognition of pleasure for its own sake, detached from procreation, Comstock's legacy fell out of fashion. "The late gorilla-like prude," *Time* magazine called him in 1936, as it defended the feminist activist Margaret Sanger's support for contraception.[52] By the 1970s, Comstock was remembered as a pathologically antisex crusader against modernity itself.

The ambitious Parrish had no desire to align himself with that legacy. Though defense attorneys attempted to link him to the ghosts of censors past, calling him "the reincarnation of either Lloyd T. Binford or Cotton Mather" in early 1976 (referencing both Memphis's own nationally reviled censor and the famously stringent Puritan), Parrish sought to lay claim to a conservative modernism.[53] His other obstacle, of course, was the iconic Monkey Trial, which had done so much damage to the image of fundamentalist Christianity in the 1920s, so Parrish had also to reconcile his own self-professed fundamentalism with an era of ambivalence toward the intermingling of religiosity and public policy.

Certainly one way Parrish echoed Comstock was in his knack for publicity. The earlier smut chaser had made his national mark going after the notorious feminist publisher Victoria Woodhull in 1872, and the Reems case played a similar role for Parrish. When compiling a hundred-page dossier on *Deep Throat* in 1973, the FBI had focused primarily on the director, Damiano; the producer, Lou Peraino (also on trial with Reems); and the star Lovelace, whose phone calls were carefully monitored.[54] The emphasis on Reems thus appears to have been Parrish's own innovation, and it succeeded in drawing attention that an ordinary obscenity trial would not have received. By late 1976, *Newsweek* was profiling him in an article called "The Memphis Smut Raker."[55]

Parrish understood the difference between pitching his rhetoric toward local juries and pitching it toward national-press readers. Trying a case in 1975, before the national spotlight turned his way, Parrish hit notes that might sound discordant to a broader audience. Unlike animals, he told the jury, humans "don't have heat or mating seasons, therefore free and open expression of sexual feelings easily could become a way of life and humans would have nothing else on their minds." Such folksy argumentation worked better in a courtroom than in the mass media, and by the time the latter arrived, Parrish had fine-tuned the language. The *Los Angeles Times* called him "a great believer in sex," adding that he "thinks there ought to be a lot more sex education than there is now. Victorian prudery, he thinks, is especially bad." Instead of linking smut to humans in animalistic heat, Parrish more intellectually criticized "depersonalized sex" and its effects on "the tone and tenor of society."[56]

Such phrasing revealed Parrish's education and urbanity. While his boss, US Attorney Thomas Turley, had bypassed law school for the old-fashioned training of reading with a lawyer and reflected deliberately homespun ways in his gruff demeanor, Parrish came from the urban Mid-South, raised in Nashville and graduated from the University of Tennessee law school. Before taking his position in Memphis, he worked for the Federal Trade Commission in Washington, DC. Though he told an antiporn origin story of taking his wife to a film in the late 1960s and being horrified by a graphically sexual preview beforehand, Parrish was no stranger to city life and the shifts it had witnessed and often sponsored during the sexual revolution.

Another way Parrish showed his modernist bona fides was by evincing a rugged manliness that distanced him from religious fanaticism. Explaining his beliefs to the *Washington Post* in late 1976, he declared that the government had no role in private morality. "It's the means" of expressing an idea, he clarified. "You can't advocate nudity by walking up Pennsylvania Avenue bare-a—d," as the paper printed it. In this, Parrish ironically paralleled the presidential candidate Jimmy Carter, who similarly employed semivulgar language in a controversial *Playboy* interview in an effort to reveal himself as no Bible-thumper. It worked—Carter won the presidential election in November—and Parrish anticipated the interview, even portending Carter's promise not to chase after fornicators in his statement, "Look, I would never argue with what a man does in private. Things that seem wrong to me—say homosexuality—it would not be my business to try to interfere with him."[57]

Whether guileless or consciously orchestrated, Parrish's performance of conservative modernist masculinity worked well. He had a higher bar to meet than did the more immediately sympathetic Reems, who faced years in prison, but Parrish won a fair amount of positive national press. While *Good Housekeeping* acclaim of the "daring young prosecutor" was perhaps to be expected, even the adversarial movie-industry paper *Variety,* using a predictable lens, described him as "Central Casting's idea of the perfect prosecutor: young, tall, handsome, well-dressed, stating his neat logic in dulcet southern overtones, mixing fact, fury and theatrical humor."[58] In the ultimate tribute to Parrish's self-presentation, the *Washington Post* reporter Henry Mitchell wrote, "You could easily imagine him attending a stag film and not paying much attention to it"; Mitchell was too charmed by Parrish to acknowledge that he sought the imprisonment of those involved with precisely such works.

If one could imagine Parrish at a stag film, one could just as well envision Harry Reems as a lawyer. A self-described "nice middle-class Jewish boy from Westchester County," the young Herbert Streicher had led a colorful life, from a brief stint in the Marines to roles in off-Broadway Shakespeare plays. He wound up in smut only by accident, when "legitimate" acting failed to pay the bills. As he detailed in his genial 1975 autobiography, *Here Comes Harry Reems,* he was not very experienced sexually when he took his first pornographic gig, and so he approached the job with a sense of wide-eyed adventurousness.[59]

A mainstay of early to mid-seventies hardcore films, Reems developed a persona generally removed from the stereotypes of pornomasculinity. Though he occasionally took such roles as his frighteningly convincing deranged Vietnam-veteran rapist in the unsettling *Forced Entry* (1973), for the most part Reems offered a gentler gender performance. He hardly embodied the role of sex-crazed, aggressive male. In *Deep Throat,* his wacky Doctor Young can't keep up with Linda Lovelace's voracious sexual appetite, going so far as to wrap his penis in a bandage in an unsuccessful effort to ward off her advances. Informed less by seedy smut men than by the Marx Brothers, Doctor Young resists the socially destabilizing sex mania Parrish feared. "How much deep throat do you think I can take," he groans midway through the film.[60]

Playing "the teacher" in his other most famous role, in *The Devil in Miss Jones* (1973), Reems embodies a soft masculinity even when telling Georgina Spelvin's title character, a spinster consigned to hell for committing suicide but allowed two days to explore the unbridled lust she has missed in her earthly existence, that he will "punish" her if she fails to conform to his instructions. Opening his robe to reveal a flaccid penis, Reems showed comfort and ease as he moves through the stages of arousal with Spelvin physically in control even as he maintains verbal command. His role as an art professor in *Wet Rainbow* (1974), also with Spelvin, allowed Reems to segue from middle-class respectability to graphic penetration shots without any suggestion that the two were in tension.

Thus, in both film and public persona Reems performed a sexual-revolution masculinity that situated carnality as one aspect of an identity that refused to be limited to it. He defused the fraught bodily semiotics of the male porn star by rounding its sexualized essence with both brains and humor. "You could call me the Shirley Temple of fuck films," he said in one interview. "I really enjoy laughing and joking and carrying on and having sex. Because it's fun."[61] This was the opposite of Parrish's standards, which would celebrate sexuality, but only when restricted to the marital bedroom, and rarely as a laughing matter.

Here Comes Harry Reems includes a passing reference to the Memphis case. "Recently, in the middle of the night, FBI agents routed me out of dreamland and arrested me," Reems wrote. "I am innocent (I hope!) I am not involved in the distribution of the film."[62] As realization of the trial's seriousness dawned, Reems launched a national publicity effort to raise both awareness and funds. A March 1976 cocktail party at an architect's house in San Francisco drew precisely the sort of publicity Reems wanted: the *San Francisco Chronicle* described him as "more like a successful insurance executive than a porno star," even carefully cataloging his "beige suit, blue shirt, maroon tie and oxblood penny loafers."[63]

Desexualizing Reems supported his public self-reinvention, the close attention to outfits helping to replace the naked, erect, and ejaculating on-screen version of his body that so many Americans knew of. His greater ambition was to distance himself from the body altogether. In a society marked by a mind-body dualism, the challenge Reems faced was something of the opposite of the challenge Parrish faced. While the prosecutor had to show himself not *anti*sex, Reems insisted that he was not *only* sex but also a cultured man of intellect and refinement.

The Harvard law professor Alan Dershowitz, joining the Reems legal-defense team in 1976, pointed the press in the right direction, landing a quote in the *New York Times* as he explained, "I expected to see a 6-foot 4-inch stud," but "instead I met an intelligent man whom I mistook for a Harvard law student."[64] Reems sometimes pushed the interpretive lens a bit hard. "He came on like a law clerk trying to show how much he knows, name-dropping Supreme Court decisions, mentioning judicial circuits," wrote a disappointed *Washington Post* columnist who would "have preferred to talk smut."[65]

With his charming demeanor and well-spoken ways, Reems drew considerable, and sympathetic, national coverage. The *New York Times Magazine* reflected the effectiveness of his press campaign in early 1977, reiterating the tropes he had so meticulously generated. "Instead of cavorting naked with Linda Lovelace and Georgina Spelvin," the paper marveled, Reems was "now in a three-piece suit, addressing college audiences and quoting Learned Hand on the first amendment."[66] Amazement that a porn star might cogitate as well as he copulated continued to mark the media's analysis, but it played to Reems's advantage, not only casting him in a sympathetic light but also reprivatizing his body and thus emphasizing his position as a victim of prosecutorial persecution.

Buttressing Reems's national campaign was a small phalanx of celebrity supporters. The actors Warren Beatty and Jack Nicholson, blocked from testifying on his behalf by Judge Harry Wellford, took to the press to deliver their testimony. "Today Harry Reems, tomorrow Helen Hayes," Beatty intoned (though the raciest thing the septuagenarian actress had been in since the Fifties was the G-rated *Airport*). Nicholson made the point more pertinent, and personal; thanks to the new local *Miller* standards, his recent R-rated hit film *Carnal Knowledge* had been found obscene in Georgia. "Accordingly I could have been put on trial," the actor told a reporter at a Reems fundraiser. Nicholson noted "all these lunatics and Bible freaks" protesting outside the event, suggesting a link between them and Parrish.[67] Even the feminist congresswoman Bella Abzug allowed her name to appear on the letterhead of Reems's fundraising mail.

Reems unquestionably drew the more positive publicity as the case dragged on in 1976. Even conservatives had a difficult time endorsing prosecution for appearing in a porn film. The *National Review* called it a "preposterous charge" but found fault with colleges using student-activity funds to pay for lectures by Reems, and when he appeared on William Buckley's *Firing Line* television show, the uncomfortable host tried his best to simply ignore Reems entirely, directing almost every question during the hour-long show at Dershowitz instead.[68]

Parrish faced a greater struggle in selling his version of modern masculinity at a time of porno chic, relaxed gender strictures, and sexual revolution, thus arguably accomplishing a greater success in largely validating his presentation as reasonable, rational, and au courant. Though he faced the occasional dismissal, as when the San Francisco columnist Nicholas Von Hoffman brushed him aside as "some Memphis maniac," overall he was treated with respect and deference by most major press organs.[69] Mainstream masculinity in the mid-seventies was flexible, accommodating, or incoherent enough to incorporate both the buttoned-up porn star and the secular-sounding fundamentalist.

FRAMING THE MEMPHIS HEAT

Harry Reems's speaking and fundraising events took him from Los Angeles to North Dakota, West Virginia to Boston. They helped him win financial support (though his trial still left him destitute) and cultural legitimacy, but they little impacted the place that mattered most. Back in Memphis, in May 1976 Harry Reems, along with his codefendants, was found guilty by a jury whose sexual sophistication lagged distinctly behind that of the teeming crowds attending *Deep Throat* screenings. "I didn't know there were so many crazy things people do, or like, or whatever it is," one juror told a local reporter. "I learned a lot of big words," she continued, "a lots of names for sex."[70] Whatever pedagogical value this imputed to *Deep Throat* itself failed to rescue the film.

The national press rushed to condemn the conviction as a display of backward-looking southern religiosity. In *Film Comment,* Brendan Gill described Memphis as located "in the heart of the Bible Belt," and Reems himself echoed the notion, calling the city "the buckle on the Bible belt."[71] Yet this narrative was rather pat. While Parrish's conspiracy charges reflected legal audacity, the core finding of *Deep Throat*'s obscene nature was hardly invented in Memphis; the film had already been found obscene at the local and state levels not only in Georgia and Kentucky but New York and Michigan too. The other notable porn show trials of the post-*Miller* seventies—those of the magazine publishers Al Goldstein (*Screw*) and Larry Flynt (*Hustler*)—occurred not in the South but in Kansas and Ohio, respectively. Indeed, in Memphis itself the local press maintained an ambivalence that predated the incursion of federal power into its porn-related tensions. In a wavering editorial, the *Commercial Appeal* expressed opposition to smut but called Parrish's approach "a tremendously costly and tedious way of attacking the problem."[72]

The easy narrative of southern Bible Belt social mores reenacting the Monkey Trial as the Fellatio Trial obscured the greater political valences of the *Deep Throat* case, which pointed to an ongoing ideological realignment that would not become fully apparent for a few more years. The coalescence of what became known as the Christian Right certainly had strong southern roots, but it also stemmed from suburban white flight and its laissez-faire politics of color blindness.[73] Depicting the Memphis Heat as a strictly southern phenomenon obscured the larger national base of support for such endeavors. Battles over pornography—as well as the other elements of the "social issues" package, which included gay and lesbian rights, abortion, and feminism—acted as sites of inscription for proper models of social citizenship for a vast number of voters.

The stakes of these contests were not yet fully understood by the broader public in 1976, when sexual politics played a fairly muted role in the presidential election, since the incumbent, Gerald Ford, and the challenger, Jimmy Carter, held similar, moderate views. In that context, the Memphis Heat could appear an orphan leftover from the Nixon years, though glimpses of its significance came from those who occupied various social margins. The Boston-based *Gay Community News* defended Reems, arguing that his case carried "tremendous ramifications for the gay press," and gay supporters included the composer Steven Sondheim, the poet Rod McKuen, and the Massachusetts congressman Barney Frank, who called the prosecution "one of the most crazy, outrageous things I've ever heard."[74] While the feminist press remained effectively silent on the indictment of Georgina Spelvin for performing sex acts on film, the radical *Women & Revolution* did link the Reems case to that of Texan Mary Jo Risher, who lost custody of her 9-year-old son because of her lesbian identity. If its call for socialist revolution against the "blood-drenched bourgeois state" found little support in the attenuated leftist politics of the 1970s, its analysis dug deeper than that of the mainstream press in understanding the interlinked nexus of reactionary sexual politics that would propel the Christian Right into the center of Republican policymaking by the next presidential campaign, in 1980.[75]

Harry Reems himself, feeling the pressure of this political transition at an intensely personal level, squeezed out of it a free man, if barely. Shortly after his conviction, Solicitor General Robert Bork confessed error in another case, from Kentucky, in which there had been a wrongful conviction under the *Miller* standards based on events that had taken place before *Miller* changed obscenity criteria. Though an outraged US Attorney Turley compared the solicitor general's office to the "monarchy of pre-revolutionary France" (leading a stunned deputy from the office to ask a reporter, "You mean to say he said that for the record?"), Reems was able to win a new trial on those same grounds. In the interim, the newly appointed US attorney, Mike Cody, reflecting the incoming Carter administration's Department of Justice priorities, which emphasized organized crime, corruption, antitrust law, and environmentalism, dropped the charges against Reems in April 1977.[76] The actor understood the symbolic importance. "I'm so happy to be restored to citizenship," he told a Memphis reporter.[77]

Cody also dropped the still-pending *Devil in Miss Jones* charges, citing the "great deal of cost to the government as well as to defendants" in his motion to dismiss.[78] With the young, liberal, former ACLU member in office, Larry Parrish resigned, citing "misgivings" about Cody's philosophy in a pointed three-page press release.[79] Acting without direct guidance from the Carter administration, Cody chilled the Memphis Heat, dropping most of the ongoing cases, though a sense of obligation led him to finish pursuing the lingering *Deep Throat* charges, sans Reems. The rest of the plaintiffs were reconvicted in 1978, in a trial that largely repeated the first, albeit without as much national attention or grandiosity. This time, the government's only expert witness was the psychiatrist Victor Cline, who once again labeled smut pathological, calling group sex "sick sex." The prosecutor, Robert Williams, went beyond Parrish's own rhetoric, telling the jury, "Memphis is a religious community. They tell you to disregard the Bible, but you can't disregard it because it is the views of those people in the community that you also have to plug in." Yet the convictions withstood several rounds of appellate review, ultimately reaching an uninterested Supreme Court, which let them stand in 1981.[80]

The end of the Memphis Heat corresponded with a broader effort by the Carter administration to downplay contentious sexual politics even as it staked out a moderate liberal stance. Carter supported *Roe v. Wade* but also the Hyde Amendment, which kept abortion financially out of reach for many women; he tentatively supported gay rights, but as quietly as possible; and he refocused obscenity investigations away from consenting adults and onto child-pornography cases. The approach was less than effective. Conservatives took each small, progressive Carter gesture as a major affront to traditional values, perhaps best witnessed in the maelstrom surrounding his 1980 Conference on Families ("Families" replacing the singular, monolithic "The Family," which conservatives preferred), while liberals chafed at his perceived timidity. As the Reagan Revolution dawned, a culture-war narrative developed that drew conservative evangelical and fundamentalist Christians into the Republican fold en masse after they had shown support for the born-again Democratic candidate in 1976.

What appeared to most as the dying gasp of Nixon justice in the Memphis Heat, then, retrospectively looked remarkably like Reaganism rising. One casualty of the culture-war narrative, however, was the competition over a contested middle ground that Parrish and Reems had engaged in. The two sides of the culture wars employed dramatically different and uneven tactics, as liberals continued to aim for that center, distancing themselves from feminist claims for abortion on demand, emphasizing gay rights only when LGBT people partook of heteronormative values and self-presentation, and remaining largely complicit in the murderous silence of the Reagan administration on the AIDS crisis, as in the bipartisan support for the homophobic Helms Amendment of 1987. The empowered Christian Right, on the other hand, saw no cause for such compromise, advocating a fiercely conservative antigay, antiporn, antifeminist agenda.

Larry Parrish reflected that hardening stance. After his bids for the mainstream in 1976, he moved further from the center. Though he still pseudoscientifically appealed to the second law of thermodynamics in explaining his doubts about evolution in 1978, the stance was firmly outside the political mainstream.[81] At a 1978 hometown talk, he likened empiricist governmental bureaucrats to communists and took a more aggressively antigay stance than his earlier comments in the national press had suggested.[82] When he declared himself "ready to lay down the sword" as he geared up for a 1979 mayoral campaign, even the local press balked, with a *Press-Scimitar* editorial wondering, "Our Ayatollah?"[83]

A Tennessee state obscenity statute that Parrish authored shortly after leaving the Justice Department was ultimately held unconstitutional by the state supreme court, and though well poised for a prominent position in the rapidly developing organizational infrastructure of the Christian Right, Parrish bypassed the Moral Majority/Morality in Media/American Federation for Decency network to remain in private practice locally in Memphis. Though the city councilman J. O. Patterson called him "an extreme fanatic" and claimed that "Memphis has suffered nationally from the Parrish prosecutions," the prosecutor's stance resonated with many local citizens—particularly white ones, since the African American community leader Patterson suggested black skepticism with a New Right moral agenda often led by figures associated with opposition to black civil rights.[84] Adrian Rogers, the white pastor of a local megachurch, for instance, played a crucial role in the 1979 internal takeover of the Southern Baptist Convention by a faction dedicated to reactionary sexual politics.[85]

After several years of the Reagan administration, the national sexual retrenchment of the 1980s left Parrish looking more prescient than obsolete. While Reagan's Meese Commission on pornography issued a laughable report in 1986 that distorted social science and co-opted feminist rhetoric to support a Christian Right antiporn agenda, obscenity prosecutions flourished, often going beyond Parrish's conspiracy approach to employ attrition tactics of multiple simultaneous venues and racketeering laws that allowed for punitive confiscations. By the turn of the 1990s, even Harry Reems was on board—not with the Christian Right, but with the born-again movement, which he joined after bottoming out on drugs and alcohol as his career and fortune waned after the Memphis trial.[86]

Though the Memphis Heat portended a larger national movement of Christian Right sexual politics, never did it achieve success in disciplining American sexual mores to its standards. *Deep Throat* remained iconic in the national cultural memory, and though it stayed "conspicuously absent" from Memphis video stores as VHS privatized porn consumption in the early 1980s, Parrish's prosecutorial impact finally proved impermanent.[87] In an ironic postscript, Harry Reems returned to Memphis in 2005 for the premiere of the documentary *Inside Deep Throat,* which cheekily charted the film's social impact. Staying at the historic downtown Peabody Hotel, Reems turned his television on after returning to his room for the night, only to encounter none other than *Deep Throat* playing on the pay-per-view channel.[88] Something had risen again, and it was not the South, exactly.

NOTES

1. Harry Reems Legal Defense Fund mailing, 17 January 1977, Joel Wachs Papers, B540, file: pornography, Los Angeles City Archives.

2. On the locations of these films, see "Adult film locations 4: In search of Miss Aggie, The Devil and Miss Jones," 19 September 2015, and "Adult Film Locations 5: Deep Throat (1972)," 10 January 2016, at *The Rialto Report,* www.therialtoreport.com/.

3. Henry Mitchell, "U.S. Prosecutor in Memphis Defends Law on Obscenity," *Los Angeles Times,* 25 December 76.

4. Daniel Williams, "Jerry Falwell's Sunbelt Politics: The Regional Origins of the Moral Majority," *Journal of Policy History* 22, no. 2 (2010): 125–47; Kevin Kruse, "Beyond the Southern Cross: The National Origins of the Religious Right," in *The Myth of Southern Exceptionalism*, ed. Matthew Lassiter and Joseph Crespino (New York: Oxford University Press, 2010), 286–307.

5. Lassiter and Crespino, *Myth of Southern Exceptionalism;* James Cobb, *Away Down South: A History of Southern Identity* (New York: Oxford University Press, 2005), 8.

6. Reuben Herring, "Southern Baptist Resolutions on the Family," *Baptist History and Heritage* 17, no. 1 (1982): 36–45, 63.

7. Daniel Williams, *God's Own Party: The Making of the Christian Right* (New York: Oxford University Press, 2010), 160.

8. James Chisum, "X," *Commercial Appeal* (hereafter *CA*), 2 May 1971.

9. On downtown decay, see Roger Biles, "Epitaph for Downtown: The Failure of City Planning in Post–World War Two Memphis," *Tennessee Historical Quarterly* 44, no. 3 (1985): 267–84.

10. James Cobb, *The Most Southern Place on Earth: The Mississippi Delta and the Roots of Regional Identity* (New York: Oxford University Press, 1992).

11. On Binford and Loeb, see Whitney Strub, "Black and White and Banned All Over: Race, Censorship, and Obscenity in Postwar Memphis," *Journal of Social History* 40, no. 3 (2007): 685–715.

12. Hugh Frank Smith, "A Visit to the Adult Center," *Press-Scimitar* (hereafter *PS*), 29 August 1969,

13. "Tidal Wave of Muck Rising to Hurricane Heights," *PS,* 26 August 1969.

14. On obscenity doctrine, see Whitney Strub, *Obscenity Rules: Roth v. United States and the Long Struggle over Sexual Expression* (Lawrence: University Press of Kansas, 2013).

15. William Green, "Sex Film Gets Green Light to Return to Screen," *PS,* 25 April 1970.

16. James Cobb, *The Selling of the South: The Southern Crusade for Industrial Development, 1936–1990*, 2nd ed. (Urbana: University of Illinois Press, 1993), 181.

17. "Mistrial Ruled in Obscenity Case," *CA,* 4 June 1972; David Flynn, "Skin Flicks at Peak of Nudity but Peaks Out on Popularity," *PS,* 2 March 1973.

18. "Explicit Sex Film Gets Knife from New York City Judge," ibid.

19. David Tucker, *Memphis Since Crump: Bossism, Blacks, and Civic Reformers, 1948–1968* (Knoxville: University of Tennessee Press, 1980), 151.

20. Williams, *God's Own Party*, 102.

21. On Nixon, see Whitney Strub, *Perversion for Profit: The Politics of Pornography and the Rise of the New Right* (New York: Columbia University Press, 2011), chap. 5.

22. Douglas Charles, *The FBI's Obscene File: J. Edgar Hoover and the Bureau's Crusade Against Smut* (Lawrence: University Press of Kansas, 2011), esp. 97–99. On tension between the FBI and Nixon, see Beverly Gage, "Deep Throat, Watergate, and the Bureaucratic Politics of the FBI," *Journal of Policy History* 42, no. 2 (2012): 157–83.

23. Kay Pittman Black, "Court Views Films Seized as 'Porno,'" *PS,* 18 May 1972.

24. Michael Lollar, "Five Movies are Ruled Obscene," *CA,* 1 September 1972.

25. Timothy Robinson, "Memphis Jury Indicts 'Adult Film' Distributors," *Washington Post,* 16 February 1973; "U.S. Pushing Campaign Against 'Obscene' Films," *Des Moines Register,* 17 February 1973.

26. *Miller v. California,* 413 U.S. 15 (1973).

27. Edwin Howard, "Will Porno Ruling Help—Or Harm?" *PS,* 29 June 1973.

28. Charles Keating, "Green Light to Combat Smut," *Reader's Digest,* January 1974, 147–50.

29. Kay Pittman Black, "'Memphis Heat' Stars in Battle on U.S. Pornography," *PS*, 20 September 1974.

30. Kay Pittman Black, "Innocent, Says Star in Obscenity Case," ibid., 16 October 1974.

31. "CLU Lawyer Calls Memphis 'Bible Belt,'" ibid., 1 August 1974.

32. "The War on Pornography," ibid., 21 September 1974; Tom Jones, "Officials Continue Obscenity Crackdown," ibid., 28 August 1974.

33. Kay Pittman Black, "Can U.S. Regulate Obscenity in Films? Trial Here Monday," ibid., 23 September 1975.

34. Michael Lollar, "Judge Scrutinizes Jurors' Sex Views," *CA*, 30 September 1975.

35. Kay Pittman Black, "Spectators Mill About as Court Movies Grind On," *PS*, 8 October 1975; Black, "Doctor Tells Anti-Obscenity Jury: X-Rated Films Can Lead to Rape," ibid., 17 October 1975.

36. "Film Distributors Fined, Sentenced," *CA*, 30 December 1975; Bailey Brown, memorandum, 30 December 1975, CR 72-207, National Archives and Record Administration, Southeast Branch, Atlanta (hereafter NARA-SE).

37. "Mistrial is Declared in Pornography Case," *PS*, 8 November 1975.

38. Kay Pittman Black, "Verdict Split in Pornography Trial," ibid., 21 February 1976; "Judge Calls Film 'Sex Exploitation,'" ibid., 19 February 1976.

39. Bruce Williamson, "Porno Chic," *Playboy*, August 1973, 159; Michael Lollar, "Jury Weighs Sex Film's Merits," *CA*, 7 October 1975.

40. Richard Rhodes, "Deep Throat Goes Down in Memphis," *Playboy*, October 1976, 181.

41. Memorandum, Gates to William O. Douglas, 26 February 1975, *Art Theater Guild v. Parrish*, 74-749, box 1683, file 3, William O. Douglas Papers, Library of Congress, Washington, DC.

42. On Cline, see Strub, *Perversion for Profit*, 235–36.

43. The convoluted trajectory of the *Devil in Miss Jones* case is contained on the US district court docket sheet for *U.S. v. DeSalvo, et al.*, CR-74-103, NARA-SE.

44. On the Little Rock case, see Timothy Nutt, "'Somebody Somewhere Needs to Draw the Line': *Deep Throat* and the Regulation of Obscenity in Little Rock," *Arkansas Historical Quarterly* 69 (2010): 91–116.

45. *U.S. v. Peraino*, CR 75-91, transcript, vol. 4, 14 March 1976, 436, 450, NARA-SE.

46. Kay Pittman Black, "Youth is 'Choked' For Bootleg Print," *PS*, 19 March 76; "Minister Testifies Film Has Value," *CA*, 21 April 1976; "Professor Calls Movie 'Obscene,'" ibid., 30 March 1976.

47. "DT Jury Expects to Begin Debate Today," *PS*, 29 April 1976.

48. Georgina Spelvin also recounted being offered immunity, which she apparently turned down, in her autobiography, *The Devil Made Me Do It* (LA: Little Red Hen Books, 2006), 141.

49. Michael Honey, *Going Down Jericho Road: The Memphis Strike, Martin Luther King's Last Campaign* (New York: Norton, 2007), 388.

50. Kirk Hutson, "Hot 'N' Nasty: Black Oak Arkansas and Its Effect on Rural Southern Culture," *Arkansas Historical Quarterly* 54, no. 2 (1995): 185–211; Barbara Ching, "Has the Bird Flown? Lynyrd Skynyrd and White Southern Manhood," in *White Masculinity in the Recent South*, ed. Trent Watts (Baton Rouge: Louisiana State University Press, 2008), 251–65; Joshua Freeman, "Hardhats: Construction Workers, Manliness, and the 1970 Pro-War Demonstration," *Journal of Social History* 26, no. 4 (1993): 725–45.

51. Elana Levine, *Wallowing in Sex: American Television in the 1970s* (Durham, NC: Duke University Press, 2006).

52. "Medicine: Sanger Milestone," *Time,* 21 December 1936.

53. Michael Lollar, "Parrish Sets Pace in Smut Attack," *CA,* 22 February 1976.

54. FBI Deep Throat file, NY 145-3400, accessed 30 August 2016, www.gomorrahy.com/deep -throat-fbi-file-ny-145-3400.pdf.

55. Merrill Sheils, "The Memphis Smut Raker," *Newsweek,* 5 April 1976, 62–63.

56. Kay Pittman Black, "Jury Brings Back Guilty Verdicts Against Two in Sex Movies," *PS,* 25 October 1975; Mitchell, "U.S. Prosecutor in Memphis Defends Law on Obscenity."

57. Henry Mitchell, "Parrish: The Strength of 44 Convictions," *Washington Post,* 12 October 1976.

58. Charles Remsberg and Bonnie Remsberg, "Dirty Movies! Dirty Books!," *Good Housekeeping,* March 1977, 103, 194–99; "Law Forces Porn to Run for Cover," *Variety,* 20 October 1976.

59. Harry Reems, *Here Comes Harry Reems* (New York: Pinnacle, 1975), 3.

60. *Deep Throat* (Gerard Damiano, 1972).

61. Kenneth Turan and Stephen Zito, *Sinema: American Pornographic Films and the People Who Make Them* (New York: Praeger, 1974), 180, 185.

62. Reems, *Here Comes Harry Reems,* 125

63. Eugene Robinson, "Harry Reems Stars at S.F. Bash," *San Francisco Chronicle,* 19 March 1976.

64. Tom Goldstein, "Notables Aid Convicted DT Star," *New York Times,* 29 June 1976.

65. Richard Cohen, "Governmental Excess Rears Its Ugly Head," *Washington Post,* 7 December 1976.

66. Ted Morgan, "United Sates versus the Princes of Porn," *New York Times Magazine,* 6 March 1977.

67. Sally Quinn, "Harry Reems: Deep Trouble," *Washington Post,* 6 March 1976.

68. Alan Crawford, "Leading Man," *National Review,* 24 December 1976, 1411; *Firing Line,* PBS, 17 December 1976.

69. Nicholas Von Hoffman, "The Deep End," *San Francisco Chronicle,* 20 June 1976.

70. Paul Vancil, "Deep Throat Jury Found Trial Educational," *PS,* 5 May 1976.

71. Morgan, "United States versus the Princes of Porn"; Brendan Gill, "Justice is Blind—and Dirty-Minded," *Film Comment,* July–August 1976, 6.

72. "DT Decision," *CA,* 3 May 1976.

73. Kevin Kruse, *White Flight: Atlanta and the Making of Modern Conservatism* (Princeton, NJ: Princeton University Press, 2005); Matthew Lassiter, *The Silent Majority: Suburban Politics in the Sunbelt South* (Princeton, NJ: Princeton University Press, 2006).

74. Neil Miller, "Civil Liberties Peril Cited at Reems Benefit," *Gay Community News,* 4 December 1976.

75. "God-Fearing Hypocrites Revile Sin and Smut," *Women & Revolution,* Summer 1976, 23.

76. Michael Lollar, "Turley Unleashes Blast at U.S. Throat Stance," *CA,* 13 July 1976; Deborah White, "Deep Throat Actor Wins New Trial," ibid., 12 April 1977; Mike Cody, phone interview by author, 20 January 2012.

77. Deborah White, "Cody to Drop Charges Against Sex Film Stars," *CA,* 15 April 1977.

78. Motion to dismiss indictment, CR 75-90 #2, box 7, 22 August 1979, NARA-SE.

79. Deborah White, "Misgivings Over Cody Spur Parrish to Quit," *CA,* 3 March 1977.

80. Otis Sanford, "Jurors Get Private Showing of Sex Film Deep Throat," ibid., 8 December 1978; *U.S. v. Peraino,* CR 75-91, transcript, vol. 36, 18 December 1978, 4678, NARA-SE. On Cody acting without guidance, see Cody interview.

81. Michael Lollar, "Ready to Drop Sword, But Who Will Pick it Up?" *CA*, 5 March 1978.

82. Henry Bailey, "Parrish Says Majority Must Stand Up to Opinion-Shapers," *PS*, 15 November 1978.

83. "Our Ayatollah?," ibid., 1 August 1979. Parrish withdrew from the race after falling short of his funding goal.

84. Clark Porteous, "Councilmen O.K. Parrish's Obscenity Law," ibid., 21 December 1977.

85. Williams, *God's Own Party,* 157.

86. Steve Dougherty, "Born-Again Porn Star," *People Weekly,* 13 May 1991.

87. Kathleen McClain, "XXX-perts deal in under-the-counter trading," *PS,* 26 May 1982.

88. Harry Reems, phone interview by author, 19 December 2011.

5

Creating the Perfect Mancation

Golf, Sex, and the Grand Strand, 1954–2010

RICHARD HOURIGAN

What do you need for a great bachelor party?" Tim McDonald, the national golf editor for *Golf Publication Syndications,* asked in 2008. "The essence is cheap digs, alcohol, and nude dancers. Myrtle Beach has all that and more. For bonus it's got the beach—to lie out and let the sun soak up the Jim Beam. . . . You can do everything you normally do at bachelor parties, then stumble out the door for limitless golf options." McDonald recommends three strip clubs, but he acknowledges, "Myrtle Beach is lousy with strip clubs; you can't turn around without bumping into one." In fact, thirty-seven strip clubs and escort services call the Grand Strand home; that is roughly one for every one thousand male residents over 18 years old. Impressed, Myrtlebeachgolf.com added the article to its website.[1]

Highlighting McDonald's strip-club recommendations is Masters Club, the new symbol of Myrtle Beach. Of all the clubs in the city, it stands out for both its prominence and its gimmick. The thirty-three-thousand-square-foot gentlemen's club is equipped with a pro shop, a driving range, and valet parking. Deriving its name from the annual golf tournament in Augusta, Georgia, it is one-stop shopping for bachelor parties. The name, though, could just as well come from the male clientele that visit the clubs, who consume the moving images of naked female flesh in a manner reminiscent of their nineteenth-century predecessors. Inside, men are truly masters.

Myrtle Beach media heavily promote these establishments. Driving around the Grand Strand, it is difficult to avoid seeing a strip club or listening to one of their tacky, sexually charged promotions. Local radio stations frequently air advertisements and contests like the one heard on Sunday, 17 May 2006, the last day of the Myrtle Beach Harley-Davidson Bike Rally. The spot reflects how important sex has become in city culture. The advertisement featured two male morning disc jockeys promoting a contest to be held the following week.

Poking fun at more conventional prize offerings, the winner in their contest would receive "dinner and a booby." After a meal, the lucky man (because only a man can win the contest) would get a private room at Masters.

In addition to golf courses and strip clubs, Horry County boasts of three breastaurants—Hooters-like restaurants designed for heterosexual men's voyeuristic pleasure—and three bike rallies, as well as the previously mentioned escort services and strip clubs. Entertainment like this makes Myrtle Beach the perfect place for a mancation, an all-male, sometimes raucous vacation typified in movies like *The Hangover* (2009) and *Mancation* (2012). Since the 1960s, white men have flocked to the region in ever-increasing numbers, taking advantage of all the activities the Grand Strand had to offer. The city became, as the historian Alecia Long notes about turn-of-the-century New Orleans, "a geographic and metaphoric safety valve—a place where southerners came to escape, if only temporarily, from the . . . religious and behavioral strictures that dominated their home communities." Today that escapism has spread beyond just southerners.[2]

The Myrtle Beach area provides insight into how many southern coastal locales turned what W. J. Cash dubbed "gyneolatry" on its head starting in the 1950s. Capitalizing on an emerging sexual culture typified by *Playboy*, Myrtle Beach boosters rebranded the city after a devastating hurricane by utilizing scantily clad women as a lure for men looking for a vacation. Other male-dominated activities soon found a welcome home in the region. By the 1990s, white women, while still worshipped, were no longer required to be the "lily-pure maid of Astolat"; instead, they were expected to play the role of a temptress to be caught and tamed by randy, white males.[3]

City leaders created a culture that encouraged white women to be increasingly sexually permissive; it provided their economic lifeblood. Key to Myrtle Beach's development and advertising was the incorporation of attractive white women in both the newspaper's and the chamber of commerce's promotional material to encourage white men to visit. It perhaps began innocently. Sometimes the messages were hidden in seemingly innocuous articles published in the *Myrtle Beach Sun*. In other instances the paper would publish photographs of beauty-pageant winners or local contestants vying for such crowns as Strawberry Queen or Miss Tobacco Festival. Published on the front page, the pictures of the early 1950s were small head shots of 18-year-olds in their pearls. Both the acknowledgment of pageant winners and the accompanying photos are typical of small-town newspapers.[4]

The *Sun,* however, went further than just printing pictures of white pageant winners. It published photographs based solely on capturing a beautiful girl on camera. As one man put it succinctly in 1958, "No story on Myrtle Beach would be complete without a photograph of beautiful young ladies enjoying the surf." For example, in its 11 August 1950 edition, the *Sun* caught Marilyn Bessent on camera coming down from a lifeguard stand wearing her bathing suit. The caption reads, "All the beauties seen on Horry County's famous Grand Strand are not imported products. Some of them are home grown. . . . Marilyn was snapped as she climbed the lifeguard tower in front of the Ocean Forest Hotel . . . noted for its gorgeous gals." The caption continues by informing the reader that Bessent attends Wampee High School and works at Doc Johnson's Crescent Beach Drug Store. She is young, local, and presumably single.[5]

Other pictures showed women in a similar light. One titled "Home Grown Talent" shows three young women in bathing suits holding hands as they emerge from the ocean. The description asserts, "In shape . . . these Myrtle Beach lovelies play on the beach and soak up sunshine for a healthy looking tan." Other photographs of women in the 1950s and 1960s specifically refer to them as a crop.[6]

Myrtle Beach promoters understood their audience. Talking about women as "crops" helped locals accept the transition from a farming-based economy to a nationally based tourist economy in ways they could understand. By the 1920s the voracious appetite of the boll weevil had taught farmers that they had to diversify to survive. Referring to women as "home-grown" and as a "crop" showed them as an economic asset, like any agricultural product. Having beautiful women grace the cover of the newspaper and the beaches of the Grand Stand did more than bring in much-needed income for the region; it diversified their economy. For the purposes of tourism, young, single women were a product, or at least a moving attraction, used to draw visitors. They were walking and talking economic diversification.

Referring to women as "crops" did more than just help farmers understand the beach's new tourist-based economy: it commoditized women. Crops are grown, bought, studied, and, if unspoiled and pretty, sold and consumed. For Myrtle Beach boosters, women fit the role of the crop perfectly. Every summer a new collection of women visited the beach. The pretty ones, assuming they were unspoiled (a.k.a. chaste), would be taken home to be married. The next year, a new collection of women would take their place.

And new females did come to the city every year. The beach attracted almost twice as many white women as it did white men. Many of these women were budget-conscious high-school and college students who found the Grand Strand to be a great place to spend their spring and summer breaks. College women came to the beach, as one spring breaker insisted, because it was "where the boys are." In 1960, the movie *Where the Boys Are,* starring George Hamilton and Connie Francis, stormed the box office, and theatergoers witnessed the story of four beautiful college women looking for love on spring break in Fort Lauderdale, Florida. Spring break and the beach became synonymous as women sought to replicate the experience for themselves, and those who could not afford to travel to Florida came to the Grand Strand. By the early 1960s, students made up 38 percent of those visiting the beach, the largest-percentage category.[7]

During the Easter weekends, white college students packed the area. The liquor laws in South Carolina were stringent; alcohol could only be purchased in quantities over a half pint and could only be consumed in one's home. Yet despite the archaic laws, students had few problems obtaining the forbidden libations. Government officials "closed their eyes" to the laws being broken in tourist hotspots such as Charleston and the Grand Strand. As early as the 1950s, officials up to and including the governor knew of Myrtle Beach businesses' refusal to comply with state liquor laws but did little to enforce them. On one visit to the city, Governor Strom Thurmond observed waiters at the Ocean Forest Hotel illegally serving liquor. Shocked at the blatant violation of state law, Thurmond asked Myrtle Beach's mayor, Jasper N. Ramsey, to crack down on the offenders, telling Ramsey, "Myrtle Beach will never amount to a thing as long as you let them serve liquor." Despite the exchange, neither the state nor city officials stopped the hotel's practice.[8]

Ocean Drive Beach, soon to become part of the town of North Myrtle Beach, was the location of much of the white college students' revelry. Jails became drunk tanks as officers arrested students for flagrantly violating the law against public intoxication, including one student arrested for stumbling down the sidewalk carrying a half gallon of bourbon. Despite the crackdown on youth drinking, local officials did little to enforce the state's ban on consumption. The head of the Myrtle Beach Chamber of Commerce, Ashby Ward, referred to the laws as "archaic" and "an embarrassment." Stringent enforcement of the law would only serve to stunt the area's growth.[9]

Myrtle Beach leaders never encouraged white youth to seek their fun elsewhere, as Fort Lauderdale and Daytona Beach leaders would do in the 1980s and 1990s; money brought in by their visits helped sustain the local economy. Every year in the spring and summer tens of thousands of high-school and college students descended on the city, filling hotels, so that many had to sleep in cars. Their arrival brought city businesses hundreds of thousands of dollars, but the youths' increasingly permissive activities and ideals profoundly changed the town. This was the *Playboy* generation, whose leader, Hugh Hefner, espoused the principles of the "swinging bachelor" as a modern-day Renaissance man, who dressed exquisitely, cooked, traveled, and read fine works. For Hefner, the bachelor was the epitome of freedom and class, able to purchase whatever he wanted without being held in check by a woman.[10]

Women, of course, were *Playboy*'s biggest attraction and the reason why its circulation had surpassed that of *Esquire* by 1959. *Playboy* got its readership not from its articles but from its nude pictures of young women. The pictorials were the most important part of the magazine and its reason for existence. These photos objectified women, posed as seductive sirens or the girl next door, allowing men to consume their naked images. As Bill Osgerby explains, *Playboy* "constructed women as the objects of a voyeuristic look," with women "being configured as items for the *Playboy* adventurer's consumption."[11]

By the late 1950s, the magazine was furnishing fashion tips to its readers in its Back to Campus feature. In 1966, *Playboy* claimed to have a circulation that included more than half of all undergraduate men. Those same white men who enjoyed *Playboy* came to the Grand Strand for their spring and summer breaks, hoping to catch a glimpse of the sexualized female they saw in the magazine and believing that the tips they had read would pay dividends with the young, scantily clad single women lounging on the beach. Myrtle Beach leaders, while they would never admit it, followed *Playboy*'s lead, using alluring, young women as spectacle. What sold magazines also sold resorts.[12]

Young women were aware of the attention their bodies received. A 1960s survey by James Fussell, a graduate student at the University of South Carolina, found that 81 percent of young females vacationed on the coast to get a tan. Women might claim that they were sunbathing to look healthy, but most were doing it to attract the opposite sex. In fact, more young women (56 percent) than men (53 percent) claimed that meeting the opposite sex was one of the primary purposes of vacationing on the strand. This same study found that "beer (chills) and kissing games (smackymouth) were more attractive to boys than girls." Fussell believed the women were lying about their desires to protect their reputation, noting, "At any rate, that is the way they reported it."[13]

Myrtle Beach, state leaders knew, had more than just fun and sun. It had a little sin as well. In 1965 Ralph Gasque, a state senator from nearby Marion, South Carolina, claimed on two occasions that high-school and college students were having "orgies" on the sands of Myrtle Beach. He further complained about the brothels that were in operation along the Grand Strand. Gasque was undoubtedly correct. Fussell seemed to confirm Gasque's claim. During the graduate student's travels he met a "very pretty young woman" who claimed that she was a prostitute and demanded that her profession be included as a reason for visiting the beach. Fussell declined her request, noting that prostitution could not exist there. There were twice as many females as males on the coast, he concluded, implying that men would not pay for something they could readily get for free.[14]

Objectifying white women for men's voyeuristic pleasure became the Grand Strand's calling card. The best example of this is Myrtle Beach's annual Sun Fun Festival. Started in 1952 by the city government, local businesses and clubs, and the chamber of commerce, the festival was a way to attract visitors to the beach in early June, a down period between the busy Memorial Day and July 4th holidays. Held until 2011, the festival usually featured B-list celebrities like Mario Lopez and the American Idol runner-up Justin Guarini to entertain guests.

One 1956 editorial extolling the virtues of the Sun Fun Festival encouraged tourists to see Myrtle Beach as a "young city with young ideas" whose spirit reflects "a virile, driving progressiveness, balanced and tempered by a gracious hospitality for its visitors." The gendered terminology is important: *young* and *virile* are words associated with a sexually prepared young man. Locals wanted their target audience, middle-class white men, to think of Myrtle Beach as a progressive place where multitudes of beautiful, sexually available white women waited to serve them.[15]

Sun Fun festivities included a parade down Kings Highway (Highway 17) complete with marching bands, floats, and local dignitaries. But this was not the typical small-town parade featuring the local homecoming queen. Every year the Sun Fun Festival organizers littered the parade with attractive young women. The 1965 fete is illustrative. Featured in the newspaper's "Beauties on Display" article were Miss America, Carolina's Carousel Queen, Miss National Rural Electrification, the WECT Pirate Girl, Miss Sun Fun, and beautiful girls chosen by governors of eleven states as far away as Alaska. The plethora of smiling, waving queens lining the parade guaranteed a large male audience composed of both locals and tourists.[16]

While the parade was part of the festivities, it was not the highlight. Like many southern fairs, the Sun Fun Festival needed to crown its own beauty queen. From 1952 to 1959 the festival was the site of the Miss South Carolina pageant. The contest was the biggest draw for the beach; people flocked to see the evening-gown and bathing-suit contests. The winner would get a chance to compete in the Miss America pageant. In 1957, Miss South Carolina took home the crown for the state. Myrtle Beach promoters took great delight in the fact that Miss America had gotten her break in their city.

Festival organizers could not hold on to the state pageant forever; the Miss South Carolina pageant officials moved the event out of the city in 1959. Myrtle Beach promoters needed another pageant to bring beauty to the beach. Sun Fun organizers started one of their own, a national contest whose winner would be dubbed "Miss Sun Fun USA." The pageant featured representatives from states all over the country. Many of these contestants represented Lions Clubs, merchant associations, or other small-town beauty contests. Qualified contestants were single women, age 18 to 25, chosen by their home states. Ideally, fifty women, one from each state, would participate. Town boosters hoped the new pageant would keep local and national coverage on the city. In 1961, *Life* magazine, the Associated Press, United Press International, and seventy-five other news organizations sent reporters to cover the event. The first Sun Fun USA pageant was held in 1960.[17]

A 1960 Sun Fun Festival brochure further focused on the event's main attraction, women. In the promotional piece, the chamber acknowledged that "beautiful girls and celebrities highlight festivities." The short synopsis of the festival mentioned only one event by name, the Sun Fun USA pageant. It was the biggest draw and the most important event. For those who did not read the pamphlet, the pictures littering the cover were easy to interpret. Of the twelve pictures, five showed beauty queens, two showed other scantily clad women, and two showed golf and fishing. It was a pamphlet designed to attract white women who desired to be beauty queens and the white men who were to chase them.[18]

The Sun Fun Festival fostered a carnival atmosphere, full of fun, games, and events, with most utilizing scantily clad, striking women to attract tourists. Even some of the competitions used the beauty of these women. A game held on 9 June 1956 is a good example. On a hot Saturday morning visitors to the Sun Fun Festival gathered to watch a battle of wits between Major General E. J. Timberlake, commanding officer of the Ninth Air Force, and Erberto Landi, producer of the first Italian television show. Radio and film crews from a national television network recorded the proceedings. The master of ceremonies, Barry Sturmer, introduced the event to the audience. The game had first been played almost five hundred years earlier between two men vying for the right to marry the daughter of the governor of the Italian state of Marostica. Before the skirmish, the local Gerard Tempest translated a proclamation written by Ernesto Xausa, mayor of Marostica, giving Myrtle Beach his blessing to reenact this "noble" event. The proclamation and history belied the purpose of the occasion.

What Myrtle Beach staged on the morning of 9 June 1956 was a game of human checkers, with twenty-four South Carolina beauty-pageant contestants as the pieces. Dressed in bathing suits with either red or black shorts the women were only required to smile and absorb the lustful stares of curious onlookers. A grainy picture taken at the event shows a crowd of roughly two hundred spectators, mostly men and young boys—a sizable number considering the early start time and the proclivities of vacationers to sleep late. Promoters reenacted the game of human checkers for the same reason that they tried to get as many beauty queens to take part in the festival and the same reason that they published contestants' measurements: to attract men to the beach. They staged this game of checkers for more than twenty years.[19]

Myrtle Beach boosters had a solution to the problem of how to attract men if these subtle messages did not get their attention: more beauty pageants. The Miss Legs contest is more instructive of how Myrtle Beach exploited women to attract male audiences. The contest was designed, as its creative title would suggest, to judge which young lady had the best legs. Competitors dressed in one-piece bathing suits and high heels to accentuate their shapely attributes. Women also wore paper bags over their heads with eye holes cut out. This was supposed to help the judges stay focused on the women's legs. No effort, however, was made to hide contestants' plunging necklines and upper bodies; nor was there any effort to learn about the contestants' personalities. This contest was strictly about the female body.

The winner, as pictured in a 10 June 1977 photo, was "crowned" by Hawaiian Tropic representatives. Unlike in a typical beauty pageant, this pageant's "crown" was a garter. The photo appearing on the front page of the *Myrtle Beach Sun News* featured two smiling Hawaiian Tropic officials easing the winning garter well over the knee of the new Sun Fun Miss Legs Queen. Racy events like these solidified Myrtle Beach's reputation as a destination for single men to visit.[20]

Myrtle Beach citizens even admitted that the Sun Fun Festival was the place to see and meet young women. In an article titled "Festival Features Accent on Women," the author acknowledged that "girl watchers are in evidence" at the Sun Fun Miss Legs Contest. There were, however, "other examples of female pulchritude ... on display." Editorials jokingly acknowledged, "We are too old for many things but looking at pretty girls is not one of them" and "You are never too old to look." By the 1970s there was no hiding that Myrtle Beach was the place for girl watching.[21]

Taken separately, the Sun Fun Festival events and promotional materials seem innocuous. Boosters' goals were to attract visitors to the beach, to give tourists an experience they would never forget, and to encourage them to come back for years to come. Together, though, these events highlight the fundamentally provocative nature of Myrtle Beach and signified that the city was a willing proponent of sexual permissiveness, but only for whites. Only on rare occasions are were African Americans pictured or included in the events. The city was not for them.

Catering to the sexualized youth culture had its consequences for women and the area. For example, there was little glamour for many of the young women participants at these beauty pageants. During the 1970 Miss Waves pageant, held as part of the Sun Fun Festival festivities in North Myrtle Beach, the audience, mainly high-school boys and college men, was overly rowdy and fueled by alcohol from a nearby beer parlor. Armed with rocks and beer cans, the unruly mob threatened to discharge their weapons if their winner was not chosen. Throughout the competition, the fourteen women heard hoots, hollers, and catcalls. After the winner was announced—fortunately, the one the crowd wanted—all the women involved vowed never to return to the beach. One contestant, glad the pageant was over, complained, "I feel like we were a bunch of cattle on the auction block." Myrtle Beach's insistence on using the promise of attractive single young women as the primary attraction had created this atmosphere.[22]

Despite leaders' best efforts, the Grand Strand was still attracting more women to its shores than men. Americans considered going to the beach a feminine desire; the mountains were the male domain. Travel magazines frequently played up the sexual stereotype in their articles, depicting men and women squabbling over where to spend their time. Women wanted to relax along the ocean and get a tan; men would rather fish for trout in a mountain stream or go hiking.[23]

One way local boosters answered this debate was by creating a spatial separation between men and women. Wives and children, they implied, could frolic along the surf, while husbands and single men could find activities further inland. Key to this was golf, a sport dominated by white men.

Developers completed the town's first golf course, the Ocean Forest Club, in 1927, but outside of locals and the very rich, for the first twenty-five years few ever heard of the locale. Jimmy D'Angelo, a golf pro from Philadelphia, was one of the first people to see the potential of the beach as a golfer's paradise. When he decided to move permanently to the town in 1948, his peers were skeptical. "Golf writers who were my friends in Philadelphia," remarked D'Angelo, "thought I had lost my mind when I moved to Myrtle Beach, a god-forsaken place that few people outside of the Carolinas had ever heard of."[24]

D'Angelo saw something in the Dunes Golf and Beach Club, a new development that George W. "Buster" Bryan was attempting to build in 1949. The proposed community was located across the highway from the Ocean Forest Club (now known as the Pine Lakes International Golf Course) and would feature a championship golf course surrounded by luxury homes. Although the site was beautiful, the plans were nonetheless ambitious. Bryan wanted to build the course right along the beach, an area covered in marshland and swamps. He enlisted some help to make his dream a reality. The famed golf-course designer Robert Trent Jones saw the area's potential and agreed to design the course. Upon completion, the course was immediately considered one of the best in the nation. As late as the 1960s, *Time* magazine marveled at its thirteenth hole, dubbed "Waterloo" for its difficulty.[25]

In November 1953, one of D'Angelo's sportswriter friends, Larry Robinson, of the *New York Telegram,* had an idea. He persuaded the Dunes Club developers to hold a dinner honoring designer Robert Trent Jones. The meal was to be held the Monday of the week of the Masters, the famed tournament in Augusta, Georgia, and all sportswriters were invited. Robinson knew the event would give Myrtle Beach free publicity, as journalists would stop for the dinner, play golf, and write a story about the city on their way to the tournament. On April 4, 1954, the Dunes held the first annual dinner for golf writers. Although only 8 attended the affair, by 1990 the "clambake" attracted roughly 120 journalists. Months after the first dinner, Time-Life sent sixty-seven executives to play golf and plan a magazine. It would be dubbed *Sports Illustrated.* The two events put Myrtle Beach golf on the map.[26]

Persuading golfers to migrate from their historic southern stomping ground, Pinehurst, North Carolina, proved more challenging. Just three hours by car northwest of Myrtle Beach, Pinehurst is a golfing Mecca, attracting thousands to its courses each year. Home to the best golf courses in the South, the city had already hosted several major tournaments, including the 1936 PGA Championship and the 1951 Ryder Cup. With the exception of Augusta, Georgia, which has held the Masters tournament since 1934, no other southern city could boast of landing a major tournament. And Augusta National's exclusionary policies made Pinehurst the place for golf lovers seeking to try their skills on the same courses that legends Sam Snead, Byron Nelson, Gene Sarazan, and Ben Hogan played. So popular was the resort location that unlike in Myrtle Beach, golfers year-round needed to reserve tee times in advance to guarantee a place on the links.[27]

Myrtle Beach leaders desperately wanted to tap into Pinehurst's popularity. City promoters tried two tactics to siphon off golfers. Since the North Carolina resort had unquestionably superior courses, boosters promised that Myrtle Beach courses were nearly equal to Pinehurst's, and they pointed out that while freezing temperatures and snow made Pinehurst unbearable and its courses unplayable in the winter, Myrtle Beach's proximity to the ocean made golfing possible there year-round. Most importantly, Myrtle Beach promoters attempted to bring golf to the masses. To play on most courses in the city, tourists did not need to be club members. In fact, several courses did not even require reservations. Playing golf in Myrtle Beach was less expensive than at other locations, including Pinehurst. Golf, a sport once reserved for the wealthy, was now affordable to the middle class in Myrtle Beach.[28]

In 1958, roughly 6 million people nationally played golf, spending more than $750 million. This was an average of $125 per person. In the same year, those engaged in boating and fishing spent less than $70 per person, including the cost of travel and the purchase of boats. Developers saw the rural coastal landscape of Horry County as the perfect place to build courses for the growing sport. Between 1949 and 1960, five courses were built in the county, and scores more were on the way.[29]

Beginning in August 1959, the chamber of commerce researched the prospect of offering travel packages. Hotels, working with airlines, could create a set monetary rate, making it easier for their male clientele to book vacations. The chamber also discussed enlisting golf courses in these package deals. Their goal was to create a total golf vacation package. With one phone call, men across the country could book a vacation complete with airfare, hotel accommodations, and tee times. In 1962, Myrtle Beach became the first city to create a golf package; the plan met with instant success.[30]

At the same time, golf's national popularity grew weekly as the rivals Jack Nicklaus and Arnold Palmer dueled at courses across the country, all captured on television. Arnold Palmer, the popular son of a greens keeper, was charismatic and a fan favorite. He was in his prime and drew a gallery in the thousands dubbed "Arnie's Army." The younger Nicklaus served as Palmer's foil. More stoic than his counterpart, Nicklaus quickly proved an equal on the links, winning the Masters in 1963, 1965, and 1966.[31]

As the sport grew in popularity so did Myrtle Beach's courses; white men wanted to experience the thrilling game they watched on television. By 1962, for the first time, golfers needed to reserve tee times in the summer to guarantee a spot on the links. Two years later, golfers alone brought in approximately $200,000 in revenue to Myrtle Beach from food, lodging, and green fees. Correctly seeing golf as an answer to its quest for a year-round economy, the chamber of commerce began making the white, male-dominated sport one of the centerpieces of its advertisements. Starting in the winter of 1964, Myrtle Beach flooded newspapers with advertisements touting itself as a golfing paradise, including spots in the three leading golf magazines, *Golf, Golf Digest,* and *Golf World.* Readers responding to the promotional blitz received golf information folders praising the city's three "championship" courses and including a list of local accommodations.[32]

In 1967, the vacation-package promotion was given its own name, the Myrtle Beach Golf Holiday. With a full-time director and four staff members, by 1992 the organization, also named Myrtle Beach Golf Holiday, was annually sending out more than eight hundred thousand pieces of promotional literature and fielding more than fifteen thousand calls, funneling golfers into one of more than seventy participating hotels. As green fees were relatively cheap, white, middle-class men flocked to the beach in ever-increasing numbers. Once dubbed the "Wal-mart of American golf resorts," by the late 1980s the county boasted more than one hundred courses. They were everywhere. As the *Sports Illustrated* senior writer Gary Van Sickle once noted, "Myrtle Beach needs another golf course like Central America needs another coup."[33]

Golf courses historically had discriminated against both African Americans and women, which perfectly suited Myrtle Beach developers' construction of leisure spaces for white men. Even the PGA (Professional Golf Association) excluded African Americans until 1961. When courses did begin to open their doors, financial barriers to learning the sport allowed only a lucky few to navigate around the links. Just playing the sport once involves shelling out money for expensive green fees, clubs, and balls, not to mention the cost of getting to the courses themselves. Even today white men dominate the number of rounds played nationally, and since 1997, when Tiger Woods broke onto the scene, no African American has earned a PGA tour card.[34]

It did not take long for businesses catering to these single, white men to find a home in Myrtle Beach. On the morning of 10 April 1974 residents awoke to shocking news. The feature story of the paper was a long story on "Stella," a Myrtle Beach businesswoman. The opening lines were meant to shock readers. "She's attractive, middle aged, and at three o'clock in the afternoon she's wearing a long red negligee. She's a mother, a grandmother and a prostitute." Stella acknowledged that she had hundreds of regular customers, all from out of town. In fact, she had so many customers that she was looking for a partner. "I wish to God there was someone working with me in the golfing season," Stella added. "If she was smart enough, I'd love to have her." By "smart" Stella meant both expensive and without a male attachment, pimp or boyfriend, who would siphon off earnings. "I've passed up more $50 tricks; you know darned well the guy's got $100. I can see if you had a bunch of golfers and they would ALL go for $50 each ... but I can't see one guy," she explains.

Stella acknowledged that it was not just single men who utilized her services. "Some of my customers have even introduced me to their wives. They say they met me at a convention," Stella acknowledges. "Then they'll sneak away later and come see me. Most men are out to have a good time, whether they're alone or with their family." If Myrtle Beach was a "family beach," its male visitors did not always subscribe to all the principles of family men.

Seeing her vocation as a business no different from a nightclub or golf course, Stella said that the sex trade was compatible with Myrtle Beach and should be protected. "Golfers—anyone who puts his money out—you are pleasing them, making them happy, entertaining them. They SHOULD pay for entertainment, ... Every Tom, Dick and Harry who comes to town wants a good time. Why should I give them free love?" explained Stella. Myrtle Beach promoters had been selling sex for twenty years, but until this article appeared, no one had stated publicly that there were buyers.[35]

By 1972 there were more than one hundred known prostitutes working the beach during the winter. Some were wives living at the Air Force base who went into business when their husbands went overseas. Many more, however, came to town in the spring and fall, when men flocked to the city, to quote the FBI agent Don Meyers, "to play golf, to drink and to find the girls."[36]

Like migrant farmworkers arriving for the harvest, call girls "follow(ed) the seasons," coming to Myrtle Beach from out of state to give the golfers some nighttime entertainment. Some came from as far away as Tampa, Florida. A local police officer conceded, "Its like tomato season.... They follow the seasons from resort to resort. They travel first class.... You can spot them around. They look like they just stepped out of a Cosmopolitan Magazine; they look like models." While this police officer could spot them, he, like other lawmen, did not arrest them.[37]

Myrtle Beach authorities turned a blind eye to the oldest profession; male entertainment was the big business of the beach. While few doubted the low estimate of one hundred prostitutes doing business on the beach, in 1972 there were only five arrests for prostitution and commercialized vice. The local police and the FBI knew about Stella and her operations but to this point had done little. Although she had been in operation for years in her beachfront house, she had only been arrested once. She had merely received a slap on the wrist. The four diamond rings she regularly flaunted showed that business was both plentiful and steady.[38]

Law-enforcement officials quickly tried to mollify shocked Myrtle Beach residents. Their response, though, yielded more information about how the culture of sexual permissiveness dominated Myrtle Beach culture by the 1970s. An area police spokesman defended the department's inaction, noting, "We don't have a big problem with prostitution at the present time.... One reason we haven't had too much organized prostitution is because of all the college girls who come here for the summer." College girls, according to the police, would have sex with anybody for free. The Horry County solicitor J. M. "Bud" Long concurred. While acknowledging that he knew there were prostitutes, he admitted surprise at the number. "We've generally felt that ... aah ... companionship ... is available—both male and female—for anyone on the beach who wanted it, without having to see a prostitute." "There's just so much free stuff," Long quietly admitted. Unlike the police spokesman, Long realized quickly the gravity of what he was saying about female visitors, hastily adding, "I hope you're not going to say that in the paper." An exasperated Stella, lamenting the influx of cheap prostitutes, who were eating into her profits, would agree. "Amateurs are messing up the business," she said.[39]

It should hardly be surprising that by the 1980s another male-dominated activity, capitalizing on the sexually charged, machismo atmosphere, called Myrtle Beach home. Virtually the entire month of May is dominated by two bike rallies: the Myrtle Beach Harley-Davidson Bike Rally and the Atlantic Beach Bikefest. "White Bike Week," as the Harley-Davidson rally is locally known, started in 1940 and as its name suggests, it attracts mostly whites. The Atlantic Beach Bikefest, started forty years later and usually held around Memorial Day, attracts mostly African Americans. The rallies bring in millions of dollars to city businesses each year, yet they have become a lightning rod of controversy.

Historically, access to Myrtle Beach's sexualized culture was open only to white men, the city's target audience, around whose desires leaders built activities. Their behavior, no matter how raunchy, was, and still is, accepted if not encouraged. Gunning their expensive Harleys and sporting leather jackets, white bikers fit perfectly with the city's image—so perfectly in fact that for the first forty-five years of the rally their arrival garnered little to no attention in the *Sun News*. Today, locals note that the attendees are older, ranging in age from late twenties to sixties, and are generally upper-class doctors and lawyers—the same men who frequent Myrtle Beach golf courses and strip clubs—who are just coming to town to unleash their wild side just as they did when they were college students. Making the rally of close to two hundred thousand sound more like a bus full of retirees visiting a casino, locals claim that white bikers are generally well behaved and harmless and that their presence, while causing massive traffic delays, is a welcome boon to the economy.[40]

The same cannot be said for African American bikers. Myrtle Beach and the Grand Strand were historically off-limits to blacks. In the 1930s, Federal Writers' Project authors noted that Horry County contained numerous "sun-down" cities. Little changed for twenty years. As the longtime resident Jack Thompson recalls, "If black people crossed Kings Highway [Highway 17] in the '30s, '40s, and '50s, they had to be going to or from a job." The one exception was the small black-owned coastal city of Atlantic Beach, nicknamed "The Black Pearl." Nestled between the cities of Myrtle Beach and North Myrtle Beach, the lightly populated, four-block town was a haven for vacationing African Americans that attracted numerous celebrities during the late Jim Crow period but lost its luster with the end of segregation. Looking to regain some of its past glory and some much-needed revenue, the town started the Atlantic Beach Bike-fest in 1980. It was a quick success. Within twenty years, more than four hundred thousand African Americans visited Atlantic Beach and the rest of the Grand Strand for the one week in May to party and participate in what Myrtle Beach leaders had carefully created, a haven for boisterous white men and promiscuous women. The event draws African Americans from similar professions and of similar ages as those attending the previous biker week, yet it also attracts tens of thousands of black youths without motorcycles who come just to party.[41]

Most mean no harm. "It is an atmosphere," acknowledges the journalist Jeffrey Gettleman, "that is more forward than raunchy, where women jump on the back of strangers' bikes for a ride and men with video cameras shoot whatever crosses their field of view." There are legitimate concerns about traffic problems and the expense of enlisting police officers from other departments to handle the crowd, which is twice the size of that attending the Harley-Davidson rally. But neither the expense nor the additional money generated by the larger crowd is what really concerns residents.

Most troubling to local whites is the overt sexuality exhibited by African Americans during the week. Every May, chat rooms and blogs explode with complaints of black women wearing little and engaging in public sex acts in what the *New York Times* refers to as "an exhibitionist's paradise." The following complaint from Sandra Davis is typical: "Several black girls actually pull[ed] down the back of their bathing suit and started gyrating while a car load of black men watched. After her filthy dance, one of the guys in the car motioned her over he felt her butt and then all the girls giggled." Others complain that the city is overrun by "pimps and "hookin," yet the crime rate is actually lower during Atlantic Beach Bikefest than during its white counterpart.[42]

These complaints are genuine and not overstated. African American promoters describe the event to prospective male visitors as a sexualized getaway, noting, "If you can imagine 175,000 sexy women, in tiny bikinis, 'droppin it like it's hot' on the back of a bike, then you should have an idea." They do the same for women. "Ladies... can you imagine 175,000 men on the hottest bikes in the county ready to give YOU a ride? If you love men on bikes and love to have fun, you won't find a larger gathering of professional chocolate men ready to show you their engines." Euphemisms aside, there is no doubt that promotions like this attract tens of thousands of young blacks who care little about bikes and more about partying, sex, and partaking in activities they cannot engage in back home—activities locals accept, if not welcome, from their white peers.[43]

Missing is the same outrage over white women engaging in comparable activities during the Harley-Davidson rally. The local club Suck Bang Blow, whose racy name serves as a double entendre for an internal combustion engine, is the center of the celebration and home to sexually charged activities similar to those castigated by Myrtle Beach residents during the Atlantic Beach Bikefest. Wet T-shirt and frozen T-shirt contests add to an already raucous event featuring indoor motorcycle burnouts and readily available beer. Bumping into a topless woman and "lots of thongs" is just as common during Harley-Davidson Week as during Bikefest. The revelry exists all over town, bringing little fanfare or contempt. Arrests of those having sex in public are treated almost as comedy. In 2010, for example, after Myrtle Beach police caught and arrested two people for engaging in sex at a local strip club during the Harley-Davidson biker week, bloggers did not respond with disgust but instead said, "Not in Myrtle Beach.... What will the golfers do?" Another blogger asked sarcastically, "Did the golfers get a group rate and I wonder how much they charge for bikers?" In Myrtle Beach, boys will be boys, provided they are white. Myrtle Beach's lure as a "safety valve" was not intended for African Americans.[44]

The Grand Strand's place as a haven for white men was intentional. Leaders desperately wanted the area to grow and thrive; utilizing the sexual allure of local white women in bathing suits appeared to be the best advertising asset. In creating a place for young southerners to relax, boosters lost control of the message, and the region developed in ways unforeseen by the early leaders. Only rarely do leaders attempt to change the area's image as a place that encourages open sexual permissiveness among whites, and even then businesses dependent on this culture fight every step. The presence of young African Americans during the Atlantic Beach Bikefest has only further complicated matters; the sexual lure of the region was never meant for their consumption.

The Myrtle Beach Convention and Visitors Bureau likes to paint the region as "one of the premier family and beach vacation destinations in the United States," yet the derisive nickname Las Vegas of the South is far more accurate. Like Las Vegas, the region is known more for its strip clubs, bachelor parties, and spotty enforcement of alcohol and prostitution laws, all male-dominated activities, than for its racial exclusionary policies. Yet, whereas Las Vegas has largely replaced the moniker Mississippi of the West with the catchphrase

"What happens in Vegas stays in Vegas," the vestiges of Jim Crow still haunt the Grand Strand.[45]

NOTES

1. Tim McDonald, "Myrtle Beach: Home of Great Golf and Wild Bachelor Parties," Myrtle Beach Golf Travel, accessed 13 March 2008, www.myrtlebeachgolf.com/departments/features /planning-bachelor-party-2508.htm; "Table DP-1. Profile of General Demographic Characteristics: 2000, Geographic Area: Myrtle Beach city, South Carolina," accessed 2 October 2008, censtats.census. gov/data/SC/1604549075.pdf; "Table DP-1. Profile of General Demographic Characteristics: 2000, Geographic Area: North Myrtle Beach city, South Carolina," accessed 2 October 2008, censtats.cen-sus.gov/data/SC/1604551280.pdf.

2. Alecia P. Long, *The Great Southern Babylon: Sex, Race, and Respectability in New Orleans, 1865–1920* (Baton Rouge: Louisiana State University Press, 2004), 5–6.

3. W. J. Cash, *The Mind of the South* (New York: Vintage Books, 1991), 86.

4. "In Tobacco Festival," *Myrtle Beach Sun,* 28 July 1950.

5. Larry Boulier, "Western Cities are Different? . . . So is Myrtle Beach," *Myrtle Beach Sun and Ocean Beach News,* 10 December 1958; "Tan Age Beauty on the Beach," *Myrtle Beach Sun,* 11 August 1950.

6. "Home Grown Talent," *Myrtle Beach Sun,* 15 May 1953; "Grand Strand Starts Harvest of Its Biggest Annual Crop," *Myrtle Beach Sun News,* 15 June 1967.

7. The movie was based on the book by Glendon Swarthout, *Where the Boys Are* (New York: Signet Books, 1960); James Richard Fussell, "Some Aspects of the Geography of Recreation in Coastal South Carolina" (master's thesis, University of South Carolina, 1966), 64–65. Housewives made up the second most populous group, at 9 percent.

8. Governor McNair, interview by Cole Blease Graham, 23 August 1982, tape 9, transcript, Governor McNair Oral History Collection, South Carolina Department of Archives and History, Columbia; Athalia Stalvey Ramsey and Jasper Ramsey Jr., interview by Sarah Bryan, 21 January 2005, folder 20, transcript, Myrtle Beach Oral History Collection, Chapin Memorial Library, Myrtle Beach.

9. Bill Black, "College Students Jam Grand Strand," *Myrtle Beach Sun News,* 18 April 1968; Roy Talbert Jr., *So Much to be Thankful For: The Conway National Bank & The Economic History of Horry County* (Columbia: R. L. Bryan, 2003), 241.

10. Bill Osgerby, *Playboys in Paradise: Masculinity, Youth and Leisure Style in Modern America* (New York: Berg, 2001), 121–78.

11. Ibid., 152, 161.

12. Ibid., 140–42.

13. Fussell, "Some Aspects of the Geography of Recreation," 65–66.

14. Ibid., 65; "'One of Cleanest Places I Know of,' Stevens Says," *Myrtle Beach Sun News,* 8 April 1965.

15. "Sun Fun The Sprit of Myrtle Beach," ibid., 6 June 1956.

16. "Beauties on Display," ibid., 3 June 1965.

17. "Many Features on Tap for the Festival," ibid., 7 June 1962; Bobby G. Thompson, "Annual Festive Event Set For Sun Fun Days," *Myrtle Beach Sun and Ocean Beach News,* 18 November 1959; "In Picking the Queen Beauty Doesn't Count," *Myrtle Beach Sun News,* 6 June 1956. There were other Sun Fun Queens before 1960. When the festival started in the 1950s, the queen was chosen at random. The first winner was a bride from Philadelphia celebrating her honeymoon at the beach.

18. *Myrtle Beach and South Carolina's Grand Strand Present the 9th Annual Sun Fun Festival,* undated brochure, Horry County Vertical Files, South Caroliniana Library, University of South Carolina, Columbia. The other pictures show clowns, an airplane, and the chamber of commerce building.

19. "Sun Fun: Flavor All Its Own," *Myrtle Beach Sun News,* 6 June 1956; "Festival Features Accent on Women," ibid., 10 June 1977. When the Miss South Carolina pageant left in 1959, Sun Fun organizers chose other attractive women to participate in the checkers game.

20. "Festival Features Accent on Women."

21. Ibid.; "Pretty Girls Make Spring Great," *Myrtle Beach Sun and Ocean Beach News,* 8 February 1961; Eldridge Thompson, "These Girls are the Prettiest I've Ever Seen," *Myrtle Beach Sun News,* 30 August 1961.

22. Tom H. Billington, "Reflections on Headlines," *Myrtle Beach Sun News,* 18 June 1970.

23. Thomas M. Heaney, "The Call of the Open Road: Automobile Travel and Vacations in American Popular Culture, 1935–1960" (PhD diss., University of California at Irvine, 2000), 83.

24. W. Horace Carter and Jimmy D'Angelo, *Jimmy D'Angelo and Myrtle Beach Golf* (Tabor City, NC: Atlantic, 1991), 67.

25. Ibid., 62–67.

26. Ibid., 91–94, 101.

27. "Golfing Gap Can Be Closed," *Myrtle Beach Sun News,* 15 March 1962.

28. Ibid.

29. Fussell, "Some Aspects of the Geography of Recreation," 65; George Fisk, *Leisure Spending-Behavior* (Philadelphia: University of Pennsylvania Press, 1963), 42; Carter and D'Angelo, *Myrtle Beach Golf,* 158.

30. "Airlines Mgr. Talks On Package Vacations," *Myrtle Beach Sun News,* 26 August 1959; "There is No Need For an 'Off Season' Along South Carolina's Golden Coast," *Myrtle Beach Sun and Ocean Beach News,* 31 August 1960; Carter and D'Angelo, *Myrtle Beach Golf,* 116–21.

31. Ian O'Connor, *Arnie & Jack: Palmer, Nicklaus, and Golf's Greatest Rivalry* (New York: Houghton Mifflin, 2008); Howard Sounes, *The Wicked Game: Arnold Palmer, Jack Nicklaus, Tiger Woods and the Business of Modern Golf* (New York: HarperCollins, 2004).

32. "Golf is Big Business on the Strand," *Myrtle Beach Sun News,* 19 March 1964; "Chamber's Advertising Program Gets Results," ibid., 2 April 1964; Carter and D'Angelo, *Myrtle Beach Golf,* 116–21.

33. Carter and D'Angelo, *Myrtle Beach Golf,* 116–21; Gary Van Sickle, "Myrtle Beach's Newest Addition," *Sports Illustrated,* 15 November 1999, accessed 13 February 2013, sportsillustrated.cnn.com/inside_game/gary_van_sickle/news/1999/11/15/underground/.

34. Paul Newberry and Doug Ferguson, "Even With Tiger at No. 1, Golf Still Mostly White," *USA Today,* accessed 16 February 2013, usatoday30.usatoday.com/sports/golf/2009-03-31-584252466_x.htm.

35. Jennifer Amor, "She's Mother, Grandmother, and Prostitute," *Myrtle Beach Sun News,* 10 April 1974.

36. Jennifer Amor, "Prostitution Found in MB," ibid., 4 December 1972.

37. Jennifer Amor, "100 Prostitutes in MB—What's Being Done," ibid., 11 April 1974; "Over 20 Arrested On Gambling, Prostitution Charges at Beach," *Georgetown (SC) Weekly Observer and Journal,* 19 August 1976.

38. Amor, "She's Mother, Grandmother, and Prostitute"; Amor, "100 Prostitutes in MB"; "It's Time to Act Against Prostitution," *Myrtle Beach Sun News,* 11 April 1974. While there were only a few arrests, South Carolina's prostitution penalties had few teeth. A first offense called for a maximum fine of one hundred dollars and thirty days in jail. Penalties for second and third offenses were precipitously stronger, but the law contained an archaic clause stating that the harsher penalties could only be given if the country were at war.

39. Amor, "100 Prostitutes in MB"; Amor, "She's Mother, Grandmother, and Prostitute."

40. Calm_Cool_and_Elected, comment on "Myrtle Beach Mayor Wants Bike Events Nixed—McBride Stands By Comments About Bikefest Attendees," Freerepublic.com, 26 May 2005, www .freerepublic.com/focus/f-news/1410688/posts; Jeffrey Gettleman, "Suit Charges Bias at Rally for Black Bikers," *New York Times,* 21 May 2003, www.nytimes.com/2003/05/21/us/suit-charges-bias-at -rally-for-black-bikers.html.

41. Federal Writers' Project, *The Ocean Highway: New Brunswick, New Jersey to Jacksonville, Florida* (New York: Modern Age Books, 1938), 122; Randall A. Wells, *Swamp, Strand, & Steamboat: Voices of Horry County, South Carolina, 1732–1954* (Myrtle Beach: Horry County Historical Society, 2004), 94–95; P. Nicole King, *Sombreros and Motorcycles in a Newer South: The Politics of Aesthetics in South Carolina's Tourism Industry* (Jackson: University Press of Mississippi, 2012), 113–49; Calm _Cool_and_Elected, "Myrtle Beach Mayor Wants Bike Events Nixed"; Gettleman, "Suit Charges Bias."

42. Jeffrey Gettleman, "Claims of Bias Cloud an American Dream for Black Bikers," *New York Times,* 25 May 2003, www.nytimes.com/2003/05/25/us/claims-of-bias-cloud-an-american-dream -for-black-bikers.html; Rich, 20 May 2009, and Sandra Davis, 27 May 2009, comments on "Myrtle Beach Bike Week. Disappointment and Anger," Cyril Huze Post, cyrilhuzeblog.com/2009/05/19 /myrtle-beach-bike-week-disappointment-and-anger/; statistics on the rally e-mailed to author by Myrtle Beach Police Department, February, 2013.

43. Free4Life11, comment on "Anyone Been to Myrtle Beach During 'Black Bike Week,'" Disboards.com, 29 March 2005, www.disboards.com/showthread.php?t=1069777.

44. Ncjail, 17 May 2010, and Victory Rider, 31 May 2010, comments on "2 Charged With Prostitution at Myrtle Beach Strip Club," Topix.com, www.topix.com/forum/city/myrtle-beach-sc/TJA02 TF6ANDOHORRQ; Long, *Great Southern Babylon,* 5–6.

45. Myrtle Beach Convention and Visitors Bureau, "About the Myrtle Beach Area," accessed 30 January 2013, www.visitmyrtlebeach.com/about/.

6

A Queer Destination

Cruising and Connecting on Florida's Redneck Riviera

JERRY WATKINS

There was "something in Florida's humid, languorous air," a writer for Fortune observed, that over the years had "attracted pirates, derelicts, remittance men, thieves, madams, gamblers, blue sky promoters, profiteers, [and] all the infections of Western life."

—HARVEY H. JACKSON III

When most people consider LGBTQ history in Florida, what often springs to mind is Miami, or Key West.[1] Other scholars have documented South Florida's queer past, yet the state's northern section, where the tourists and locals enjoyed a more "down home" southern existence, has received precious little scholarly attention.[2] People call this section of Florida, from Pensacola in the west to Tallahassee in the east, by several names: the Gulf Coast, the Redneck Riviera, the Panhandle, even the Gay Gulf Coast or the Gay Riviera. People and ideas have ebbed and flowed through the spaces of North Florida throughout the twentieth century; in this dialectical process, locals and visitors have created a colorful tapestry, weaving together the sleazy and the upstanding, the queer and the straight-laced.

World War II began a transition in Florida tourism that continued into the long 1950s. Though the southern part of the state had been a tourist destination for America's wealthy from the last half of the nineteenth century, the state's northern section did not fully embrace its tourist potential until after the war. As the country settled into a peacetime economy, attracting tourists to Florida generally became enshrined as civic virtue. Florida boosters, politicians, and business owners were heavily invested in selling what is officially titled "The Sunshine State"—the imagined tropical paradise of sun, fun, thinly veiled sexuality, and release from the worries of "back home." This essay uses the full official title to convey that in addition to a descriptor of the weather, or of what was possible in Florida, "The Sunshine State" was an intentional, carefully crafted, tightly managed, and heavily policed version of Florida that salespersons, government officials, local boosters, police forces, and advertising agencies sold to the outside world. What makes this section of the state unique is the rapidity with which tourism became a primary economic driver. Unlike Miami, Los Angeles, Provincetown, and other famous coastal destinations with long-established reputations, the Gulf Coast became a nationally known tourist destination less than ten years after World War II, a situation that created stiff competition among municipalities along the coast.

Concurrent with the drive for tourists was the Cold War quest for uncovering communists and "undesirables." To this end, politicians, law enforcers, and newspaper editors practiced a politics of exposure. In theory, exposing and then publicly shaming individuals would deter future deviance and subversion. The national practice, enacted through so many congressional committees and blacklists, was taken up by states in their own crusades. Selling "The Sunshine State" placed Florida under added pressure to police the boundaries of respectability as "many lawmakers recognized the economic need to maintain the state's positive national image for the sake of attracting tourists, residents, and businesses," according to the historian Stacy Braukman in her book *Communists and Perverts under the Palms*.[3] Thus, the long 1950s is characterized by countless "moral" panics, as municipal and state-level authorities sought to ferret out undesirables in order to project and refine a "family-friendly" image of Florida as "The Sunshine State" and ensure the benefits of postwar capitalism for all.

As the United States enjoyed unprecedented prosperity, automobile ownership was on the rise. All of those new cars, financed through easy credit, paid for by jobs that men trained for thanks to the GI Bill, brought tourists and migrants to Florida on roads that were New Deal paved and military maintained.[4] This new kind of tourist—generally southern, rural, and working class—traveled throughout the state, though their impact was most acute along the Redneck Riviera. These southerners helped to continually construct and refine the Redneck Riviera as they sought to re-create their home environs on the beach. As the scholar Harvey H. Jackson has stated, "Along this coast folks from the lower South found a way of life, a culture and context, much like the one they left back home—segregated (where blacks existed at all), small town, provincial, self-centered, and unassuming. Only the landscape was different."[5]

The massive influx of visitors and new residents brought about an identity crisis of sorts. How did a region whose reputation had been built on selling sun, fun, and a release from the cares of home stop itself from becoming a haven for the debauched, the criminal, and the queer as more and more people became mobile? By 1961, surveillant authorities (local and state) interested in growing the northern Gulf Coast's reputation for so-called good, clean fun began crackdowns on the most obvious sites of queer socialization—public restrooms, bars, even beaches. Newspaper editors, law enforcers, and city boosters conspired not only to arrest men and women engaged in consensual, albeit illegal, sexual activity but also to humiliate them as part of a larger effort to demonstrate vigilance to potential tourists and migrants and assure the benefits of capitalist commerce. In the context of a dynamic regional economy rapidly becoming a tourist monoculture after World War II, queer individuals circulated, congregated, made contact, and had sex—and were at times punished for it. Yet, the communication networks, advancements in transportation, and the lure of the beach lifestyle, which made Florida so attractive to visitors, also made it attractive to queer men and women. Information networks, from national magazines to local graffiti, pointed the way to queer hot spots, while better roads and vehicles made them easier to reach. Despite the culture of persecution, queer men and women used the spaces around them to construct a queer political economy and claim their place in "The Sunshine State."

THE COMMITTEE

Any history of sexuality in Florida after World War II that did not discuss the Florida Legislative Investigation Committee (FLIC) would be incomplete given the committee's far-reaching implications. This committee was the state-level institutionalization of more nebulous persecutions of integrationists, political dissidents, and homosexuals in the late 1950s. Formed by the state senator Charley Johns in 1956, the committee sought to block or slow the process of racial integration by linking the National Association for the Advancement of Colored People (NAACP) with domestic communism. By practicing a politics of exposure, which had been so successfully deployed against communists nationally through the House Un-American Activities Committee and the Senate's McCarthy hearings—in which Senator Joseph McCarthy accused on television a variety of agencies and individuals of communist sympathies—FLIC members, and by extension their supporters, hoped to forestall the process of integration. The language of subversion that began in the national hunt for domestic communists propelled the committee beyond the NAACP because it created new enemies. According to Stacy Braukman, this "allowed southern conservatives to construct other enemies in those terms: homosexuals as secret infiltrators, polluters and corruptors, and integrationists as secret race mixers and statists."[6] The committee was unique among its Deep South counterparts, such as Mississippi's Citizens' Council; it went well beyond its original anti-NAACP remit to tackle the "problems" of homosexual teachers, pornography and indecent literature, student peace and civil rights groups, and even academic freedom in the guise of "liberal professors."[7]

Committee members spent nine years traveling throughout Florida conducting investigations that usually involved closed hearings, secrecy, and the intimidation of witnesses, entrapment, and warrantless wiretapping. In addition to their investigations at Florida's universities and colleges, the committee assisted local law-enforcement agencies throughout the state with their own localized investigations. Despite the dreadfulness of their creation, the records left by the FLIC provide valuable insights into Florida's queer past. However, the population from which they were drawn, namely, men arrested for engaging in public sex, confirmed the committee's worst fears. Braukman writes, "The very nature of the furtive, anonymous bathroom encounter meant that the committee often ended up interrogating men who were deeply conflicted about their sexual desires."[8] Though the records predominantly record the criminal actions of queer individuals, by reading between the lines it is possible to use the testimonies as a base from which to construct a vibrant queer history of the Redneck Riviera.

RAY AND HENRY HILLYER

Though Florida's government and many Floridians bought into the homophobic rhetoric of the FLIC and supported the committee's efforts, certain queers quietly flourished in the 1950s despite the pressures against them. Ray and Henry Hillyer, adopted brothers and lifelong lovers, were just such men. Over the years, the couple became important figures in North Florida's queer history. Both men grew up in Texas, but the couple settled in Pensacola after Ray completed his Air Force service at Hurlburt Field. Through the years, the couple became quietly famous in Pensacola and in the South more broadly. Both men were involved with local theater and worked on costume design for the

Festival of Five Flags, as well as the various Mardi Gras krewes. The couple was socially well connected, and they enjoyed the privileges that came with their class and race positions—white and middle class.

In the 1950s, as fear and paranoia swept the country and served to closet many men and women, the Hillyers wanted to connect with larger homophile discourses and other homosexuals across the country. In the 1950s this was not an easy task. According to Joshua Jones, a friend of the Hillyers', "They heard that the local Post Office was keeping a list of men receiving the publications [e.g., *ONE* magazine] and sharing the list with the police, who in turn would target and harass those on the list."[9] The Hillyers were aware that the public shame heaped on men arrested for receiving obscene material could devastate their careers.

The Hillyers invented a creative way to thwart postal inspectors. They enlisted the help of a female friend in New Orleans to rent a post office box under the nondescript fictitious name Emma Jones—"'Emma' because it was such an awful name, 'Jones' because it was so common."[10] Every month this friend retrieved the packages and delivered them to Ray and Henry, who in turn shared the books and other publications with their friends.[11] The Emma Jones Society, which began as a secretive book club, was the beginning of a phenomenon that would put Pensacola on the American LGBTQ map.

The social options for LGBTQ people in Pensacola at midcentury were limited and usually secretive. Men could cruise for sex in public parks or on the streets of downtown. Trader Jon's was famously known as the unofficial watering hole for the US Navy and was immortalized as TJ's in the film *An Officer and a Gentleman.* The large number of sailors, in conjunction with an uncharacteristically tolerant owner, meant that gay men often socialized and cruised there. Both Bob Shaw, of the *Miami Herald,* and Bill Rushton, of the *Advocate,* call Trader Jon's the site of the first openly public gatherings of gays in Pensacola. Lesbians in uniform and lesbians more broadly also socialized at Trader Jon's. There existed as well a network of private house parties, if one was lucky enough to secure an invite. However, these parties were subject to "illegal raids conducted by both military and civilian police."[12] The queer population (regular and visiting) of Pensacola grew year after year. According to Rushton's *Advocate* article, "fine, white beaches and naval meat rack" drew many to Pensacola.[13]

The Hillyers regularly hosted out-of-town friends at their spacious home, and they saw the distinct areas of "community" of Pensacola not as separate

Fig. 6.1. "Miss Emma" mimes the female part of "Indian Love Call," a song originally written for the musical *Rose-Marie* by Oscar Hammerstein II and Otto Harbach, and recorded by numerous artists since its premier in 1924. The legend upon which the song is based has the male calling down from above to the woman he intends to marry. In the show, it is Miss Emma who calls from atop Mount Rushmore, thereby queering the legend. Photo in author's collection, courtesy of Kurt Young, friend of Ray and Henry Hillyer.

but as in need of connection. The Fourth of July has long been a traditional beach holiday for those who living close to the coast. Together with friends, the Hillyers designed and distributed invitations to a private beach party for members of the Emma Jones Society. The first year, they distributed fifty invitations, and one hundred people showed up at the beach.[14] The timing of the parties had to do with more than convenience. According to one of the society's founders, "The real theme was patriotic. It was, we're Americans. This is our Fourth too. Thank God we're in America where we can be independent enough to be gay."[15] The Hillyers, because of their time spent reading publications ordered under Emma's name, were well aware of other homophile groups across the country that used the Fourth of July holidays to make a statement about their place in, and right to, America.[16]

What began as a simple gathering of friends on the beach quickly morphed into a full-scale weekend event that took over the San Carlos Hotel. The events at the San Carlos included a drag show, "The Red, Hot, and Blue Review," comprising patriotic-themed acts. One year the show was titled "Emma Jones'

Fig. 6.2. Queering the Founding Fathers. With hands on hips and waving handkerchiefs, the actors reenact the signing of the Declaration of Independence with a camp sensibility. Photo in author's collection, courtesy of Kurt Young.

Tribute to the Golden West." In it, "Miss Emma," dressed in red, white, and blue, mimed "Indian Love Call" from atop and then around a model Mount Rushmore (fig. 6.1). In another year's show, was titled "Emma Jones Proudly Presents the United States of America," "the signing of the Declaration of Independence featured all the actors with their hair tied up in bows, dripping with lace, and cruising the drawing room as if it were a bar" (fig. 6.2). For each year's finale, "a silver drag Statue of Liberty [was] dollied around the San Carlos' ballroom, throwing flowers while the Kate Smith recording of 'God Bless America' pronounced the show's finale" (fig. 6.3).[17]

As can be seen in figure 6.1, the shows and the larger parties were racially diverse. According to the *Advocate,* "The purchase of Manhattan was a composite minority-consciousness *tour de force:* a black drag affecting a New York Jewish accent, tap dancing and pretending to be an Indian princess while our 'straight' forbearers attempted to win her favors."[18] Despite the advances made nationally by the civil rights movement, at least one man who spoke to John Loughery for his book *The Other Side of Silence* commented on how uncom-

Fig. 6.3. In what became a staple of the "Red, Hot, and Blue Review," a drag Statue of Liberty is dollied around the ballroom to patriotic songs. Because of issues such as privacy and outness, the author has intentionally blurred faces that are easily recognizable. Photo in author's collection, courtesy of Kurt Young.

mon and unexpected the racially diverse crowd was. Pensacola was a progressive city in some ways, but it was also very much a part of the Deep South.

The party could not go on forever. As it grew in importance and notoriety, it attracted the attention of the city. The final straw was the announcement by a local DJ that the area would play host to "a convention of 3,000 homosexuals where Mr. Gay USA will be named." This posed significant problems for a city that had built its tourist reputation on "family friendly fun."[19] Beginning in May 1974, local police launched a series of raids on cruising grounds and bars with the expressed intention of cleaning up the city's image. The founders canceled the official celebrations, but men and women came anyway. There were more arrests and more raids. Emma was never about flaunting, but that is just what the weekend had become. According to the *Advocate,* "Delicate Miss Emma Jones suffered a terrible and ultimately irreversible seizure." Or, according an anonymous source in the same article, she "died in the streets of Pensacola on July 4, 1974. She was 17."[20]

The Hillyers and the Emma Jones Society are a key component of Florida's queer past. The society represents an attempt to overcome the stigmatization and isolation experienced by many gay men and lesbians throughout the country. In a time when many gay men met one another by cruising public parks and restrooms and socializing in public was conducted subject to the whims of bar owners or municipal authorities, the Emma Jones parties were an opportunity to socialize with other gay men and lesbians from around the South. In the process of making Pensacola a regional hub for LGBTQ tourism, the Emma Jones Society parties spawned innumerable friendships, launched the careers of a number of drag performers, and gave many the courage to come out and live openly.

CARRYIN' ON

Ray and Henry Hillyer were not the only people to host parties with queer guest lists. The phenomenon of "gay parties," as such events were called at the time, was well known in this era.[21] John Howard and Allan Bérubé have both shown that gay parties were a key social element for those who adopted LGBTQ identities and those who did not.[22] The distances some attendees traveled show how important the parties were to their social lives and that they formed important nodes in the deterritorialized community of the Gay Gulf Coast, and the ability to travel those distances illuminates the link between postwar mobility and queer networking.

Unlike an apartment shared with multiple people, the individual private home (or apartment) greatly opened up sexual and social possibilities for queer individuals. If one met a potential partner while out cruising, one could bring that person back to an ostensibly private space away from the prying eyes of law enforcement. If one had a network of queer friends, one could invite them over to socialize in a relaxed atmosphere. These private parties were not completely safe from police harassment, as John Howard showed in his article "Place and Movement in American Gay History."[23] If a party became too public or too boisterous, police had an arsenal of "public order" statutes that allowed them to shut down gay parties and then publicly shame the attendees. In addition, the FLIC was well aware of the gay party scene in Tallahassee and Pensacola and deeply concerned about race mixers at such parties. In the years before Emma Jones threw her beach parties, civilian and military police regularly raided private events held by "known homosexuals."[24]

The phenomenon of gay parties in this era drew upon a long tradition of queer socialization. According to the historian Allan Bérubé in *Coming Out Under Fire,* "At all of these private gatherings, newcomers who had just moved into town or who had been recently discovered or 'brought out' by someone in the group were socialized into the gay life."[25] These functions were especially important in small towns with no publicly established gay or lesbian nightlife, such as the Gulf Coast in this era. A small and intimate gathering of friends provided a place for gay men and lesbians to socialize in a way that they often could not outside of a private home. According to Mike Nelson, a resident of Tallahassee, "The atmosphere is supposedly cozy and all that bit—lights turned down low and everything—there's a hi-fi going and about three-fourths of the party was sitting around in conversation and naturally in conversation with all of one kind, the conversation was usually homosexual."[26] In the public sphere, one guarded one's conversations for fear of eavesdroppers. Individuals also policed their behavior to avoid drawing unwanted attention to a group of homosexual friends. Yet, in the space of a gay party, a certain level of trust was inherent, and individuals could conduct homosexual-themed conversations more openly.

In addition to providing a local space in which to deepen friendships and relationships with other homosexuals, gay parties in North Florida were a reason to travel. People routinely traversed the Panhandle to attend gay parties in Tallahassee and Pensacola. According to Jackson Williamson, a Tallahassee resident whose housemate hosted several gay parties, "Usually to a large extent, they would be constituted by out-of-town people."[27] Another man from Tallahassee who came before the FLIC stated, "There is a . . . [redacted] who holds gay parties, to which I have been. There were two people who were present there from Panama City."[28] The two men to whom he referred traveled one hundred miles each way in order to attend a gay party. Making such an excursion speaks to the importance of these events in the men's lives.

The available evidence for this area would seem to indicate that gay parties were a largely white phenomenon. Despite the FLIC's best efforts, it could not find the so-called race mixers it sought in Tallahassee. However, there is a tantalizing mention of a party on the other side of the Panhandle, in Pensacola, in a transcript from a FLIC interrogation. On 17 October 1962, R. J. Strickland and John H. Sullivan, both investigators for the FLIC, interrogated David Carter in the county solicitor's office in Pensacola. Though the party referred to was ostensibly a Halloween party, Strickland produced several nude photos of Williams and other young men engaged in homoerotic poses.[29] Williams stated, "I remember . . . [redacted] had some made sitting in one of the boy's laps and then had some made with a dress on and that's all I remember seeing, I see in this naked one."[30] Carter's interrogation makes clear that gay parties ranged in character from quiet, civilized affairs to erotically charged events.

Because of gay parties, people forged friendships and made connections that spanned the South. According to Williamson, people from as far away as Atlanta and Miami attended the parties held at his home. The mixing of so many people from different locales is an example of the mobility afforded by the postwar economic boom. The connections afforded by mobility and travel meant that queer affective networks could spread across the South as never before. Yet, how did one secure an invitation to a gay party? Often, cruising for sex was the first entry point into a larger queer world in this era.

CRUISING NORTH FLORIDA

The practice of men cruising for sex is well known in the field of queer history.[31] Sometimes men simply needed a quick release in a place where they could shed other identities; at other times, they sought longer-term connections.[32] "Men young and old," writes John Howard, have made outdoor cruising grounds a vital form of community initiation, imitation, and belonging, especially in warm southern climes."[33] Cruising for sex in this era could provide men with a circle of gay friends. An essential component of cruising for sex in North Florida was the automobile, though public restrooms and parks often proved fertile as well.

The automobile fundamentally changed human mobility and interaction, especially in the economic boom of the 1950s, when automobile ownership exploded in the United States, and improved roads meant easier access to far-flung places. The ability to access and use an automobile opened up new possibilities in many areas of life, especially for queer people, as men and women enjoyed the freedom of mobility offered by automobile use. As John Howard explained about queer southerners, "The ability to travel, both to nearby rural areas and to other cities, provided a means of escape from familial pressure and police persecution."[34] Greater automobility also fundamentally changed cruising. In addition to providing a means of conveyance by which men traveled to cruising destinations, the automobile became a "private" space where sexual acts could take place.

The automobile, the people using it, and the spaces that the automobile occupied open up vast analytical possibilities when considering queer uses of space in the South. Unlike in the larger cities so typical in much LGBTQ history, in the cities of North Florida the sense of space was different for queers. When men came together, these events often involved an automobile.[35] Exploring what happened within the space of the automobile, around the automobile, or with the assistance of the automobile decenters the urban cruising ground in favor of a wider network of highways, parkways, streets, and rural, dirt roads. For men who met in a bar or a public restroom, the automobile gave them a secluded spot where they could take their partners. In Tallahassee, the highway leading to the airport was a favorite spot, as were the roads that led to "a pond at the end of the road; down at the bottom of a hill."[36] Panama City's Carl Gray Park was popular with car cruisers, and a lovers' lane was located near the community of Millville.[37] In Pensacola, desolate stretches of highway between the city and the beaches and between the city and the navy yard became popular spots to park, and car cruising at the city marina grew in popularity.

Some men drove great distances to find sexual partners. Tallahassee police officers arrested James Smith, of Valdosta, Georgia, in the Greyhound Bus Station in 1962. Smith had driven from his home in Valdosta for one purpose: "to be done and I came to Tallahassee.... I come for the purpose of being given a blowjob."[38] Smith's employment as a glass technician involved a great deal of travel throughout Florida, Alabama, and Georgia, so he was accustomed to driving great distances. For Smith, driving two hours in search of sexual release was no great sacrifice. Yet, for many men, fear of exposure in their home environs made them more than willing to make such a drive.

Certain cars seemed destined to be spaces for sexual activity. Tom Baker, of Panama City, and Charles Taylor, of Tallahassee, both preferred station wagons over other types of cars. Taylor recalled that the station wagon was "pretty well set up for the act in the way of blankets and stuff."[39] Tom Baker stated, "[I] had a station wagon... big station wagon. Put the back seat down and make a bed out of it. I always loved station wagons to go out cruising."[40] Though some preferred station wagons, any car could be turned into a queer space when desire struck.

More than a conveyance between two points or a space in which to have sex, a man's automobile could be the deciding factor in a cruising encounter. One man interviewed by the FLIC stated about his sexual partner, "If [he] had of been driving a '55 or '56 Chevrolet, I wouldn't have done anything with him because I've had those guys approach me before and that was the only reason... about cars like that. That was the only reason."[41] This young man was questioned because of his involvement with a helicopter pilot stationed at nearby Fort Rucker, Alabama, who drove a 1963 Ford Galaxie XL convertible. When investigators interviewed this man in December 1962, the pilot's Galaxie was a brand-new car. According to the young man, conversation about the car began the couple's initial encounter, though desire clearly kept the two together over multiple weeks.

In the car culture of the time, the automobile became the primary identifier for men who practiced car cruising. Numerous FLIC interrogations show that men did not necessarily remember a sexual partner's face but often remembered every detail about his car. The FLIC interrogated Bill Jenkins in February 1963. Jenkins was in possession of business cards that incriminated him. It seems from the testimony that he went so far as to write down the make and model of men's cars when he exchanged information with men he met while out cruising.[42]

Beyond the automobile, certain men located in Florida's coastal areas enjoyed an advantage over men in other parts of the country when it came to cruising. The story of the Pensacola resident Mark White, who came before the FLIC on 13 December 1962, is illuminating about the ways that water and Florida's tropical climate aided cruising. The investigator John H. Sullivan sat down with White to discuss homosexuality in Pensacola's junior college, yet his testimony went far beyond the college.[43] The conversation between White and a man named Jack Faust began innocently enough. White remembered, "Well I was just walking down the street, he walked beside me and started talking to me, things, asked me if I worked downtown, said he saw me downtown often, nothing out of the ordinary."[44] Over the next several days, Faust sought out White and repeatedly invited him to his house at Oriole Beach (west of central

Pensacola) for skiing and swimming. White accepted the invitation, and by that weekend White and his friend, known only as "Bill," were at Faust's for a day of drinking, boating, and skiing.[45] Here, the weather and the water played key roles in Faust's approach. The extended summer season, with warm temperatures and more daylight hours, allowed him to use his boat as an enticement for White, and likely for other men as well.

Much like the space of the automobile, the space of the boat on the water provided a sufficient amount of privacy. While in the boat, "[Faust] looked back to see if Bill [White's friend] was looking, he didn't, and then he reached over and grabbed me."[46] The privacy afforded by the boat out on the water gave Faust the opportunity to literally reach out to White. In addition to an enticement, the boat served as a physical space of queer connection or attempted connection, if White's testimony is taken at face value.

In Florida's Panhandle, women also benefited from owning an automobile. Jane Boyles, who was stationed at Eglin Air Force Base, near Pensacola, possessed the only car in her friendship circle. The air force discharged Boyles during a purge of lesbians at Eglin, and she later settled in Pensacola with a friend whom she had met while in service. During her time at Eglin, Boyles and her friends routinely used her car to travel to local beaches and bars. Sometimes she allowed her friends to utilize her car. Because she owned the only car in her squadron, Boyles was popular among her peers. Given midcentury gender expectations, Boyles's car represented freedom and the possibility of a life off the base.

The practice of cruising for sex in the South at this time must be understood within the matrix of the region's regime of racial segregation. Florida's northern Gulf Coast was more aligned with the racial policies and attitudes of its Deep South neighbors. In fact, maintaining racial segregation was regarded as a civic virtue, despite the moderate image Florida politicians tried to project.[47] Public facilities across this part of Florida were legally segregated under Jim Crow. They often remained practically segregated well into the 1960s. As activists tore down the walls of segregation, the separation between black and white queer experiences slowly became less clear. As John Howard wrote in *Men Like That,* "Parallel black and white queer realms cautiously intermingled after the early sixties . . . whereas before, same-sex interracial intercourse usually involved advances by white men of privilege on their black class subordinates."[48] Throughout the contested spaces of the South, black and white queers intermingled, complicating our understandings of segregated queer experiences.

One of the most visibly contested spaces in the Jim Crow South was the intercity bus station. Public restrooms at these stations were among the most active cruising grounds for white men. Though a number of directives, rulings, and laws legally desegregated bus stations, the actual desegregation of such spaces took time.[49] Despite multiple rulings by the Federal Interstate Commerce Commission and the US Supreme Court, bus stations, restaurants, and other public accommodations in much of the South remained segregated in practice until the Civil Rights Act of 1964.

The Greyhound Bus Station in Tallahassee, and its public restroom, most clearly show the slow integration of cruising in the Jim Crow South. A December 1961 memorandum from R. J. Strickland reproduced a report from Officer Burl Peacock, of the Tallahassee Police Department. On 30 November, Peacock had observed four African Americans "just sitting in the section for whites, although two asked for service at the food counter and were refused but left quietly, after being told to do so."[50] At the time of this incident, white sections of bus stations had been banned (again), so Officer Peacock's actions were illegal. Dismantling segregation in Tallahassee was clearly a slow process.

The desegregation of bus terminals and facilities should have created a multiracial cruising ground, as men of all races could technically use the formerly white-only restrooms at the Greyhound Bus Station. According to the arrest records that survive in the FLIC collection, the integration of cruising in the bus station's public restroom was in line with Howard's assertion that the black and white queer worlds cautiously intermingled. The majority of arrests at the bus station occurred between December 1961 and February 1962. According to records, the Tallahassee Police Department arrested only white men in the bus station restrooms until 1964, when the first racial designation other than "white" or "cauc" appeared in the records.[51] Given the degree of surveillance placed on African Americans in sites where segregation was contested, it is reasonable to assume that *if* African American men cruised the white public restrooms after the autumn of 1961, they would appear in the arrest records in much higher numbers.

Thanks to the increase in mobility after World War II, the automobile and the bus brought an unprecedented number of tourists to the Gulf Coast. They also extended the range that men could travel to find a sexual partner, as in the case of James Smith, or to socialize with other queers, such as at gay parties in Tallahassee. Whether queers were driving for business or pleasure, the automobile and better roads helped them connect with one another. Because of the connections the automobile made possible, it was an essential component of the region's deterritorialized community and is essential to understanding the Panhandle's queer history.

CONNECTING BUT NOT CURING

The Florida State Hospital at Chattahoochee was the institution in Florida through which authorities sought to "reform" homosexuals. The attempted psychiatric treatment and cure of those "suffering" from homosexuality has a relatively short history.[52] Lobotomies, debilitating aversion therapies, and electroshock treatments formed just part of the arsenal available to psychiatrists.[53] Not all homosexual men and women in Florida fell victim to the rehabilitation system, though. The vast majority of people arrested, interviewed, tried, and sentenced for homosexual acts never became part of the mental-health system. Judges generally sent homosexuals through the penal system.[54] Until 1962, when the available records stop, the Florida State Hospital never held more than twenty patients categorized as "sexual deviants" at one time.[55]

One might ask why I include a discussion of the state hospital, where homosexual men and women were forcibly confined and horribly mistreated in an effort to "cure" them, in an essay about connections and the expansion of queer networks. Leaving aside the violence done to individuals for a moment, I argue that it is possible to use the mental hospital to show the ways that state-sponsored oppression could give people a language with which to talk about their desires and connect them with national homophile discourses and other queers.[56] As Allan Bérubé wrote, "Sometimes drawing on their ability to 'camp,' gay patients developed a sense of camaraderie, privately helping each other overcome the demoralization and boredom of psych ward life."[57] The experience of James Ogier serves to illustrate the potential of the mental hospital as a site of connection. In an institution designed to cure their "problem," queer men exchanged ideas, shared feelings (and possibly beds and intimacies), and made connections that allowed access to regional and national communities and networks.

Ogier was a resident of the state hospital for two years, from 1964 to 1966.[58] Authorities in Pensacola sent Ogier to the state hospital based on what he claimed was circumstantial evidence.[59] Though he spent a total of two years in the hospital, nine of those months were devoted to grappling with the bureaucratic morass necessary to secure his release. After release from the institution, which according to Ogier involved a monumental deception, he returned to Pensacola, where he secured a job and housing that was mostly paid for by the state's rehabilitation program. However, this support was contingent on "good behavior." According to Ogier, this meant a near-constant surveillance of his life, including his reading habits and postal correspondence, by those responsible for administering the program. Despite the surveillance of his life, he was able to come out and make connections with national organizations and quite possibly Emma Jones.

In July 1966, Ogier wrote a letter to ONE, Inc., the Los Angeles–based homophile organization. "I heard of your organization while I was an inmate of Florida State Hospital, a mental institution," he wrote.[60] Ogier's letter to ONE, Inc., acknowledged his homosexuality and served as a discreet coming out. Apparently, before entering the hospital Ogier had not publicly revealed his sexual identity. "All of my friends and family had completely turned against me upon receipt of my admission diagnosis."[61] Further, according to Ogier, after leaving the hospital, he could not be open about his sexual identity because of the "good behavior" conditions necessary for his release and the continued support by the state's rehabilitation program. Therefore, his contact with ONE, Inc., was initially the only public acknowledgment of his sexual identity.

Gaining the courage to come out after encountering *ONE* is a refrain repeated often in queer history of the mid-twentieth century. Craig Loftin wrote in *Masked Voices*, "*ONE* undoubtedly politicized some of its readers for whom a pro-gay attitude might have been unimaginable before encountering the magazine."[62] Ogier had a certain level of consciousness of his desires as a result of his sentence to the state hospital and what he describes as the deception necessary to secure his release. He knew what he was, and he knew how to act in order to persuade the authorities that he was not that. It is unlikely that the incident that landed him in the state hospital was his first encounter with law enforcement. These homosexual acts may not have led him to an understanding of an incipient identity, given the various scenes and social opportunities available to men in Pensacola. He calls the two years he spent in the institution needless "but rather enlightening."[63] This "enlightenment" seems to have included both his identity formation and his knowledge of ONE, Inc., and other political organizations.

It was the encounter with fellow patients at the hospital that prompted Ogier's identity formation. He was exposed to ONE, Inc., *because of* his time in the state hospital. It is possible that he would eventually have become aware of ONE, Inc., or other homophile organizations and publications; however, at this time newsstands and bookstores in the Panhandle did not stock *ONE* magazine. According to Ogier, "I cannot purchase any of your publications in this area."[64] Through his incarceration with other queers (mostly men, according to the available hospital records), he became aware of the national homophile movement. In the place where state authorities detained and experimented on homosexuals for the purpose of "curing" them, or at least separating them from society, homosexual men shared information about themselves and clearly about the larger homophile movement, thereby raising the consciousness of some.

It is important to realize that the state *created* a space where homosexuals could congregate as homosexuals (even if the label was initially applied *to* them rather than self-acknowledged), the very thing that officials tried to avoid. Confining gay men (and some lesbians) in a segregated space made coming out and connecting with others easier. Ogier's experience opens the hospital to a different reading, as a place of contact. More time must elapse before there is adequate research into the confinement of homosexuals in the mental-health system, given the strict privacy laws that prevent access to medical records.[65] However, letters such as Ogier's suggest that the space of the hospital and the incarceration of patients enable queer contact that could move beyond the confines of the institutions and bring queers together in national, state, and local queer networks.

ADVERTISING THE GAY GULF COAST

Beyond bus stations, public parks, or gay parties, two bars in the Panhandle developed reputations as meeting places for homosexuals in the 1950s and early 1960s. The Cypress Lounge, in Tallahassee, and Trader Jon's, in Pensacola, both gained national reputations as sites of connection, though neither was considered a "gay bar" in the sense that neither was owned by a gay or patronized primarily by gays. The Fiesta Room Lounge in Panama City, the region's first openly gay bar, opened its doors in 1965. Other bars came and went during the remainder of the twentieth century, but the Fiesta stayed. With the growth of the gay print media and the national increase in specific kinds of gay and lesbian visibility, these bars and their patrons (both local and visiting) helped to construct the Gay Gulf Coast as a tourist destination for gay and lesbian individuals.

In July 1960, Gordon E. Wilkinson, of Buffalo, New York, wrote a letter to ONE, Inc., in which he enclosed a five-page list of bars across America where homosexuals were likely to meet others like themselves. Wilkinson listed twenty bars in South Florida, most of which were clustered around Miami and Fort Lauderdale. Jacksonville and Jacksonville Beach listed three bars, and only two were listed for Daytona Beach. The only listing for the Panhandle was the Cypress Lounge in Tallahassee.[66] On the surface, the Cypress Lounge seemed an unlikely candidate for Wilkinson's list. It was attached to the Floridan Hotel, and according to Lynn Homan, it was the after-hours home of the Florida legislature, yet its inclusion on the list meant that it had a certain level of recognizability—or "cruisy-ness," in common parlance—among gay men.[67]

For gay men and lesbians at this time, the recognizability of bars and nightclubs posed significant risk. In times of social stress, bars that were known homosexual hangouts risked raiding and closure by moral crusaders or overzealous police officials.[68] For this reason, owners and managers often policed the behavior of their patrons. In other instances, gay men and lesbians were subject to harassment and watered-down drinks in mafia-owned venues with enough capital to bribe police officials—as was the case with New York City's Stonewall Inn. Yet the inclusion of the Cypress Lounge on Wilkinson's list meant that the bar had become "officially recognized/designated" as a queer space to a certain segment of the gay and lesbian population insofar as any queer space in this era could be sanctioned as safer for gay and lesbian individuals. However, if one simply happened upon the bar, it likely would not have appeared to be a bar that allowed homosexuals.

By 1966 the Cypress Lounge was no longer the only "officially recognized" queer drinking establishment in the Panhandle. According to *The Address Book,* compiled by Bob Damron, Le Roc (another hotel lounge, just two blocks from the Cypress) was also viable as a site of connection. In addition, Damron's guide included Trader Jon's and the Fiesta at the San Carlos Hotel in Pensacola.[69] The distribution of lists with an ostensibly national circulation meant that gay men and lesbians could more easily navigate their way to queer spaces when they found themselves in North Florida. Relying solely on lists such as Wilkinson's or Damron's was risky given the frequency with which the winds of tolerance shifted, but possessing a reliable guide could minimize that risk.

Until 1965, gay men and lesbians (and otherwise queer individuals) socialized in private homes or in the sometimes-tolerant bars across the Panhandle. In that year, the Fiesta Room Lounge, a small, unassuming bar, opened in the downtown section of Panama City where gay men and lesbians could socialize as homosexuals. Though intimacy or even dancing with a same-sex partner still carried a risk, a bar owned by a gay man and opened for the benefit of homosexual people represents a massive shift in the social possibilities along the Gulf Coast. Over the years of its existence—sadly it closed after the death of its owner in 2015—it expanded to take over two buildings, and its growth tracked with the growth of the Gay Gulf Coast.

Initially, only rumor and innuendo guided homosexually inclined people to the inconspicuous door at the end of Harrison Avenue. However, by the early 1970s certain southern gay publications took notice of the bar and other gay and lesbian happenings on the Gulf Coast. Because *ONE* magazine, the *Ladder,* and the *Mattachine Review* opened the door to gay and lesbian publications through various legal challenges against censorship, other, often localized publications aimed at gay men and lesbians increased in number throughout the 1960s and 1970s, a trend that continues today, though online resources have replaced many print publications. In addition to the national gay press, various local magazines appeared in cities across the United States that had sizable gay communities.[70] These magazines were locally or regionally based and generally funded by advertisements. They kept residents and visitors apprised of their respective local "gay scenes," to use the parlance of the day. In addition to local information, magazines routinely featured stories that dealt with travel and highlighted nearby areas.

Some of the Gulf Coast's queer offerings were well known by the mid-1960s thanks in part to Bob Damron, Gordon Wilkinson, and *ONE* magazine. Those publications went a long way in pointing the way to certain places along the Gulf Coast here. However, it was not until southern gay publications proliferated, attendance at Emma Jones's increased exponentially, and bars that catered to "the gay crowd" flourished that the discourse changed. Rather than just a few bars or active public parks, the whole Gulf Coast became a gay and lesbian tourist destination. In showcasing activities, publications based in the South constructed an image of the Gay Gulf Coast as a tourist destination in the minds of landlocked southern gays.

In 1976 a new magazine that catered to gay men and lesbians appeared on the scene in Atlanta. *Cruise: The Entertainment Guide to Gay Atlanta* promised to provide "an up-to-date Guide to all of those bars, restaurants, lounges, discos, baths, cinemas, book stores and other places of entertainment that welcome the gay crowd."[71] In recognition of the explosive growth in the number of businesses and events that catered to lesbians and gay men in Atlanta, the publishers began publishing a weekly social calendar in addition to the monthly magazine. Soon, the publishers realized the need for a publication that covered gay happenings throughout the South. At certain times, the guide to gay Atlanta became *Cruise: The Guide to Gay Entertainment in the South*.

In 1977 Richard Kavanaugh, a reporter, and Bob Swinden, a photographer, set out on a tour of the Gay Gulf Coast. The resulting article's title proclaimed, "It's Hot! Hot! Hot! This Summer on the Gay Gulf Coast." The grand gay tour took Kavanaugh and Swinden from Tallahassee, to New Orleans, with stops in Panama City, Pensacola, and Biloxi, Mississippi. Kavanaugh wrote, "The area between Tallahassee, Florida on the east, and New Orleans on the west is always fun, but during the summer the beaches become the place to go for summer vacations, weekends or just a day off if you live close enough."[72] He made clear that not just non-gay southerners but gay and lesbian southerners as well chose the Gulf Coast for its proximity and ease of travel.

According to the article, Tallahassee boasted two gay bars: the Panhandle Mining Company and the Foxtrot. Kavanaugh did not mention the Cypress Lounge, a fact that is telling in the post-Stonewall era. It is likely that men still cruised at the Cypress Lounge and the Greyhound Bus Station. Yet, because of the shift in focus to an identity politics based on outness after Stonewall and the Gay Liberation Front, coupled with a decrease in municipal harassment of gay establishments, the article focuses on bars that were owned, operated, and frequented by gays rather than just tolerant of gays. This should not obscure the myriad ways that queer men and women continued to find one another to form relationships and networks, though like the Fiesta, it does speak to the changing nature of socialization on the Gay Gulf Coast. Shifting to Panama City and its beaches, Kavanaugh advised readers that in addition to the fun on offer at the Fiesta Room Lounge, there was fun available on or near the sand. According to Kavanaugh, one could rent boats, ski, play golf, swim, or simply soak up the sun on the sugar-white beach. At night the action moved inland to the Fiesta Room. Though mostly college-aged men populated the bar, Kavanaugh wrote that "as in any town with only one gay bar, you'll find a few people of all types."[73]

Kavanaugh then moved on to Pensacola after a one-paragraph description of a bar in Fort Walton called the Lobby, which attracted a "mixed crowd."[74] Kavanaugh listed four bars in Pensacola: the Red Garter, Quiet Village, the Aquarian, and the Fiesta at the San Carlos Hotel. Though gay men remember the Fiesta as a very cruisy bar, it was not a "gay bar" in the same way that the other bars were. Yet, the Fiesta and the San Carlos Hotel, because of their association with the Fourth of July events thrown by the Emma Jones Society, certainly qualified for a mention in a gay guide. Pensacola was also interesting, then as now, because it had the only bar that caters to the lesbian crowd, according to Kavanaugh.

Because of the publicity and word-of-mouth advertising that endeared the Gulf Coast to southerners generally, Panama City and the entire coastal area held a special place in the hearts of gay and lesbian southerners as well.[75] Robert Bosch, a gay resident of Atlanta, remembered that "all of gay Atlanta went to Panama City when they wanted to go to the beach."[76] Kavanaugh believed that many southerners echoed that sentiment. "Guys and gals from Georgia and other south-eastern states head for the Florida beaches."[77] In the same way that print media and word-of-mouth advertising in conjunction with local business, municipal boosters, and the state government created and sold the Gulf Coast as a tourist destination, the gay media, gay and lesbian southerners, and locals created and sold the idea of the Gay Gulf Coast.

The Gulf Coast's gay reputation continued to grow over the last quarter of the twentieth century. In 1994, an author who called himself Randy Mann wrote an article for *Steam* entitled "Pensacola, Florida and nearby Gulp [*sic*] Coast Playgrounds."[78] In the article, he covered the coastal cities from Panama City to Mobile, Alabama, describing the cruising and other sexually based opportunities for tourists and locals along the coast. *Steam* was published in San Francisco on a quarterly basis and distributed via mail order around the United States. Its tag line read, "A Quarterly Journal for Men," and it was explicitly dedicated to "sex—all kinds of sex, but especially public, publicly disapproved, *exciting* sex."[79]

Beyond the search for sex, Pensacola had something for everyone, according to Mann:

The Festival city of Pensacola, with 200,000 residents, has several positive things going for it: a very good bar scene, outstanding gay-owned and operated restaurants and business . . . a large Navy base, a large Air Force community, thousands of horny tourists, and a law enforcement attitude of "hands off the gay tourists because they pump $$$ into the economy." All of these factors combine to produce a unique and colorful time for the gay traveller in search of the perfect cock.[80]

Mann was unaware of Pensacola's pushback against LGBTQ tourists and their business, and his assertion of law enforcement's lax attitude is surprising. According to other publications at the time, there was a great deal of pushback from city officials against Pensacola's growing reputation as the Gay Riviera.[81]

As Pensacola attracted more and more tourists and residents, it drew ever-increasing numbers of gay men and lesbians. It seems that Pensacola had something for everyone. For those wishing to partake in the outness of a gay community of bars and restaurants, they were on offer in Pensacola. For those searching for different kinds of connections, Pensacola and the surrounding beaches offered them as well. Thanks to the Emma Jones Society and the beach parties held regularly in Pensacola, the Memorial Day, Fourth of July, and Labor Day weekends were memorable experiences for many gay men and lesbians (though Mann only wrote about men). According to Mann, "You will find thousands upon thousands of guys out there during the day . . . by some strange quirk of nature, men and boys have found their way to this beach for those nocturnal sojourns year after year after year, without any interference from 'outside' sources."[82] However, it was not a quirk of nature, and there was plenty of interference from outside sources. Mann wrote his article in 1994, at a time when municipal authorities were once again attempting to erase the area's queer past because of the publicity associated with Memorial Day and "gay fest."[83] It is unclear whether Mann simply never experienced interference or was attempting to paint a more positive, almost fantastic picture of Pensacola.

The various publications that informed southerners about all the gay opportunities along the coast helped to construct an image of the Gay Gulf Coast. In fact, Richard Kavanaugh coined the term. Each article written about the Gulf Coast, coupled with the remembrances of satisfied gay visitors, reinforced an image of a tourist destination for gay men and lesbians. For those who could not afford, or lacked the inclination, to travel to Miami, Fire Island, or Provincetown, the Gay Gulf Coast provided a beach holiday that was nearby and easily affordable for southern gay men and lesbians.

CONCLUSION

In what Phil Tiemeyer has called America's most homophobic decade, men and women who were gay and lesbian (and even those who did not articulate those identities) managed to find one another.[84] Pensacola, Panama City, and Tallahassee were nodes in the trans-Panhandle queer networks, and the roads between were the arteries that connected them. In their cars and on buses, queers traveled from throughout the South to attend gay parties, find sexual partners, or simply go to the beach. In ones, twos, and small groups, queer movement was multidirectional, characterized by circulation and networks.

While queers found themselves and one another, surveillant authorities and municipal boosters tried to build and then maintain the region's reputation for family fun. According to Harvey H. Jackson, "In the evolution of the region one can see how efforts to build a tourist economy led to new and innovative ways to promote the Gulf Coast. However, the new and innovative ultimately altered, threatened, and even destroyed the simple, laid-back, guilt-free enjoyment of tropical indolence that attracted lower South southerners at the start."[85] Practicing a politics of visibility and public shaming, newspapers and law enforcers sought to ferret out and expose corruption, crime, and vice in the region in an effort to assure residents and visitors that the region was safe and enforce a particular vision of morality and propriety along the Gulf Coast.

Like southerners generally, gay and lesbian southerners enjoyed vacations along the Gulf Coast because of its proximity and the low cost. As homosexuals around the country came out in ever-increasing numbers after the 1960s, they chose Gulf Coast destinations because of the number of gay amenities. Despite the continued backlash against gay men and lesbians, the Gay Gulf Coast continued to grow year after year. Queer individuals adapted to the spaces around them. Rather than abandoning a largely racist and officially homophobic Florida, these men and women built friendships, found lovers, and claimed their place in the Sunshine State.

NOTES

1. I deploy the term *queer* to encompass the various nonnormative or oppositional ways of being or behaving along Florida's Gulf Coast in this time. Where appropriate, I use *gay, lesbian,* or *homosexual* to connote a certain kind of identity politics.

2. Stacy Braukman, *Communists and Perverts under the Palms: The Johns Committee in Florida, 1956–1965* (Gainesville: University Press of Florida, 2012); Fred Fejes, "Murder, Perversion, and Moral

Panic: The 1954 Media Campaign Against Miami's Homosexuals and the Discourse of Civic Betterment," *Journal of the History of Sexuality* 9, no. 3 (July 2000): 305–47.

3. Braukman, *Communists and Perverts*, 25.

4. Harvey H. Jackson III, *The Rise and Decline of the Redneck Riviera: An Insider's History of the Florida-Alabama Coast* (Athens: University of Georgia Press, 2012), 2.

5. Ibid., 13.

6. Braukman, *Communists and Perverts*, 4.

7. Ibid., 3.

8. Ibid., 71.

9. Jessica Forbes, "Queer and Here: The Long History of Gay Tourists on Pensacola Beach," *Independent News*, 23 May 2013, 1–13.

10. Bill Rushton, "Killing of Emma Jones—III: Only memories remain for once-gay Pensacola," *Advocate*, 15 January 1975, 10–11, ONE National Gay and Lesbian Archives, Los Angeles.

11. Forbes, "Queer and Here," 11.

12. Rushton, "Killing of Emma Jones—III." See also Bob Shaw, "The Discreet Lovers of Emma Jones," *Tropic*, supplemental Sunday magazine of *Miami Herald*, 16 March 1975, 8–14, 28, 29, clipping, Billy Jones Collection, Atlanta Gay and Lesbian History Thing Papers and Publications, MSS 773, James G. Kennan Research Center at the Atlanta History Center, Atlanta.

13. Rushton, "Killing of Emma Jones—III," 10.

14. Forbes, "Queer and Here," 11.

15. Shaw, "Discreet Lovers of Emma Jones," 12.

16. Marc Stein, "'Birthplace of the Nation': Imagining Lesbian and Gay Communities in Philadelphia, 1969–1970," in *Creating a Place for Ourselves: Lesbian, Gay, and Bisexual Community Histories,* ed. Brett Beemyn (New York: Routledge, 1997), 253–88.

17. Descriptions of the shows from Rushton, "Killing of Emma Jones—III," 11.

18. Ibid., 16.

19. Shaw, "Discreet Lovers of Emma Jones," 28.

20. Bill Rushton, "The Killing of Emma Jones—1: Gay Pensacola becomes a nightmare of corruption and bigotry," *Advocate,* December 1975, 35–36, ONE National Gay and Lesbian Archives, Los Angeles.

21. Though the parties are much like other house parties, I use the term *gay parties* because that is how those involved conceived of them and spoke of them, as well as to differentiate them as social spaces for individuals identified as gays and lesbians.

22. John Howard, "Place and Movement in Gay American History: A Case from the Post–World War II South," in Beemyn, *Creating a Place for Ourselves,* 211–26. See also Allan Bérubé, *Coming Out Under Fire: The History of Gay Men and Women in World War Two* (New York: Free Press, 1990), 155–60.

23. Howard, "Place and Movement," 217–18.

24. Rushton, "Killing of Emma Jones—III."

25. Bérubé, *Coming Out Under Fire,* 112.

26. Florida Legislative Investigation Committee (FLIC), series 1486, carton 11, folder 8, 12, State Archives of Florida, Tallahassee.

27. Ibid., carton 8, folder 29, 11.

28. Ibid., carton 9, folder 47, 5.

29. Without access to the original photographs or any graphic description of the activities pictured, it is impossible to be more precise. However, it is clear that the pictures were homoerotic enough to warrant attention by investigators.

30. FLIC, series 1486, carton 10, folder 139, 5.

31. Mark W. Turner, *Backward Glances: Cruising the Queer Streets of New York and London* (London: Reaktion Books, 2003). John Howard has also written extensively about the practice of cruising in *Men Like That: A Southern Queer History* (Chicago: University of Chicago Press, 1999).

32. Laud Humphreys, *Tearoom Trade: Impersonal Sex in Public Places* (New York: Adline, 1975).

33. John Howard, "Southern Sodomy; or, What the Coppers Saw," in *Southern Masculinity: Perspectives on Manhood in the South since Reconstruction,* ed. Craig Thompson Friend (Athens: University of Georgia Press, 2009), 196–218.

34. Howard, "Place and Movement," 212.

35. Ibid., 221.

36. FLIC, series 1486, carton 9, folder 59, 7.

37. Tom Baker, interview by author, 12 July 2011.

38. FLIC, series 1486, carton 9, folder 60, 4.

39. Ibid., folder 47, 3.

40. Tom Baker, interview by author, 19 July 2011.

41. FLIC, series 1486, carton 11, folder 31, 6.

42. Ibid., folder 47, 4.

43. Ibid., folder 29.

44. Ibid., 1.

45. Ibid., 3.

46. Ibid., 4.

47. Irvin D. S. Winsboro, introduction to *Old South, New South, or Down South: Florida and the Modern Civil Rights Movement,* ed. Winsboro (Morgantown: West Virginia University Press, 2009).

48. Howard, *Men Like That,* xvi.

49. "Civil Rights Timeline," accessed 10 July 2012, www.civilrights.org/resources/civilrights101 /chronology.html. This is the clearest picture of national legislation, though the best civil rights history for Tallahassee is Glenda Alice Rabby, *The Pain and the Promise: The Struggle for Civil Rights in Tallahassee, Florida* (Athens: University of Georgia Press, 1999).

50. FLIC, series 1486, carton 1, folder 12.

51. Ibid., carton 13, folder 34. Here I have assumed that the two men listed as "C" are African American ("colored"), given that the only other racial designations are "W" and "cauc," for "white" and "Caucasian."

52. Jennifer Terry, *An American Obsession: Science, Medicine, and Homosexuality in Modern Society* (Chicago: University of Chicago Press, 1999), 5.

53. Blanche M. Baker, MD, introduction to *Gay Bar: The Fabulous, True Story of a Daring Woman and Her Boys in the 1950s,* by Will Fellows and Helen P. Branson (Madison: University of Wisconsin Press, 2010), 13.

54. FLIC, series 1486, carton 1, folder 11, 2. According to this FLIC report, 400 men and 60–70 women were incarcerated in Florida's prison system for offenses relating to homosexual activity.

55. Federal Census for Public Mental Hospital Records, 1933, 1942–62, Record Number 000841, series 1068, carton 2, State Archives of Florida, Tallahassee. The majority of "sexual deviants" were

likely homosexuals, though this number could include rapists or those convicted of sex crimes involving minors.

56. Bérubé, *Coming Out Under Fire,* 201–27.

57. Ibid., 210.

58. James W. Ogier, letter to ONE, Inc., 25 July 1966, ONE Correspondence, box 33, folder "Mue-P," ONE Incorporated Records, COL2011-001, ONE National Gay and Lesbian Archives, Los Angeles.

59. Ibid., 5.

60. Ibid., 1.

61. Ibid., 2.

62. Craig Loftin, *Masked Voices: Gay Men and Lesbians in Cold War America* (New York: SUNY Press, 2012), 8.

63. Ogier, letter, 1.

64. Ibid., letter, 7.

65. In Florida, patient records are sealed for fifty years after the patient's death unless release can be secured from the person's next of kin. For more general information about incarceration, the period is fifty years from the date of confinement.

66. Gordon E. Wilkinson, letter to ONE, Inc., 25 July 1960, 4. ONE Editorial Correspondence 1954–1964, Box 46, Folder 9. ONE Incorporated Records, COL2011-001, ONE National Gay and Lesbian Archives, Los Angeles.

67. Lynn M. Homan and T. Reilly, *Tallahassee* (Mt. Pleasant, SC: Arcadia, 2005), 56.

68. Fejes, "Murder, Perversion, and Moral Panic." See also George Chauncey, *Gay New York: Gender, Urban Culture, and the Making of the Gay Male World, 1890–1940* (New York: Basic Books, 1995); and Fellows and Branson, *Gay Bar.*

69. Bob Damron, comp., *The Address Book,* 1966, ed. Hal Call (San Francisco: Pan Graphic, 1966), ONE National Gay and Lesbian Archives, Los Angeles.

70. The idea of a singular "gay community" in any city is problematic given differences of class, race, and gender inherent in even the most inclusive of spaces. I deploy the term here with its popular usage to mean a sufficient number of individuals with gay and lesbian identities who patronize bars, restaurants, and so on, with those of similar interests.

71. Wesley Chenault and Stacy Braukman, *Gay and Lesbian Atlanta, Images of America* (Mt. Pleasant, SC: Arcadia, 2008), 71.

72. Richard Kavanaugh, "It's Hot! Hot! Hot! This Summer on the Gay Gulf Coast," *Cruise: The Guide to Gay Entertainment in the South* 2, no. 8 (July 1977): 57–61, box 4, folder 3, Lesbian, Gay, Bisexual, and Transgender History Serial Collection, Atlanta History Center, Atlanta.

73. Kavanaugh, "Gay Gulf Coast," 58.

74. Ibid., 58.

75. In addition to Robert Bosch, John Howard, in "Place and Movement," documents that a certain set of gay and lesbian southerners from Birmingham, Alabama, routinely spent their vacations in Panama City and other locations along the gulf coast.

76. Jerry T. Watkins III, "Underneath the Rainbow: Queer Identity and Community Building in Panama City and the Florida Panhandle, 1950–1990" (master's Thesis, Georgia State University, 2008), 81.

77. Kavanaugh, "Gay Gulf Coast," 57.

78. Randy Mann, "Pensacola, Florida and nearby Gulp Coast Playgrounds," *Steam* 2, no. 2

(Spring 1994): 201–4, Subject Files, "Films—Florida," ONE National Gay and Lesbian Archives, Los Angeles.

79. Don Schwamb, "Steam Magazine," The History of Gay and Lesbian Life in Milwaukee, Wisconsin, collection, www.mkelgbthist.org/media/print/steam.htm.

80. Mann, "Gulf Coast Playgrounds," 203–4.

81. Tanya Dewhurst and Hannah Thompson, "Fahrenheit: Where the Girls Are," *Our World: International Gay and Lesbian Travel,* November 1993, 36–44, Canadian Lesbian and Gay Archives, Toronto, ON. Also, the *Christopher Street South Quarterly* regularly features articles and editorials urging readers to indicate that they are gay or lesbian travelers to illustrate the economic impact of LGBTQ tourism.

82. Mann, "Gulf Coast Playgrounds," 203.

83. Dewhurst and Thompson, "Fahrenheit."

84. Phil Tiemeyer, *Plane Queer: Labor, Sexuality, and AIDS in the History of Male Flight Attendants* (Berkeley: University of California Press, 2013), 60.

85. Jackson, *Redneck Riviera,* 4.

7

The *Mandingo* Effect

Slavery, Sex, and Contemporary Cinema

KATHERINE HENNINGER

As Shelley Stamp Lindsey's work on white slave films of the second decade of the twentieth century demonstrates, for as long as there has been a cinema, filmmakers have known that sex slavery sells.[1] Up until the 1975 release of Richard Fleischer's revisionist slave spectacular, *Mandingo*,[2] however, the dominant depiction of sexual desire within race-based American slavery revolved around the supposedly uncontrollable lust of black slave men for any and all white women. Based on Kyle Onstott's 1957 sensationalist novel of the same name, and starring James Mason, Susan George, Perry King, and the boxer Ken Norton in his first film performance, *Mandingo* has perhaps done more than any other film to reverse the sexual logic of classical Hollywood films such as *The Birth of a Nation* and *Gone with the Wind* in the American popular imaginary. With graphic specularity, *Mandingo* posits slavery as primarily a sexual institution, and the South as a cauldron of both barely sublimated and openly exploitative, perverse sexual desire, primarily of slave owners for their (male and female) slaves.

While *Mandingo* was not the first film to offer such imagery, its revisionist strategies were particularly effective, and they continue to influence popular representations and understandings of the South to the extent that they constitute what I call the "*Mandingo* effect." In this essay, I examine these strategies, their sources, and the *Mandingo* effect as it functions within contemporary cinematic portrayals of American slave history, such as Quentin Tarantino's revenge fantasy, *Django Unchained* (2012), and Steve McQueen's Oscar-winning drama, *12 Years a Slave* (2013). In its attempted manipulation of generic pleasures, including those of blaxploitation and sexploitation, *Mandingo* has in turn created a new set of generic conventions for slavery films, conventions that—for better or worse—these contemporary films employ as visual shorthand in their own grapplings with white sexual and scopic privilege. Paying special attention to issues of repetition and revision, repression and disavowal, I trace *Mandingo*'s lasting cinematic effects, ideological and otherwise, arguing that both its "campy" (i.e., *Django*) and "serious" (i.e., *12 Years*) descendants walk *Mandingo*'s jagged line, representing the sexual degradation of slavery in the context of a white pleasure that ultimately frames and contains the history of slavery for the nation as a whole.

In her 2005 book, *Hollywood Fantasies of Miscegenation,* Susan Courtney helpfully analyzes the history of mainstream filmic representations of interracial intimacy as an attempt to manage and mitigate intertwined white racial and sexual anxieties, using historically specific cinematic strategies of displacement and the manipulation of spectatorial pleasure. *The Birth of a Nation*'s 1915 classical fantasy of "black beast" males attacking white women, for example, Courtney argues, represents a repression of early twentieth-century white masculine anxieties of being beaten by black men. *Birth* effects this repression not only through plot but by cinematic assertion of a transcendent white male vision contrasted with a hypercarnal African American vision and intensely embodied to-be-looked-at, suffering white women. With regard to sexuality within and in the immediate aftermath of slavery, of course, such a repression replaces actual histories of white rape of black female slaves, along with economic motives for white force, with phantasmic images of inherent black male sexual aggression toward white women desperately in need of white male protection. (This is the same rhetorical move made by white "chivalric" groups such as the KKK, whose "birth" is chronicled in *Birth of a Nation*.) While such imagery and technique would come to be known as conventional in "classical" cinema, Courtney's research shows it to be part of a "musical chairing" of Hollywood miscegenation fantasies, in which "perpetually shifting and recurrent paradigms are revised and resurrected over time."[3] Thus, films such as *Gone with the Wind,* which were subject to the 1930–56 Production Code, forbidding even a suggestion of interracial sex, relegate slave labor and slave sexuality to the realm of the comic (e.g., Prissy's indolence and Mammy's red petticoat), maintaining strict racial divisions that, as Courtney might argue, help to buttress its exploration of white gender anxieties (e.g., Ashley v. Scarlett). And films such as a proposed 1939 reissue of *Uncle Tom's Cabin,* with its implied and explicit interracial desire, were not permitted at all.[4]

That *Mandingo* sets out consciously to radically overturn the classical imagery of slavery and its sexualities represented by *Birth of a Nation* and *Gone with the Wind* is abundantly evident beginning with the film's promotional poster (figs. 7.1 and 7.2). Allegedly hiring the same artist that had designed the poster for *Gone with the Wind, Mandingo's* marketers replaced Rhett and Scarlett's passionate embrace with not one but two interracial clutches.[5] Promising "the savage," "the shocking," "the sensual," and "the shameful," as well as to reveal "all that the motion picture screen has never dared to show before," the poster constructs an audience that should above all "expect the truth" and proclaims them now "ready for 'Mandingo.'" In a Foucauldian incitement to discourse— or as Linda Williams has phrased it, "noisy confession"—a public finally, "now" ready to see (and pay to see) the "reality" of slavery will burst free of decades of systemic and psychic repression and confront "real" interracial desire.[6]

The truth that *Mandingo* purports to offer follows two main threads: first, replacing romanticized images of slavery with "realistic" images of slavery's extraordinary brutality, and second, exposing the sexual dynamics of race-based slavery, including but not limited to coercion, rape, concubinage, and racial fetishism. *Mandingo* was not the first film to pursue these "truths" in conjunction—the blacklisted director Herbert Biberman's 1969 independent film, *Slaves,* appears to hold that honor[7]—but it was the first Hollywood movie to do so, using Hollywood techniques even as it sought to overturn Hollywood imagery for Hollywood purposes (to make an entertaining and profitable film). Eschewing Hollywood studio influence but aiming for maximum cultural impact, Biberman's *Slaves* serves as both an important cinematic source for *Mandingo's* film version and a measure of the *Mandingo* effect functioning well before that film graced the silver screen. A brief look at this nearly forgotten film is thus illuminating.

While *Slaves* reaches back to before *The Birth of a Nation,* to Harriet Beecher Stowe's 1852 novel *Uncle Tom's Cabin* as its primary source text, Biberman's film functions equally as a response to *Mandingo,* Kyle Onstott's bestselling novel of 1957, which infamously framed the sexual exploitation of slavery in terms of white fantasy of mutual desire. *Slaves* retains the basic elements of Stowe's plot and her systemic, national analyses of slavery's corruptive effects, updating them for modern sensibilities by incorporating Black Power rhetoric (including a jester slave character, Jericho, "like the walls") and radically extending her critique of slavery's sexual economy to address *Mandingo's* phantasm. In Onstott's novel, whites admire and desire black bodies, which have been rendered always accessible by slavery, *but the feeling is mutual.* Slaves, male and female, are portrayed as desiring and even competing for

Fig. 7.1. The 1967 theatrical re-release poster for *Gone with the Wind* (Selznick International/Metro-Goldwyn-Mayer, 1939).

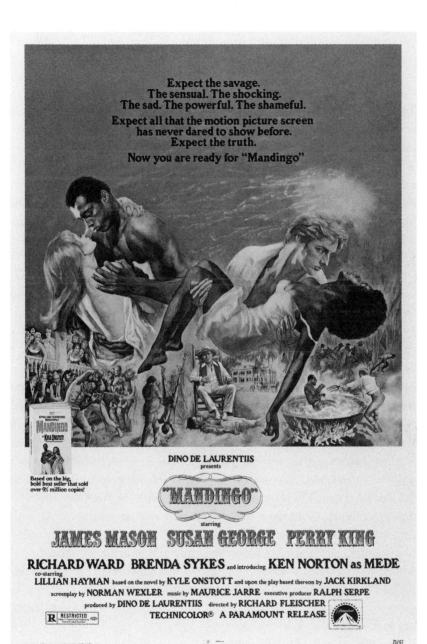

Fig. 7.2. Theatrical release poster for *Mandingo* (Paramount, 1975).

sexual attention from male masters. Though Onstott frequently claimed that his novel was based on fact, his literary mode is sensational, not realist.[8] Biberman redresses Onstott's sensationalism, as well as Stowe's sentimentalism, with a hardcore realism. Under Dionne Warwick's soulful title song, *Slaves's* opening sequence portrays a slave auction at which male and pregnant female bodies are prodded and ogled by a white trader, while the camera lingers on the etched faces of local extras Biberman hired from the jobless rolls of Shreveport, Louisiana.[9] *Slaves* features brutal beatings, ragged clothes, shackles, and most all, slaves' discontent with their condition and treatment. Sexual abuse of slaves by the master (a self-aware, sadistic, northern transplant named MacKay, played by Stephen Boyd) is depicted as just that: one of MacKay's field hands dies giving birth to his child, and his favored concubine, Cassy (Warwick in her first movie role), spits in his face as he forces her to the bed.

In bringing Stowe's slavery saga "up to date," *Slaves* and its marketers sought to appeal to audiences primed for a revisionist history not only by the insights of the Black Power and (to a lesser extent) the feminist movement but also by the "insights" of *Mandingo*. Posters for the film's original release exploit both registers, touting slaves' courage and masters' desire, offering a defiant quotation from Cassy, while inviting viewers to gaze with MacKay at her naked body (fig. 7.3). *Slaves* proved to be neither the critical nor the commercial success Biberman had hoped, but as a precursor to the blaxploitation era and a cinematic source text for *Mandingo's* film adaptation six years later, it did make a lasting impression. While most critics panned the film for its poor production, acting, and didactic script, at least some, including *Slaves's* script cowriter, John O. Killens, tied its failures to *Mandingo's* influence: Killens felt that Biberman had become "too fascinated" with the MacKay-Cassy relationship, diluting his focus on the larger picture of slave resistance.[10] Though Biberman's treatment of slavery's sexual power dynamics is clearly intended to counteract any hint of romanticism, the film's undeniable "fascination" with these relationships reflects and fosters a new expectation that they be addressed, indeed foregrounded, as the key truth of the plantation economy. As the chief purveyor of this "fascination" in popular culture of the time, *Mandingo* undoubtedly affected the movie that *Slaves* came to be.

But just as surely, *Slaves's* realism and its tone regarding slavery's sexual "truth" affected the type of film *Mandingo* was to become.[11] By the time *Mandingo* was filmed, blaxploitation cinema had become a full-fledged industry, and several other B movies dealing with slavery had been made.[12] *Slaves's* fu-

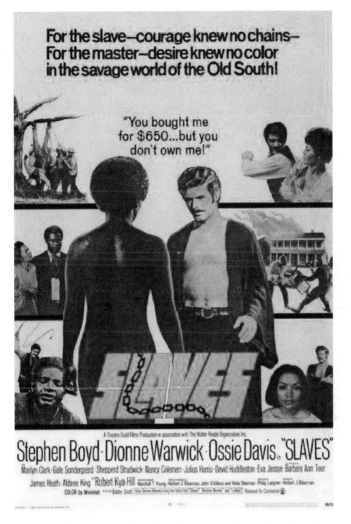

Fig. 7.3. Theatrical release poster for *Slaves* (poster number 69/216; Continental, 1969).

ture influence would be channeled through *Mandingo*'s more lasting effects. In what could easily be taken as an homage to Biberman's film, *Mandingo*'s opening shots similarly dispense with Dixie and Tara, substituting Muddy Waters singing "Born in this time, to never be free" to introduce the decrepit mansion, Falconhurst, as the site of a slave auction. Sexual violation of blacks by whites is introduced from the outset, as the business of Falconhurst is revealed to be not the expected cotton farming but slave breeding and flesh peddling. We see a line of shoddily clothed slave men offered for sale to a vulgar slave trader who peers into orifices and feels groins for "altering." The agony of families separated by sale, the automatic beatings for offenses such as learning to read, the conspicuous Black Power rhetoric of consciousness-raising slaves—all are additions to Onstott's novel, and all have a cinematic source in *Slaves*. However, *Mandingo* the film would reframe these elements with a different set of revisionist strategies, establishing a cinematic legacy that is ongoing.

As in the novel, in a direct reversal of classical miscegenation fantasy, the main symbol of *Mandingo*'s truth-telling—standing both for racial brutality and sexuality—is the figure of the lascivious slave master. *Mandingo* features several, both male and female, whose intertwined business interests and sexual desires only rarely collide with conventional notions of white southern honor and racial purity. Indeed in the film's southern mise-en-scène, slave owners' sexual use of their slaves is endemic and matter-of-fact, attaining the status, at best, of an open secret. As did Onstott's original novel, *Mandingo* the film follows the family saga of the Maxwells, father and son slave owners whose main activities include bedding and breeding their slaves, forcing incest, and arranging homoerotic slave fights (for gambling and male bonding purposes). Responding to pressure from his father to produce a "real" heir, young Hammond Maxwell (Perry King) takes a white wife, his cousin, Blanche (Susan George), who he soon discovers is "not pure" due to an incestuous relationship with her brother. Incensed by her husband's sexual rejection and by his overt preference for his black "bed wench," Ellen (Brenda Sykes), Blanche hatches a plan that is in equal parts revenge and sexual self-gratification: she commands Hammond's prized "fighting Mandingo buck," Mede (Ken Norton), to her bed. And though Hammond seems truly to care for both Ellen and Mede and is generally portrayed as a "good master," when Blanche gives birth to a dark-skinned baby, he casts Ellen to the ground as nothing but "a nigger," poisons Blanche, and boils Mede to death, pitchforking him for good measure. But whereas Onstott's novel ends with whites firmly in power, if a little humiliated, *Mandingo* the film features a new element of comeuppance for the white masters: at the culmination of the boiling scene, the senior Maxwell (James Mason) is shot to death by his lifelong black manservant, Agamemnon (Richard Ward). Cursed by Mede's dying words as being nothing but "just white," Hammond is left in the ruins of his patriarchal kingdom, staring into the void of tragedy.

Though its cartoonish characterizations, hokey dialogue, and soft-porn gothicism were roundly condemned by film critics, *Mandingo* was a tremendously popular film, the eighteenth highest grossing of 1975.[13] Its notoriety was and still is its power: in the years since, the word *Mandingo* has entered the popular lexicon, both as a noun, for black male sexual prowess, especially in the context of sex with white women, and as a verb, for interracial sexploitation (as in Catherine Clinton's decrying the "Mandingoization" of plantation history, or in the case of a film being touted as out-Mandingoing *Mandingo*).[14] Long derided by academics as a campy mess, *Mandingo* has more recently received renewed critical attention not only for its representation of ostensibly mutual sexual pleasure between masters and slaves, white and black southerners, but for its purposeful manipulation of cinematic pleasure, which, Lisa Hinrichsen has argued, "position[s] its viewers into an uncomfortable yet provocative relation to the racial and sexual traumas of the plantation past."[15]

In the remainder of this essay, I want to outline what I see as the chief source of "provocation" in *Mandingo* and its contemporary revisionist slave film descendants, such as *Django Unchained* and *12 Years a Slave:* a tension between a liberal desire for a "realist" re-presentation of slavery's sexual brutality and longstanding cinematic traditions of scopic pleasure in race-sex transgression. This tension is resolved, to the extent that it can be, through a new series of repressions and displacements, embodied by some of the same "perpetually shifting and recurrent paradigms" that Susan Courtney documents in the first half of the twentieth century, "revised and resurrected over time."[16] While I find psychoanalytic and even Hegelian readings of *Mandingo*'s master-slave dynamics compelling, I argue that the repressions and displacements effected by *Mandingo* and its descendants are more directly in the service of the shifting narrative needs of American national identity. Destroying certain pleasures and heightening others, these films ultimately preserve a national pleasure, through equally familiar strategies of the liberal gaze and the diverted gaze of sexual and regional containment.[17]

Mandingo disrupts the traditional pleasures of the classical Hollywood plantation romance even as it compensates with the pleasures of contemporaneous blaxploitation and sexploitation films such as Gordon Parks's *Shaft* (1971) and Russ Meyer's *Black Snake* (1973). Seeking to appeal to black urban audiences as well as white, the film offers powerful black male and naked female bodies as *openly* fetishized objects, to be looked at by desiring white eyes and admiring black eyes alike. Black male sexual potency, or hypersexuality, so feared in *The Birth of a Nation,* is in *Mandingo* a "purity" to be coveted, in explicit contrast to white corruption and disability (embodied by Hammond's limp). As in *Slaves,* anachronistic slave dialogue asserting black brotherhood and black power occurs alongside the "noisy confession" of white masters' open preference for "black meat," male and female. Seeking to lure audiences away from their TV sets by offering images that to this day cannot be broadcast, *Mandingo* features frequent full and partial nudity, of men (notably Hammond Maxwell) but especially of black women, and of course the infamous sex scene between Blanche and Mede, in which his nude body, much more than hers, is objectified. While the narrative tone of these revisionary scenes is consistently sympathetic to the slave perspective, in terms of cinematic technique the framing remains white. In one of the rare shots conceivably emanating from a black point of view, one of Hammond's slave concubines regards him as he comes to bed. The camera angle, however, is from beneath the actress's armpit, with the effect of framing the shot with her naked breast—the object of Hammond's regard, and the audience's. This "frame," shall we say, "contextualizes" what the slave woman sees: Hammond's nude body in the process of seeing, and coming to possess, his naked property, for his own pleasure.

Hammond's sexual use of slave women is repeatedly contrasted, however, to the brutality of the *typical* slave master. While at Falconhurst it is the "duty" of the masters to de-virginize slave girls, when Hammond and his cousin Charles are offered two "wenches" while traveling, Charles rejects the one who is a virgin because sex with her would be "too much work." Instead he takes the more "experienced" slave woman from behind, whipping her with his belt as foreplay. When Hammond expresses shock equally at Charles kissing a "nigger" on the mouth and at his extraordinary violence, Charles replies, "It makes a man feel good." Hammond's own sexual encounter with the virgin, who turns out to be Ellen, is, by contrast, a study in romantic mutuality. Unlike the dark brute Charles, Hammond is a sensitive, dreamy blond, and when Ellen is clearly desirous but reluctant to look at him (direct gazes by slaves at masters being strictly forbidden), Hammond commands, then *asks* her to do so and even overcomes his aversion to kissing before the camera discreetly cuts away. Indeed, *Mandingo* strives mightily to render Hammond a sympathetic character. Left limping as the result of a childhood injury, he is consistently "soft" with the slaves, blanching at his father's harsh punishments and unable to carry out beatings himself. Interracial sexual intimacy, particularly with Ellen, seems to *increase* Hammond's humanity toward his slaves, as he promises Ellen eternal fidelity and freedom for their future child. But Hammond's "humanity" is predicated on a painful lack of self-awareness, a romantic streak that obscures to him—and perhaps to the film's audience—the degree of his own thrall to mastery. *Mandingo* evokes the possibility of a white progressive—a good and perhaps redeemable master—only to destroy it. If the audience, along with Mede, imagines that Hammond is "somehow better than a white man," when Hammond shows his true colors in his murderous rage, we are meant to recognize that he indeed is "just white."

Blanche, with her overdetermined name, is "just white" throughout the film, and it is with her rape of Mede that the slippage between realist critique and white scopophilia is most pronounced. Using the full force of her very limited sphere of mastery, Blanche threatens to deploy *Birth of a Nation*'s black-beast rapist mythology to put Mede literally in danger of his life if he does not fulfill her sexual desires. Perversely echoing Hammond's "asking" of Ellen to put her eyes upon him, Blanche wheedles Mede, asking, "Ain't you ever craved a white lady?," to which he makes no response. The camera lingers on Mede's body, ostensibly mirroring Blanche's gaze as she disrobes him, then herself, and presses herself against him. From there, the camera focuses on Blanche's ecstatic reactions to sexual gratification from a slave who Hammond has earlier declared "so big he'll tear the wenches." While there are cuts and angle shifts, there is no discreet camera fadeaway from this encounter but rather an insistence on seeing—confronting—its "facticity" through to the end. The shot of Mede's face as he appears to climax is intercut to suggest Blanche's point of view; indeed, seeing his apparent orgasm appears to seal her own satisfaction. But it is of course the audience's pleasure that is courted here—a voyeuristic pleasure exponentially enhanced by the degree of race-sex transgression involved. As Linda Williams has argued, following Georges Bataille, the erotic charge of a transgressed taboo is directly proportional to the level of knowledge of the taboo and of the fear used to enforce it.[18] In this sense, Hammond's violent reassertion of his mastery at film's end constitutes a retelling of *Birth*'s origin story for the taboo of interracial sex (what "did" happen and, if the audience is lucky, might happen again). Blanche's noisy confession—through cries of pleasure—of her sexual gratification via Mede prefigures the lasting cultural resonance of the film, whose title is so often invoked as shorthand for the risky, risqué pleasure of interracial sex.

Mandingo has added equally to the American cinematic lexicon. Overturning classical Hollywood fantasies of slavery-era miscegenation, *Mandingo* has created a new set of Hollywood conventions, a visual shorthand that remains powerful in contemporary slavery films as they do—or do not—interrogate white sexual and scopic privilege. The years following Barack Obama's election to a second term saw something of an explosion of films that represent race-based slavery, particularly in the southern United States. In 2013 alone, seven such feature-length films were set to be released in the United States, including the Oscar-nominated *12 Years a Slave*.[19] These followed hard upon the 2012 blockbuster successes of Steven Spielberg's *Lincoln* and Quentin Tarantino's *Django Unchained* and preceded later television offerings, such as 2014's *American Horror Story: Coven* and the 2015 Canadian miniseries *The Book of Negroes*. Much of the critical commentary greeting these releases, particularly on the Internet, focused, reasonably enough, on the question why so many films featuring slavery now (particularly in the time of a black president), with answers tending to focus on immediate political and/or ideological motivations and effects, or lack thereof, rather than on the longer view of visual culture studies. By way of taking this longer view, I want to offer a brief but, I hope, suggestive outline of *Mandingo*'s lasting legacy in *Django Unchained* and *12 Years a Slave*, two films that are otherwise about as different as can be. My argument is not that these films in any simple sense replicate *Mandingo* but that they *rely* upon it, or rather upon the cinematic strategies and their cultural resonances that I call the *Mandingo* effect. Sometimes as foil, but often as buttress, these films depend upon and in the process perpetuate the *Mandingo* effect to advance their own re-visions of American slavery and America.

Neither *Django Unchained* nor *12 Years a Slave* could be said to "out-Mandingo *Mandingo*," but in certain respects they do seem to try. Taking wildly different tones, both films not only embrace the realism-by-brutality mandate thrown down by *Slaves* and brought to mass audiences by *Mandingo* but enhance it. Tarantino, known as a champion of blaxploitation films and a master of cinematic allusion, cites directly *Mandingo*'s slave fight-to-the-death scenes and adds his own innovation with graphic scenes depicting a slave who is no longer able to fight torn apart by dogs as punishment. *Django Unchained* announces its particular revisionist strategy in its opening moments: like *Mandingo* and *Slaves*, the film opens with a miserable slave coffle, but the moment of sale is disrupted by the comedic murder of the two slave traders, the first by the mysterious German bounty hunter who had proposed the sale, who then encourages and enables the second, committed by the enslaved themselves. In this scene, and throughout the film, slavery's violence against

African Americans is explicitly and (hyper)realistically rendered, whereas the deaths of whites are cartoonish, with comically flying bodies and spurting blood that reflect both the most advanced special-effects technology and Tarantino's retro aesthetic.

Steve McQueen in *12 Years a Slave* shuns any hint of comedy or camp but repeatedly demonstrates similar filmmaking virtuosity in his depictions of violence against African Americans. Most notably, or notoriously, in a five-minute scene accomplished in one long take encompassing multiple perspectives, the slave girl Patsey's blood and bits of flesh fly beneath the whip's lash. Less bloody but equally harrowing, the film's protagonist, Solomon Northup, is shown hanging from a tree with only the tips of his feet touching the ground in a four-minute scene that (compellingly) represents several hours—slaves move about their chores in the background, children play, only one slave woman offers him a sip of water. McQueen uses such violence to push the dehumanizing effects of slavery dramatized by *Mandingo* to greater heights of physical and psychological realism, precluding even the possibility of effective slave resistance, intimacy, or even community.[20] Both directors have received criticism for the degree of graphically depicted violence in their films, and both have responded with rationales similar to those offered by Richard Fleischer on the making of *Mandingo:* brutal realism is necessary not only to convey the truth of slavery but also to counteract previous romanticism or erasure.[21] Through the shock of realism, *Mandingo* becomes, as Robert Keser has appropriated John Berger's phrase to suggest, "the eye we cannot shut."[22]

From their diverse locales—Django is first unchained in the Texas backcountry, and Northup is kidnapped in Washington, DC—Tarantino and McQueen use graphic violence to introduce the "truth" of slavery as an exercise in brutal physical oppression. Once these films enter the Deep South space of the plantation, however, they join *Mandingo's* tradition of spectacular sexualization of that violence. Decidedly, it is Hammond Maxwell's thoroughly interpellated ghost, rather than *Slaves's* didactically self-conscious Nathan McKay, that hovers around both films' imagery of lascivious slave owners: unthinkingly sadistic yet physically attractive male masters who openly prefer black slave women for their sexual "partners."[23] Having joined forces with the German bounty hunter who has freed him (Dr. King Schultz, played by Christoph Waltz), and having demonstrated natural talents for shooting guns and riding horses, Tarantino's protagonist, Django (Jamie Foxx), rides with Schultz into Mississippi to rescue Django's wife, Broomhilda (Kerry Washington), from the clutches of Monsieur Calvin Candie (Leonardo DiCaprio), owner of the no-torious plantation Candyland. Although the big house at Candyland shares many physical attributes with Tara, the former is curiously devoid of crops or field workers. Instead, the primary business of Candyland appears to be Mandingo fighting and opulent, interracial revelry. Upon learning that Broom-hilda has been sold to Candie, Django immediately avers that she will be made into a "comfort woman," as the *R* (for "Runaway") burned into her cheek has rendered her unfit to be one of the bevy of finely dressed slave beauties who appear constantly at Candie's table. Indeed, slave women appear to be the main candy at Candyland, serving as a complement or embellishment to the second-order, if higher-stakes, entertainment of Mandingo fighting.[24] Though Calvin Candie exhibits none of Hammond Maxwell's "soft-heartedness" in punishing his slaves, he clearly shares Hammond's hegemonic preference for "black meat."

By *Mandingo* standards, *Django Unchained* is a remarkably chaste film. There are no sex scenes and only brief moments of nudity: Django's back (un-der Schultz's gaze) as he casts off his slave blanket in the opening minutes of the film; Broomhilda's naked body as she is removed from the "hot box" to which she has been consigned after running away; and Django's backside again, suspended nude, spread-eagled, and upside down (an image borrowed directly from *Mandingo*). In this respect, Tarantino favors the generic conven-tions of spaghetti westerns rather than blaxploitation or "slavesploitation" films; however, I suggest that the cultural resonance of such films, particularly *Mandingo,* infuses *Django* to such an extent that graphic re-representation is unneeded. Indeed, *Django* relies upon *Mandingo*'s lasting effect to make the nature of Tarantino's own re-vision of American slave history clear. When someone enters the room where Broomhilda cowers on a bed, face to the wall, and approaches her from behind, she—and the viewer—know what to expect: *Mandingo*'s set piece of slave rape. Instead, it is Django come to effect Broom-hilda's rescue before completing his apocalyptic revenge against the entire house of Candie, and the two share the one passionate (and pointedly intra-racial and marital) kiss in the film. And if it is the head house slave, Stephen (Samuel L. Jackson), who casts Sheba back into her place as nothing but a "nig-ger" after Candie's death, Stephen who devises the worst possible punishment for Django, the cinematic context of *Mandingo*'s Black Power rhetoric makes clear that it is not only white-power but black-race betrayal that supports slav-ery's power structure, leading some slaves to do their master's dirty work. If

Stephen never comes to Mede's final moment of black consciousness, his spectacular, literally explosive death at the hands of Django does give viewers a release of cathartic violence for their own raised consciousness.[25]

Based on Solomon Northup's 1853 memoir, *12 Years a Slave* visualizes and literally fleshes out scenes to which Northup's nineteenth-century decorum would only let him allude. Taking a resolutely higher tone and employing a modernist aesthetic, McQueen has positioned *12 Years* as far removed from previous portrayals of American slave history,[26] but his film nonetheless depends upon some of the key tropes and rhetorical gestures used by *Mandingo,* not only for contrast but also to cement its own affective register. Raised a free man in New York, the historical Solomon Northup was lured to Washington, DC, on business and then kidnapped and sold into slavery, where he suffered for twelve years before being located and rescued by family members. Northup's account of his ordeal, written and published the year after his return home, proceeds in a linear fashion, chronicling his adult and family life before enslavement, the degradations he and others experienced, and the circumstances of his return. By contrast, McQueen and the screenwriter John Ridley's adaptation begins *in medias res* with a montage of scenes meant to set the stage and major thematics of Northup's enslavement. Comprising images straight from Northup's memoir—the backbreaking labor of cutting cane, squalid living conditions and meager rations, fruitless attempts to manufacture ink—the montage ends with an innovation: a sex scene. In a one-room cabin crammed with sleeping bodies, a female slave wordlessly compels Northup (played by Chiwetel Ejiofor) to bring her to orgasm manually and then turns away from him, sobbing.

Significantly, McQueen and Ridley introduce sex into their representation of slavery in a very un-*Mandingo*-like way: a (quasi-)consensual act between two African American slaves, ostensibly free from the watchful eye or desire of white masters. When interviewed by Nelson George, McQueen characterized this scene as an attempt to add "a bit of tenderness—the idea of this woman reaching out for sexual healing in a way.... She takes control of her own body. Then after she's climaxed, she's ... back in hell, and that's when she turns and cries."[27] More than portraying slaves as tender or agential, however, the scene establishes two core premises of the film: first, that Northup is heroically faithful (it is the woman's desire, not at all his, that manifests here); second, that sexuality is firmly contained within, and indeed an intrinsic part of, slavery's matrix. The silence of this scene and of the montage as a whole—there is no conversation, no reciprocity, no actual evidence of "tenderness" between slaves—is contrasted to the mutual regard and desire of marital love, as the postcoital desolation of the slave cabin cuts to a flashback of Northup and his wife in a clean bed, looking into each other's eyes and smiling before Northup blows out the light (a later "prequel" return to this scene makes it crystal clear that they are about to make love). If Northup is at all aroused, it is to think of his wife; from the position of voyeur, however, audiences may respond to the erotics (*tenderness* strikes me as a euphemism here) or raw sexual desire on offer in the scene, no matter how sternly they are guided away by McQueen's editor. The sterility and degradation of lust, the miserable (yet visually exciting) process of compelling others to gratify it, the perversion of the rights and pleasures of matrimony—these, along with graphic physical violence, are the structural, primary components of plantation slavery. This is not so far from *Mandingo*'s ground, after all.

Indeed, the cabin encounter is the only representation of sexual contact, much less intimacy, between slaves in *12 Years a Slave*. McQueen conducts his exploration of the constituent role of sex in slavery on much more familiar territory, using two tropes introduced to popular cinema by *Mandingo:* the sexually voracious slave master and the wife driven to violent jealousy by his preference for black female bodies over her own. Hammond Maxwell's skin-deep tenderness and core violence are split between two characters in *12 Years:* Northup's seemingly decent but ultimately treacherous first master, Master Ford, and the unrelentingly sociopathic Master Epps.[28] As played by Michael Fassbender, Epps is a hard-eyed but disturbingly handsome bundle of religious righteousness, physical cruelty, economic greed, and sexual compulsion. The locus of his overriding obsession in all these respects is a slave girl named Patsey (Lupita Nyong'o). *12 Years* is more forthright in its depiction of slave labor and masters' economic interests in it than any film since *Slaves*— scenes of labor and accounting abound—but the economic motive for slavery is ultimately overshadowed by the depiction of Epps's psychosexual struggles.

When Epps waxes dreamy over Patsey's extraordinary cotton-picking ability, all the while edging suggestively behind her, it is clear that he sees those abilities as an extension and confirmation of his masterly sexual prerogative, his God-given right (fig. 7.4). The power of Fassbender's performance lies in the transparency with which he conveys Epps's inner process of forming a coherent narrative of mastery. Faced with a bewildering contradiction between religious righteousness and sexual desire, for example, he appears to search

Fig. 7.4 Promotional film still for *12 Years a Slave* (Fox Searchlight Pictures, 2013).

inward for a moment before landing on a tortured justification (usually a justification for torture). McQueen has characterized this struggle as a "madness" brought on by Epps's contradictory "love" for Patsey,[29] but its primary effect is the confirmation of a premise offered first by *Mandingo:* plantation slavery is *at core* a psychosexual drama on the part of masters, the primary variation between whom is the degree to which they seek to delude themselves that honor or love is involved at all. In Epps's sadistic rape scene with Patsey, he appears a weird hybrid of Hammond Maxwell and his cousin Charles, with Epps's apparent desire or need to have Patsey's eyes upon him during sex and his even more apparent need to beat and strangle her for sexual gratification. Once again, the scene takes place mostly in one long take, starting with a close-in two-shot at face level, positing an objective viewer and privileging neither character's experience. Yet increasingly, it is Epps's eyes we can see, his emotions that are on offer, while Patsey attempts her only possible escape, to look away. She is allowed to be no more successful in this than is the audience (the scopic pleasure of race-sex transgression another eye we cannot shut); eventually it is the camera that pans away, to focus on Epps solely.

Depicting Epps's brutal pleasure, foregrounding his sexual desire as the cornerstone of his character and masterly motivation, *12 Years* engages *Mandingo*'s central premise: that slavery is fundamentally about sexual power. If McQueen repudiates even the red herring of romance (save perhaps what may be in Epps's deluded fantasy),[30] the "truth" of slavery that *12 Years* offers, and that audiences have come to expect post-*Mandingo,* is preserved. Stopping himself one moment shy of asphyxiating Patsey (perhaps remembering her extraordinary economic value to him), Epps looks around wildly and leaves her gasping on the woodpile, nothing but a "nigger." While McQueen successfully and significantly refutes *Mandingo*'s aesthetics, the camera staying with Patsey, he does not dismantle the erotic presumption on which even contemporary understandings of slavery rest.

Unlike the final scenes of *Mandingo,* Epps's actions here have no force of revelation: his degradation is evident from the first and only deepens with each scene. Equally one-note is Sarah Paulson's portrayal of Mistress Epps, who is introduced surveilling Patsey from the upper gallery of her plantation and who takes every opportunity viciously to malign and injure her competition. Where Lara Lee Candie-Fitzwilly is a veritable model of tolerance for her brother's open interracial philandering,[31] Mistress Epps is created in the mold of Blanche Maxwell, a toxic combination of gendered economic dependency, pathetic emotional hurt, and racist venom. The depth of her own unfulfilled sexual need, and her attempt to compensate for it with racial prerogative, is evident as she berates Epps as "manless" and "a damn eunuch," positing her own bed as "too holy for [Epps] to share." Very much like Hammond Maxwell, Edwin Epps refuses his wife the consolations of white-lady privilege, responding to her threat to leave with a humiliating (in front of the slaves) reminder of the "hog's trough" she came from and an assurance that he would more willingly rid himself of her than of Patsey. Ultimately, however, McQueen appears no more interested than Tarantino in exploring the character or condition of the slave mistress, much less in making explicit analogies between mistresses and their slaves à la Biberman and, to a lesser extent, Fleischer. To be sure, the parallels drawn in these earlier films were facile and reflected a second-wave feminist fantasy as anachronistic as Black Power dialogue. But what cultural need is reflected by slave mistresses who have inherited Blanche's situation and her savagery without *any* of her pathos or sexual agency?

The roots of an answer are again suggested by later films' engagement with tropes and rhetorical strategies popularized by *Mandingo.* The different but equally strong cathartic aims of *12 Years a Slave* and *Django Unchained* are achieved both by borrowing *Mandingo*-esque tropes and by revising them, particularly with regard to the notion of a black male protagonist in a southern-plantation setting. The image of Mede's exceptional physical and sexual prowess lurks behind the exceptionalist images of Django and Northup (both of whom are explicitly identified as "exceptional niggers") even as it is strictly channeled into their single-minded determination to return to the sanctity of heterosexual marriage, and even then represented *only* in the most chaste terms. Though emphatically virile, neither character offers the faintest hint of sexual interest in other women, much less white women—*and there is no hint of white women desiring them*. Refuting the image of the black-beast rapist, Mede must be coerced with the threat of death to have sex with Blanche. Removing the sexual power and desire of slave mistresses ensures that neither Django nor Northup is at risk of such coercion and, thus, the dilution of his conjugal masculinity. At the level of cinematic discourse, however, both films borrow from *Mandingo*'s Hollywood playbook, casting extraordinarily attractive stars to invite a familiar scopic pleasure in the black male body for audiences, even while repressing its diegetic expression, at least in the plantation context.

And the plantation context is key. For all the evocation of interracial desire and violence, for all the invitations and repressions of race-sex scopic pleasure, the major repression effected by *Mandingo* and its descendants is slavery's *national* history. Aggressively asserting slavery as a psychosexual dynamic represses altogether the enormous structural, national economic motive for maintaining slavery (as it did *Birth of a Nation*'s Reconstruction-era race relations). For *Mandingo,* slavery is a closed sexual system. The only production at Falconhurst is the sexual reproduction of more slave bodies, and the few outside contacts involve selling and buying more of those bodies (including Blanche's). With only the briefest images of field slaves as a backdrop, *Django*'s Candyland plantation is foremost a playground (and profit center) of slave fighting and interracial sex. *12 Years* reintroduces the profit motive of slaves' physical labor in the southern plantation economy, only to subsume this line of inquiry in its obsession with Epps's obsession with Patsey. In none of these films is there the briefest suggestion of the structural role of northern capital in the slave system, and indeed the later films move even more aggressively to portray and contain the evils of that system as southern.

For although Stanley Fish has praised *12 Years a Slave* for foreclosing any safe outlet for audience sympathy or hope within—"no way out"[32]—there is of course a way: go South and go sexual. I argue that the most lasting of *Mandingo*'s cinematic effects, even more so than the "provocative" tensions between realist violence and scopic pleasure, is the time-honored strategy of regional containment. This too is yet another resurrection and revision of a paradigm used in earliest cinema. While the wildly popular *Birth of a Nation* sought to salve Civil War divisions by appealing to white unity over blackness, the wildly popular *Mandingo* worked in the post–civil rights era to acknowledge white sexual and moral depravity in race relations, but to firmly define and confine it as southern. The dynamic appeared if anything heightened in the age of Obama. Audiences can leave Hammond Maxwell righteously, in the patriarchal ruin of his southern empire. *Django Unchained* and *12 Years a Slave* go a step further, contrasting their wholly corrupt southern masters with wholly "good," resolutely moral white men, who are pointedly not from the South and pointedly not interested in sleeping with black women. Looking away to Dixie—and at an exclusively sexualized race system—enables looking away from national complicity. This gaze South, which has been such an important component of the liberal gaze regarding US slavery, enables a complex set of audience pleasures: voyeurism and disavowal, shame and pride, a justified appetite for ever more graphic "realism" about slavery's sexual brutality and a way to quarantine it within a liberal notion of American national identity. The plantation South is, in this rubric, the only place where white sexual desire for the black other is available on demand for white pleasure, except perhaps in the contemporary cinema of slavery.

NOTES

1. Shelley Stamp Lindsey, "Is any girl safe? Female spectators at the white slave films," *Screen* 37, no. 1 (Spring 1996): 1–15.

2. *Mandingo*, dir. Richard Fleischer (Paramount, 1975).

3. Susan Courtney, *Hollywood Fantasies of Miscegenation* (Princeton, NJ: Princeton University Press, 2005), 6.

4. Courtney cites correspondence from Joe Breen, director of the Production Code Administration (PCA), rejecting the proposed reissue of a silent *Uncle Tom's Cabin* (apparently Universal Studios's 1928 version) because of the "serious problem of miscegenation, both as to Casey, the older woman, and as to Liza, toward whom Legree is making overtures of an obviously sexual nature," as evidence of the PCA's "anxiety about depicting slavery's sexual economy." She concludes, compellingly, "Insofar as that economy produced the interracial combination that had been most historically prominent [white masters raping black slaves] . . . we could well read fantasies that

recalled such encounters—the sins of white fathers that could still return to haunt their white and not-as-white sons—as the real 'Hamlet's father' that beset those charged to enforce the Code's miscegenation clause." Ibid., 125.

5. Edward D. C. Campbell Jr., *The Celluloid South* (Knoxville: University of Tennessee Press, 1981), 185.

6. Linda Williams, "Skin Flicks on the Racial Border: Pornography, Exploitation, and Interracial Lust," in *Porn Studies,* ed. Linda Williams (Durham, NC: Duke University Press, 2004), 272.

7. *Slaves,* dir. Herbert Biberman (Theatre Guild, 1969). One of the "Hollywood Ten," Biberman (1900–1971) was imprisoned for contempt of Congress for six months after refusing to answer questions from the US House Un-American Activities Committee. He chronicles this experience, and the making of the 1954 film for which he is best known, in Herbert Biberman, *Salt of the Earth: The Story of a Film* (Boston: Beacon, 1965). *Slaves* was his next, and last, film.

8. Paul Talbot, in *Mondo Mandingo* (New York: iUniverse, 2009), offers a selection of Onstott's comments on the facticity of the novel. Searching for a potential publisher for *Mandingo,* Onstott's son wrote, "The book doesn't have any significance, but it's like eating peanuts." Quoted in Earl F. Bargainnier, "The *Falconhurst* Series: A New Popular Image of the Old South," *Journal of Popular Culture* 10 (1976): 299. The entertainment value of slavery is what is important here, as it ties into the national cultural dynamics in which *Mandingo* takes part.

9. Herbert Biberman, "We Never Say Nigger in Front of Them," *New York Times,* 19 January 1969, D1.

10. Keith Gilyard, *John Oliver Killens: A Life of Black Literary Activism* (Athens: University of Georgia Press, 2011), 249. *Slaves* premiered in competition at the Cannes Film Festival in 1969. Representative critical reception includes Vincent Canby's verdict in the *New York Times* that *Slaves* was "a kind of cinematic carpetbagging project in which some contemporary movie-makers have raided the antebellum South and attempted to impose upon it their own attitudes that will explain 1969 black militancy." "Screen: 'Slaves' Opens at the Demille," *New York Times,* 3 July 1969, www.nytimes.com/movie/review?res=9E00E5DA1E3AEE34BC4B53DFB1668382679EDE; and *Box-office,* 19 May 1969, which found *Slaves* "banal, predictable and technically inept, with the editing faintly reminiscent of St. Vitus Dance." www2.boxoffice.com/the_vault/issue_page?issue_id=1969 -5-19&page_no=157#page_start. Critics were also less than kind to Killens's 1969 novelization of *Slaves* (New York: Pyramid Books), which *Publisher's Weekly* declared read "like the black answer to *Mandingo,*" finding that Killens "countered a simplistic, psychologically underdeveloped tale of black sexual animals lusting more after whites than after freedom with an equally simplistic, psychologically underdeveloped tale of slaves obsessed *only* with freedom." Gilyard, Gilyard, *John Oliver Killens,* 247.

11. Fleischer's rationale for including scenes of brutal violence and sexuality in his film is strikingly similar to Biberman's: "The whole slavery story has been lied about, covered up and romanticized so much that I thought it really had to stop. The only way to stop was to be as brutal as I could possibly be, to show how these people suffered. I'm not going to show you them suffering backstage—I want you to look at them." Quoted in Ian Cameron and Douglas Pye, "Richard Fleischer on *Mandingo,*" *Movie* 22 (February 1976): 24.

12. *Mandingo* arrived in theaters near the end of the blaxploitation film era, which flourished between 1970 and 1975. Made to exploit black audiences, these films featured strong black characters (and often mocked white ones) and were made by white and black filmmakers alike across a variety of genres: action, crime, comedy, horror, drama, musical. Popular with white audiences as well,

blaxsploitation films evoked issues, as well as stereotypes, from the African American past and present, including racism, slavery, prostitution and pimping, and drug use. Plantation slavery–related movies included *Pleasure Plantation* (1970), *Quadroon* (1971), *The Legend of Nigger Charley* (1972), and most notoriously, *Addio Zio Tom* (*Goodbye Uncle Tom*), a 1971 mockumentary that the "mondo" filmmakers Franco Prosperi and Gualtiero Jacopetti conceived of as "*Mandingo* as a documentary." *The Godfathers of Mondo,* dir. David Gregory (Blue Underground, 2003), DVD.

13. Campbell, *Celluloid South,* 172. Campbell provides a long list of contemporaneous bad reviews, which included characterizing the film as a racist "conspiracy of depraved minds" that presented nothing but "the most salacious miscegenation-inspired sex fantasies" (189). More recently, Andrew DeVos has surveyed white and black press reactions to *Mandingo* (finding that both condemned the film) and comparing these with the reactions of black audiences (considerably more positive) as documented in street interviews and other anecdotes from 1975. DeVos, "'Expect the Truth': Exploiting History with *Mandingo,*" *American Studies* 52, no. 2 (2013): 5–21. To date, no one has attempted a regional analysis of these reactions.

14. Catherine Clinton, *The Plantation Mistress* (New York: Random House, 1982), 226. Perhaps not surprisingly, the promotional poster for *Drum* (1976), based on the second novel in Onstott's Falconhurst series, declares: "It scalds. It shocks. It whips. It bleeds. It lusts. It out-Mandingos *Mandingo!*"

15. Hinrichsen advances this claim in an as yet unpublished essay, "The Reel South: Screening Southern Fantasy in *Mandingo.*" I am grateful to Hinrichsen for sharing this important work. While most critics were, and remain, dismissive of *Mandingo*'s aesthetics, the first positive critical academic assessment was offered as early as 1976 by Andrew Britton, who judged the film "a great and achieved work of art" for its diagnosis of the racial and sexual conflicts at the heart of America. Britton, "Mandingo," *Movie* 22 (February 1976): 1–22.

16. Courtney, *Hollywood Fantasies of Miscegenation,* 6.

17. Jennifer Rae Greeson, in *Our South: Geographic Fantasy and the Rise of National Literature* (Cambridge, MA: Harvard University Press, 2010), and Leigh Anne Duck, in *The Nation's Region* (Athens: University of Georgia Press, 2007), offer insightful histories of this gaze in the antebellum and modernist periods, respectively.

18. Williams, "Skin Flicks on the Racial Border," 275.

19. Reflecting the vagaries of the film industry, only three of these films (*12 Years, Belle,* and *Savannah,* the latter of which only tangentially addresses slavery) saw actual release in the United States. The others (*Tula, Freedom, The North Star,* and *The Keeping Room*) either were released only overseas, were delayed until 2014, or are still awaiting release.

20. While *Mandingo* could hardly be said to offer compelling or even coherent visions of slave community or intimacy, its moments of slave interaction, particularly in the anachronistic Black Power sequences, do offer a suggestion of communal resistance entirely precluded in *12 Years*'s chronicle of individual survival.

21. See, e.g., interviews with Tarantino (2012) in the *Guardian,* www.theguardian.com/film/2012/dec/07/quentin-tarantino-slavery-django-unchained; and McQueen in Nelson George, "An Essentially American Narrative: A Discussion of Steve McQueen's Film '12 Years a Slave,'" *New York Times,* 11 October 2013, www.nytimes.com/2013/10/13/movies/a-discussion-of-steve-mcqueens-film-12-years-a-slave.html. In an interview with the United Kingdom's Channel 4 News on 10 January 2013, Tarantino credited his portrayal of slavery's violence with opening a needed conversation:

"I am responsible for people talking about slavery in America in a way they have not in 30 years." www.channel4.com/news/quentin-tarantino-im-shutting-your-butt-down.

22. Robert Keser, "The Eye We Cannot Shut: Richard Fleischer's *Mandingo*," *Film Journal* 13 (2006), brightlightsfilm.com/greatest-film-race-ever-filmed-hollywood-richard-fleischer s-mandingo/#.V32Cr_krKM9. In a 1972 essay, John Berger used the phrase "the eye we cannot shut" to describe typical justifications (which he goes on to refute) for publishing the war photography of Donald McCullin: "Such photographs remind us shockingly of the reality, the lived reality, behind the abstractions of political theory.... [They] are printed on the black curtain which is drawn across what we choose to forget or refuse to know." Berger, "Photographs of Agony," in *About Looking* (New York: Pantheon, 1980), 42. Interestingly, Keser reframes Berger's characterization of the realist mandate to serve as a justification of *Mandingo*'s "provocative" formulations of sexuality and brute power: "The eye we cannot shut," in his formulation, is "the persistent vision of competing powers—the slave's physical strength (and by extension sexual potency) against the master's sovereign power to define reality and decide life or death." Keser, "The Eye We Cannot Shut." I critique the implications of this argument below.

23. Both Leonardo DiCaprio and Michael Fassbender have made multiple appearances on *People* magazine's "Sexiest Man Alive" lists. The visual rhetorical effect of the choice of such actors in relation to theme is dramatically illustrated by the different actors chosen to play Hammond Maxwell in *Mandingo* (Perry King) and its 1976 "sequel," *Drum* (a much older and dissipated-looking Warren Oates).

24. The first scene of "Mandingo" fighting (the "tribal" name is taken directly from Onstott/ Fleischer) culminates with a close shot of multicolored candy balls apparently spilling from the apron of one of Candie's slave-girl attendants as she gasps in horror at the bloody conclusion of the fight. Candie's favored concubine, Sheba (Nichole Galicia), is more often at Candie's side than even his widowed sister, Lara Lee Candie-Fitzwilly (Laura Cayouette); one might surmise that the exaggerated display of love and compliments he showers upon Lara Lee is Candie's way of buying her silent acquiescence to the openness of his "relationships" with slave women, although truly she has no choice in the matter. More than one critic has characterized the relationship between Candie and Lara Lee as incestuous. Analysts of southern culture going back at least to W. J. Cash, however, might recognize Candie's behavior as typical southern "gyneolatry," an elaborate performance of white-female worship designed to mask and compensate for white male desire for black women.

25. Tarantino has repeatedly defended the extraordinary violence in the film as "cathartic" and as a chance for "black revenge." Several critics have argued, however, that the catharsis and revenge fantasy in *Django* is actually offered to white viewers. See, e.g., David J. Leonard, "Django Blues: Whiteness and Hollywood's Continued Failures," in *Quentin Tarantino's "Django Unchained": The Continuation of Metacinema,* ed. Oliver C. Speck (New York: Bloomsbury, 2014), 269–86.

26. See, e.g., McQueen's interview by Calum Marsh, www.film.com/movies/12-years-a-slave-s teve-mcqueen-interview.

27. George, "Essentially American Narrative."

28. Master Ford (Benedict Cumberbatch) expresses moral revulsion over a slave trader's refusal to sell a slave girl along with her mother, whom Ford intends to buy because her mixed-race beauty will bring the trader a fortune on the sexual market in a few years. That Ford proceeds to buy the mother (and Northup) from this trader anyway is the first hint of his moral precariousness.

29. Quoted in George, "Essentially American Narrative."

30. While McQueen has explicated this scene as Epps attempting "to destroy his love for [Patsey] by destroying her," Epps's religious belief that "God give her to me" would suggest a simpler motivation, a version of Charles's "It makes a man feel good."

31. The Candie siblings' relationship, with its whiff of incest, shows its only moment of strain when Calvin crosses an invisible line by stripping Broomhilda to display her back at dinner. Lara Lee's desperate flirtation with Dr. Schultz, which he consistently ignores in favor of Broomhilda, provides the barest suggestion of the uncomfortable parallel of the widow and slave that Lara Lee may be reacting to here.

32. Stanley Fish, "No Way Out: '12 Years a Slave,'" *New York Times,* 25 November 2013, www.ny times.com/2013/11/26/opinion/fish-no-way-out-12-years-a-slave.html?_r=0.

8

"I Just Cain't Wait to Get to Heaven"

Nostalgia and Idealized Queer Community in Fried Green Tomatoes at the Whistle Stop Café *and* Fried Green Tomatoes

ABIGAIL PARSONS

P opular narratives of queer history in the United States have frequently compartmentalized the development of queer identities, politics, groups, and movements into two distinct phases: before and after Stonewall. According to these narratives, the Stonewall riots, which took place in Greenwich Village in the summer of 1969, ushered in a new era of activism and awareness in which the visibility of queer issues and queer Americans increased exponentially. In the national consciousness, Stonewall became the watershed moment that sparked a widespread rebellion against the laws that criminalized gay, lesbian, transgender, and transsexual people, highlighted the violence and intimidation perpetrated by the police and members of the public, and led to the emergence of visible queer social scenes.

Of course, a model that reduces queer history to two distinct periods has limitations. The before-and-after model oversimplifies the concept of visibility, suggesting that prior to the riots queer Americans lived in secrecy, isolation, anguish, and fear of being outed. By contrast, pride, visibility, community, radicalism, and public displays of defiance characterize representations of the post-Stonewall era and the gay liberation movement.

In celebrating Stonewall as the impetus for radical change, the popular discourse of queer history has given woefully inadequate attention to the many instances of protest and resistance that occurred prior to 1969. The effect of this oversimplification is that pre-Stonewall instances of activism, resistance, and community formation become inexplicable anomalies rather than essential components of queer sociopolitical development as a whole. In the before-and-after model, the homophile movement is confined to the pre-Stonewall era, while the more radical gay liberation movement becomes a separate and distinct post-Stonewall phenomenon, even though there was much overlap between the two. Prominent homophile organizations that formed in the 1950s, such as the Mattachine Society and Daughters of Bilitis, become noted for the covertness of their operations and their assimilationist approach to seeking equality and respect.[1] The gay liberation movement, on the other hand, is recognized for the formation of the Gay Liberation Front, the first advocacy group in the United States to use *gay* in its name,[2] and the beginning of annual Gay Pride marches in major cities on the East and West Coasts in 1970.

In short, the before-and-after model inspires a series of binaries—closeted/out, euphemisms/explicit language, assimilationist/resistant—that misrepresent the complexity of queer history in the United States. Popular representations of twentieth-century queer history have tended to overemphasize the roles that white gay men and lesbians played in crucial historical moments while downplaying or even denying the contributions of transgender, transsexual, gender nonconforming, and bisexual people, especially people of color. The result of this erasure is yet another pair of reductive binaries—gay/straight, white/other—that shore up the oversimplified dichotomous framework within which (predominantly white) activists, artists, and scholars have conceptualized the most visible queer historical narratives.

But despite the problematic constraints of the before-and-after model and its attendant binary oppositions, it has often become the default lens through which to view queerness in the twentieth-century United States. For example, the award-winning documentaries *Before Stonewall* and *After Stonewall,* the PBS production *Stonewall Uprising,* and historiographies by Martin Duberman and David Carter attempt to give voice to some of the lesser-known actors in the history of queer social and political movements but still reify the binary model in the process.[3]

Dominant cultural and historical narratives have also deployed a troublesome spatial binary that has worked in tandem with the before-and-after-Stonewall model to suppress and distort the reality of queer lives in certain regions of the country. The fixation on Stonewall and the bicoastal activism that immediately succeeded the riots secured New York City and other major urban centers such as San Francisco, Washington, DC, Philadelphia, and Los Angeles as the primary hubs of queer sociopolitical transformation. The result is the creation of an uneven rural/urban binary that privileges cities—East and West Coast cities in particular—as sites of progress while naming the space between as the locus of repression and silence, in essence making the rural United States "America's perennial, tacitly taken-for-granted closet."[4]

While extensive community studies in the fields of anthropology, sociology, and history have sought to understand how spatial relations have influenced the development of gay and lesbian identities, politics, social groups, and modes of communication, the vast majority of these studies have limited their scope to urban areas in the Northeast and on the East and West Coasts. Studies of the Buffalo lesbian bar scene by Elizabeth Kennedy and Madeline Davis, San Francisco's gay leather clubs by Gayle Rubin, and Philadelphia's gay and lesbian neighborhoods by Marc Stein are just three examples out of many that reinforce the assumption that same-sex relationships and gender nonconformity can more easily become visible and legible in the city.[5]

The emphasis on urban communities in studies such as these reflects the predominance of another narrative of queer American history that works to divert attention away from the most marginalized queer populations: the urban-migration narrative. Kath Weston's landmark essay, "Get Thee to a Big City: Sexual Imaginary and the Great Gay Migration," suggests that queer people have migrated from rural to urban areas because they assume cities will provide less judgment and surveillance from families, friends, and neighbors; a larger dating and social scene; greater acceptance because of a more diverse population; and access to queer facilities such as clubs, bars, and social organizations.[6] In the urban-migration narrative, "urban queers" pity the "sad and lonely" rural queers, who "might be thought of as 'stuck' in a place that they would leave if they only could."[7] The luckier rural queers can leave the oppressive small towns in which they were raised and move to the city, where a warm welcome and a plethora of social, political, and sexual opportunities await.

If proponents of urban migration viewed rural areas across the United States as generally incompatible with nurturing queer subjectivities and relationships, then the rural South especially, with its perceived regressive and conservative tendencies, became an entirely hostile space, inimical to queer possibility. The renowned Washington, DC–based activist Frank Kameny recalls that he and his peers in urban gay-rights organizations referred to the space between the East and West Coasts as a "vast desert." Such was the perceived dearth of queer visibility or activism in the "hinterlands" in the 1950s and 1960s. But Kameny also claims that their perception of the South in particular was that it "remained a 'desert' for long thereafter,"[8] not daring to contribute to any sort of queer movement or embrace a collective national identity until the latter part of the twentieth century.

The preoccupation with the urban-migration narrative, coupled with what James Sears calls the "bicoastal bias,"[9] has long undermined the capacity of rural areas, especially those in the South, to generate and sustain queer communities and relationships. In his study of gay men in Mississippi, John Howard urges us to "listen and look closely" in order to learn stories that counter the assumptions made in urban-migration narratives. He suggests that by scrutinizing the lives and stories of gay men from the South, "not only can we hear the words of those who utilized privilege to craft a gay life away from home, but we also can see the interactions between men who experienced and acted on queer desire within a small, localized realm, men who never took on a gay identity or became part of a gay community or culture."[10]

Howard is one of a growing number of scholars who are turning their attention to the archives, conducting interviews, and scrutinizing cultural texts in search of queer traces in the South's historical record. Patti Duncan's interviews with LGBT Asian and Pacific Islander Americans in Atlanta, E. Patrick Johnson's oral-history project with southern gay black men, and James T. Sears's biographical essay on the life of the Charleston transsexual Dawn Langley Simmons are just some examples of the intersectional, nuanced, and exciting projects emerging from the small but ever-growing field of queer southern studies.[11]

But despite the recent, substantial expansion of the field, however, there continues to be a relative dearth of research on the stories and representations of queer women and other female-assigned queer people in the region. This critical inattention is especially surprising given the extent to which fictional and creative texts have persisted in writing such forms of queerness into existence. These include novels by Dorothy Allison, Alice Walker, Carson McCullers, KI Thompson, Cynthia Webb, and Ann Shockley, poetry by Minnie Bruce Pratt, memoirs by Laura Milner, Mab Segrest, and Rita Mae Brown, and films, particularly, though not exclusively, adaptations of novels by queer female authors, such as Walker's *The Color Purple,* Allison's *Cavedweller* and *Bastard Out of Carolina,* and McCullers's *The Member of the Wedding* and *The Heart Is a Lonely Hunter.* In addition to portraying a range of queer female-assigned bodies and identities, many of these texts address and challenge the sexist, racist, and homophobic sociopolitical structures that operate in the South and that have historically suppressed certain kinds of queer voices and images.

What follows is an examination of Fannie Flagg's 1987 novel, *Fried Green Tomatoes at the Whistle Stop Café,* and the 1991 film adaptation, *Fried Green*

Tomatoes, directed by Jon Avnet.[12] Both join a growing number of creative and fictional texts, counterhistories, and oral-history projects that insist upon offering a corrective to the phenomenon of queer female erasure in representations of the South. Flagg's novel and Avnet's film inscribe same-sex desire and gender nonconformity onto times and spaces often considered incompatible with the flourishing of queer lives and communities. In doing so, they expose the artificiality and limitations of multiple binaries that structured dominant cultural narratives about queerness in the twentieth century. Working around and within the discursive space of the pre-Stonewall rural South, Flagg and Avnet begin to unfasten the binary oppositions that have produced simple and coherent if flawed and incomplete narratives.

Set in Birmingham, Alabama, in the mid-1980s and the nearby fictional town of Whistle Stop in the first half of the twentieth century, the novel tells several intertwining stories using a variety of narrative strategies. Evelyn Couch is a frustrated and underappreciated housewife whose life is transformed for the better when she goes with her husband to visit his elderly mother in a nursing home. There she meets the aptly named Ninny Threadgoode, a lovable and chatty but slightly scatterbrained old woman who dreamily reminisces to Evelyn about her life growing up in Whistle Stop, a small railroad town in rural Alabama. The narrative action jumps back and forth from the nursing home in the present day to the Whistle Stop of Ninny's flashbacks. Ninny's flashbacks revolve around her fond memories of her sister-in-law, Idgie, and Idgie's best friend/companion/lover, Ruth. The two women set up a home and café together after Idgie rescues a pregnant Ruth from her abusive marriage and brings her back to Whistle Stop, where they also raise Ruth's son, Stump. They become de facto community leaders; their café serves as the epicenter of the small town's diverse and inclusive social scene, with the two women hosting town events and celebrations and defying law and custom to take in and serve black and homeless patrons. In the imaginary town of Whistle Stop, threats of prejudice and harm come from the outside, from cities, while inside the small town, residents establish safe and nurturing kinship systems predicated on cooperation and interdependency.

The third-person narration of the flashbacks and the scenes with Evelyn and Ninny is interspersed with the first-person narration of the *Weems Weekly,* Whistle Stop's newsletter, penned by the local resident and busybody Dot Weems. Occasionally, more formal and detached news bulletins from Birmingham and Valdosta intervene to fill gaps in the plot. The contrast in tone between the *Weems Weekly* and the city newspapers reflects the different social climates of the two kinds of locale. Dot Weems writes with a gossipy tone that conveys her familiarity with all the residents of Whistle Stop, whereas the Birmingham and Valdosta publications report stories in a way that distances the nameless and neutral reporters from the stories' subjects. Weems's conspiratorial tone lends credence to the claim that in the small town everyone knows everyone else's business. A central premise of urban-migration narratives is that the lack of privacy in small towns drives people to the city, where they hope anonymity will bring them the freedom to explore new identities and experiences, in addition to greater economic opportunities.

Urban migration for social reasons is not a pattern that is exclusive to queer populations in the United States, a fact that Flagg weaves into her story. The Great Migration, which occurred in the first half of the twentieth century, saw a mass movement of black people from rural areas in the South to cities in the North, Midwest, and West as well as in the South.[13] According to Louis Kyriakoudes, their reasons for migrating were not entirely based on labor. Rather, Kyriakoudes claims, for many black southerners relocation to the city was part of a "fundamental social process," because, like their queer counterparts, they perceived social conditions to be more favorable for them there.[14]

In Whistle Stop, however, transparency and social intimacy among the residents breeds its own desirable qualities not found in the city, such as faithfulness and a collective pride in the community. Flagg's strategy of inverting the urban-migration narrative is central to her premise that rural spaces can be inherently liberatory and affirming for marginalized groups, unlike the urban spaces, which she depicts as antithetical to freedom and safety. Whistle Stop is not the final destination on the railroad but a place that trains pass through on their way to more industrialized cities and regions, a place that progress has seemingly bypassed. Yet Flagg implies that the city, for all its promises of excitement, growth, self-discovery, and opportunity, is a far less desirable place for minority groups, especially black and queer people, than the underdeveloped town of Whistle Stop.

A subplot involving Artis Peavey, the son of Idgie's black employees, is another example of how Flagg reworks dominant narratives about urban migration as liberating. Filled with wanderlust and harboring contempt for the stifling nature and tedium of small-town life, Artis leaves Whistle Stop for Birmingham. Upon arrival in the big city, Artis seeks out Slagtown, "the Harlem of the South," which is "all too much for the seventeen-year-old black boy in overalls who had never been out of Whistle Stop."[15] Flagg captures the excitement and promise of the city with vivid descriptions of its "towering skyscrapers and steel mills that lit up the sky with red and purple hues, and its busy streets buzzing with hundreds of automobiles and the streetcars on wires."[16] Slagtown is at once colorful, bustling, sensual, liberating, and dangerous. Artis, experiencing for the first time a town in which black people are seemingly economically, socially, and creatively autonomous, "knew he was home at last."[17]

But Artis's exhilaration is short lived. Jailed over a misunderstanding, Artis soon learns that the city is rife with injustice and that even black communities such as Slagtown are not immune from externally imposed racist oppression by a white-supremacist judicial system. Paradoxically, the anonymity of the city that allows Artis a chance to reinvent himself as a sophisticated and worldly man about town also deprives him of a support network that would have protected him. It is not until Idgie travels to Birmingham with Whistle Stop's white sheriff to speak on Artis's behalf that he is released from prison. Artis is duped by false promises of riches, glamour, and excitement in the city and pays for his error in judgment with his freedom.

While the train repeatedly passing back and forth through Whistle Stop succeeds in tempting Artis to the city, Ruth, Idgie, and their black employees remain impervious to its pull. Instead, they attempt to construct a space in the rural South that is always already inclusive and liberatory, negating the need for them to migrate to urban areas. The residents of Whistle Stop create and honor kinship systems and a "progressive reworking of 'family'"[18] that supplant the nuclear family as the foundation of the town's social order. In Flagg's imaginary small southern town, a masculine woman can create a chosen family comprising a married woman with whom she parents an amputee son, a black family that includes a baby found abandoned at a train station, and an alcoholic vagrant, all without fear of judgment or reprisal. In Flagg's descriptions of these contrasting locales, Whistle Stop engenders solidarity, warmth, protection, and safety, while Birmingham is rife with loneliness, disloyalty, crime, and injustice.

Flagg therefore portrays Whistle Stop as an idealized tight-knit community whose members are bound by a loyalty to one another that transcends racial and sexual boundaries and by a desire to protect themselves from nefarious external forces. When the dangers of the city threaten to infringe upon the relative tranquility of Whistle Stop, the small-town community bands together to dispatch troublemaking outsiders; Whistle Stop's Sheriff sends away a Valdosta contingent of the Ku Klux Klan, Sipsey kills Frank when he tries to break up Ruth's new queer family, and the residents conspire to thwart detectives' efforts to capture Frank's killer. When Sipsey's son, known as Big George, stands trial after being wrongly accused of Frank's murder, the people of Whistle Stop convene in the courthouse to protest his innocence. Reverend Scroggins, the town's curmudgeonly minister, goes so far as to lie under oath to secure Big George's freedom. In flouting the law, Scroggins makes it clear that the need to preserve the cohesiveness and stability of Whistle Stop's community supersedes the legal imperative to tell the truth.

Flagg's vision of a pluralistic and cooperative small town in the Jim Crow, pre-Stonewall South is an improbable fantasy, but it functions as an important counternarrative that proposes alternatives to the dominant urban-migration narrative for both queer and black people. The novel aligns both populations in a reinvented rural society in which everyone, especially those belonging to marginalized groups, works to ensure others' protection from destructive outside forces.

Indeed, *Fried Green Tomatoes at the Whistle Stop Café* appears to normalize Ruth and Idgie's relationship to the extent that the other characters find two women falling in love and setting up a home together to be entirely unremarkable. No one in the novel expresses surprise or offers comment of any kind upon learning that Ruth and Idgie are a couple; instead, they accept their atypical family setup as a mundane component of the community as a whole. Given the dominance of representations that map silence, isolation, and repression onto the pre-Stonewall rural South, Ruth and Idgie, as a romantically involved couple, seem to enjoy a heightened level of visibility and acceptance that seems unlikely, if not impossible.

So how does Flagg convincingly normalize a queer relationship that would surely have provoked extreme hostile reactions had it been so publicly visible in real life? Or to use the words of Jennifer Church, how has Flagg turned a story about a "tomboy's life of playing poker and drinking, defying the Ku Klux Klan, recapturing her lesbian lover from a violent marriage, and murdering and cannibalizing the husband" into a much-loved bestseller that even garnered high praise from the *To Kill a Mockingbird* author, Harper Lee?[19] *Fried Green Tomatoes at the Whistle Stop Café* does not comport with dominant narratives about the pre-Stonewall South, yet it somehow succeeds in making queerness appear to be an intrinsic and unexceptional occurrence.

The answer lies in Flagg's use of nostalgia, the mechanisms of which foster acceptance of a queer relationship among the characters (and perhaps among the readership, which kept the novel on the *New York Times* bestseller list for thirty-six weeks). Although the novel is everything that Church described, it is also a sentimental and palatable tale about "a sweet old woman in a rest home telling stories of a distant past to a middle-aged housewife."[20] Ninny's flashbacks re-create a story of queer love, interracial harmony, and an impotent patriarchy in her imagined past. As the omniscient and subjective narrator, Ninny filters out her most undesirable memories, leaving only those memories that accord with her rose-tinted vision of her youth.

Peter Applebome describes the South as "a place congenitally geared to looking toward the past in a nation rushing headlong into the future,"[21] an observation borne out in Flagg's novel. Ninny laments the disaffected state of modern life, claiming that people are not happy "like they used to be,"[22] and she recalls that "those Depression years" were "the happy times, even though we were all struggling."[23] Instead of emphasizing Ninny's memories of Klan violence, the devastating effects of poverty and hunger, and the decimation of the region's agricultural industry and primary source of livelihood, the novel uses the repetitive motif of southern cooking to tie the story firmly to the region, a motif that also enhances the text's nostalgic quality. Ninny's memories invoke the affective and sensory properties of southern food with vivid, mouth-watering descriptions. She remembers fondly how Sipsey's dumplings "were so light they would float in the air,"[24] and she tells Evelyn that she would "pay a million dollars for a barbecue like Big George used to make, and a piece of Sipsey's lemon icebox pie."[25] Food appears throughout the novel as a way for characters to show affection and respect for one another, consequently strengthening Ninny's romanticized Whistle Stop community. Ruth and Idgie contravene regional custom by selling their food to black people, an effort to promote interracial harmony in the idyllic Whistle Stop of an otherwise racially fractured South. Their food also brings comfort and nourishment to Smokey Lonesome, a starving hobo who shows up at the café looking for work and a place to stay.

Southern home-cooked food is not the only nostalgic device that emerges in flashbacks. In Ninny's recollections, the residents of the town become flawless and idealized. Ruth is beautiful, selfless, and virtuous, while Idgie is charming, hilarious, and fearless, the kind of person "everybody wanted to be around."[26]

White and black people are devoted to each other (at least in the skewed white southern fantasies that see good white folks absolve themselves of any blame for racism), and the Threadgoodes welcome anyone into their extended family. Even as she looks toward her death, Ninny expresses excitement at the prospect of reverting back to her previously happy family life when she is reunited with her loved ones in the afterlife, telling Evelyn, "Sometimes I just cain't wait to get to heaven. I just cain't wait."[27] Ninny's selective and subjective memories dictate the course of the narrative, meaning that much of the evidence contradicting her memories is left unknowable.

The film theorist Pam Cook calls nostalgia "a state of longing for something that is known to be irretrievable, but is sought anyway." Nostalgia is also, according to Cook, "rooted in disavowal, or suspension of disbelief" and "generally associated with fantasy."[28] Certainly, Ninny's remembrances of Idgie and Ruth's relationship require the reader to push dominant narratives to one side and conceive instead of a queer southern history that is not real and hidden but imagined and desired. Cook also claims that "nostalgia plays on the gaps between representations of the past and actual past events, and the desire to overcome the gap and recover what has been lost."[29] Flagg uses Ninny's flashbacks to offer a desirable view of the past that contradicts much of what we know about the visibility and acceptance of queer people in the early twentieth-century Deep South. At the same time, she attempts to compensate for a lost history by writing queer lives into existence, however inconceivable they may be. That Ninny's flashbacks may be inaccurate or even fantastical is not as important as the fact that Ninny highlights her memories of Idgie and Ruth as worthy of recovery and preservation in the first place. Only with the suspension of disbelief that nostalgia engenders can we envision an early twentieth-century, rural southern community that does not just tolerate but embraces a same-sex couple and their chosen extended family.

The nostalgia in the novel, however, also produces a vision of the past that is stripped of certain key political associations. The novel is set decades before Stonewall and the onset of a visible gay liberation movement, in a region far removed from the queer subcultures then found in West Coast and Northeast cities. For the residents of Ninny's imagined Whistle Stop, there is no homophobic political or pathological discourse available for them to recognize the kind of queerness that Ruth and Idgie embody or to mark their sexuality out as deviant. By situating Ninny's memories in a prepolitical or apolitical milieu, and by framing those memories as the selective nostalgic and wistful reminiscences of an old lady, Flagg can place a queer couple at the front and center of her story without ever confronting the possibility that they might experience opposition from a homophobic society.

Deborah Barker describes how *Fried Green Tomatoes at the Whistle Stop Café*, its film adaptation, and similar contemporary southern chick flicks can use nostalgia to bypass the historical moments of civil rights, second-wave feminism, and gay liberation, effectively depoliticizing the South in the first half of the twentieth century. In the 1980s, Evelyn Couch tries "to raise her son to be sensitive, but [her husband] had scared her so bad, telling her that he would turn out to be a queer, she had backed off and lost contact with him."[30] That Evelyn and Ed are raising a son not just in the post-Stonewall era but in the midst of the AIDS crisis means that Evelyn reacts to a warning about her son's perceived feminization with horror and anxiety. Evelyn is forced to think about her son within the context of a political and historical moment characterized by the fear and othering of gay people, whereas Ninny's reminiscences leapfrog over that moment so that Ruth and Idgie can be fondly idealized. In other words, by creating an imagined past divested of the gender and sexual politics of the present, "a pregnant woman (Ruth) can leave her abusive husband (Frank) for another woman (Idgie) with whom she lives, works, and raises a child without being labeled feminist or lesbian."[31]

The flashbacks, nostalgia, and erasure of political context also produce a temporal flux that contests the linear progress model of popular queer-history narratives. Thus, certain principal images in the novel and film can be dislodged from their original historical context and meaning and then resignified within readings that prioritize queer interpretations. Perhaps the most striking example in Flagg's novel and in the film adaptation is the reading of Idgie's tomboyism as a symbol of her queerness. The tomboy is a curious cultural figure that, depending on how, when, and where it is deployed, can be a harmless symbol of youthful vigor and adventure or a worrisome precursor to adult homosexuality and cross-gender identification. In the late nineteenth century, tomboyism was considered an antidote to Victorian female frailty, a way of preparing girls for the rigors of childbearing in adulthood.

Charlotte Perkins Gilman championed tomboyism in her 1898 treatise, *Women and Economics:* "The most normal girl is the 'tom-boy'—whose numbers increase among us in these wiser days,—a healthy young creature who is human through and through; not feminine till it is time to be."[32] Gilman points to a crucial assumption about tomboyism, namely, that it reaches its natural conclusion at the onset of adolescence, when any traces of masculinity are superseded by conventional, feminine characteristics that include the desire to be a mother. Furthermore, the tomboy is, according to Gilman's reading, an asexual or perhaps presexual being whose masculinity is benign because it is not configured within the "adult imperatives of binary gender" that conflate adherence to traditional roles with heterosexuality.[33] In Gilman's imagining, the tomboy is playfully and appropriately experimenting with cross-gender behaviors before succumbing to inevitable adult femininity.

However, Gilman does not address what happens to the tomboy who does not grow out of her masculinity and does not consider the possibility that tomboyism might in fact be a precursor to a transgender or butch identity later in life. Lee Zevy critiques the tendency to view childhood as a presexual state, claiming that such a tendency "fails to acknowledge the developmental continuum of lesbian sexuality."[34] Autobiographical essays by lesbian, transmasculine, and transgender adults certainly shore up Zevy's theory that queer sexual development begins in childhood and that tomboyism in young girls can morph into adult masculinity. Sara Cytron describes how she "anxiously submerged the feminine" as a young tomboy, while Judith Halberstam recalls asking for boxing gloves for her thirteenth birthday, believing "that these accoutrements of masculine competitions signified for me a way to keep adult womanhood at bay."[35] As a child, Idgie is the archetypal tomboy but does not face a similar mandate to undergo a feminine transformation upon reaching puberty, and thus she remains in a suspended state of youthful, roguish masculinity throughout her adult life.

The young Idgie possesses many traits typically associated with tomboyism, including "a proclivity for outdoor play (especially athletics), a feisty independent spirit, and a tendency to don masculine clothing and adopt a boyish nickname."[36] Ninny recalls a special occasion for which Idgie—named Imogen at birth—was made to wear "a brand new white organdy dress." Taking issue with this forced feminization, Idgie "stood up and announced . . . 'I'm never gonna wear another dress as long as I live!'" and then "marched upstairs and put on a pair of [her brother's] old pants and a shirt."[37] In an effort to prevent similar disruption at the wedding of Idgie's older sister, Momma Threadgoode lets Idgie wear a green velvet suit to the ceremony. Ninny's description of the young Idgie highlights the child's most masculine characteristics: "Seems like Idgie was always in overalls and barefooted. It's a good thing, too. She would have ruined any nice dresses, going up and down trees like she did, and she was always going hunting or fishing with Buddy and her brothers. Buddy said that she could shoot as good as any of the boys. She was a pretty little thing, except after Buddy got her hair all bobbed off, you'd swear she was a little boy."[38]

In adolescence, when Idgie is expected to submit to the social pressures of heterosexuality and gender conformity, she shows no interest in dating men and persists with a masculine gender expression that often causes others to forget or misread the fact that she was assigned female at birth. After Idgie causes a scene in a barbershop, where she threatens to kill Frank for beating Ruth, the barber reads her as male, saying to the other patrons, "That boy must be crazy."[39] Later, when Idgie performs in drag with a group of male friends as part of a fundraiser for the local school's sports teams, Dot Weems announces in her weekly newsletter that their skit will feature a "womanless wedding,"[40] evidently reading Idgie as just one of the boys. Halberstam finds that tomboyism can be "encouraged to the extent that it remains comfortably linked to a stable sense of a girl identity,"[41] but in the fantasy world of Ninny's flashbacks, Idgie's womanhood is consistently negated without penalty.

Idgie's masculinity is perhaps most salient when she becomes a parent to Stump, taking on a paternal role rather than becoming an adoptive mother figure. When Stump is born, Idgie's mother exclaims, "Oh look, Idgie, he's got your hair!"[42] effectively erasing Stump's biological father and inserting Idgie into the role. Moreover, her joke that Stump bears a physical resemblance to Idgie implies that Ruth and Idgie had the capability to conceive him together naturally, which hints not only that the two have a sexual relationship but that Idgie is somehow masculine enough to overcome the anatomy and physiology with which she was born. Even Poppa Threadgoode acknowledges Idgie's masculinity when he perpetuates the idea that she is Stump's natural father. Ninny recalls that Poppa "sat Idgie down and told her that now that she was going to be responsible for Ruth and a baby, she'd better figure out what she wanted to do, and gave her five hundred dollars to start a business with,"[43] demanding that she fulfill responsibilities typically attributed to husbands and fathers. As Stump grows up, Idgie sees him through several masculine rites of passage, coaching him in football, leading his Cub Scout troop, and even giving him advice about dating and sex.

Idgie thus complicates both traditional narratives of tomboyism, which presume that the tomboy will grow into a feminine and heterosexual adult woman, and queer readings, which suggest that tomboyism is a precursor to butchness, lesbianism, or transgender identity in adulthood. In either case,

Idgie was assigned female at birth but is masculine presenting and known to engage in romantic and sexual relationships with women, rendering her undeniably queer in gender and sexuality.

In contrast, Ruth is almost excessively feminine, with "light auburn hair and brown eyes with long lashes, and was so sweet and soft-spoken that people just fell in love with her on first sight."[44] In effect, the romantic and demure Ruth plays the part of the southern belle to Idgie's roguish young suitor, initially rebuffing Idgie before surrendering to her charms. Ruth thus queers the image of the belle by entering into a same-sex relationship while still possessing the features that make the belle recognizable, a maneuver the film adaptation succeeds in replicating.

The film of Flagg's novel, *Fried Green Tomatoes,* remains quite faithful in its portrayal of Idgie and Ruth. Ruth is first seen at a party at the Threadgoode house dressed in a pale pink gown and a bonnet with flowers on it. Her strong southern drawl further marks her out as an archetypal belle, but crucially, Ruth is a belle divested of the compulsory heterosexuality that has characterized many of her real-life and fictional counterparts. The novel and the film perform important critical work on this famously southern image by suggesting new possibilities for the belle, one being that she possesses lesbian potentiality when read as a femme character in relation to Idgie's butchness.

The young Idgie in the film is seen climbing trees, throwing her frilly dress on the floor, and disrupting every family occasion with practical jokes and mischief. Even when Idgie's mother dresses Idgie in a frilly white frock and oversized hair ribbons, the tomboy's scraped knees, cheeky smile, and unkempt hair undermine her mother's attempts to force femininity upon her.

In adulthood, Idgie, played by Mary Stuart Masterson, manages to retain the appearance and demeanor of the youthful tomboy, occasionally affecting a theatrical but undeniable hypermasculinity. When Stump is born, it is Idgie who proudly announces to their friends and family waiting in the parlor, "It's a boy!," before exclaiming, "Goddamnit to hell sonofabitch, she did it!" Idgie then promptly initiates the paternal ritual of wetting the baby's head and smoking a cigar. When she performs in drag as part of the town follies, Idgie easily slips into a confident performance of excessive masculinity by slicking her hair back, donning a suit, and adopting a swagger. The rest of the time, she keeps her playfulness and her juvenile sense of humor by playing pranks on the residents of Whistle Stop, and she persists with her adventuresome ways, most notably by climbing out of her bedroom window to sneak out on a date with Ruth, train hopping in the middle of the night to steal food for the poor, and venturing across the railroad tracks to visit her friends in the black enclave of Troutville. Idgie bears a striking resemblance to another famous icon of southern fiction, appearing as a kind of Huck Finn character, with her pants rolled up, feet bare, face muddy, and a fishing pole slung over her shoulder. She spends much of her free time by the river or roaming around outdoors, teaching herself how to find food in the wild and shunning the confinement of the domestic sphere.

Jan Whitt suggests that in preventing Idgie's tomboyism from growing into an explicitly adult female masculinity, the film actually affords some viewers an opportunity to read Idgie's queerness as nonthreatening, even nonexistent. She notes that "even though Idgie is a lesbian and chooses to wear pants, suspenders, ties, and vests, it is still possible for members of the audience to refer to Idgie as a 'tomboy' and avoid dealing with her lesbianism entirely."[45] Keeping Idgie as a tomboy makes it less problematic that she has not yet succumbed to adult femininity, the operative word being *yet*. As long as Idgie's masculinity remains in a state of suspended adolescence that permits and even encourages gender experimentation, there is always a possibility that she will grow out of it eventually and assume a more feminine identity.

But the softening of Idgie's masculinity has drawn criticism from viewers who had hoped to see a film that was as unambiguously queer as the novel from which it was adapted. *Fried Green Tomatoes* has divided critics on the subject of queer visibility. In one review, a critic concedes that "of course some compromises were made in bringing *Fried Green Tomatoes* to the screen," presumably hinting at the constraints that filmmakers, studios, and investors place on queer content in a Hollywood film that they hope will be commercially successful. The critic advises, "For those of you expecting romantic themes to be played out, prepare yourself for some heavily restricted voyeurism."[46] The film critic Rita Kempley calls the film "a parable of platonic devotion," while Jennifer Church writes that "the most common response in the mainstream audience . . . was that [Ruth and Idgie] had a deep emotional tie."[47] Even Fannie Flagg, herself an out lesbian, downplayed claims that the film is about a queer relationship, despite the claim by her ex-girlfriend, the renowned lesbian author Rita Mae Brown, that Idgie was based on Flagg's lesbian aunt.[48] According to Flagg, the story "is about love and friendship. The sexuality is unimportant. . . . We are looking at them from 1991. [The 1930s] were a totally different time period. There were very warm friendships be-

tween women."[49] Even though Flagg and others participated in a critical un-
queering of the film, *Fried Green Tomatoes* won the Gay and Lesbian Alliance
Against Defamation Award for Outstanding Depiction of Lesbians in Film in
1992.[50] Other critics have been similarly generous, highlighting the ways that
queerness does appear in recognizable forms in the film. Naomi Rockler, for
example, suggests that the film relies on "strategic ambiguity" to represent
Ruth and Idgie's relationship, showing interactions that can be interpreted as
constituting a lesbian love story or a platonic buddy movie, depending on the
position, investment, and intent of the viewer.[51]

The screenplay undeniably dilutes some of the novel's more explicit queer
content, in particular in the dialogue, but does not dispose of it altogether,
making it difficult to reduce the film to just another buddy movie. In the novel,
Flagg writes that Ruth and Idgie's displays of affection were so obvious that
"even Sipsey razzed [Idgie]," saying, "That ol' love bug done bit Idgie."[52] Flagg
portrays Ruth as being similarly enamored, writing that "she had no idea why
she wanted to be with Idgie more than anybody else on this earth, but she
did."[53] In the film, there is no talk of crushes or "be[ing] with" someone, but
Ruth's desire for Idgie is palpable when she tells Idgie, "All the guys must be
wild about you," and then nervously asks, "Got a fella yet?" Later, once the two
women have started a business and family together, Idgie reassures Ruth that
her wandering days are over: "I'm as settled as I ever hope to be." Throughout
the film, their conversations are supplemented with intense, longing gazes and
affectionate, often sensual caresses and embraces that, along with the spoken
declarations of love and commitment, make it easy to understand why GLAAD
recognized the film for its depiction of "lesbians."

I too read Ruth and Idgie as a queer couple and use their relationship to
examine how the interplay of queer aesthetic and narrative cues with southern
iconography produces a queer romance that contributes to the cultural imagination of the region. Placing the belle in a queer context by having her leave
her husband to establish a home and family with a woman with whom she
enjoys a visibly romantic relationship is just one example of how *Fried Green
Tomatoes* manipulates images that are fundamental to dominant narratives
about the South. The film deploys many other signifiers of southern culture to
ground this queer love story firmly in the region, from the Threadgoodes' gran-
diose plantation-esque home to the swampy, bluesy locale of the speakeasy that
Idgie frequents. The repetitive shots of southern geographical icons—especially
the verdant rural landscapes and Victorian architecture—and the sweeping

orchestral score align *Fried Green Tomatoes* with other southern nostalgia films of the late twentieth century, such as *Driving Miss Daisy, Steel Magnolias,* and *Forrest Gump,* while the occasional blues and gospel refrains are a nod to the African American musical roots of the region. Moreover, these southern signifiers are often used to facilitate the development of queer characters and stories. For example, the blues provides a seductive soundtrack to Ruth and Idgie's most intimate scenes, the Baptist church attempts to reform Idgie's rebellious, prankster ways (although not her queerness), and the undeveloped rural landscape encourages Idgie to express her adventurous tomboy spirit.

As in the novel, the tantalizing images of food invoke sentimental memories of the South in a bygone era. There are lingering camera shots of cherry pie, green tomatoes frying in the skillet, and pork simmering in the barbecue pit. But food in the film is also used to convey sensuality and to facilitate the closest thing to a sex scene that a Hollywood film about a queer couple in the 1930s Deep South is likely to show. The director, Jon Avnet, claims that in his vision for the film, "the food fight would be an improvisational scene that would really allow the audience to see two people making love,"[54] and it is this scene that has attracted the most attention from critics performing queer readings of the film.

The scene begins with close-ups of bowls containing plump, juicy berries and smooth, creamy chocolate frosting. A sultry blues number plays in the background. Ruth and Idgie are cooking in the café, Idgie attempting to make fried green tomatoes, which Ruth deems "terrible." Idgie, feeling slighted by the remark, exacts revenge by throwing water into Ruth's face. When Ruth asks, "What did you go and do that for?," Idgie replies flirtatiously, "I just thought you needed a little coolin' off." From there, a food fight breaks out, with the shrieking and giggling women smearing berries and chocolate onto each other's faces and chests. As the two women grapple and wrestle each other to the ground, their skin flushed and moistened with sweat, they transform playful teasing between friends into a deeply sensual display of erotic desire.

Grady Kilgore, the town sheriff and a longtime admirer of Idgie's, is sufficiently motivated by both outrage and jealousy to threaten the women with arrest for disorderly conduct. Grady therefore functions as a representative of two interlocking systems of law that attempt to suppress queerness by regulating what kinds of gender and sexuality are permissible. As sheriff, he represents the legal-juridical system that interprets Ruth and Idgie's behavior as deviant and endows him with the authority to intervene and put a stop to it. Grady also symbolizes a system of heteropatriarchal law that works to destroy affective and erotic bonds between women as a means of upholding the power and authority of the heterosexual male and regulating the social order over which he presides. Therefore, Grady's intervention in Ruth and Idgie's food fight seeks to restore order, not only by enforcing calm and decent public conduct but also by turning the women's attentions away from each other and redirecting them toward a proper (male) object.

Yet, in the queer-affirming, nostalgic utopia of Whistle Stop, Grady is comically ineffective in his efforts to enforce the laws. When he confronts the women about their conduct, they respond by taking a bowl of chocolate frosting and smearing it over his face and shirt while they continue to laugh hysterically. Similarly, the detective who comes from Valdosta to investigate Frank's disappearance becomes the subject of Idgie's derision. Idgie gets the better of him for five years, teasing him for taking so long to catch Frank's killer and tricking him into eating Frank, whose body was disposed of in the café's barbecue pit. Even though the detective confidently claims that "you can't beat the law" and eventually arrests Idgie and Big George for Frank's murder, Idgie and her allies manage to outsmart the system at every turn. Because of Idgie's quick-witted responses in court, which make a mockery of the prosecutor's interrogation tactics, and the testimony of Reverend Scroggins, who provides a false alibi for her and George, the legal-juridical system fails to break up their queer kinship system. In fact, it is in court that Ruth and Idgie's love is most publicly cemented, with Ruth's declaration that she left Frank for Idgie because "she's the best friend I ever had . . . and I love her." With those words, Ruth defiantly refutes the alleged authority of heteropatriarchal law and the legal-juridical system by suggesting that her relationship with Idgie is invested with more meaning and value than her legal union with Frank.

As in the novel, the Valdosta detectives and court officials are interlopers who try to impose their views on morality and justice on a small town that they deem immoral and lawless. They constitute oppressive and menacing forces that threaten to throw the harmonious Whistle Stop community into turmoil, but they are ultimately unsuccessful because the Whistle Stop residents' collective investment in upholding the town's unique ethos makes their community impervious to interference from outsiders. Even those in the town who, by definition, should be upholding and enforcing externally imposed laws and social standards prioritize their devotion to their community over the demands of their jobs: Grady advises Idgie to flee before he can arrest her for Frank's murder, and he even enjoys socializing with other residents in the drinking and gambling den at the river, while Reverend Scroggins lies in court to save Idgie and Big George from execution. Whistle Stop adheres to its own code of conduct, which favors intracommunity cooperation, mutual respect, unconditional acceptance, and vigilante justice over compliance with a biased and corrupt legal system and social order.

The insular and unified community is an integral part of the imagined past that Flagg and Avnet have created. The novel and the film each produce a fantastical space so that queer-affirming counternarratives can develop without having to confront or negotiate the cultural and political realities of the time and place in which they were set. The *Fried Green Tomatoes* texts situate representations of female masculinity, desire between women, and alternative family configurations at the center of a story about life in the rural South before the advent of a publicly visible and accepted queer community. In doing so, these texts shift the discourse of queer southern history away from reductive and misleading binary models and instead offer nuanced interdependent narratives that reveal the complexity of how queer behaviors, cultures, and relationships might have been developed and practiced.

NOTES

1. Neil Miller, *Out of the Past: Gay and Lesbian History from 1869 to the Present* (New York: Alyson, 2006), 310; Marcia Gallo, *Different Daughters: A History of the Daughters of Bilitis and the Rise of the Lesbian Rights Movement* (Emeryville, CA: Seal, 2007).

2. Joanne Myers, *Historical Dictionary of the Lesbian and Gay Liberation Movement* (Lanham, MD: Scarecrow, 2013), 176.

3. *Before Stonewall: The Making of a Gay and Lesbian Community*, dir. Greta Schiller and Robert Rosenberg (First Run Features, 1985), DVD; *After Stonewall*, dir. John Scagliotti (First Run Features, 2010), DVD; *Stonewall Uprising*, dir. Kate Davis and David Heilbroner (First Run Features, 2011), DVD; Martin Duberman, *Stonewall* (New York: Plume, 1994); David Carter, *Stonewall: The Riots that Sparked the Gay Revolution* (New York: St. Martin's Griffin, 2010).

4. Mary Gray, *Out in the Country: Youth, Media, and Queer Visibility in Rural America* (New York: New York University Press, 2009), 4.

5. Madeline Davis and Elizabeth Kennedy, *Boots of Leather, Slippers of Gold: The History of a Lesbian Community* (New York: Penguin Books, 1993); Gayle Rubin, "The Catacombs: A Temple of the Butthole," in *Leatherfolk: Radical Sex, People, Politics, and Practice*, ed. Mark Thompson (Boston: Alyson, 1991), 119–41; Marc Stein, *City of Sisterly and Brotherly Loves: Lesbian and Gay Philadelphia, 1945–1972* (Philadelphia: Temple University Press, 2004).

6. Kath Weston, "Get Thee to a Big City: Sexual Imaginary and the Great Gay Migration," *GLQ: Gay and Lesbian Quarterly* 2 (1995): 253–77.

7. Judith Halberstam, *In a Queer Time and Place: Transgender Bodies, Subcultural Lives* (New York: New York University Press, 2005), 36.

8. Frank Kameny, foreword to *Rebels, Rubyfruit, and Rhinestones: Queering Space in the Stonewall South*, ed. James T. Sears (New Brunswick, NJ: Rutgers University Press, 2001), ix–xii.

9. James T. Sears, *Lonely Hunters: An Oral History of Lesbian and Gay Southern Life, 1948–1968* (Boulder, CO: Westview, 1997), 1.

10. John Howard, *Men Like That: A Southern Queer History* (Chicago: University of Chicago Press, 1999), 14.

11. Patti Duncan, "Claiming Space in the South: A Conversation among Members of Asian/Pacific Islander Lesbian, Bisexual, Transgendered Network of Atlanta," in *Out in the South,* ed. Carlos Dews and Carolyn Leste Law (Philadelphia: Temple University Press, 2001), 26–55; E. Patrick Johnson, *Sweet Tea: Black Gay Men of the South, An Oral History* (Chapel Hill: University of North Carolina Press, 2008); James T. Sears, "Race, Class, Gender, and Sexuality in Pre-Stonewall Charleston: Perspectives on the Gordon Langley Hall Affair," in *Carryin' On in the Lesbian and Gay South,* ed. John Howard (New York: New York University Press, 1997), 164–202.

12. *Fried Green Tomatoes,* dir. Jon Avnet (Universal Pictures, 1991), DVD.

13. Howard, *Men Like That,* 13.

14. Louis Kyriakoudes, "Southern Black Rural-Urban Migration in the Era of the Great Migration: Nashville and Middle Tennessee, 1890–1930," *Agricultural History* 72, no. 2 (Spring 1998): 342.

15. Fannie Flagg, *Fried Green Tomatoes at the Whistle Stop Café* (London: Vintage, 1992), 117.

16. Ibid., 118.

17. Ibid., 120.

18. Shameem Kabir, *Daughters of Desire: Lesbian Representations in Film* (London: Cassell, 1998), 128.

19. Jennifer Ross Church, "The Balancing Act of *Fried Green Tomatoes,*" in *Vision/Revision: Adapting Contemporary American Fiction by Women to Film,* ed. Barbara Tepa Lupack (Bowling Green, IN: Bowling Green State University Popular Press, 1996), 193.

20. Ibid.

21. Peter Applebome, *Dixie Rising: How the South is Shaping American Values, Politics, and Culture* (Orlando, FL: Mariner Books, 1996), 10.

22. Flagg, *Fried Green Tomatoes at the Whistle Stop Café,* 250.

23. Ibid., 248.

24. Ibid., 48.

25. Ibid., 302.

26. Ibid., 80.

27. Ibid., 325.

28. Pam Cook, *Screening the Past: Memory and Nostalgia in Cinema* (New York: Taylor & Francis, 2005), 2.

29. Ibid., 3.

30. Flagg, *Fried Green Tomatoes at the Whistle Stop Café,* 31.

31. Deborah Barker, "The Southern-Fried Chick Flick: Postfeminism Goes to the Movies," in *Chick Flicks: Contemporary Women at the Movies,* ed. Suzanne Ferriss and Mallory Young (New York: Routledge, 2008), 102.

32. Charlotte Perkins Gilman, *Women and Economics: A Study of the Economic Relation between Men and Women as a Factor in Social Evolution* (Berkeley: University of California Press, 1998), 56.

33. Judith Halberstam, "Oh Bondage Up Yours! Female Masculinity and the Tomboy," in *Sissies and Tomboys: Gender Nonconformity and Homosexual Childhood,* ed. Matthew Rottnek (New York: New York University Press, 1999), 179.

34. Lee Zevy, "Sexing the Tomboy," in ibid., 181.

35. Sara Cytron, "Butch in a Tutu," in ibid., 210; Judith Halberstam, *Female Masculinity* (Durham, NC: Duke University Press, 1998), 267.

36. Michelle Ann Abate, *Tomboys: A Literary and Cultural History* (Philadelphia: Temple University Press, 2008), xvi.

37. Flagg, *Fried Green Tomatoes at the Whistle Stop Café,* 31.

38. Ibid., 34.

39. Ibid., 189.

40. Ibid., 278.

41. Halberstam, *Female Masculinity,* 6.

42. Flagg, *Fried Green Tomatoes at the Whistle Stop Café,* 192.

43. Ibid., 193.

44. Ibid., 80.

45. Jan Whitt, "What Happened to Celie and Idgie? 'Apparitional Lesbians' in American Film," *Studies in Popular Culture* 27, no. 3 (April 2005): 50.

46. Maria Vetrano, "Chopped Tomatoes," *Gay Community News,* 23 February 1992, 10.

47. Rita Kempley, "Fried Green Tomatoes," *Washington Post,* 10 January 1992, www.washingtonpost.com/wp-srv/style/longterm/movies/videos/friedgreentomatoespg13kempley_a0a28a.htm; Church, "Balancing Act of *Fried Green Tomatoes,*" 193.

48. Rita Mae Brown, *Rita Will: Memoir of a Literary Rabble-Rouser* (New York: Bantam Books, 2009), 325.

49. Quoted in Jeff Berglund, "'The Secret's in the Sauce': Dismembering Normativity in *Fried Green Tomatoes,*" *Camera Obscura* 14, no. 342 (1999): 149.

50. Kelli Pryor and Sharon Isaak, "Women in Love," *Entertainment Weekly,* 28 February 1992, www.ew.com/article/1992/02/28/women-love.

51. Naomi Rockler, "A Wall on the Lesbian Continuum: Polysemy and *Fried Green Tomatoes,*" *Women's Studies in Communication* 24, no. 1 (Spring 2001): 91.

52. Flagg, *Fried Green Tomatoes at the Whistle Stop Café,* 82.

53. Ibid., 89.

54. *Fried Green Tomatoes: The Moments of Discovery,* dir. J. M. Kenny (Universal Pictures, 1991), DVD.

9

"I Wish I Had a Daddy Good as You"

Fay *and the Rough Sex of Larry Brown*

TRENT BROWN

Larry Brown's novel *Fay* (2000) represented something of a departure for the Mississippi writer best known for his gritty portrayals of contemporary rural white southern men who drink Budweisers while cruising dirt roads in their pickups, a gun under the seat or in the gun rack, all the while confronting challenges that demand they man up and "face the music," as one of Brown's early short stories puts it.[1] Most obviously, this novel differs from nearly all of Brown's earlier work, including the prequel, *Joe* (1991), in that its protagonist is female. Brown explained that *Fay* began with his desire to know what happened to Fay Jones after she literally walked out of *Joe* in the middle of the novel. "It was around 1984 or '85," wrote Brown, "that I started writing a long novel about a family of migrant workers who had found themselves in Mississippi. . . . I published that book in 1991, and never did cease wondering what happened to [Fay]. . . . This is her story."[2] However, this decision to structure the novel around a woman hardly meant that Brown had abandoned the basic concerns or altered the moral universe of his earlier masculinist fiction. Indeed, some readers of Brown's fiction have seen more than realistic consistency across the rough South of Larry Brown. "The author's scrupulous refusal to judge his whores, batterers, and garden-variety losers," wrote one reviewer of *Fay*, "suggests not merely a propensity but a philosophy."[3]

Whether propensity or philosophy, the narrative voice and plot of *Fay*, as in much of Brown's other fiction, are informed by an intense focus upon physicality, violence, and sex. In the novel *Fay*, the body of the main character herself, Fay Jones, is a text upon which social, cultural, and other conflicts and story lines are written. The use of the female body—particularly a sexualized body—as a signifying text in this novel and in Brown's other work is relatively unexamined, in part because the bodies with which he usually worked were male and the action upon them was violence, whether actual physical violence from another character or violence from a constant use of alcohol, tobacco, and other drugs.[4] Thus, while critics are right in noting the physical and emotional harshness of the rough South of Larry Brown, this essay focuses upon the female body as a locus of that violence, sexual or otherwise.[5]

Further, this essay seeks to demonstrate that the narrative voice, and not merely the action of the plot, works that violence upon Fay. It is not my purpose here to insist that the sexual content of the novel is outré or inappropriate or offensive. Nor do I assert that the novel operates in destructive ways upon readers or southern women. Such an argument would be difficult indeed to support. What is possible, however, is to suggest that the masculinist world of Larry Brown here is built by action upon women's bodies—not only Fay's but those of other women in the novel, both primary and minor characters, as well—and that the action is performed both by the narrator and by his male characters. The women are observed, catalogued, penetrated, impregnated, shot, struck, and killed. Such a litany constitutes not merely realism of a naive documentary sort but an esthetic that asserts the body as an establishing, fundamental text. Indeed, the violated body might be said to define Larry Brown's South in the way that the past might be said to define Faulkner's work; or grace, O'Connor's; or the magical and lyrical, Lewis Nordan's, to take only a few examples of southern writers who work, especially the latter two, with and upon white characters.

Brown's published work deals almost exclusively with the working-class white South, and Brown is attentive to the ways in which social class informs and drives his characters.[6] How, specifically, does social class shape the world of Fay Jones? When the 17-year-old beauty abandons her dirt-poor family and her abusive father, she does not neatly climb from or within Brown's male-dominated world of physical violence, heavy drinking, and tarnished heroism. Her movement, or progress, through the novel is not very concerned with social-class mobility, despite her outsider origins and consequent ignorance of much of the world into which she subsequently moves. Wherever she goes, geographically or economically, masculinity and the male gaze in the novel, whether of other characters or of the narrator, follow her. Thus, the positions of the male observer and the male actor operate upon Fay as fundamentally as anything else in the novel. So despite the suggestion of middle-class respectability or at least material comfort for Fay that is dangled before the reader early in the novel, Brown never establishes the story as one in which Fay seems poised to escape from one sort of universe into another, whether moral or material. Fay's movement is launched by her desire to learn how best to escape the violence and potential degradation with which her life began. Over the course of this novel, that means learning to survive the men who people Brown's fiction and who represent his greatest interest, which is reconciling masculinity and morality, distinguishing right action from base action (largely among men) in a world that asks us to understand and accept as facts of life a world inhabited by law breakers, adulterers, and drunks.

Thus, the female protagonist in this novel seems potentially to allow a critique of a fictional world and novelistic vision that are masculinist in their representations of violence and sexuality. There is no reason, of course, to believe that Larry Brown wrote with such a critique in mind. Nevertheless, the novel's deliberate choice to tell Fay's story, defined and operated upon within this masculinist world, invites the reader to consider Fay throughout against the ethos that so strongly informs the novel. However, this critique is not stable or ultimately a compelling argument for how best to view the novel within the body of Brown's fiction, because of Brown's handling of the character Fay. For Fay herself is not a fully realized or developed character. Is she an innocent against whom we are to read the world in which she moves? Innocent and ignorant she largely is, but not in ways that operate critically. That is, Fay's innocence does not operate as a critique of the world in which she moves, as in Henry James or Dostoevsky.

While Brown clearly works in the realist and naturalist tradition, he has difficulty here creating a believable female perspective. Despite the realist mode, Brown is so obviously invested here (as in his earlier fiction) in painting a sympathetic portrait of the masculinist working-class white South that any attempt to read the novel as an internal critique of that masculinity is complicated, because the female protagonist is working against the larger current of the fiction, which seems deeply wary of women as rational actors or moral agents. Realism thus wars here with a predisposition on the narrator's part to stack the deck in favor of his men. One character cannot change fate, as Thomas Hardy's characters ultimately learn. Here, Fay cannot swim against the tide of Brown's larger narrative voice. This narrative voice, which so resembles the working-class white male characters of Brown's other texts, trades in misogynistic stereotypes, or perhaps better put, projects a voice that establishes women's bodies as the material from which the plots of novels, as well as sexual gratification or masculinist curiosity, are built.[7]

Creating convincing fictional innocents is tricky enough, particularly when their innocence is sexually charged, as is Fay's. These days, we are used to sexual precociousness. But the narrator in *Fay* seems both pruriently fascinated and repelled by the physicality of women's bodies. Indeed, the novel's treatment of women as vessels and objects often seems drawn from what used to be called locker-room stories, particularly those involving a female character's bodily functions and consequent humiliation, compounded here by having the woman herself tell the story. After Fay sips an unfamiliar soft drink, "two spurts of it shot out of her nose." In an anecdote that seems hardly relevant to the situation, the woman who gave her the drink comforts her: "I had a date with this boy one time and we'd been swimming, went in this beer joint to get some ribs and I sat down on the chair and farted in my wet swimming suit and you could hear it all over the room." She adds, "Shit happens" (51). Continuing to establish this vision of women as creatures from whom and into which fluids and substances spurt, spew, or flow, the narrator describes Fay in the act of urination: "[Fay] saw the commode and stepped inside and shut the door, raised her skirt and lowered her panties to her knees and sat down. She closed her eyes and breathed a long sigh of relief and leaned forward until she was through.... She dabbed at herself with some tissue she pulled off the roll and got up and fixed her clothes and flushed the commode" (23). Presumably, the men in the novel urinate too, but the narrator is not interested in watching them do it. We know that they have genitals, but the narrator never seems interested in looking at them, as he does at Fay's, "thinly pelted" as they are (117). Thus, the difficulty in establishing sympathy with Fay as a fully realized character stems largely from the narrator's fascination with and unease around women's bodies.

In the novel's introduction to the character Fay, we first encounter the problems that Brown will face throughout the novel in handling a female character at such length. These problems initially manifest themselves as tonal ambivalences. "She came down out of the hills that were growing black with night" (9), writes Brown, in a passage that manages to evoke both the noir fiction of Raymond Chandler, for instance, and several of Faulkner's women, such as the traveling innocent Lena Grove. But what precisely is Fay, and what is the nature of the world in which she moves? Early on, Brown wishes to establish both Fay's innate morality and her unconsciousness seductiveness. At times Fay seems a childish primitive with essentially good longings. Seventeen years old, in interior monologues she expresses a desire for domestic stability defined in terms of material consumption. Walking along a road at night, Fay looks into a lighted window, observing a family at the dinner table. In their yard she sees bicycles and a swing set, and she notes that the table is full of food (14). Such a scene is for Fay the dream of middle-class stability, which she seems to think she wants through the first half of the novel. She compares this scene of family and stability to one she observed on a television screen viewed through a store window in Florida, an image that reinforces both the fictiveness of such dreams of domesticity and their tendency to hang out of reach. But that longing for domesticity does not seem to be the novel's main concern for Fay and has dissipated well before the novel's end.

So how are we invited to view Fay's story, if not as a frustrated quest for order and stability? In the end, Fay's story becomes one of survival in a world whose operation we are meant to view as rough but realistic. Because of Brown's realistic mode of representation throughout the novel, however, the reader almost inevitably weighs the narrative in terms of plausibility. Often that plausibility simply does not work. For instance, almost unbelievably for a character raised in the South, Fay fails to recognize that a building she enters seeking food and water is a church, believing it to be a dwelling house, as older Mississippians still call it. Recognizing representations of Jesus and the Cross, Fay realizes where she is: "It's a church for rich folks" (12). After helping herself to chicken and potatoes from the church kitchen, Fay leaves one of her two dollars as payment, or as an offering. Why place Fay in a church and show that she would not steal food even when hungry? For all his reputation as a writer of grit(ty) realism, Brown maintained that it was a writer's task to give his characters "the moral feelings they're supposed to have."[8] Are we truly asked to consider Fay's actions as examples of right or wrong conduct? Are we to judge Fay on her responses in terms of "moral feelings" she is supposed to have, as Brown put it? The narrator's handling of Fay, particularly of her body, does not allow the reader to do so. For Fay and the other female characters in the novel simply are not represented as capable of moral choice.[9]

So what accounts for Fay's inability to stand as a moral agent whose actions we are to weigh, again to take Brown's own estimation of his task? Fay's morality, or at least her ethical sense, which Brown wishes to establish, seems to stand in an uneasy tension with her sexuality, which he most assuredly does establish. Why, one might ask, should an ethical sense and a woman's sexuality necessarily exist in such a tension? The answer might be as simple as that, as the narrator insists, there is something fundamentally dirty or shameful about women's bodies, so that the achievement of a real ethical and moral position is a challenge that really faces only men. Ethical or moral, or not, Fay is initially modest, or at least wary, holding her knees together when riding in the back of a truck or when men touch her. She is sexually inexperienced, her virginity intact despite the malign intent of her father. She is aware enough to know that men are attracted to her and, moreover, what they want from her: "People were always looking at her, men, boys like this" (18). At 17, then, she is no sexual naif, at least when defined as an awareness that men want to do things to her body. There is certainly nothing problematic or unrealistic about a novel's representing a sexually active or aware 17-year-old; we are not Victorians, at least not in this sense. What is problematic is the relation of the narrator to the character. The narrator's eye lingers upon her, noting her physicality in ways that focus upon her sexuality: her long legs, her puckered nipples, her "titties" themselves, as the third-person narrator, not one of the characters, calls them. Placed against Fay's childish desire to ride a bicycle, this representation begins to look Lolita-like. But Fay cannot be a convincing Lolita; she is at the same time too experienced and too innocent, and of course too old. Perhaps most important, she never self-consciously deploys her sexuality in a way that would mark her as a Lolita-like, let alone a femme fatale, character.

Brown had worked before with female characters, in both his fiction and his nonfiction. Yet in only one short story, "Kubuku Rides (This is It)," in his first collection, *Facing the Music* (1988), does he allow a female character to so dominate the perspective. That character, Angel, well realized and convincing, is an African American alcoholic. Her story is crisp and harrowing. But Brown did not repeat this experiment, particularly of crossing both gender and racial lines; Fay was his first experiment with a female protagonist, then, in more than twelve years. Brown preferred to work with a third-person narrator, as he does in *Fay* and in this short story. In the earlier story, all the characters, as well as the third-person narrator, speak in Brown's representation of rural Mississippi black dialect ("Angel hear the back door slam. It Alan in from work" [11]). But literary realism has not worn well as an excuse for white writers using black dialect, particularly one in which the third-person narrator speaks in dialect. In later works, Brown basically steered entirely clear of black characters. Brown did not comment widely on his own fiction, so we do not know why he chose to avoid women as main characters or as narrative voices, though perhaps the answer is as simple as Brown's desire to work with material and a voice with which he was familiar, and which consequently is clearly very often his own voice.[10]

The narrative voice in *Fay* can be devastatingly cutting to unsympathetic women and seems to suggest that women neglect the gendered demands of home and family at their peril. Early in the novel, for instance, Fay accepts a ride with three young men and goes to a trailer owned by one of them. Linda, the wife of one of the three, is a slovenly housekeeper and a bad mother. While lighting a cigarette, she drops her baby, whose head makes "an ugly sound" when it strikes the ground. Also revealing as a marker of Linda's unsympathetic nature is use of the racial epithet *nigger*. "I ain't got nothing against a nigger if he'll act right," she allows (26). While it may seem unremarkable that a truly drawn picture of rural Mississippi life would include racial slurs, the fact is that in Brown's six books prior to *Fay* the word *nigger* almost never occurs. One exception is the prequel to *Fay—Joe—*in which the word is used by Fay's father, one of the most unambiguously evil characters in Larry Brown's world; and like many southern writers, Brown readily recognizes that evil does exist. Fay's father has menaced her sexually, prostituted her sister, terrorized her mother, stolen from and physically abused the family, and even traded a baby for an automobile. So Brown appears to reserve the use of the word *nigger* for characters he wishes to mark as particularly degraded—this woman, for instance. Linda leaves her baby with Fay and takes her bad mothering and "wide ass," as the narrator puts it, away, to engage in a three-way sex scene that seems a particularly broad example of Brown's wish to mark Linda as a bad woman. Good mothers watch their children, the novel suggests. Bad ones pursue their vices and pleasures. Men do too, of course, but the punishment of the children in this novel is a blame clearly laid at the feet of bad mothers.

That judgmental or punitive attitude toward women characters, somewhat surprising in a novel that justifies itself in terms of a naturalistic aesthetic, seemed contagious. Perhaps following the narrator's lead, the initial reviewers of *Fay* occasionally made coarse statements about Fay, with one reviewer describing her as "a busty piece of Southern poon."[11] While this may seem a matter for which Brown ought not to be held responsible, reviews of *Fay* sometimes seemed to characterize or replicate the tone of the novel and do reflect the manner in which the reviewer perceived that the character ought to be treated. The reviewer Rodney Welch, who viewed Fay as "Southern poon," also insightfully points out the compulsion of male writers to capture female subjectivity, a description that seems particularly applicable to *Fay:* "It has something to do with a sense of penetration—to forge a being from the whore house of one's own imagination who can rise above its crude point of origin, live and breath its own air, and whose creation shows no strain; a woman, in other words, who exists on the page as unself-consciously as if her maker were Jane Austen or George Eliot."[12] As we shall see, however, the sense of penetration that the narrator achieves with Fay is most often less a matter of the psyche than it is of the body. Reviewers generally seemed interested in and indeed possessive of Fay's body: "She is tan and long-legged and a natural at sex—good men and bad want to keep her for their own. Every reader should picture his or her own mythical beauty; I see Laura Dern, circa 1987, wearing Egyptian-goddess eyeliner and bathed in a golden light."[13]

Other odd and seemingly small details in the novel lend to the instability of Fay's character—of Brown's failure to craft a character whose "creation shows no strain," as Rodney Welch put it. As an innocent, and innocent of so many quotidian details (restaurants, laws, movies, how to drive a car), Fay becomes for each man who meets her his own Pygmalion, an educational project. For instance, Sam, one of the novel's main characters, introduces Fay to Coca-Cola. And despite Fay's poverty, it is difficult to believe that a contemporary southern child has never tasted a soft drink. Fay does not like Coke, she says, claiming that it fizzes in her nose. Instead, she prefers beer. Her preference for beer is useful to the plot, allowing Brown to give her too much beer and place her in dangerous situations. While a preference for beer is of course in part just a matter of taste, it is certainly more convenient for the main drive of the plot: toward trouble for Fay, trouble often reckoned in terms of the threat to her body. Still, though, her taste for beer seems both naive and precocious and unintentionally humorous. One can imagine the joke: "Have you heard the one about the 17-year-old girl who drank only beer?" And what man in the rough South of Larry Brown would not like such a girl, with her long, muscular legs, puckered nipples, available body, and beer-hazed sense of judgment, as the narrator carefully describes her?

The novel follows a plot as old as the English novel itself. Not only is it a picaresque but it is also a progress, in which a character and plot move linearly through time, place, and adventures. In this case, Fay Jones traces the three hundred miles or so from northern Mississippi to the state's coast of the Gulf of Mexico. She moves not only geographically but also from man to man, in a series of seemingly serendipitous encounters that lead to sexual liaisons that lead to dead men and dead women. One of the early, most central, and most problematic relationships is that between Fay and Sam, a married, 40-year-old Mississippi state trooper. Their first encounter begins innocently enough, with Sam offering Fay a ride, feeding her lunch, and inviting her home, all from high motives, we suppose, whether professionally or paternally inspired. As fate, or the narrator, would have it, Sam and his wife Amy have recently lost a teenage daughter of their own. The couple takes to Fay, giving her a room in their house, clothes, and plenty of food and beer. Fay plays at the lake, drinks beer, lounges, enjoys the clothes and other things Sam and his wife buy for her; she has no responsibilities. She lives, in short, a teenager's ideal of adult domestic freedom, or even a bourgeois Eden. "I wish I had a daddy good as you" (87), Fay tells Sam, a line that is at once touchingly innocent and honest and disturbing, with readers knowing what they know about Fay and her experience with daddies. Indeed, readers unfamiliar with *Joe,* the first in what Brown said would be a trilogy of the Jones family (never completed), are at a certain disadvantage in reading *Fay* if they suppose that Fay might achieve here what she seems to think she wants. One might be tempted to hope that Fay and Sam can make a life together in the Edenic lake house with its fishing boats and sunny afternoons filled with endless cigarettes and ice-cold beers. But as Larry Brown would say, "It's just impossible for me to write a happy ending."[14]

Despite their material success—not a small consideration, it seems, given the narrative's admiration of the good life—Sam and Amy are not happily married. They have no sex life, Amy is a drunk, and Sam is having an affair with a woman on the other side of the lake. In short order, Amy dies in a car accident, Fay and Sam have sex, Fay becomes pregnant, and Sam's other woman determines to kill Fay; Fay kills her instead, in self-defense. Much like many other naturalist characters, Fay ends up, through no design of her own, pretty much where she wanted to go, in Fay's case the Gulf Coast. In Biloxi, Fay is found by—and the passive voice does seem appropriate in describing Fay's meeting men—Aaron, a strip-club bouncer. While Sam promised his own version of middle-class respectability, Aaron is less wholesome, down to his live-in ex-stripper mother and his brother, the budding pornographic-movie entrepreneur. Yet Aaron still manifests the cigarette-smoking, strong but taciturn, decent-to-women-in-his-own-way model of white masculinity that Larry Brown so frequently portrays. In the overdetermined ending, so foreseeable, obvious, and avoidable as almost to suggest that Fay might have willed it, Aaron and Sam kill each other in a shootout. Fay leaves before the police arrive, escaping both legal entanglements and any apparent sense of guilt or responsibility.

The progress of Fay from man to man suggests, almost in *bildungsroman* like fashion, that her character might develop throughout the novel. Here again the novel betrays a profound uncertainly about how to handle Fay, or more precisely, a serious generic uncertainty. What conventions rule its protagonist? Is this indeed a *bildungsroman,* in which case we might assume that Fay's travels and experiences will awaken her and cause her to develop morally? Is this picaresque, in which case (as in *Huck Finn*) the character's travels will operate as a critique of the peoples with whom she comes into contact? Not likely in Brown, as I have suggested, as invested as he is in sympathetic representations of rural and working-class white Mississippians. Or is this a rogue's tale? Is she a female seductress like Defoe's Roxana or Dreiser's Carrie Meeber, who uses up men as she moves along? The ending suggests the last reading, but if so, the bulk of the novel seems confusing or at least confused.

Critics and reviewers have praised the novel for its pitch-perfect dialogue, exciting plot, and realistic depiction of Sam, the state trooper who, one suspects, is the sort of man Brown admires.[15] Reviewers are most concerned, though, with Fay's own character: How "realistic" is she? Is she a seductress responsible for the havoc she causes or a naïf who moves innocently from one disastrous situation to the next? Neither of these questions elicits a very complex response to this novel. Such questions assume a moral universe in which characters have options and make choices. To a much greater degree than even *Joe, Fay* must be read as a work of naturalism rather than realism, for the plot is driven by an inevitability that does not allow for much freedom of will. Throughout his earlier fiction, on the other hand, Brown gave men the dignity of choice. Even if the choices were grim or repugnant, men were allowed to choose and face the music. But not Fay.

While the novel *Fay* is striking as Larry Brown's fullest fictional representation of a woman, the text also spends a great deal of energy establishing models of men and masculinity as well, as is the case with Brown's larger body of work. As in Brown's examination of Fay, though, he is not simply playing the realistic observer when it comes to men's lives; he presents a certain model as admirable. Consider Sam, the state trooper, Fay's educator and sexual initiator. Why is Sam a state trooper? Brown gets more masculine bang by combining Sam's natural male authority with that of the law. Sam drives the roads of Mississippi like a cowboy, using his grit and character to distinguish the bad from the mischievous from the innocent, enjoying carrying a gun. Brown's narrator shows clear and undisguised respect for Sam the lawman. But even as the narrator describes Sam on the job, his misogyny is never far from the surface. In one episode, for instance, Sam and other troopers sit around the dispatch room discussing recent events. In the space of four pages, Brown gives us two references to bestiality, one metaphorical ("He'd fuck a snake if somebody would hold his head" [134]) and one actual ("A farmer had caught him fucking one of his goats in the dark of his barn one day" [137]). Further, Brown the narrator—not one of the troopers—observes of the dispatcher, "She had an enormous set of titties that stretched out the front of her uniform almost beyond belief" (135). Lest we miss the narrator's attention to the character's breasts, he notes, "She moved back a little, but not enough to keep him from bumping up against one of her huge knockers" (136).

Finally, the troopers tell the story of a colleague in trouble. The story line could be drawn from urban legend or from pornography and surely has nonfictional analogues: The officer pulls over a drunk woman who "worked it out" to trade sex for dropping the drunk-driving charges. While dressing after their tryst, the woman accidentally kicks the trooper's gunbelt; the gun "went off and shot her right in the damn eye" (134). What purpose do such anecdotes serve? Realism? Frankness? Yes, one might allow, but the story of the wounded woman also suggests that in Larry Brown's moral universe, the whorish woman receives her punishment, typically bodily punishment.

This is not the only episode in the novel in which a woman's body is mutilated, seemingly as punishment for sexual activity. Fay recalls Barbara Lewis, a girl in one of the migrant-worker camps where Fay and her family lived for a time. Although Lewis is a very minor character in the novel, she is deemed worthy of this sort of exposition. Unable to work because of her "crooked legs," Lewis exchanges sex for food. In itself, the bargain is not inherently degrading, one could possibly imagine. Yet Brown chooses to make the transaction as grossly comic as it is unlikely: "They would climb on while their friends watched and waited for their turns, while she lay on her back and scooped her hand into the box [of food and candy that the boys provided] and stuffed the candy into her mouth and chewed it as they did what they did with her" (147). Lewis could scarcely be more disengaged from what is happening to her. However, the disengagement seems less willed than animal-like; the boys might as well be having sex with a cow eating grass. And again, Brown physically punishes women for their sexual activity: Lewis's father beats her savagely when he discovers "one of the boys on top of her" (148). Her food-for-sex game ended,

Lewis throws herself into the path of a truck, leaving her body "broken and bleeding" in the road.

Leaving aside for a moment the treatment of sex and sexuality in the novel, it is apparent not only that Brown writes here about white men and their South but also that he is writing through a sympathetic aesthetic that ultimately compromises his ability to write very critically or even searchingly about the men he spent so much time chronicling. In *Fay,* the narrator suggests that coming home, as Sam does, to a boat, a beer, and a large set of breasts is indeed a satisfying ending to a workingman's day. The taste and range seem limited, but *à chacun son goût.* What is not simply a matter of taste or realism is Brown's insistence that Sam and, later in the novel, Aaron possess an inner decency and a fiber that no woman in the novel displays. Fay simply *is.* She lives by instinct and in the moment. Sam and Aaron are strong, silent types, but they possess some inner moral mechanism. Indeed, by allowing Sam to anguish over Fay's killing of his mistress and the legal consequences that may befall him, Brown gives Sam a depth that the perpetually infantilized Fay cannot reach.

Whatever else Fay may be in the novel, in her sexual and other domestic arrangements with Sam she is infantilized and sexualized, a combination that makes it difficult to view Sam with the sort of moral complexity or sympathy or approval that Brown seems to wish his readers to do. Sam's relationship with Fay is inescapably disturbing on several levels. First, Fay is 17 years old. Sam and his wife provide alcohol to Fay; and Fay and Sam eventually have sex. Since the death of their daughter, Sam and his wife Amy have endured a loveless, sexless marriage. Karen drinks to numb her pain; Sam takes a large-breasted Lebanese mistress. Sam brings Fay into their home as casually as he would a stray puppy. They install Fay in their dead daughter's bedroom, and soon Karen is giving Fay an allowance. Fay admires Sam's fathering skills. By turns, then, Fay is represented as a little girl and a replacement child, which raises echoes of incest after Karen dies and Sam and Fay have sex.

When women in the novel other than Fay are considered, the narrative voice of *Fay* seems systematically misogynistic. More specifically, the narrator seems uninterested in anything other than the women's bodies, consistently represented as either objects to be dominated or parts to be assessed. Even more than Fay, the other women in the novel are animal-like spewers of blood and other fluids; the narrator notes their "titties," "knockers," and "asses." Men "get on top of them," establishing the power and submission that the narrator seems to see in sexual relations. The broader question is why Brown gives such a voice to the novel. The answer is elusive. Brown never explained his choice of narrative voice in *Fay*. Nor would his answer necessarily have settled the matter. To say that the narrative voice embodied Brown's own prejudices and convictions is hardly a useful critical statement, and it is unfair given Brown's reputation as a genuinely decent man. One might argue that Brown deliberately chose this narrative voice to represent the ethos surrounding Fay and the other characters. That is, Brown meant for the realism of the novel to be supplemented by a narrative voice approximating life as Fay and the other characters would find it. Yet the fact remains that the narrative voice renders women as objects of violence or degrades them or fails to allow them the agency of the male characters.

Nothing in the novel suggests that the narrator should be seen as unreliable. Nothing would lead the reader to see the narrator as subverting himself in any way. In the end, then, Fay moves through a world in which fate is a man, a man deeply suspicious of women and their ways. "And men. Why did they act the way they did?" (434). Loretta, the state patrol dispatcher, asks that question when thinking about how Sam turned down her offer of sex. But her question is really one of the central questions of the novel for two reasons: first, the novel seems to posit that men act, while women react or are acted upon; second, it underscores the seeming contention throughout the novel that women consequently cannot really understand men. Thus, Loretta's statement is less a critique of men's fickleness than it is of women's obtuseness about men and things generally.

Aaron and Sam, the two men who kill each other over Fay, seem almost complementary types of southern manhood. Through much of his fiction, Brown enjoyed creating paired male characters, notable in *Dirty Work* and *Father and Son*.[16] Sam's badge seems to be the only boundary separating him and Aaron. We first see Aaron through the eyes of the drunken stripper Reena, who befriended Fay after her arrival on the Gulf Coast. This friendship, incidentally, allows Brown to dangle before the reader the possibility that Fay will doff her clothes: "What do you have to do?" Fay asks Reena. "Nothing much. Just take off your clothes and dance in front of a bunch of perverts" (165). After a few beers, Fay asks, "How hard is it to learn that dancing?" (168). Several chapters later the pregnant 17-year-old Fay is still considering sex work. "I hadn't really decided what to do," Fay tells Reena (218). Fay is spared the choice, and the reader the spectacle, when Fay meets Aaron the bouncer. Like her relationship with Sam, Fay's time with Aaron ends when she decides to leave him. These are decisions in which men take the brunt of the responsibility and are left holding the bag (or in Aaron's case, his bleeding guts) for Fay's actions.

Aaron exclaims when he finds that Fay has stolen his gun and is prepared to leave him, "All you fucking whores are *alike*" (484). By this point in the novel, Fay has recognized her kinship with Reena, Wanda, Gigi, and the other women whom Aaron "went through." He would use her up as well if she stayed with him, whatever his protestations of love. But Aaron is merely the novel's most extreme example of how men in Brown's universe determine the lives of women, whom they see mostly in sexual terms. Though Sam is consistently represented as a basically good man who pays the price for some poor decisions about women, his actions toward the 17-year-old transient are predatory from the beginning. That their relationship begins as that of father and daughter is not reassuring in a novel that begins as the protagonist flees the father who has tried to rape her.

While the title of the novel and the bulk of the narrative establish that Fay is the center and subject of the text, Brown spends a considerable amount of time, as I have suggested, creating various models of white southern masculinity. Indeed, many of the women in the novel, including Fay herself, seem objects or occasions for the development of manhood. Consider Sam's involvement with Alesandra, his alluring but dangerous Lebanese mistress. She seems a comically flat and predicable character, fatally attracted to Sam and emotionally unstable: "He hoped she wouldn't cry again. Or threaten him with something" (74). Alesandra's soap-opera femme-fatale flatness is initially somewhat puzzling. Is Brown really so incapable of drawing a believable female character? While the question is difficult to answer categorically, it does seem clear that in this case Brown simply is not interested in the nuanced representation of a female subject. Alesandra is merely an object. For one thing, she demonstrates the chaotic essence of woman against the solidness of man. And she suggests just what kind of woman is naturally drawn to a Larry Brown hero, as she models some of Brown's favorite physical characteristics and habits: she is large-breasted, she drinks a lot, and she is highly sexed. She also demonstrates Brown's penchant for having women of wealth fall for working- or middle-class men, which seems not harmless fantasy but a reflection of a desire to discipline and control women in terms of class as well as gender. Consider first her wealth: "The Chris Craft with its curved glass windshield and that big Mercury inboard was a high-dollar ride on this lake" (74). Again, the third-person narrator, not Sam himself, seems at the same time to admire the quality of the boat and to see it primarily, perhaps slightly resentfully, in terms of its price and what it says about the social class of its owner.

The plot of *Fay* is driven by violence inscribed upon and inflicted upon the bodies of the characters, both main and supporting. Indeed, Fay's progress, traced by threats to and the use of her own body, is marked by a trail of broken and dead bodies, both male and female. Fay's progress can be measured by her passing from man to man and by her use, passive though it may be, of them as she moves geographically from North Mississippi to the Gulf Coast to New Orleans. But her body is used as well by the narrator. As I have noted, her body is exposed, penetrated, observed, used, and threatened by a variety of men, from her father to the first boys she encounters to Sam to Aaron to her customers in a French Quarter strip club to which she silently walks at the end of the novel.

But any use of men to effect Fay's rise, more deliberately understood by the narrator than by Fay herself, it seems, should not distract one from the instrumental use of violence upon women's bodies that seems both so central to the plot and also at times so secondary to the plot's main action but in its own way also so telling. Consider Sam Harris, for instance. Of the women connected to his own body in one way or another, three die: Sam and Amy's daughter, Karen (dead before the novel opens), Amy herself, and Sam's mistress, Alesandra. The latter two are killed in a violent, gruesome, and slightly far-fetched (if only in terms of convenience for the narrator, or inconvenience for Sam) manner. Of the deaths in the novel, that of Sam's daughter, Karen, is handled perhaps the most sensitively, at least in terms of narrative attention to the effect of her death upon her body. Sam tells Fay that while he was working (naturally) and Amy was not attending to their daughter (naturally), Karen "slipped out" of the house to rendezvous with her boyfriend and was killed in an automobile accident. An on-shift Sam "happened" to be the highway patrolman closest to the scene of the reported accident. Sam crawled through the window of the old wrecked Plymouth Duster and wrapped his daughter's body in a blanket. "Wasn't a mark on her nowhere," he tells Fay, "but her neck was broken she just looked like she was asleep" (84). The boyfriend too was dead, of course, but the condition of his body is untold. Of all the descriptions of all the broken bodies in the novel, this one is certainly the most reticent. Again, the question here ought not to be one of taste or suitability or even plausibility, although this description is unremarkable on all those scores. Instead, the tenderness and even absence of apparent violence upon Karen's body is noteworthy mainly because of the ease and quickness with which both Sam and Amy accept Fay as a surrogate daughter—before Sam's interest in this surrogate daughter turns sexual.

Indeed, Amy too treats Fay's passive body tenderly as she prepares it for rest of a different sort. On the night Sam brings Fay home, Amy helps Fay prepare for bed in their dead daughter's well-preserved room. "Amy helped her undress in a room papered with roses; a bed with pillows trimmed with lace, a child's dolls sitting in a toddler's rocking chair. . . . Amy brought her a nightgown and Fay held her arms over her head and let her pull it down over her shoulders, her waist. . . . She closed her eyes and felt one soft kiss upon her cheek" (59). His dead daughter's body serves Sam in a variety of ways: it opens both a paternal and a sexual space that can be filled by Fay. Fay literally moves into his daughter's room, and Amy begins shopping for clothes for her, shopping being one of the activities that *Fay*'s narrator apparently believes is natural to women. After Karen's death, Amy has retreated into an alcoholic haze, one that leads to her timely death. Consequently, Sam seeks solace and pleasure, ultimately in the arms of his daughter/lover Fay but also with his physically alluring but dangerous mistress, Alesandra.

What motivates Alesandra? On the one hand, the question hardly seems relevant. She is necessary in the novel because her death at Fay's hands and Sam's cover-up of that death lead to the destruction of the familial and sexual idyll that Sam and Fay enjoy after Karen's death and before the real consequences and responsibilities of Fay's pregnancy become inescapable. In the short term, the purpose of Alesandra seems to be that of another idyll, that of consumption and its pleasures: the consumption of women's bodies and of material goods, both of which Sam uses in a curiously passive manner (by this point, Alesandra pursues him, and Sam enjoys the cake of his troubled conscience and the eating of that cake in the form of a lusty, rich Lebanese femme fatale).

Alesandra arrives, *diabolus ex machina,* to summon Sam aboard her Chris Craft. Consider again the description of the boat. It is a "high dollar ride," notes the narrator (74), perhaps for those who do not appreciate the self-evident desirability of the boat that some readers might see as the apotheosis of Big 1980s, *Miami Vice*–style crass conspicuous consumption. "I've been expecting you," says Alesandra in a line that gives one as much aesthetic pain as just about any other in the novel (74). We receive Alesandra in pieces, as Sam for unexplained reasons takes hold of her foot—"he couldn't help himself" (75).

Like all the other grown-ups in the novel, she drinks and operates machinery. What attraction does she hold for Sam? Her thighs, for one thing, are, naturally enough, "velvet" (75). She smokes cigarettes, again naturally enough for one of Larry Brown's characters, although we are told without amplification and with at least a suggestion of a cause and effect, perhaps, that she smokes only "five cigarettes a day, and could squeeze him so tightly inside her that it took his breath" (75). Or perhaps the non sequitur is simply intended to take away the reader's breath too. A high-dollar ride indeed. Alesandra asks Sam if he is seeing someone else, adding, "I catch you with somebody else I'll kill her" (75). Rightly enough at this point, and perhaps in anticipation of readers' questions, the narrator explains, "He didn't know if what he felt was love" (75).

Perhaps it is unfair to subject Alesandra to this sort of critical scrutiny. On the one hand, she is clearly a femme fatale, beautiful but deadly, as another masculinist writer said of such a dame. Yet one should also note that Alesandra is the one who dies, although her death sets Sam on a path to his destruction, as he begins his pursuit of Fay. What strikes an odd note here is not so much the existence of a femme fatale but rather her construction, her deployment, and her end, and what she tells us both about Sam and about the larger moral or ethical questions of the universe they all inhabit. Simply put, the novel seems to assert that there is no point in being much concerned about such questions. No character seems to be, nor does the narrator.

If this were a conventional *bildungsroman,* concentrating on the moral or intellectual development of its main character, one might expect some pattern, order, or point to the men Fay encounters. But this is not the case in *Fay,* for one main reason: the primary focus here is not on her development from innocence through experience, although at first glance one might be tempted to read the novel that way. After all, isn't Fay painfully naive about sex at the beginning of the novel—not recognizing a three-way sex encounter and being ignorant of birth-control methods—but much less so by the end, having learned about sex, pregnancy, rape, murder, prostitution, and pornography? The answer might be yes, but only if the novel really did focus on Fay's education in the world of the rough sex of Larry Brown. Instead, Fay's development seems coincidental to the narrative's real interest: the representation of a world driven not by the development of a character but rather by the use, penetration, and exposure of women's bodies, including Fay's. Most important, Fay seems not to learn much from her encounters. She guesses. She believes. She wonders. But nothing that happens serves as a revelation equal to Huck Finn's

"I'll go to hell, then" decision when he destroys the letter that would betray the location of his friend Jim. Fay's lessons never rise to the level of moral lessons or even cautionary lessons that she can use. She continues to be surprised by the perfidy of men, but in the end she survives and continues to move without its being apparent whether she has changed very much from the country girl whom Sam initiated into sex after having taken her into his dead daughter's bedroom.

What, then, is the fruit of Fay's progress? Bodies, male and female, upon which violence and suffering have been wrought, but from which Fay seems to have learned very little, even in a behaviorist sense of a burned child learning to dread the fire. By the end of *Light in August,* by comparison, Lena Grove is able rightly to declare that she had come a "fur piece." Not so with Fay. She begins the novel and ends it under the scrutiny of questioning, voyeuristic male eyes, on her way to strip for men to earn her money. Her own body, then, despite sexual initiation, pregnancy, and rape, is a progress that is more apparent than real. Her journey comes at the cost of a great deal of blood and suffering. But to what end? To become the object of more men's desire. She is less a femme fatale, although she trails bodies in spades, than she is a continuing and exposed example of the southern sexual faux naif: a Eula Varner without the dignity of realizing the cost for which she has been sold, a Dewey Dell Bundren without the dignity of realizing the pain of having been used by men.

But one should quickly note that the text does not operate, even obliquely, as a feminist critique of the objectification of women. The narrative is largely an objectification of bodies—male and female—without the larger justification of telling us of a world without good or mercy. Brown's representation of Sam, whom he seems to want to preserve with a sort of honor, perhaps as a surrogate for himself, but at least as a character with whom the reader is invited to sympathize, keeps the naturalism from assuming its natural level. Is Sam tragic? He has at least experienced a fall, and he certainly suffers because of decisions that he makes. Fay, however, is not allowed that kind of dignity or even that kind of a voice.

The significance of Fay's relationship with Sam is so great that it threatens to dominate the text. After all, Sam introduces Fay to domesticity, consumption, and love of a sort, as well as sex, pregnancy, and homicide. But Fay's time with Aaron is just as important, occupying half of the text. Fay encounters Aaron only when her geographical journey is nearly complete, when she arrives on the Gulf Coast after leaving Sam to deal with the fallout from Alesandra's death. Fay's time with Aaron is also punctuated by death, after Fay learns more about the rough sexual world of violence, use, and exposure. At a Denny's restaurant, however, Fay first meets Reena, a waitress, stripper, and prostitute. Fay remains the naif, ignorant of the meaning of a tip, a trick, or a pervert. Of some of these she will learn, again via a toll taken upon women's bodies—Reena's and to a much lesser degree her own. "You ever turned a trick?" Reena asks Fay. "You mean like trick or treat?" she replies. "Naw, they never did let us do that" (167). Reena, she of the good tan and shiny, clean hair, explains: "I mean fucking a man for money. Sucking him off or something" (167). Fay is repelled by the suggestion, a curious moral sticking point by this time in the text, and one that serves mainly to mark Reena as morally lower than Fay.

This response to Reena highlights a major difference between the men and the women in the text. There is a clear pattern of class and even moral declension in Fay's encounters with women, one that is absent from her movement through men. In part, this occasional expression of shock or disgust from Fay toward other women seems similar to Brown's decision, whether or not the larger narrative works against such questions, to try to maintain Sam as a morally sympathetic or at least morally aware person. Not so with Fay's women. From Karen to Amy to Alesandra to Reena the stripper/prostitute to Gigi the porn actress, one can follow a clear path toward the sexual and the unsympathetic and even depraved. Against each of those women, and certainly by default and not through any positive action, Fay serves to highlight the degradation of women through sexual activity and especially through sex itself as a commodity in trade. Fay, recall, ends as a stripper, but only after Brown has established through Reena and Gigi just what sort of nasty and characterless women take part in such activities. Men in *Fay* are punished for sex only when they take it by force. Women are punished for sex by pregnancy, death, and rape, not to mention objectification by and within the text, merely through participation in sex without the sanctioned tutelage and daddyness of a man like Sam, or even with it.

Brown also notices bad mothering by his women, whereas he never similarly takes men to task for bad fathering or even recognizes it. A bad mother is one who fails to watch properly (Karen dies when Amy is sleeping, for instance) or to shield her children from unsavory men. For Brown, fatherhood seems more about providing the right sort of male model for a son. Quotidian tasks of cleaning, feeding, baby care, and other mundane things are seemingly by definition women's work, and he registers disapproval or worse when a woman fails to keep her children away from dangerous things. Men such as Aaron are among those dangerous things, while providing an opportunity for the narrator to task a woman for bad mothering.

At bottom, Fay's attraction to Aaron is similar to what she felt for Sam. He seems to her a man who can protect her and provide material things for her. The trail of destruction that Fay leaves in her wake should not obscure the fact that through the great bulk of the novel, Fay has relied upon the kindness of strangers, principally Sam and Aaron, to get by. The women Fay meets have been weak, psychotic, self-destructive, poor mothers, and poor providers—the latter two seem always to come in tandem. Reena is a particularly weak person and also an object of violence and a sexual commodity. When Fay first makes her way into the trailer park where Reena lives (and fails to provide well materially for her children), Reena is turning a trick, accompanied by a thinly squeaking trailer that shakes "very gently," as the narrator surprisingly puts it. Shortly afterwards, Reena is visited by a man that we, but not Fay, recognize as her pimp, who beats her—Fay hears "the thud of a body hitting the floor" (193)—and who emerges with money in his hand only to try to entice Fay, improbably at that moment, into the line of work to which Reena has just introduced her. This scene represents a departure from Brown's usual method of driving the plot by exposing a body that is inscribed with violence. In this case, Reena is never seen and not even heard, except for the sound her body makes as her pimp throws her around the trailer. Why this seeming reticence about exposing Reena as she is screwed and beaten? But it is not reticence here that keeps Reena from exposure—her body is clearly violated and battered; rather, her exposure is not necessary to drive the plot. In fact, to focus the narrative upon her body might even risk exercising sympathy from the reader. Instead, her beaten and used body simply does not matter except as a plot device for introducing Fay to the world of turning tricks and to dismiss Reena as another weak woman.

In a realist novel, with its bourgeois values and emphasis upon psychological development for the sake of moral betterment, Fay might be blamed for the deaths of Alesandra, Aaron, Sam, Chris Dodd, and possibly Amy. But not here. Fay does indeed learn as she moves through the novel; she is not merely the object of male desire or a siren upon whose rocks men destroy their lives. But what she learns are the limitations of her place in the world, the degree to which as an uneducated and poor but beautiful woman she is destined to a life as a sex object if she is to live at all. She becomes educated in the ways of

Brown's world, which is determined by white, working-class masculinity. In the last scene of the novel, Fay walks by herself through the familiar French Quarter. Men smile at her, but she is pointedly alone on her way to work at a strip club.

By the end of the novel, Fay's body count is formidable: Amy, Alesandra, and Chris Dodd, a man who tried to rape Fay the first night she arrived in Biloxi. The latter is spectacularly killed by Aaron, her protector by this point in the novel, who shoots Dodd's plane out of the sky, explaining that no real man would fail to do much the same for a woman like Fay. Sam has trailed along, of course, delaying what one imagines will be a significant day of reckoning with various law-enforcement agencies. Even Aaron's quasi-chivalrous revenge upon Fay's rapist is bookended by narrative reflections upon the penetration of Fay's body. Just before shooting down Dodd's plane, Aaron and Fay "had lunch at three o'clock after showers and some hard fucking on the couch" (315). Thinking of Dodd's death, Fay reflects: "She thought about it like this: A person who had been inside her was now dead" (31). One might note here that his being "inside her" had been a rape carried out on a drunken teen-aged girl, although Fay's bland but typical response here would allow one to forget that fact.

It is perhaps no surprise that Aaron the strip-club bouncer pays a great deal of attention to Fay's body—or more particularly, to her breasts, a seeming fetish not only of Aaron, one should note, but of Sam and the narrator as well. In *On Fire*, Larry Brown remembered a woman in a bar (the woman has no name, one notes; the bar does) with "a set of breasts that are spectacular, that are not to be believed . . . [that are] are as big as my head" (61). Recall too that one of the novel's opening scenes dwells upon the detail of Fay's puckered nipples. Aaron too is a breast man. "He could feel one of those big titties pressed up against his arm like a puppy dog's nose. He glanced at her and saw the swell of her breasts against the thin cloth of the dress" (361). A few chapters later, Aaron's hand "reached around and touched one of her breasts, squeezing it tightly" (393). While Fay later falls down stairs, suffering a conveniently timed miscarriage, at this point in the novel the full breasts and attractive nipples that charm Aaron are those of a pregnant teenaged woman. Aaron continues his tactile examination of Fay: "His fingers reached around and touched one of her breasts, squeezed it tightly. She had to admit she liked it. His fingers moved around and stroked one of her nipples through the cloth. Her insides stirred. She leaned her head back on the seat while her rubbed her like a pet cat" (393). Titties like puppy dogs' noses and a body that responds as sensually and passively as a relaxed pet cat—such is the body upon which and through which so much sex and violence are carried through the novel to so little effect upon the psychological development of the characters, Fay included. Hers is a body upon which men enact their beliefs about control, protection, and erotic satisfaction. And so Fay ends as she begins, with men and a narrator observing her and certainly inscribing their own narratives of manhood and sexuality upon her body. And Fay's body, with its puppy-dog "titties" and catlike passive sexuality? Such are the things, the novel seems to say, that dangerous but irresistible little girls are made of.

Ultimately, though, in considering sex and sexuality in Fay, it is vital not to be misled by the question of realism. That is to say, sex in the novel ought not to be held to a standard of plausibility or believability. Such an approach says as much about the reader as it does about the novel. So we must proceed as if the adventures of Fay were possible, as they surely are. Nor is it useful, I think, to consider what Larry Brown meant or intended by representing Fay's sexual landscape as it is. Readers of Erskine Caldwell and William Faulkner rightly are dismissive of concerns about the image of the South that the novelists portray. In sum, neither Brown nor his rough South can profitably be psychologized or evaluated at the level of their effect, if by effect one means the good or the end of that portrayal. Words like *gratuitous* or *shocking* have no place in a useful consideration of the novel. One person's vice is another person's pleasure, after all. But does this mean that the best way to think about sex in the novel is with a jaded tolerance? That Fay's sexual nature and practices are central to the plot and to her character cannot be dismissed. Also important here is the fact that Brown himself has chosen to work in a highly realistic vein, as he did in the great bulk of his work. So what we make of sex in *Fay* and what we make of Fay and of *Fay* are difficult to separate in any useful way. Brown gives us his imagined South as it is, so to speak, and we can do nothing but assess Fay in the terms the novel deliberately sets out.

Brown's working within the tradition of naturalism, then, allows us to ask whether Fay "works" in the terms that he establishes for her and how sex fits into and works upon the larger constellation of forces of fate and character that drives this world. Certainly Brown's attention to Fay's body as corpus thus is noteworthy, as is his elision, ignorance of, or eroticization of social-class boundaries and markets in the rough South of Fay. Sex, both as a represented act and also as an inherent quality subject to narrative scrutiny, is also useful as a tool with which to compare Fay with male characters in the novel. To the degree that sexual praxis or the narrator's attitude or approach toward the subject sets Fay apart from other characters, one must ask what we are to make of that fact. Consider the narrator's early, carefully naturalistic description of Fay's nipples, as well as other pieces and parts of her. Is it frankness at work here? Or prurience? And what is one to make of the fact that a reader can make her or his way through five hundred pages of the novel without reading a close description of a male character's penis or buttocks? Or anything else about a man that is presented so cynically or voyeuristically. Simply put, Fay's body is exposed, as is the female body through the text, in multiple ways, and certainly in ways to which male bodies are not subjected.

It is doubly striking, moreover, to consider the relative lack of black characters in this novel and in Larry Brown's other fiction, given his emphasis upon violence and the body. Even the language itself treats mildly or largely fails to treat black characters, when one might well argue that the history of violence upon black bodies is one of the chief things that has made the South distinctive.[17] So much, then, for any assessment of Brown's fiction that explains his representations of sex and women simply as functions or consequences of a realistic aesthetic.

What broader significance are we to draw from the tale of Fay Jones? What does it say about sex and sexuality in the American South? First, one ought not to sell Larry Brown short as a documentary realist in the naturalistic vein. As a chronicler of the white working-class South as he knew it in North Mississippi, Brown has few literary equals. Unlike Faulkner, to draw the inevitable if unfair comparison, Brown neither in his statements about his art nor in the art himself ever claimed to be speaking of eternal verities, of the heart or otherwise. Brown's best work is that in which he drew it as he saw it. That is far from saying, however, that he is a naive realist, a sort of condescending diagnosis that afflicts many southern artists whose achievements seem otherwise unaccountable to critics. For realism is art of a high degree when done well, as it consistently is in Brown. And it is finally because Brown's writing is both great art and realistic that students of sex and sexuality in the South ought to read it carefully.

Fay is written out of and about a world in which women have long been objects of lust, violence, or paternal care. All of these modes—and they most certainly are not discrete categories—see and work upon the bodies of women. Sometimes, it is claimed, the discipline of the body is for their own good.

And sometimes the use of the body occurs without that justification. Brown's fiction, then, is about a world that was and is real for the Fay Joneses of the South. Larry Brown's biographer, Jean Cash, has argued that *Fay* "does offer a significant evocation of what has happened or failed to happen in the lives of lower class American women at the end of the twentieth century and into the twenty-first,"[18] and Cash is surely right. That is why the novel matters, for students of southern literature but also for students of southern culture. To assess the novel in this manner is not to criticize Larry Brown as a man or to criticize the novel as "bad" in any reductive sense. Rather, it is to recognize that Brown did in fact offer here and in most of his other work a well-realized and perceptive account of the rough South that operates upon Fay Jones.

NOTES

1. Larry Brown, *Facing the Music* (Chapel Hill: Algonquin Books, 1988). Breasts, which feature so prominently in *Fay*, figure largely in the title story of this collection, in which a man steels himself to have sex with his wife, who has lost her breasts to cancer.

2. Larry Brown, "Author's Note from Larry Brown," in *Fay: A Novel* (2000; reprint, New York: Simon & Schuster, 2001). The parenthetical page references to *Fay* in this essay are to this edition.

3. "Passions of the Trailer Park," *Economist*, 15 April 2000, 13.

4. For a collection of essays examining Larry Brown's novels, stories, and nonfiction, see Jean W. Cash and Keith Perry, eds., *Larry Brown and the Blue-Collar South* (Jackson: University Press of Mississippi, 2008). The collection is often frankly celebratory. Rick Bass eulogizes "My friend Larry Brown" and claims for *Joe* the status of "the second Great American Novel," after *The Great Gatsby* (vii, xi). On *Fay*, see esp. Robert Beuka's essay in the same volume, "Hard Traveling: *Fay's* Deep-South Landscape of Violence." See also Erik Bledsoe, "The Rise of the Southern Redneck and White Trash Writer," *Southern Cultures* 6, no. 1 (2000): 68–90.

5. I draw the phrase *rough South of Larry Brown* from the documentary *The Rough South of Larry Brown*, dir. Gary Hawkins (Durham, NC: Center for Documentary Studies, Duke University, 2002).

6. For an anthology that sets Brown among other contemporary writers with similar interests, see Brian Carpenter and Tom Franklin, eds., *Grit Lit: A Rough South Reader* (Columbia: University of South Carolina Press, 2012).

7. See Jay Watson, *Reading for the Body: The Recalcitrant Materiality of Southern Fiction, 1893–1985* (Athens: University of Georgia Press, 2012). Watson argues that "a more careful, thoroughgoing consideration of the body's complex and prominent role(s) in southern writing has been slow to emerge in southern studies" (10).

8. Larry Brown, *Conversations with Larry Brown,* ed. Jay Watson (Jackson: University Press of Mississippi, 2007), 7.

9. Larry Brown's biographer, Jean Cash, has praised the "richness of the development" of female characters in Brown's earlier fiction. However, these characters she describes as "nurturers" and

"good cook," which I would maintain is evidence of Brown's comfort with women who stay in their (nonsexualized) place. See Jean W. Cash, *Larry Brown: A Writer's Life* (Jackson: University Press of Mississippi, 2011), 167. And Cash notes that Brown's editor Shannon Ravenel noted of a draft of *Father and Son* that "the female characters were not complex enough" (156).

10. Jay Watson writes in his introduction to *Conversations with Larry Brown,* "In many of the interviews surrounding the publication of *Fay* in 2000, Brown seems as eager to talk about the writing cabin he was building for himself beside a small pond near Tula as he is to discuss the challenges of creating a female protagonist for his new novel" (xv).

11. Rodney Welch, "Larry Brown's Road Trip," review of *Fay,* accessed 23 February 2005, www .free-times.com/Reviews/fay.html. Another reviewer more circumspectly describes Fay as possessing a "quick wit and a good body." See Roger Boylan, "Review of *Fay,*" *Boston Review,* 1 April 2000, www.bostonreview.net/fiction/roger-boylan-review-fay.

12. Welch, "Larry Brown's Road Trip."

13. Virginia Vitzthum, "Review of *Fay,*" *Salon,* 4 April 2000, www.salon.com/2000/04/04 /brown_5/.

14. Brown, *Conversations with Larry Brown,* 167.

15. See Diann Blakely, "Shades of Brown: Mississippi Writer's Latest Novel Affirms His Depth as a Story Teller," *Nashville Scene,* 14 August 2000, www.weeklywire.com/ww/08-14-00/nash_8-books .html. Blakely asserts that Brown's "comprehension of women sets him apart from the crowd," but Blakely also characterizes Fay as "a siren in tennis shoes and a too-tight dress."

16. Larry Brown, *Dirty Work* (Chapel Hill: Algonquin Books, 1989); Brown, *Father and Son* (Chapel Hill: Algonquin Books, 1996).

17. On Larry Brown and race, see Suzanne Jones, "Refighting Old Wars: Race Relations and Masculine Conventions in Fiction by Larry Brown and Madison Smartt Bell," in *The Southern State of Mind,* ed. Jan Norby Gretlund (Columbia: University of South Carolina Press, 1999), 107–20.

18. Jean Cash, "Larry Brown's *Fay,*" in *Still in Print: The Southern Novel Today,* ed. Jan Norby Gretlund (Columbia: University of South Carolina Press, 2010), 117.

10

Freaknik

Intersectional Perspectives on the Politics and
Discourse of Public Space in Atlanta

MATT MILLER

Freaknik, an annual spring-break gathering of African American college students in Atlanta, took place from 1982 to 2000. Over the course of these years, it was transformed from an event contained within and impacting almost exclusively black neighborhoods to one that played out in much more central parts of the city, including the downtown business district and the predominantly white Midtown neighborhood, around Piedmont Park. As its size grew in the early 1990s, so did its impact on city residents, and a raging public debate developed between supporters and opponents of the event. The public discourse around Freaknik in Atlanta was intense and conflictive during the years 1994–99, with opponents pointing to gridlocked traffic, crime, and the harassment or assault of women, while supporters argued for the potential economic impact of the event and the right of the students to use and enjoy public space in the city. While the opposing camps in the debate were far from racially exclusive, they quickly took on racialized identities. White opponents of the gathering denied any racist motivations, although at times these were undeniably paramount. For their part, African American supporters of the gathering often framed their arguments in the context of the civil rights movement and Atlanta's status as a known center of African American history and culture. By the year 2000, the anti-Freaknik camp had scored a decisive victory, as the event dwindled to the point of nonexistence, ending not with a bang but with a whimper.

While avoiding the oversimplified and polarized rhetoric for and against the event, subsequent commentators and scholars have also been challenged to understand the multivalent nature of the phenomenon. Some have called attention to issues related to gender and social class in the discourse around the event, as well as to the impact of ideas of (hetero)sexuality upon the collective experience of Freaknik by the citizenry of Atlanta. More so than gender (as narrowly defined) and class, the influence of sexual orientation or preference or the experience of young LGBT African Americans has been largely ignored in analyses of Freaknik and its implications. The failure to acknowledge the presence and participation of gay, lesbian, or bisexual students and young people in the event likely contributed to the climate of runaway heterosexual machismo that became one of Freaknik's most expensive liabilities. Despite the documented homophobia of the fraternity culture from which the event grew, the ways in which this manifested in the activities and discourse around Freaknik have received scant attention. While some Freaknik supporters condemned the misogyny and victim-blaming that excused men's abuse of women participants, the voices of LGBT supporters or participants in the event were largely silenced.

In this essay, I present a history of Freaknik and the racialized discourse that surrounded it within an intersectional framework derived from black feminist theory. As Patricia Hill Collins put it, "As opposed to examining gender, race, class, and nation, as separate systems of oppression, intersectionality explores how these systems mutually construct one another."[1] In addition to gender, class, and race, I add consideration of sexuality and the politics of its expression or repression to enrich the historical perspective on Freaknik and the discourse around it. I wish to explore the ways in which what Kendall Thomas labels the "jargon of racial authenticity" employed in defense of Freaknik produced and endorsed the near invisibility of African American LGBT participants in the event.[2] Ultimately, Freaknik represented a missed opportunity for Atlanta's political and civic elite to address lingering racism in the city and a similar failure on the part of the black collegiate community and African Americans in general to address entrenched homophobia.

I am interested in the ways in which the polarization of opinion and discourse along racial lines obscures other important dynamics that have an undeniable impact on the phenomenon. The simplification of the Freaknik controversy into a black-white racial conflict obscured the influence of other modes of identification, which, as Collins noted, are mutually constructed with race. Because of its inherently spatial nature, the story of Freaknik brings to the fore the "ongoing issues of inclusion plaguing the Black community and the gay community alike" in modern Atlanta.[3] It reveals how the discourse around public space in Atlanta operates according to ideas of belonging or citizenship that are essentially reductive in nature. Either unconsciously or consciously (in the name of strategy), gray areas are ignored and conflicts are simplified into black/white, male/female, and gay/straight binaries. As Thomas observed, "To understand that antiracist and antihomophobic politics are informed by a common ethical interest is to create the possibility of coalition across difference."[4] In this regard, the story of Freaknik is one of missed opportunities and the reinscription of isolated and disempowered forms of identification that belie the complexity and intersectionality of the urban experience.

x x x

Freaknik began in 1982 as a small, one-day picnic in John A. White Park (located in southwestern Atlanta) for members of the D.C. Metro Club, an organization of Atlanta University Center students who hailed from the Washington, DC, area. In 1989 the event was held at Washington Park, in the Hunter Hills neighborhood, and featured a live band playing DC's go-go music, drawing twenty thousand attendees. With increased attendance came complaints from residents of neighborhoods in southwestern Atlanta and parts of Dekalb County concerning excessive traffic, noise, littering, and public drunkenness. Because the problems occurred in predominantly black areas of town, the concerns of residents failed to garner much attention from mainstream media outlets or civic leaders. Recalling this experience, the *Atlanta Journal-Constitution* reader Sharese Shields wrote in a 1994 letter to the editor, "Those residents raised sand, to no avail. It wasn't until last year, when some Midtown residents complained . . . that city officials expressed newfound sympathy."[5]

After a decade of organic, gradual growth within the largely black middle-class neighborhoods around the Atlanta University Center (a grouping of historically black colleges and universities located to the west of downtown Atlanta), Freaknik burst its previously inscribed boundaries in the early 1990s. For most of the city's white residents, this was when Freaknik intruded into their consciousness, in the form of increased traffic and congestion on roads and the unsettling presence of large groups of young, rowdy African Americans. As noted by Sharese Shields above, the penetration of Freaknik into the Midtown neighborhood—"Atlanta's oldest and most widely recognized center of visible LGBT activity" and home to the venerable Piedmont Park—was a watershed moment in terms of consciousness outside the African American community of Freaknik's existence and the problems surrounding it.[6]

By 1993 Freaknik drew approximately one hundred thousand to Atlanta; the 1994 event saw a doubling of that number. Cruising the streets and socializing became the principal activities of attendees in spite of countless attempts by civic authorities, student organizers, and event promoters to draw revelers into more contained events and venues. Once confined to black neighborhoods, in 1993 and 1994 Freaknik spilled over into mostly white areas such as Midtown and the area around Piedmont Park. The African American mayor, Bill Campbell (elected in 1994), tried to straddle the growing divide between (mostly white) Intown property owners and business interests and (mostly black) supporters of the students' right to gather. Many white opponents of Freaknik were less than successful in concealing the racial baggage they brought to the debate, while black supporters often appealed to racial solidarity in their arguments.

In 1957, the black sociologist E. Franklin Frazier asserted that "the role of Negro politicians has been restricted to attempting to satisfy the demands of Negro voters while acting as the servants of the political machines supported by the propertied classes in the white community," a statement that accurately describes Bill Campbell's ambiguous stance on Freaknik.[7] In 1994, Campbell made the mistake of openly discouraging the revelers from coming to the city, a position he quickly abandoned. After that year, Campbell combined a strategy of zero-tolerance policing of the event with a public position that blandly asserted that "everyone is welcome, but we expect them to obey the laws."[8] Lambasted from all sides for his waffling, Campbell still survived an electoral challenge in 1997 from the president of the city council (and on-the-record Freaknik opponent), Marvin Arrington, and eventually saw the festival's attendance reduced to nothing before he left office. In his public statements, especially those to mostly black audiences, Campbell used careful wording to try to minimize his political vulnerability on the issue. He emphasized to black audiences that "everyone is welcome," while assuring Intown property owners that "the city of Atlanta is not going to host Freaknik."[9]

As the Freaknik tradition picked up steam in the early 1990s, political and civic leaders expressed growing concern over some of its problematic aspects. According to the reporter Kathy Scruggs, the "laissez-faire approach to crowd control" of Atlanta's African American chief of police, Eldrin Bell, resulted in "an unusually peaceful Freaknik weekend" in 1994, although several sexual assaults against women were reported.[10] The *Atlanta Journal-Constitution* reported that "at least one young woman was sexually assaulted in Downtown," and "a police officer working the crowd on Marietta Street said a second woman was assaulted, but he would not provide details."[11] Anecdotal reports of women's unpleasant experiences at the 1994 Freaknik also began to trickle into press reports. Jillet Earnest, an Emory University freshman, complained that "guys were extra-wild and overly friendly."[12] As the problems with Freaknik escalated well beyond issues of traffic control, Campbell's increasingly stern rhetoric regarding the festival seemed justified to many residents. At least by 1994, sexual harassment and assault of women by men had been reported at the events, a trend that seemed to worsen as the annual tradition moved into the late nineties. In addition, the 1995 Freaknik had descended into the looting of mall stores at Underground Atlanta, and violent crime (almost always directed against Freaknik participants themselves) increasingly marred the gathering.

During the Freaknik festivities, both men and women used handheld camcorders—"the accessory of choice"—to engage fellow participants and to document their own experience. While many women performed willingly for groups of men holding cameras, there are indications that some women did not appreciate the invasive nature of the practice. Darrius Watson claimed that "a few of the girls I've met trip out and pretend to be shy when I turn the camera on them . . . but you just know they're really not. Nobody's shy during Freaknik."[13] Watson's confidence that "you just know" that girls really weren't shy is disturbingly reminiscent of the attitude of men who cannot seem to understand a woman saying no to a sexual proposition. Newspaper articles such as one referring to "a group of men with cameras [who] coaxed a woman at Underground Atlanta to dance the booty wop" in 1994 often portrayed the voyeuristic practice as simply part of the collegiate fun, but as incidents in later Freaknik gatherings would demonstrate, "coaxing" and "encouraging" easily gave way to demanding and forcing.[14]

This aspect of intrusive male sexuality was certainly present in the Freaknik celebrations after (and perhaps even before) 1994. A description of a sexual assault from the 1995 gathering was published in the *Journal-Constitution* in 1999, as Andrea Harvey recalled how she "found herself surrounded by at least 40 guys" in the food court of South Dekalb Mall. "They engulfed me. Pulled my dress off. Groped me in places," said Harvey. "I was pretty hysterical, but no one heard my screams." The article notes that "although most of the faces were unfamiliar, she saw at least two people she knew from high school."[15] Significantly, Harvey remained silent about the assault for years, perhaps because of the tendency observed by Johnnetta Betsch Cole and Beverly Guy-Sheftall: "When

Black women 'break the silence' about our experiences with Black men, especially sexual ones, there is intense anger in our communities."[16] Harvey's advice to future Freaknik attendees remained mixed despite her bad experience: "I didn't talk about it for a while," she said. "Now, when the discussion comes up, I'll talk about it. I don't know if I would advise people not to go, but I would advise them on the situation they put themselves in by just being there."[17]

The lawlessness, rowdyism, and sexual abuse associated with Freaknik helped the case of those who advocated a zero-tolerance approach, and as the 1990s came to a close, the numbers of attendees gradually dwindled. By 2000 Freaknik was a fading memory for Atlantans, pleasant or unpleasant depending upon one's perspective. The controversy over young black college students' gathering and claiming public space moved on to other locales, such as Myrtle Beach, South Carolina (Black Bike Week), Daytona Beach, Florida (Black College Reunion), and Biloxi, Mississippi (Black Spring Break). Nonetheless, the story of Freaknik reveals much about the racialized tendencies in politics, governance, and media in Atlanta and their troublesome intersections with other modes of identification.

Scholars who have analyzed Freaknik, including the media scholar Marian Meyers and the art historian Krista Thompson, have pointed to a racial divide that played a central role in the discourse and attitudes about the gathering. They have also called attention to the ways in which ideas around gender, class, and sexuality impacted the discourse around Freaknik. Additionally, they have theorized a connection between the racialized discourse and reception of Freaknik and a growing trend of violence against and harassment of women within the annual event.

In a 2004 article, Marian Meyers uses black feminist theory in an effort to understand how "the convergence of gender, race, and class oppressions" impacted media representations of Freaknik. For media commentators and local officials, this complex of oppressions "[minimized] the seriousness of the violence" against black women and relied upon victim-blaming rhetoric that revealed the lower social capital commanded by black women in the public sphere. Meyers also identifies "a racialized context that blamed locals rather than students for any acts of violence." For Meyers, understanding the media discourse around the event requires thinking outside a simplistic black-and-white framework and accounting for the impact of other forms of identification, although the latter were often folded into a racialized discourse. As Meyers shows, the fact that young black women were the targets for most of the harassment and violence skewed the media coverage of the event. The author further points to the important role of class in the portrayal of the event: poorer "locals" often took the rap for violent or criminal behavior, while middle-class college students were tacitly absolved from blame.[18]

According to Krista Thompson, the increased police presence and the higher number of arrests that characterized the Freaknik gatherings after 1994 fostered an increasingly hostile climate for women participants. In her 2007 article, Thompson shows how the event's public image of black female sexual display and performance emerged in conversation with the surveillance and repression of the event by authorities and the mainstream media. Thompson focuses on the intertwined effects of race, gender, and class in the public discourse around Freaknik, asserting that "the sexualized behavior of young women" and "the constant videotaping of women by male participants" that defined the event in the mainstream media after 1994 should be seen as embodied protest against "local government officials' sustained attempts at controlling space and imposing order on the bodies of black youth within Atlanta." Thompson argues that "specific spatial divisions in the city based in race, gender and class affect minority groups in particular ways and transformed the city more broadly." Thompson theorizes a link between the prevalence of videocameras, the rise in violence against women, and the increasingly repressive response by the police and the media: "The constant videotaping of women by male participants suggests that the authorities' culture of surveillance surrounding Freaknic generally was reproduced or redirected, on a microlevel within the event, on the black female body."[19]

x x x

An understanding of the social and demographic history of Atlanta sheds light on the politics and discourse around Freaknik. Over nearly two centuries of existence, Atlanta has been the site of numerous conflicts and tensions between racialized groups around the use of public space. Like slavery, racism, and segregation generally, these conflicts often involved important dimensions related to other modes of identification, including gender, sexuality, and social class. The 1906 Atlanta Riot, in which mobs killed at least twenty-five blacks and two whites, was inflamed by reports in local (white-owned) newspapers about alleged sexual crimes committed by black men against white women, a common rationale for mob violence against blacks throughout the South.

The lynching of the middle-class Jewish factory owner Leo Frank in 1915 revolved around claims that he had sexually attacked and murdered a young working-class Christian white woman. While whites justified violence against blacks and other minorities with the purported sexual threat to white women's virtue, the protest movements that were in turn fueled by this violence often resorted to a masculinist discourse of rights (e.g., "I *am* a man"), in which the specific concerns of black women and gay men were subordinated, reinscribing the sexism, patriarchy, and homophobia of mainstream American society. As Patricia Hill Collins observed, "Maintaining racial solidarity at all costs often requires replicating hierarchies of gender, social class, sexuality, and nation in Black civil society."[20]

Just as the African American struggle for civil rights has at times been conceptualized by its middle-class, heterosexual, college-educated male leaders in reductive and exclusionary ways, the image and self-identity of particular places have also been the products of oversimplification and have relied upon the invisibility of entire communities of people. The "new South" imagined by the urban booster Henry Grady in the late nineteenth century was imagined for the benefit of and represented by the same class of people who had ruled the region during slavery times, upper-class white men. In spite of the growing numbers of black arrivals in Atlanta in response to the transformation of the agricultural system throughout the twentieth century, it took the civil rights movement and the elimination of de jure segregation (and the resultant white flight) to allow Atlanta to be seen, as in Parliament's 1975 song, as one of America's "Chocolate Cities."

From the election of the city's first black mayor in 1974 to the emergence of Atlanta as a "black mecca" for migrants fleeing declining Rust Belt cities in the 1990s, the last few decades of the twentieth century saw the city redefine itself as one in which African Americans not only formed a majority percentage of the population but also held positions of power and influence. While "white flight" populated the northern suburbs, a thriving black business establishment and a cluster of historically black colleges and universities around the Atlanta University Center formed an anchor in the urban center for the city's growing black middle class. But Atlanta was not just a magnet for blacks; seeking increased economic opportunity and liberation from constraining small-town values, large numbers of gay men and lesbians from around the South flocked to the city in the later decades of the twentieth century. By 2006, 12.8 percent of the city's population identified as LGBT, making Atlanta the home to the nation's third largest (behind San Francisco and Seattle) per capita gay population.[21]

Because Freaknik involved black students, and because many of its opponents were white residents of Intown neighborhoods, the issue of racism quickly became central to the public debate. Many black residents of Atlanta were skeptical of the energetic assertions by whites opposed to the gathering that racism or fear of blacks had no effect upon their position, suspecting, as Sean C. Gooden did, that "the root of their concerns . . . is purely racial."[22] A review of the anti-Freaknik letters to the editor leaves little doubt that racism—specifically, fears of young black people, and especially young black males—informed the views of many white opponents of the event. The common understanding of opposition to Freaknik was expressed by the Lithonia resident Richard Kenyada, who wrote in a letter to the editor that "perhaps had the students been blond, blue-eyed, Ivy League types, Freaknik would have been perceived for what it was—just another college romp."[23] While there is undoubtedly some truth to his assertion—many of the letters to the editor that condemned Freaknik often did so by way of barely concealed racial stereotypes—this representation of opposition to Freaknik as racially motivated led to a tendency among many in the African American community to write a blank check of support for the college students and their activities.

Tensions ran high around the subject of Freaknik, and the discursive strategies mustered for and against the gathering suffered from significant limitations. African American supporters of Freaknik often allowed questions of race to dominate, to the exclusion of other important issues of oppression that were in fact affecting the event and its reception by the public and the city government. Ultimately, this narrow focus upon race, together with the related reluctance to recognize some of the more problematic aspects of the gathering, served to undermine their position and helped the anti-Freaknik forces banish the event from Atlanta's streets. At the same time, African Americans who opposed the event often employed arguments that relied upon patriarchal notions of propriety and male control of women's bodies and expressions. Defenders of the event were often reluctant to address the problematic gender dynamics of Freaknik, as racial solidarity took precedence over serious or extended engagement with issues related to gender, class, and sexual orientation. This development would only serve to complicate a debate that, on the pro-Freaknik side, had been reduced largely to racial terms for both strategic and historical reasons.

Despite the willingness of some African Americans to acknowledge or condemn the problematic aspects of Freaknik, a general tendency of racial solidarity prevailed among many commentators. In an editorial following the 1994 gathering, Cynthia Tucker referred to the harmful potential of this unqualified support. Describing Freaknik as Atlanta's "own racial Rorschach test," Tucker claimed that "while there are those white citizens who tolerate it as an amusing outing by college students and there are those black citizens who view it as an unwelcome intrusion, those are not the typical reactions."[24] In her editorial, Tucker did not specifically address the fact that such racial solidarity often comes at the expense of other concerns within the black community, such as those around gender, class, and sexuality, although concerns for the safety of women during Freaknik would preoccupy her in every subsequent editorial that she wrote on the gathering.

Tucker's perception of a tolerant attitude toward Freaknik on the part of Atlanta's black community—combined with or perhaps even driven by a suspicion that opposition to the festival was largely due to racism—was more or less confirmed in a poll taken by the *Atlanta Journal-Constitution* in the wake of the 1995 event. Fifty-seven percent of the black respondents (as opposed to 22 percent of the white respondents) agreed with the statement that "most of the opposition to Freaknik is the result of racism," and only 31 percent of black respondents thought that the gathering was a "bad thing" for the city. The poll reveals other interesting distinctions between black and white public opinion on the issue. Of those who were opposed to Freaknik (31 percent of the black respondents and 76 percent of the white respondents), black respondents were more likely than their white counterparts to cite "lewd behavior" as the principal problem, as opposed to "crime" or overly large crowds. Of those who supported the gathering, blacks were more likely than whites to cite "good for business" and "attracts future residents, businesses to city" as rationales, whereas a greater percentage of the white supporters believed that the festival "projects [a] fun, energetic image for [the] city."[25]

The focus on racism and the perception of a black-white divide in support for Freaknik contributed to a general silence around issues of gender and sexuality among the defenders of Freaknik and allowed or encouraged problems to worsen over the course of the late nineties. By 1998 and 1999, fewer women were attending the gathering, and reports of rapes and sexual assaults were growing, giving vital ammunition to those who would ban the gathering from city streets. The emphasis upon racial solidarity on the part of black defenders of Freaknik led to a downplaying of what was going on between black men and black women on the streets of Atlanta during the gathering. Furthermore, the emphasis upon racial solidarity made any discussion of the possible role of gay black men and women in Freaknik completely impossible. As Cole and Guy-Sheftall observed, "Rarely, except among a small group of feminists and other gender-progressives, is there serious consideration of the importance of moving beyond a race-only analysis in understanding the complexities of African American communities and the challenges we face."[26]

This analysis is important for understanding the public debate around Freaknik among African Americans in Atlanta. Especially in Freaknik's early years, advocates devoted much effort to criticizing the underlying racial motivations of those who would ban the festival from Atlanta's streets. Despite some early warning signs from female participants, little effort was made to understand or change the dynamics around gender and sexuality involved in the event. Some prominent African Americans, especially members of the editorial board of the *Atlanta Journal-Constitution,* tried to draw attention to the persistent problems of male harassment of women during Freaknik, but others—including university administrators, members of the clergy, and college students defending the festival—seemed blind to the reality that Freaknik was, over the years, becoming increasingly dangerous to black women. None expressed any concern about the fact that the gathering's basis upon a notion of African American community left little to no space for LGBT participants, making their participation more or less invisible.

The problems associated with Freaknik were evident, in a much more subtle form, from the early days of the festival. In fact, for some, the name of the festival itself speaks to the degradation of women. In his article "The Language of Soul," Claude Brown includes *freak* in a group of "certain soul terms which, no matter how often borrowed, remain in the canon and are re-activated every so often."[27] Whatever its historical meaning, by the 1980s *freak* was generally understood within the African American youth subculture as referring to a sexually willing, uninhibited female. Most versions of the early history of Freaknik presented in the *Atlanta Journal-Constitution* do not delve into the specific meaning of *freak* within contemporary and historical African American culture, instead positing that particular songs (Chic's "Le Freak" and Funkadelic's "Freak of the Week") or dances served as the inspiration for the name, an etymology repeated in Thompson's 2007 article.[28]

This tendency to refer to song titles instead of to the less tangible subcultural meaning of *freak* effectively downplays the sexual connotations of the name Freaknik. Still, observers of the gathering and authors of letters to the editor bring a more negative connotation to the *freak* in Freaknik. In 1994, G. Edward Brown wrote in a letter to the editor, "I dislike intensely our young men and women being labeled as freaks. Yet, evidently some are, based on what I witnessed at last year's event."[29] An article on the 1993 gathering quoted Kim Yates, a 22-year-old Spelman senior, as saying that "a lot of brothers come to the event expecting to see the type of women the name suggests." The article went on to claim that "at least one brother revealed that the event's name refers to sexual activity." In the same article, the Morehouse junior Kevin Bowling claimed, "It's not a celebration of anything, just ignorance and nothing relevant."[30] These comments demonstrate that even in its early days Freaknik—and the celebration of "freaks"—did not enjoy unqualified support from African American students.

Concerns over the negative gendered connotations of the word *freak* were probably behind various debates over the past and present names of the festival. Miriam Y. Morris wrote to the *Journal-Constitution* to challenge previously published histories of the event that had traced its origins to the first 1982 D.C. Metro Club event, claiming, "Freaknik in all its glory stems from the early Umoja Festival days of [historically black colleges and universities] Clark, Morehouse, Spelman and Morris Brown."[31] Although Morris embraced the new name Freaknik in her letter, others were concerned that it set the tone for sexualized, exploitative, and potentially embarrassing behavior. This was the motivation behind several attempts to change the name of the gathering. Among the proposed replacements for Freaknik were FreedomFest (to link the gathering with Atlanta's civil rights legacy) and the more purely descriptive name Black College Spring Break Weekend.[32]

By the early 1990s the gathering seemed to be stuck with the name Freaknik, along with the set of attitudes about gender and sexuality that came with it. Still, well-intentioned reformers continued their efforts; in 1999, Byron Amos, a member of a municipal committee appointed to "examine" the gathering, claimed, "We are trying to convert Freaknik into Black College Spring Break, which is a more productive and respectable event."[33] In an effort to grapple with Freaknik's problems at a more substantive level, a group of Atlanta University students calling themselves Black Men for the Eradication of Sexism staged a demonstration during the 1995 gathering "in protest of the sexism and misogyny that have become hallmarks of Freaknik."[34] An article in the nationally circulated black women's magazine *Essence* told of the genesis of the now-defunct group: "The group was born shortly after 1994's Freaknik... when, at Spelman during a presentation in Professor Gloria Wade-Gayle's class on Images of Black Women in the Media, several sisters described their experiences of being nearly raped, fondled and called out of their names [i.e., addressed with offensive epithets]. Since then, they've been bonding around ways to fight date rape, sexual harassment, pornography, freak-me music videos and paternalism in Black organizations."[35]

The success of efforts such as this to raise consciousness of the problematic nature of gender relations during Freaknik is hard to gauge. While opposition to the climate of misogyny and abuse that was beginning to characterize the annual gathering was somewhat evident within the black college community, expressions of these sentiments by black collegians in citywide forums such as the editorial pages of the *Journal-Constitution* were few and far between, and little to no mention was made of the possible role of LGBT participants in Freaknik. While black columnists such as Cynthia Tucker, Jeff Dickerson, and Fredrick Robinson were more or less unanimous in their condemnation of Freaknik, many black women, college age and older, wrote to the newspaper to express their support for the event.

Typical of these letters was one on the eve of the 1994 Freaknik by Kimberley Shepherd, "a black female college student who has never been to Freaknik," who wrote that "when black people are involved, there seems to be an extra hint of anger and intolerance." The Decatur resident Valerie Thompson, eloquently describing herself as "an African American feeling once again the sting of unjustified racial panic," wrote, "I can't tell what it is the students have done in past years that justifies being treated as poorly as they have been."[36] The city councilwoman Carolyn Long Banks, one of the most prominent defenders of Freaknik among black public officials during the period 1994–95, was roundly criticized by Tucker, Dickerson, and various authors of letters to the editor for her "narrow-minded, racially divisive focus."[37] The emphasis on racism and the polarization of the public discourse around Freaknik along racial lines was a powerful distraction from a fact that was becoming clear by 1995, namely, that those put at greatest risk during Freaknik were young black women.[38]

As sexual assaults upon women became a more common feature of Freaknik during the mid-1990s, observers from both the pro- and anti-Freaknik camps fell back upon classic rationalizations for excessive male behavior. In an interview on the eve of the 1995 event, the black police chief, Beverly Harvard, lamented, "It's really sad we would have black women, young girls out there, who have no more respect for themselves. We had some of them out there totally taking off their tops and pulling up their dresses and skirts and dropping their pants in public. That's the kind of stuff that's got to go."[39]

This statement drew a harsh response from Christina Drake, an Atlanta resident, who called Harvard's implication "that women are responsible for the lewd, hostile, violent and illegal treatment many of them received at the hands of men . . . a classic case of blaming the victim for the crime." Drake also noted that "news coverage on sexual assault at Freaknik was way too limited. Grady Rape Crisis Center reported 10 rapes within a 12-hour period this weekend. It is highly probable other rapes went unreported because many of the women attending Freaknik were from out of town and very young." Drake concluded, suggestively, that the downplaying of sexual assaults and the emphasis on coverage of looting incidents at Underground Atlanta and Greenbriar Mall could be taken to mean "that theft prevention is a higher priority in this city than the safety of women."[40]

A reluctance to focus on the responsibility of African American men and a corresponding emphasis on the "type of women" who attended Freaknik seemed to hobble any efforts to come to terms with what was really happening at Freaknik. The Florida resident and police major Angel Crawford cited her concerns about "the assaults and the type of women who come up there" as her rationale for forbidding her daughter Porsche from attending Freaknik.[41] Other black parents also expressed their desire to protect their daughters from the excesses of Freaknik: in a 1999 column, Jeff Dickerson wrote that "two things must happen before the dawn of [his infant daughter Lia's] teen years: I must construct a tall fort, and Freaknik must go far, far away."[42] Dickerson's and Crawford's attitudes, while somewhat understandable, also have undertones of patriarchal control of female children. Especially disturbing in this context is Dickerson's reference to a "tall fort" that would presumably isolate his daughter from contact with the outside world, with the ultimate goal of controlling her sexuality.

Some whites who wrote in support of Freaknik seemed to want to build racial harmony or understanding on the backs of women participants. Paul Howle, in an editorial for the *Journal-Constitution* after the 1994 event, decried the racist fear that kept whites away, while endorsing some of the more questionable practices around issues of gender. His initial trepidation about walking the streets as an older white man during Freaknik evaporated when

he and a middle-aged black man were both captivated by a spectacle of female sexual display: "Suddenly, our racial identities just fell away. We weren't
black or white anymore. We were just men, doing what men have been doing
since the dawn of time: girl-watching."[43] In Howle's narrative, an experience of
gender-based male solidarity in the consumption of female sexuality leads to
the elimination of "racial identities." Despite Howle's admirable intention to
dispel the rumors that the event was dangerous for white people, the climate
of "girl-watching" that he celebrated was one of Freaknik's most problematic
features, centrally connected to the strongly heteronormative character of
the event.

As a group, black women apparently were not entirely comfortable with
this state of affairs, and by the late nineties their attendance at Freaknik started
to drop off. In 1997, Jeff Dickerson foresaw the role that decreased female attendance might have upon Freaknik: "America's young black women, who have
far more self-respect than the hiphop culture gives them credit for, will grow
tired of being chased and squeezed and groped and worse on the streets of
Atlanta." Dickerson concluded, "When the young honeys start to stay home,
this party's likely to last as long as, well, the Million Man March."[44] In 1999,
the *Journal-Constitution* reported that "fewer black college-age kids showed
up, and fewer still were female. The aggressive and too-often abusive behavior
of many male participants in earlier years had apparently scared off many
women, and for good reason."[45]

During the 1998 Freaknik, four rapes and six sexual assaults were reported,
although it is likely, as suggested by Christina Drake above, that many more
actually occurred. By 1999 the festival was on the wane, and from all reports,
female attendance had dropped dramatically. Dickerson, reporting on the
1999 event, claimed that "young women, so badly treated in Freakniks past,
got smart and stayed away." Dickerson cited Nicole Gibson of Spelman College,
who claimed that "there were 10 to 20 guys to every girl (in Grant Park) and
they were really rude and disrespectful."[46]

In an editorial for the *Atlanta Journal-Constitution,* John Head wrote that
he was "especially proud of the Spelman College students who publicly said
they would not take part this year and urged other women to boycott, too."
The Spelman students "wore buttons saying, 'I am not a Freak'—'Freak' being
a slang term for a woman who is nothing more than a sex object."[47] The president of the Atlanta City Council, Robb Pitts, while still hewing to the insistence of "isolated incidents" rather than a pervasive climate of misogynistic

abuse, claimed that "the word got out among women on some of the isolated incidents of some of the negative things that happened to women." Pitts continued: "If the women aren't here, the men stop coming. I think we're finally seeing the final chapters of Freaknik in Atlanta."[48]

This raises the rather interesting question of what really ended Freaknik in Atlanta. Was it young black women's voting with their feet, as it were? Was it the deliberate throttling down of the party through increased law enforcement? Mayor Bill Campbell, whose two terms of office covered the years of the event's major presence in Atlanta, is often credited with achieving the impossible: bringing an end to the "roaming party" without alienating the black voters of Atlanta, who often saw opposition to Freaknik as "a conspiracy of white racists and Uncle Toms trying to spoil their wholesome fun."[49] However, the decrease in female attendance seems to have been a key reason why the enthusiasm for Freaknik died out in the black collegiate community.

Based upon Cole and Guy-Sheftall's assertions that "Black women are often victimized by the sexism of Black men who may be compensating for the ways in which racism disempowers them and makes them feel unmanly," one might conclude, as did Krista Thompson above, that the atmosphere of confrontation between the police and the revelers actually stimulated the increase in sexual assaults, which in turn discouraged female attendance and ultimately ended the gathering. Cole and Guy-Sheftall assert that "the resentment, hostility, and disdain that many young Black men feel towards the police and 'the System' have been directed at Black females."[50] If this was indeed the mechanism by which the zero-tolerance policy led to the end of Freaknik, Mayor Campbell and Police Chief Harvard may have had less to be proud of than is commonly assumed. Still, the ways in which such problematic gender dynamics doomed Freaknik to failure seemed to be mostly lost on those who wrote in defense of the gathering during the late 1990s.

While many African American commentators, particularly those who supported the event, either minimized the seriousness of the attacks against women participants or blamed the victims for their treatment, issues around social class were seen as a more acceptable subject of debate. A prominent aspect of this discussion was the assertion of difference in intent and wholesomeness between black collegians and nonstudents. Following the 1995 event, in which stores at Underground Atlanta and Greenbriar Mall were looted, Jacquelyn A. Anthony wrote that while the "college students . . . basically act like all college students act," the real problems were the result of "the local unsavory element that decides to join the fun." Anthony continued: "The incidents last weekend were not caused by students but by city riffraff. The looters were home-grown. It's not the fault of college students that we can't control our own."[51] In 1996, an unsigned anti-Freaknik editorial in the *Journal-Constitution* claimed that "nonstudent thugs and predators predictably attach themselves to the event and have been primarily responsible for the lootings, shootings and rapes."[52] Taking its cue from local sources, the *New York Times* reported, "A brief flurry of looting occurred Friday night but officials said it was carried out by 'a group of local, dedicated, free-lance hoodlums.'"[53]

However, not all African Americans were convinced by this argument. Nathan Williams, a 24-year-old black man from Powder Springs who by his own admission had "been to Freaknik three times," claimed that "the common refrain" was that locals were responsible for "the looting, senseless acts of ag-gression and random acts of violence." Williams's response to those who would blame local thugs was: "Don't fool yourselves. College students aren't innocent in these occurrences. When a young woman wears what amounts to under-wear to take a stroll, it is not a given that she wants to be fondled or harassed. She may be exhibiting bad taste, bad judgment and a lack of self-esteem, but not a willingness to be attacked by men."[54]

While locals doubtless participated in the various criminal acts that oc-curred during the festival, Williams is probably correct to insist upon the participation of black college men—often portrayed as the nation's "best and brightest" young African Americans—in the misdeeds of Freaknik. Still, those who saw connections between the atmosphere of sexual assault and harass-ment of women and the fraternity culture from which the event grew were decidedly in the minority in the public debate over Freaknik. In a 1997 arti-cle in *The Fire This Time,* an African American student magazine published at Emory University, Robert Watson made the somewhat hyperbolic compar-ison between black college fraternities and black gangs, observing as a point of correspondence that "violence is another gang characteristic commonly associated with African American Greek organizations."[55] While Watson was referring specifically to the male-on-male violence of hazing, which has been associated with these organizations, his observation is especially germane to the discussion of sexual abuse of women.

Abusive and exploitative treatment of women is, unfortunately, an all too common feature of fraternity life, whether black or white. Those who pro-moted the questionable distinction between "local thugs" and the "best and brightest" collegians—which is reminiscent of E. Franklin Frazier's observation that "Negro students were supposed to be differentiated in their morals as well as in their manners from the Negro masses"—often let black college men off the hook for the Freaknik transgressions.[56] Failing to acknowledge the problematic nature of this argument was yet another way in which members of the black community (especially those who supported Freaknik) overlooked or chose to ignore a variety of factors in the interest of collective resistance to racism.

Among the African Americans who opposed Freaknik—a group that included all of the blacks on the editorial staff of the *Journal-Constitution* and a minority of black letter writers—social class seemed to be less of an issue than perceived generational differences with regard to appropriate behavior by blacks in public spaces. Perceived generational differences were often expressed through appeals to the "dignity" of the heroes of the civil rights era (even though many members of the civil rights generation, including Hosea Williams, were actually Freaknik supporters). Samuel Adams expressed a common view among black opponents of Freaknik when he wrote that "it is becoming painfully evident that there is a fissure between African American elders, who protested and died for their community, and African American youth, who have not internalized the struggles of their ancestors."[57]

On the eve of the 1995 Freaknik, Jeff Dickerson made the presumptuous assertion that various prominent black icons—Ida B. Wells, Paul Robeson, Malcolm X, Martin Luther King Jr., Andrew Young, Oprah Winfrey, and Johnnetta Cole—had in common the fact that "nary a one of them would be caught dead shaking their booties on the hood of a car on Peachtree Street." Dickerson went on to say that black students "have an obligation, a racial duty" to present a dignified image while in Atlanta.[58] The Reverend Joseph Lowery wrote in response that neither he nor Dickerson could say whether these individuals had engaged in such behavior in their youth, and he pointed out that "one of those he [Dickerson] mentioned [Malcolm X, to whom we should add Lindy-Hopper] was a drug pusher at one time but matured and became a useful citizen."[59] Instead of arguing against patriarchy, many Freaknik critics like Adams, Dickerson, and Eric Abercrumbie—who claimed that "Freaknik is a mockery to our ancestors"—often harnessed its power through an appeal to a masculinized discourse of ancestral sacrifice and struggle.[60]

Those who invoked the civil rights struggle failed to acknowledge some of the most painful sacrifices of that era, namely, those made by gays like

Bayard Rustin, whose contributions to the movement were made invisible in the name of strategic racial solidarity and conservative, religiously derived norms of identity and behavior. In their contributions to the public discourse around Freaknik, supporters failed to appreciate the ways in which the "understanding and consideration of minorities who simultaneously operate within marginalized racial and sexual statuses" might have helped their cause. Freaknik and the harassment of women that came to characterize it took place against a backdrop of heterosexual normativity.[61] The consideration of the influence of sexual "orientation" or preference was almost completely obscured under the race-dominated discourse that swirled around Freaknik. While gay men and lesbians were almost certainly among the crowds from the beginning, their invisibility was achieved through statements and attitudes such as that expressed by the attendee Keith Bloodsaw: "What Freaknik is all about is men meeting women."[62]

Rather than promoting an inclusive vision of Freaknik in which gay participation was welcomed, African American letter writers more often posited gays in an oppositional role within their arguments, reinscribing "the heteronormative logic that conditions the ascription of 'authentic' black identity on the repudiation of gay and lesbian sexualities."[63] When they did refer to Atlanta's large LGBT community, it was to suggest that black youth celebrating Freaknik were not being treated as well as the similar number of people who attended Atlanta's yearly Gay Pride festival. Andrea Harris, of Decatur, betrayed some conspiratorial suspicions when she asked in 1993, "Why did the paper make such a big thing about the trash and traffic problems at Piedmont Park during Freaknik, but there were no such reports after the Gay Pride celebration?"[64] In an otherwise sensible defense of Freaknik in which he touched upon blacks' right to use public space and the racism-tainted politics of urban planning, the civil rights activist Gus Howard resorted to lurid imagery of "Lesbian women . . . walking around bare-breasted" and "Men . . . kissing and fondling each other in public" to argue that Gay Pride attendees received more lenient treatment than Freaknik attendees: "Campbell is saying that gays are welcome to Atlanta and black college students aren't."[65]

Howard's antigay bias was revealed not only by the implication of equivalency between consensual, nonaggressive acts and sexual assaults and harassment but also by the implication that the Gay Pride celebrants were less deserving of a warm welcome because of their supposed inadequacy in terms of biological or social reproduction: "The students at least represent a future, but what about the gays?"[66] The Atlanta resident Avis Crockett voiced a similar sentiment, contrasting the treatment of black students with that of Gay Pride attendees: "We do not give these students—the cream of the crop of our black students in America—the rights that they are afforded, yet Atlanta welcomes the gay movement—more than 300,000 folks at the Gay Pride festival in June— with open arms. For these black students—two of whom are my magna cum laude sons—to be treated the way they were at this year's Freaknik is embarrassing."[67] Such rhetoric contributed to the divide between the mostly black Freaknik partiers and the mostly white Midtown gay community. Attitudes such as these stood in the way of compromise and tolerance and only hastened the demise of Freaknik in Atlanta.

For its part, Atlanta's gay community—which is well represented in the In-town neighborhoods where Freaknik intruded after 1993—made little effort to reach across the lines of race and heterosexism that delineated Freaknik. Many seemed to see the same blacks-versus-gays opposition as the black letter writers quoted above. In 1994, Christopher Johnson, of Atlanta, wrote that "it's a shame Atlanta's guests for Freaknik can't behave as well as those for Gay Pride," while in 1996 Anthony Vicari asked, "Why, Mr. Mayor, are you willing to let a bunch of students overrun the most gay area of town, forcing the gay bars to close, for a total net loss of upward of several million dollars?"[68] Several writers, however, made more constructive criticisms as they responded in 1997 to charges of city favoritism of gays over blacks: "The organizers of Freaknik (if there are any) should learn from the organizers of Gay Pride."[69]

The issue of homosexuality and the staunch resistance to discussion or acknowledgment of its presence on the campuses of historically black colleges and universities came to the fore in a dramatic way in June 2003, when Aaron Price (son of a conservative Chicago minister) used a baseball bat to brutally attack a fellow Morehouse student in the shower after what he perceived as homosexual flirtation. The response of Morehouse, critics asserted, reflected an atmosphere in which "gay men—who didn't have a recognized student group until this semester—often have to fend for themselves, getting support from other gay students or in the local gay nightlife. Morehouse touts values such as diversity and tolerance, but gay and straight students alike said the administration is largely silent about homosexuality."[70] Given that the black collegiate community is only now beginning to attempt to discuss and resolve this issue, it is not hard to imagine the ways in which the invisibility of gay, lesbian, or bisexual students impacted the character of Freaknik in the early to mid-1990s.

The heterosexual machismo that came to define the celebration became one of Freaknik's most expensive liabilities.

There is little doubt that Freaknik exposed an ugly undercurrent of racial tension between blacks and whites in Atlanta, one in which black youths are subject to increased scrutiny, surveillance, and criticism when they enter the public sphere. This tension continues to exist below the surface of debates about cruising, noise ordinances, and the closing times of the Buckhead bar district. And despite a few Freaknik success stories of racial harmony, acceptance, or understanding, the event generally did not help bridge the divide between blacks and whites in Atlanta. While one may find some slight consolation in the fact that Freaknik probably did not increase racial tensions, the entire saga of the festival and its support and opposition represented an enormous expenditure of effort and emotion on all sides. If any positive results are to come from Freaknik, the lessons must be embraced rather than avoided. Because of the manner in which the public debate unfolded—with white opponents generally attempting to minimize the intrusion of issues of race and racism into the discussion and black supporters attempting to bring questions of race to the fore—these lessons are also different for each group, although related in a very basic way.

On the side of the white opponents, coming to terms with the Freaknik phenomenon should consist in an acknowledgment of the potential role of fear in their interactions with and perception of young black people. While the disclaimer "This is not about race" became a mantra in the letters of those opposed to the festival, none of them acknowledged the simple (and painfully obvious) fact that *some* of the reaction to Freaknik on the part of Intown white residents *was* determined by racism and stereotypes. Some comments leave little doubt on this score, as they rely on classically racist images of black disorder. Such was the case in a shrill 1993 letter to the editor from the Atlanta resident Claude H. Grady III, who raised the specter of "innocent people stuck in traffic being terrorized by 'gangs' trying to roll their cars over just for fun" and concluded ominously that "these people did not come to party in Atlanta; they came to destroy it."[71] These expressions of racism—some more blatant than others—were often framed within the historical stereotype of blacks as out-of-control sexual beings.

Despite the all too common reliance upon such images, however, the fact remains that racism was probably a much less significant reason for opposition to Freaknik than the massive inconvenience and disorder that the party caused. Still, to deny its effects entirely is to engage in dissimulation. The refusal on the part of white anti-Freaknik commentators to acknowledge that some of their allies in the cause were driven by racially based fear or bias may have been strategically justifiable, but it resulted in an atmosphere of tension between themselves and black citizens, many of whom were understandably frustrated by the fact that white people seemed unable to face up to the facts of racism. Unfortunately, more recent letters to the editor about the Buckhead bar district show that some white citizens of Atlanta are still unable to conceal their racism and fear of blacks, even for strategic reasons. The cycle of fear and resentment is likely to be repeated.

With material such as that provided by Mr. Grady, it cannot be a surprise that many black commentators focused on the role of racism in the opposition to Freaknik. But in the drive to call attention to the role of white racism and stereotypical views of blacks in the debate, they often failed to recognize the importance of other factors—most centrally the relationship between black men and black women but also the views of black college students within the black community and the lack of any measurable space within the black college scene for gay men and lesbians. With the white-influenced Atlanta political establishment coming down on Freaknik, many in the African American community closed ranks behind the black college men (many of them part of the Greek system), whom they perceived as the central victims of the circumstance, at the expense of black women and gays.

Perhaps it is to engage in idle speculation (or wishful thinking) to imagine what Freaknik might have been like if black gays and lesbians had been able to claim a public space in the celebration or if the celebrants had taken the time to hear the protests of Black Men for the Eradication of Sexism. While closer attention to these issues from the outset probably would not have been enough to save Freaknik—gridlocked car traffic was always the most common subject of complaints from Intown residents—it might have at least increased the goodwill toward the festival among potential allies, such as Cynthia Tucker. By privileging the experience of heterosexual men, many of the African American supporters of Freaknik effectively encouraged some of the abusive behavior that ensued, behavior that ultimately resulted in the ending of the festival. The tactic of race-based solidarity and the minimization of differences in the face of organized and government-supported racism served African Americans well (but not without some costs) in the era of the civil rights struggle. Now, however, in the period in which we grapple with what Patricia Hill Collins calls "the new racism," such strategies hold as much peril as promise for the black community as a whole.[72]

NOTES

1. Patricia Hill Collins, "It's All in the Family: Intersections of Gender, Race, and Nation," *Hypatia* 13, no. 3 (Summer 1998): 63.

2. Kendall Thomas, "'Ain't Nothin' Like the Real Thing': Black Masculinity, Gay Sexuality, and the Jargon of Authenticity," in *Traps: African American Men on Gender and Sexuality,* ed. Rudolph P. Byrd and Beverly Guy-Sheftall (Bloomington: Indiana University Press, 2001), 332.

3. Marcus Anthony Hunter, "All the Gays Are White and the Blacks Are Straight: Black Gay Men, Identity, and Community," *Sexuality Research and Social Policy* 7, no. 2 (June 2010): 81.

4. Thomas, "Ain't Nothin' Like the Real Thing," 336.

5. Sharese Shields, letter to the editor, *Atlanta Journal-Constitution,* 22 April 1994, 18A.

6. Zachary Adriaenssens, "Mapping the Lesbian, Gay, Bisexual and Transgender Community in Atlanta" (School of City and Regional Planning, Georgia Institute of Technology, Applied Research Paper, 6 May 2011), 43.

7. E. Franklin Frazier, *Black Bourgeoisie* (New York: Simon & Schuster, 1997), 105.

8. Bill Campbell, quoted in "Campbell's Flip-Flop on Freaknik Disappoints," *Atlanta Journal-Constitution,* 23 March 1995, 14A.

9. "The Bottom Line on Freaknik," ibid., 24 March 1995, 16A.

10. Kathy Scruggs, "Freaknik: a Wild Weekend: Cops 'Chill,' Help Crowd Stay Cool; Chief 'Moved to Tears' by Officers' Performance," ibid., 25 April 1994, 4B.

11. Kathy Scruggs and Ellen Whitford, "Freannik [sic]: a Wild Weekend: Revelers Linger as Party Drags On," ibid., 5B.

12. Ronald Smothers, "Spring Break Puts Atlanta's Party Spirit to the Test," *New York Times,* 25 April 1994, 12A.

13. A. Scott Walton, "Freaknik: What's Going On: Just This Weekend, Students Are 'Frontin'" for Attention," *Atlanta Journal-Constitution,* 23 April 1994, 3B.

14. Robert J. Vickers, "Freaknik: What's Going On: Sights, Sounds, Spontaneity All Part of 'Freaky' Weekend," ibid., 24 April 1994, 7H.

15. Ernie Suggs, "Bad, Good Sides of Freaknik Expected; Spring Break: Rowdy Behavior Foreseen for Annual Atlanta Gathering, but Some Dispute that Event Is Out of Control," ibid., 11 April 1999, 1D.

16. Johnnetta Betsch Cole and Beverly Guy-Sheftall, *Gender Talk: The Struggle for Women's Equality in African American Communities* (New York: Ballantine Books, 2003), 99.

17. Suggs, "Bad, Good Sides of Freaknik Expected."

18. Marian Meyers, "African American Women and Violence: Gender, Race, and Class in the News," *Critical Studies in Media Communication* 21, no. 2 (June 2004): 96, 105, 102.

19. Krista A. Thompson, "Performing Visibility: Freaknic and the Spatial Politics of Sexuality, Race, and Class in Atlanta," *TDR: The Drama Review* 51, no. 4 (Winter 2007): 34, 38, 26.

20. Collins, "It's All in the Family," 67.

21. Adriaenssens, "Mapping the Lesbian, Gay, Bisexual and Transgender Community," 6.

22. Sean C. Gooden, letter to the editor, *Atlanta Journal-Constitution,* 18 April 1996, 10D.

23. Richard Kenyada, letter to the editor, ibid., 29 April 1993, 17A.

24. Cynthia Tucker, "Freaknik Illustrates Atlanta's Own Racial Fault Line," ibid., 27 April 1994, 15A.

25. Darryl Fears, "Opinions of Festival Are Split along Racial Lines," ibid., 10 May 1995, 6B.

26. Cole and Guy-Sheftall, *Gender Talk,* xxiv.

27. Claude Brown, "The Language of Soul," in *Rappin' and Stylin' Out: Communication in Urban Black America,* ed. Thomas Kochman (Urbana: University of Illinois Press, 1972), 138.

28. Mara Rose Williams, "News for Kids: How it Began," *Atlanta Journal-Constitution,* 12 December 1994, 3A.

29. G. Edward Brown, letter to the editor, ibid., 21 April 1994, 12A.

30. S. A. Reid, "Freaknik '93 Lures Blacks to Atlanta; City Becomes Daytona Beach of Sorts as Students Kick It Up, Max and Relax," ibid., 23 April 1993, 1D.

31. Miriam Y. Morris, letter to the editor, ibid., 22 April 1994, 19A.

32. Charmagne Helton, "Freaknik '95: Freedomfest Gets Verbal Support, But Little Else," ibid., 13 April 1995, C2; Cynthia Tucker, "My Opinion—Freaknik: Kids Will Be Kids, but Gray-Heads Ought To Be Adults," ibid., 16 April 1997, A12.

33. Suggs, "Bad, Good Sides of Freaknik Expected."

34. Cynthia Tucker, "Respect Yourselves," *Atlanta Journal-Constitution,* 26 April 1995, 15A.

35. "Black Men for the Eradication of Sexism; Fighting Misogyny," *Essence,* May 1996, 56.

36. Kimberley Shepherd and Valerie Thompson, letters to the editor, *Atlanta Journal-Constitution,* 21 April 1995, 20A.

37. Robert Sheppard, letter to the editor, ibid., 21A.

38. Scruggs, "Freaknik: a Wild Weekend."

39. Beverly Harvard, quoted in "Preparing for the Bash; Police Chief Says Partyers Should Obey Laws and Respect the City," *Atlanta Journal-Constitution,* 20 April 1995, 17A.

40. Christina Drake, letter to the editor, ibid., 27 April 1995, 15A.

41. Suggs, "Bad, Good Sides of Freaknik Expected."

42. Jeff Dickerson, "Misogynistic Madness; Freaknik Provides Partygoers with License to Act like a Fool," *Atlanta Journal-Constitution,* 13 April 1999, 10A.

43. Paul Howle, "They'll Be Back, Atlanta: Freaknik: We Might As Well Learn to Grin and Bear It," ibid., 26 April 1994, 10A.

44. Jeff Dickerson, "Event Is Running Its Course; Is Freaknik a Hiphop, or College, Happening?," ibid., 15 April 1997, 16A.

45. "Daytona, Atlanta Feels Your Pain," ibid., 7 April 1999, 16A.

46. Jeff Dickerson, "Focus on Dignity, History; With Freaknik on the Wane, Civil Rights Beacon Can Shine," ibid., 20 April 1999, 12A.

47. John Head, "My Opinion; Party Detour: Women's Rebuff Puts the Final Brakes on Freaknik," ibid., 23 April 1999, 18A.

48. Carlos Campos, "Freaknik '99; Event's Subdued Tone May Signal End; Positive Change: Fewer Arrests, Job Fair a Success," ibid., 18 April 1999, 6H.

49. Bill Campbell, quoted in S. A. Reid, "Atlanta Unveils Plan, Brochure for Freaknik," ibid., 8

April 1998, 1C; Fredrick D. Robinson, "It's Just a Matter of Time; When Today's Students Get Mortgages and Have Kids, They'll Hate Freaknik, Too," ibid., 24 March 1995, 17A.

50. Cole and Guy-Sheftall, *Gender Talk,* 203, 186.

51. Jacquelyn A. Anthony, letter to the editor, *Atlanta Journal-Constitution,* 27 April 1995, 15A.

52. "Keep Calm in Freaknik Storm," ibid., 14 April 1996, 6B.

53. Ronald Smothers, "Black Students Revel in Atlanta Despite Cool Welcome," *New York Times,* 23 April 1995, 28A.

54. Nathan Williams, letter to the editor, *Atlanta Journal-Constitution,* 28 April 1995, 17A.

55. Robert Watson, "Black Greeks or Black Gangs," *The Fire This Time,* October/November 1997, 11.

56. Frazier, *Black Bourgeoisie,* 77.

57. Samuel Adams, "In My Opinion; Black Youngsters, Get Serious," *Atlanta Journal-Constitution,* 8 April 1998, 15A.

58. Jeff Dickerson, "A Racial Duty; Do Centuries of Suffering Translate Into Freaknik?," ibid., 19 April 1995, 14A.

59. Joseph E. Lowery, letter to the editor, ibid., 25 April 1995, 11A.

60. Suggs, "Bad, Good Sides of Freaknik Expected."

61. Hunter, "All the Gays Are White," 82.

62. John Blake, "Freaknik '93 Lowers Volume, Hits the Road," *Atlanta Journal-Constitution,* 26 April 1993, 2B.

63. Thomas, "Ain't Nothin' Like the Real Thing," 330.

64. Andrea Harris, letter quoted in Betty Parham and Gerrie Ferris, "Q&A on the News," *Atlanta Journal-Constitution,* 15 July 1993, 2A.

65. Gus Howard, letter to the editor, ibid., 13 October 1994, 6K.

66. Ibid.

67. Avis Crockett, letter to the editor, *Atlanta Journal-Constitution,* 24 July 1997, 10A.

68. Christopher Johnson, letter to the editor, ibid., 16 June 1994, 18A; Anthony Vicari, letter to the editor, ibid., 18 April 1996, 10D.

69. Keith Sherwood and Patrick Miltimore, letter to the editor, ibid., 31 July 1997, 18A.

70. Craig Seymour, "Gays Feel Left Out of Morehouse Brotherhood," ibid., 29 December 2002, 1A.

71. Claude H. Grady III, letter to the editor, ibid., 30 April 1993, A15.

72. Patricia Hill Collins, *Black Sexual Politics: African Americans, Gender, and the New Racism* (New York: Routledge, 2004), 7.

11

"A Bonfire of Chastity"

Christian Girl Culture, Feminism, and Sexuality, 1970–2000

KRYSTAL HUMPHREYS

In the mid-1990s it was not uncommon to witness a True Love Waits ceremony in a conservative Christian church, particularly in the southern United States. The program became so widespread that one reporter claimed it would create a "bonfire" of chastity and purity, turning teens away from sexualized popular culture and society.[1] No matter which denomination you happened to belong to, the principle was the same. Young women waited anxiously in their pews for their turn to walk with their father or sometimes with both parents to the front of the church, where they would participate in the purity-ring ceremony, promising to save their virginity for their future husband and receiving their rings, a constant reminder of their promise to both God and their family. The tension in the auditorium or sanctuary was palpable as these young women fretted over the state of their hair and makeup, the appropriateness of their Sunday dresses, and the awkwardness of sharing such a private decision—the choice to preserve one's sexuality—with both their parents and an entire congregation of friends, family, and fellow Christians.

For many of these young women, the decision to declare publicly one's intention to remain sexually pure until marriage was a deeply spiritual one. For others, the decision was prompted by a desire to be part of Christian girl culture, to maintain or acquire the demure, innocent image associated with that identity. Women have long been considered the guardians of morality, those most fit to transmit Christian and democratic notions from one generation to the next; thus young women are often held to a very high standard and are subject to a great deal of public scrutiny. As the conservative activist Phyllis Schlafly, one of the best-known conservative voices in the 1970s and 1980s, stated, "It is on its women that a civilization depends—on the inspiration they provide, on the moral fabric they weave, on the parameters of behavior they tolerate, and on the new generation that they breathe life into and educate."[2]

For young Christian women, image has always been of the utmost importance, particularly with regard to sexuality. This essay examines the pressure placed on young women to conform to a traditional, conservative lifestyle, to be the "positive woman" that Phyllis Schlafly described, knowing full well that if they failed in this effort, their reputations and their identity as Christians could be called into question. This essay also analyzes subtle generational shifts between women who came of age in the 1970s, the 1980s, and the 1990s and the effect that conservative politics has had on the lives of Christian women. Young women have often found themselves stuck in between the ideals of their mothers' generation and the realities of society, trying to reconcile their faith with their everyday lives, all under intense supervision and scrutiny from their elders. This "new sexism," described by the historian Keira Williams, appeared in the 1980s and 1990s and used the rhetoric of family values to insist that women remain in their proper place as wives and mothers. In other words, conservatism sought to reinstate prefeminist notions of femininity and the roles of women in an effort to protect the family.[3] Despite the difficulties and contradictions inherent in growing up as a Christian young woman, these women, sometimes following and sometimes rejecting the advice of their mothers' generation, were able to form their own ideas and opinions about their faith and the ways in which they would relate to society and to their families as Christians.

THE IMPORTANCE OF IMAGE

Much of this generational tension centers on the importance of image to the experience of growing up as a young Christian and a woman. As Sue Lees, an author and feminist activist, explained in 1993, "Young women face a complicated problem as they move into adulthood, caught between the idea of adolescence and the definition of femininity.... They don't get to be moody, reckless, and scruffy like boys, if they do they gain a reputation. If they conform too much to feminine standards then they are seen as old-fashioned or prudish. To excel academically or to reject stereotypes makes them deviant or masculine."[4] Although Lees is describing a secular image of young womanhood, the contradiction applies to the Christian experience as well. Young women from a conservative Christian background struggle to be seen as feminine without crossing the line into immodesty. While they are encouraged to express their faith, to use their God-given talents to evangelize others, they must be careful not to forget their role as women. Their sexuality must also be evident but guarded, saved for the appropriate heterosexual marital relationship.

Physical beauty has been the focus of much scrutiny and advice for Christian women striving for that perfect image. The importance of beauty was a common theme in literature written for Christian women throughout the 1970s and 1980s. According to such fundamentalist Christian authors as Joyce Landorf and Viola Walden, appearance is the most noticeable indicator of femininity, and physical attractiveness is the best means of getting and keeping a man.[5] As with most advice books directed toward women, in the 1970s and 1980s those written by men were much more moderate in tone than those written by women. According to Gene Getz, for example, physical beauty is good, but it is less important than inner beauty. Women should take care to be worthy of respect, avoiding activities and entertainment that stimulate the "carnal appetites." Inner beauty includes numerous factors, according to Getz. Women should not be malicious talkers or gossips; they should be temperate with regard to alcohol use; they should be trustworthy, self-controlled, gentle, quiet, and good role models.[6] Another male author, Robert Wolcott Smith, also emphasized the importance of inner beauty but put a bit more emphasis on the benefits of a pleasing physical appearance, writing, "Some women always seem to look like last year's bird nest." He specifically called out unfeminine women, explaining that women should have a gentle and quiet spirit, in contrast to that of the "dominant, officious female one sometimes encounters."[7]

The unfiltered, harsh truth about Christian women's beauty came from women writers, generally wives and/or daughters of men who held leadership positions in the Christian community. In *The Fragrance of Beauty*, Joyce Landorf, a talented Christian vocalist and daughter of a Christian minister, insisted on the importance of beauty to the marital relationship. She described a conversation with a concerned young wife in her congregation. The young woman was worried about her marriage, convinced that she was doing something wrong despite being a good cook, a faithful wife, and a good mother. She complained that her husband seemed uninterested, never looked at her anymore, and never told her he loved her. Landorf's unspoken response, but one she included in the book, was this: "You're wrong about your husband never looking at you. Actually he has looked at you, and when he caught a glimpse of your Phyllis Diller hairdo and Mama Cass figure, he didn't feel he wanted to look any further. He didn't have any incentive to express his love."[8] By 1980 Landorf's book had seen twenty printings. Landorf conducted interviews with a variety of individuals, mostly men, whom she asked what they would change about women if they had the opportunity. Most of the complaints supported Landorf's thesis that although God looks on the inside, "man has nowhere else to look but on the outward appearance!"[9] Several respondents claimed that women should put more care into their looks, be "less militant," and stop nagging. One said, "I'd like women to fix up their outward looks and go on diets." Another went against the grain and responded, "I'd like women to be outspoken and talk more." The author's response to this was, "This one really puzzled me until I realized that this man is married to an absolutely gorgeous angel who has a quiet, gentle nature. He doesn't know what he's got!"[10]

Joyce Landorf also discussed the tendency of Christian women to equate plainness with spirituality. She explained that in earlier decades women had strived to maintain a plain, "ugly" appearance. Landorf attributed a shift in this attitude, beginning in the 1930s, to the radio evangelist Aimee Semple McPherson. Sister Aimee wore makeup to church and dressed fashionably in vibrant colors.[11] Landorf was certainly accurate with regard to the timeline, but she presents this shift in the acceptance of cosmetics from a biased and modern perspective. The historian Kathy Peiss presented a much more nuanced view of this shift in her book *Hope in a Jar*. According to Peiss, in the nineteenth century Americans as a whole had a different ideal of female beauty: "For nineteenth-century Americans, lady and hussy were polar opposites and the presence or absence of cosmetics marked the divide."[12] Painted faces defied traditional Victorian notions of beauty and morality. By the 1930s, the use of cosmetics was widespread among American women from all walks of life. Landorf was writing her book in the wake of feminist critiques of the beauty industry, critiques arguing that the overly commercialized beauty industry placed limitations on women's success by directing their attention to beauty and appearance. This religious emphasis on beauty can be attributed to attacks on feminism and the spreading of the notion that women should be content with their own physical characteristics rather than trying to live up to societal standards of beauty.

Much like Landorf, other Christian authors sought to inform women about the benefits of beauty but also to guide them in the process of beautification. In *Woman to Woman*, Viola Walden provided answers to many beauty questions. Many Christian women questioned whether the use of makeup was biblical. Walden quoted Beverly Hyles, who wrote, "I remember as a little girl I watched women of a certain religion who didn't believe in make-up. I was really repelled by their appearance. I do not think they glorified God." Hyles went on to say that beauty was an important factor in evangelism. "This gives one a better chance to be a real ambassador for Christ. Our God made everything beautiful and being ugly purposely doesn't make us spiritual."[13] This emphasis on makeup as a tool for evangelism is relatively recent. In the first half of the twentieth century and certainly prior to that, makeup was not considered acceptable for moral, Christian women.

Clothing and proper fashion were also often cited as important to Christian beauty and evangelical efforts. Most of these authors agreed that women's clothing should be beautiful and becoming, clean, appropriate for any occasion, and modest. Most importantly, however, it should be feminine. Advice on clothing choices displays an obvious bias against women who wear pants and an outright rejection of homosexuality as an inappropriate, even dangerous lifestyle. Joy Martin explained: "Men and women have different roles, so they are to dress differently. I believe this Scripture (Deuteronomy 22:5) also is a warning against homosexual practices ... even the length of the hair is a definite symbol of masculinity or femininity. The unisex idea in appearance and action is displeasing to God." She also suggested, "In our culture, the most distinctive womanly apparel is a dress. Unless a man is perverted, he wouldn't be caught dead in a dress! Why not make this basic symbol, a dress, our standard attire!"[14]

Christian women of the 1970s and 1980s were also urged to watch their weight. In *Born Again Bodies* R. Marie Griffith examines the religious association of sin with obesity or excess weight. She writes, "Fat was the embodied mark of disobedience and distance from God, while weight reduction signified the restoration of holiness."[15] Griffith shows that Christian diet culture exploded in the 1960s and 1970s with the publication of books such as *More of Jesus, Less of Me* in 1976 and *Help Lord ... The Devil Wants Me Fat!* in 1977. These books were aimed at women, indicating that women were more often the victims of gluttony and were therefore the tempters of others, responsible for the weight problems of their husbands and children.[16]

Many of these authors advised women on how to control their weight and eating habits, a direct contradiction to the message of the feminist movement. In the 1970s, feminists were attacking the idea that physical beauty is connected to a woman's self-worth, an idea later reinforced in fundamentalist writings. In Walden's book, Dr. Cathy Rice offered guidelines on how to maintain a healthy weight that might be found in mainstream books on the subject. But it was the message behind Rice's guidelines that was destructive to a woman's self-worth. Not only Rice but Christian writers more broadly equated gluttony and being overweight with sin, implying that it was a sin against God to have a less than perfect figure. According to Rice, women should look in a full-length mirror every day in order to "see all those bumps that need to come off; note the rolls of fat, the flab that needs to go."[17]

Overall appearance, according to the majority of these authors, is an absolute necessity for marital bliss, and arguments from earlier decades are frequently revived. One participant in the Weigh Down Diet, a Christian diet program created in the early twenty-first century by the nutritionist Gwen Shamblin, claimed that the plan had saved both her life and her marriage: "I was in despair. I felt ugly and fat, and my husband had lost all interest in me. He made it quite clear that he did not want to touch me until I got the weight off. I thought I may as well just end it, you know. Life that fat just didn't seem worth living."[18] Betty Malz, author of *Making Your Husband Feel Loved,* tells men, "Do yourself a favor. Buy this book for your fiancée before she becomes your wife. Or, if you're already married, mail it anonymously to your wife." To her women readers she gives a variety of advice, much of which is on beauty. She writes, "One of the ways you express love for your husband is by how you eat, exercise, and take care of yourself." She adds, "Eat light, lose weight if necessary. Take care of yourself. You can be replaced."[19]

Following this advice was not always a surefire way to avoid criticism. In the 1980s, the era of unisex hair and the woman's power suit, some evangelists took this advice to the extreme in an attempt to recover a lost feminine image, insisting that more was better and putting a somewhat comical face on definitions of Christian beauty. Tammy Faye Bakker, the televangelist and wife of Jim Bakker, was commonly mocked and criticized for her over-the-top makeup and hairstyles, an image so often equated with campy, drag style. A quick Google search for Tammy Faye returns results such as "How to avoid having the Tammy Faye Bakker make-up look" and numerous articles and opinion pieces referring to her as clownish. She has even been the subject of look-alike competitions among members of the gay community. In the documentary *The Eyes of Tammy Faye,* her brother joked that even though she was raised in a climate in which she was "scared into staying close to God," the person who sold her her first set of makeup at a garage sale was Tammy Faye's real savior. She herself was quoted on more than one occasion as saying, "Without my eyelashes I wouldn't be Tammy Faye!"[20] Tammy Faye lived with constant pressure to present the image of a good Christian wife, mother, and female role model. This pressure and the fallout from her husband's very public sex scandal ultimately led her to drug usage, rehab, and divorce. In the early 1990s, Tammy Faye appeared on *The Roseanne Show.* When the host, Roseanne Barr, commented, "Your makeup is extreme," Tammy Faye replied, "I think I look ugly without it." Roseanne chastised her, saying that that was the wrong way to think.[21] After her divorce from Jim in 1992, Tammy Faye could never quite get her career restarted. She was excluded and shunned from the Christian broadcasting community. Pat Boone, a popular singer and television personality in the 1950s and 1960s, commented on her situation and the ridicule that she has received over the years, saying, "Christians are one army who kill their wounded."[22]

In such a contradictory and overly critical environment, it was not uncommon for female Christian role models to fall victim to harsh criticism or outright rejection. In the 1980s, nothing symbolized Christian youth culture so well as music. Contemporary Christian music (CCM) exploded in the late 1970s, an outgrowth of the folksy, coffeehouse style made popular by Jesus music artists such as Larry Norman. CCM was meant to appeal to a broad audience, while offering an alternative for Christian young people who enjoyed secular musical styles but were uncomfortable with secular lyrics. The genre became a vehicle for young women who wished to move beyond the church choir to express both their musical talents and their faith in the public arena. Amy Grant was CCM's first superstar, sometimes referred to as the queen of Christian pop, and she is still CCM's best-selling artist. Grant was born in 1960 in Augusta, Georgia. She began singing at an early age, learning the guitar by the time she reached her teens. In 1973 Grant left her Church of Christ roots and joined a charismatic church in Nashville. The church, which ministered to former hippies and musicians, ran a Christian coffeehouse, where Grant gave her earliest performances. By 1976 she had signed with the Myrrh label and released her first album. By the early 1980s she had three albums under her belt and was a participant in the Billy Graham Crusade. Her albums feature songs written by her and songs by other artists. One of her most popular tracks was "Father's Eyes," written by her future husband, Gary Chapman, whom she married in 1982.

Grant's most important album, *Age to Age,* was released in 1982 and garnered her several awards. *Age to Age,* whose cover showed an attractive young woman with feminine hair and makeup, also drew the attention of the secular music market. It was not until 1985, with *Unguarded,* that Grant crossed over onto the secular charts, however. *Unguarded* had a different tone than her previous albums. The cover featured Grant in a leopard-skin coat, and the music had a much more aggressive sound, far from that of the demure, modest young woman Grant's Christian fans had fallen in love with. As with many other Christian crossover artists, Grant's most popular songs often replaced the word *God* with *love* in order to appeal to secular audiences.[23] The first song to make it into the secular Top 40 was "Find a Way," from the album *Unguarded*. It is easy to see why this particular song, with its emphasis on relationship issues with friends and men, appealed to secular audiences.

> You tell me your friends are distant
> You tell me your man's untrue
> You tell me that you've been walked on
> And how you feel abused.[24]

The answer to these problems, as presented in the song, is God's love and the Christian lifestyle.

Instead of focusing on larger social issues and the application of Christ's teachings to a variety of world problems, a common characteristic of the earliest Jesus music, Grant's music emphasized the usefulness of God and an internal spirituality as a solution to the everyday life problems of American youth, especially young women. This is unsurprising given the changing political climate in the United States as Ronald Reagan sought to improve the outlook of many Americans by focusing on the rhetoric of family values as a means to capture the hearts and minds of those who had grown disillusioned in response to rights movements of the 1960s and 1970s. Those enamored with Ronald Reagan believed the United States could appear strong again, with a president who would resurrect white middle-class "silent majority" values as the answer to economic and political decline. In the realm of popular culture and music, Amy Grant best characterized this response thanks to her image as a wholesome, southern sweetheart. She was an idealized image of how a Christian young woman should be: honest, deeply spiritual, pretty but modest. Unlike her Jesus music predecessors, she was not revolutionary or socially motivated, but certainly influenced by the conservative culture Keira Williams describes, which stressed sexual restraint and heteronormativity in the face of feminism, gay liberation, and the sexual revolution.[25] She was a good role model, and her fans were more than willing to spend their hard-earned money making her a superstar, with more than 30 million albums sold worldwide.[26]

Grant's extreme popularity and her ability to make money stemmed from her ability to appeal to both Christian and secular audiences. However, being accepted by mainstream popular culture can have a negative effect on Christian artists, and being one of the few female stars of the genre left her open to a great deal of scrutiny. When Grant crossed over and became popular among nonbelievers as well as believers, she was harshly criticized in some circles. Some said she had sold out for money.[27] Others accused her of being "too worldly or too sexy."[28] After her divorce from fellow artist Gary Chapman, rumored to be the result of an extramarital affair, and her subsequent marriage to the country artist Vince Gill, Grant took even more heat from her Christian audience. Her music disappeared from Christian bookstores and radio stations, and she was not invited to high-profile Christian events.[29] She has since returned to her gospel roots in an attempt to win back her Christian fans.

The criticism of Amy Grant was not an isolated incident. One of CCM's first major female stars also became the subject of one of the industry's first scandals.[30] The singers Russ and Marsha Stevens helped establish Christian pop, paving the way for artists such as Grant. The Stevenses toured with their group, Children of the Day, from 1971 to 1979. Children of the Day has been referred to as one of the first CCM groups; however, most references to the group have since been removed from texts that chronicle the creation of the genre. Marsha and Russ Stevens divorced in the late 1970s, leading to a scandal in the industry, but when Marsha came out as a lesbian, churches tore her songs out of their songbooks and eliminated all references to her as an artist. Andrew Beaujon writes, "As far as most Christian music institutions are concerned, Marsha never existed."[31] Now Marsha Stevens-Pino, she runs her own music ministry, BALM (Born-Again Lesbian Music), and says on her ministry's website, "Does the church really need another middle-aged female Christian singer? Check out the CD racks! I write and sing contemporary Christian music for the GLBT community. It may be a narrow field, but hey, it's wide open!"[32] It was Marsha's image, not her music or her devotion to God, that changed and lost her a place in the CCM history books.

The rejection of Marsha Stevens-Pino highlights another fear coming out of the 1970s and 1980s, that of homosexuality. Some historians have argued that the gay liberation movement of the 1970s was set into motion by the events that occurred at the Stonewall Inn in 1969. Others insist that everyday rebellions such as patronage of gay bars and participation in the disco craze engendered the movement.[33] What is certain is that the coming out of gay culture in the United States sent shockwaves through conservative families. Fears of homosexuality spread quickly in the wake of the gay liberation movement, particularly in the public school system in the 1970s. Women such as Anita Bryant, a former Miss America and a spokeswoman for Minute Maid orange juice, made public their fears of homosexual educators and the effect they could have on impressionable children. In a highly publicized debate over this issue in the schools of Miami, Florida, Bryant used her femininity to gain support for her campaign against gay and lesbian teachers. Anita Bryant was not unique in her opinions. On the opposite side of the country in 1978, the Briggs Initiative sought to ban gays and lesbians from working in public schools. The measure was defeated thanks to the persistent campaigns of politicians like Harvey Milk.

Conservative Christian writers in the 1970s and 1980s, such as Bill and Nancie Carmichael, wrote extensively on the dangers of homosexuality. They wrote, "Our society has been bombarded by militant homosexuals and lesbians proclaiming their 'freedom' and their 'superior' lifestyle."[34] The Carmichaels also gave tips to concerned parents on how to recognize homosexual tendencies in their children. They insisted that boys who were too eager to please and overly polite and who didn't care for sports and avoided fights were at risk. They placed the blame for this problem on overly concerned mothers. For a girl, they explain, "tomboy characteristics are no grounds whatever unless accompanied by other symptoms," such as saying she wants to be a boy, habitually refusing to play with dolls, being frightened of normal interactions with boys, not wanting to play house, being generally more competitive than other girls, having temper tantrums against her mother, and having a general disdain for men. They compared homosexuality to cancer and emphasized the need for a cure. Barring that, they urged caution and prevention, writing, "Homosexuality can be prevented. People are not born homosexuals."[35]

Teens of the 1990s were bombarded with information about homosexuality in school and in the medias. In 1993, one school in Seattle voted that no openly gay students could participate in student government, the goal being to preserve the "high moral standards" of the school.[36] Given the amount of literature written on the topic and the intensely passionate debate surrounding it, it is unsurprising that young Christians had questions, some of which they directed to advice columnists. One young woman wrote that she was having feelings for other girls and asked for guidance. The advice was short and simple: homosexuality is a choice; God made us to be attracted to the opposite sex.[37] Another teen wrote in asking how she could help a boy from church who wanted to be a girl. Writers responded by explaining that something traumatic must have happened to him, and the only advice they gave was to pray for him.[38] Because of the numerous letters seeking advice on this issue, at least one of the advice books of the period included some expert advice. In *What Hollywood Won't Tell You About Sex, Love, and Dating*, Susie Shellenberger and Greg Johnson admitted that since they had no experience in the subject, they had talked to a former homosexual, a man stricken with AIDS. This man claimed that many of the homosexuals he knew had been molested at a young age, had been exposed to pornography, or were somehow paying for the sins of their fathers.[39] For young women, he argued, molestation by men led to disgust and lesbianism. A bad relationship with their mother was often a cause of homosexuality in women. Once again, the book and the expert explained that "being attracted to the same sex isn't a chromosomal thing, but a spiritual thing" and that "God doesn't cause someone to be a homosexual."[40]

Ultimately, the advice given in these books and by Christian organizations such as Focus on the Family, a nondenominational parachurch organization founded by Dr. James Dobson, is that homosexuality is not natural but a sin and that it can be both forgiven and cured. In this particular instance, authors provided contact information for an ex-homosexual ministry. For some families, this advice did little to shape their experiences. Morgan, a young woman from western Texas interviewed for this study, related the story of her younger sister's coming out as a lesbian while in high school, surprising her conservative Christian family. Rather than confront the issue, her family refuses to talk about it. While they believe her sister's lifestyle is wrong, they simply choose to ignore it.[41]

Youth programs of the 1990s, such as True Love Waits, designed to prevent premarital sex among teens, depended on the participation of youth ministers, who were charged with confronting prevailing attitudes in society not only by teaching the value of abstinence but also by "denying that homosexuality is an unchangeable lifestyle." Youth ministers were urged to show unconditional love to those who were struggling with an attraction toward members of the same sex. Richard Ross, the founder of the campaign, pointed out that even those who had had a series of sexual encounters with members of their own sex could still be saved with the help of Christian counselors. The important thing to remember was that homosexuality is not an inalterable lifestyle.[42]

True Love Waits was one of a number of Christian campaigns meant to educate young people about the so-called dangers of homosexuality.

Growing up in an atmosphere that demonized "tomboy characteristics" and so-called unfeminine behavior placed even more pressure on young women to conform to a traditional notion of femininity, particularly as they entered young adulthood. Mothers of teenage girls in the 1990s sought to advise them by passing on elements of their own upbringing with regard to femininity, beauty, and the roles of women, tempering that advice to make it more modern. Mothers urged their daughters to be beautiful, but much of that advice centered on inner beauty, the importance of being kind, generous, and modest, perhaps reflecting frustration with the high beauty standards of their own generation. Anamarie, a young woman raised as part of a conservative Christian family in Alaska, said that while her mother had always taught that physical beauty was not important, she had instilled in her a sense of fashion and style.[43] Kira's mother, a western Texas native who raised her daughter in a conservative Christian environment, also stressed the importance of inner beauty but simultaneously encouraged her daughter to wear makeup and dress well so that "boys would like her."[44] Looking back, Kira believes that she was given this advice because she did not date much in high school. Despite the focus on inner beauty, young Christian women still struggled with issues relating to physical appearance, trying to maintain a balance between what society deemed beautiful and what they felt was necessary to maintain one's spirituality.

Much of the new advice directed toward women in the 1990s reflected both the influence of conservative religious thought from the 1970s and 1980s and the influence of feminism on those who had come of age during and immediately following the feminist movement of that period. In many ways, though, while advice guides of the 1990s strayed far from the fundamentalist guides published in those earlier decades, they also reflected the "new sexism" of the decade that accompanied conservatism in American society.[45] The focus on beauty and femininity in order to win a man was greatly reduced, however. Girls were reminded that boys enjoy a challenge and were urged to compete with them honestly, not just allowing them to win.[46] This advice was not the same as that given to young wives in the 1970s and 1980s, which stressed allowing one's husband to be the strong one in order to reinforce his masculinity. In 1974, for example, the author Darien Cooper had insisted that a woman should develop an interest in the activities her man enjoyed but should never become an expert. If she did, she would threaten his masculinity.[47] However, emphasizing one's femininity was still stressed as an important element of the courtship process for young women in the 1990s. Advice books told young women to compliment their dates to make them feel manly. One girl who asked how to get a shy young man to ask her out was told that "guys like to be needed so ask him questions about the homework assignment" and that she should "bake a batch of cookies for him or compliment him. This will show him you really care about him."[48]

DATING

Dating and relating to the opposite sex were central concerns for young Christian women. They also formed the single most talked about problem that young Christian girls faced in their daily lives throughout the 1980s and 1990s. The position of a young woman in Christian culture can be a precarious one. The rejection of formerly revered role models like Amy Grant emphasized that young women who did not follow the rules, who did not live up to the expectations placed on them by their parents and their faith, could be rejected or looked down upon. To avoid losing their reputation, girls sought advice on many issues that they encountered on a daily basis in school or with their friends, but they were especially concerned about dating and relating to the opposite sex. The advice columnists Susie Shellenberger and Greg Johnson, working for Focus on the Family, received so many letters that they compiled them into several advice books solely on dating. The titles themselves hint at the motivation behind publishing the books, offering up *258 Great Dates While You Wait* and implying that these were wholesome date ideas to prevent teens from having sex. This particular guide received a celebrity endorsement from Gary Chapman, who provided stories about his courtship with his then wife Amy Grant in order to provide a real-life example for young people to follow, obviously published before their breakup. While the book was primarily a collection of date ideas, advice to real young people who had written in asking for help was interspersed throughout the pages.

Most of the advice for young women was reminiscent of advice guides going back to the 1950s and earlier. Physical beauty and modesty have often been equated with spirituality, for women and girls have historically been given the responsibility of guarding both their own and their date's morality. The authors of advice guides in the 1990s stressed that "whatever you wear, don't wear it too short, too tight, or too low" and asked, "Why tempt the guy you're with? Encourage him to be a gentleman by the way you dress." After all, "loose dress reveals a loose heart."[49] Joshua Harris, author of the controversial (or perhaps simply misunderstood) book *I Kissed Dating Goodbye,* argued that it was the girl's responsibility not to tempt her date; rather, she should guard his purity by being modest and not drawing attention to her body.[50] Rebecca St. James, a Christian recording artist known for her advocacy of abstinence and purity, urged young women to follow her example by not showing too much skin and making sure to protect young men from allowing their thoughts to stray.[51] Parents of these girls offered similar advice, reminding their daughters to dress modestly, forbidding them from wearing makeup until a certain age, and placing age restrictions on dating.[52]

Young women were frequently taught that choosing the right person to date was essential for future happiness. They were reminded that they should seek dates from other Christians and not be "yoked with non-believers."[53] In other words, the only way to date successfully was to make certain that one's date's values were also Christian. For some young women, this was a rule instituted by their parents, and many never considered breaking it.[54] Regardless of whom a young woman chose to date, she was advised to pay close attention to his behavior, to make sure that his lifestyle was Godly.[55] Shellenberger and Johnson even offered up a list of questions to ask dates if monitoring their activities had yet to give a clear picture of their spirituality. Perhaps the most important thing to know about potential dates was their opinion regarding premarital sex. In every book of advice for Christian teens, writers added a chapter on the value of abstinence and the dangers of premarital sex. They presented the "facts" about premarital sex:

1. Premarital sex breaks up dating couples more than any other factor.
2. Those who have premarital sex are more likely to have extramarital affairs later on.
3. Premarital sex leads to bad marriages.[56]

The major emphasis on abstinence seemed to center on potential future problems, such as extramarital affairs and/or divorce. This is not surprising given the social and political climate of the 1990s. Fears of family decline were common and led to concerns about what children were exposed to on television, in addition to the behavior of political and religious leaders. The Christian community was rocked with sexual scandal in the 1980s and 1990s. In the late 1980s the televangelist Jimmy Swaggert exposed the marital infidelity of two of his fellow televangelists, Marvin Garmin and Jim Bakker, before becoming embroiled in his own scandal. After apologizing to his congregation in 1988 for soliciting prostitution and sinning against God, he was caught with a prostitute again in 1991. Protection of American children became a top priority for conservative politicians in the late 1980s and early 1990s. Unlike the political battles over obscenity in the seventies and eighties, which were often billed by supporters of "family values" as necessary to protect children, the conflict of the 1990s focused on sheltering children from learning about sex in the classroom.[57] In 1991, Senator Jesse Helms argued that the Senate faced a choice: "support of sexual restraint among our young people or support for homosexuality and sexual decadence."[58] The 1998 White House sex scandal involving President Bill Clinton and the intern Monica Lewinsky, which led to the impeachment of Clinton, fueled an already near-hysterical national debate over the exposure of young Americans to a sex-crazed media and seemed to confirm fears of American parents that had been building for more than a decade.[59] In the wake of the scandal, it was not uncommon to hear teens justify their sexual behavior by asking, "If the President can do it, why can't we?"[60]

For Christian parents, it seemed that marital problems and sexual infidelity were running rampant alongside teenage pregnancy in American society. For conservative Christian families, their religious beliefs helped them deal with their fears about unrestrained teenage sexuality. As Kristin Luker has explained, "Religious faith provides both boundaries and a community that supports those boundaries."[61] A few advice books devoted entire chapters to "divorce-proofing" one's life, stressing that if one did not stay pure until marriage, one's future would be in jeopardy. As Rebecca St. James put it, "Premarital sex is not just about you and the person you are with. It is about you, your future spouse, the person you are with, and his or her future spouse."[62] Sex, in the appropriate marital context, was often portrayed as the culmination of a fairy-tale romance. According to some sources, sex after waiting did not often live up to the hype. One young woman from a conservative Christian background lamented that "if I'd waited until my honeymoon, I probably would have been depressed the entire time"; in her view, teaching teens to wait romanticizes the idea of sex and marriage in a detrimental way.[63]

Christian writers and organizations such as Focus on the Family occasionally brought in Christian celebrities as role models for young teens to stress the emotional dangers of premarital sex rather than the physical ones. Kirk

Cameron, of *Growing Pains* fame, arguing that there was no such thing as safe sex, was quoted as saying, "A condom can't protect you from a broken heart."[64] In *I Kissed Dating Goodbye*, which had sold nearly a million copies by 2001, Joshua Harris focused less on abstinence and more on purity in both thought and action.[65] Harris argued that to love the way God intended us to love, one must put others first, guarding the hearts of those one cared about by not becoming too intimate (either physically or emotionally) until one was ready for true commitment (marriage).[66]

Christian writers were not the only ones discussing the emotional risks associated with premarital sex. In 1995, *Mother Jones* magazine devoted an entire issue to the subject of sex education and teenage sexual behavior. Nell Bernstein, a journalist and advocate for American youth, included a piece entitled "Learning to Love," in which she asked, "What are we offering those kids left all by themselves in a downstairs bedroom? A *'True Love Waits'* button or a condom—neither of which addresses the underlying loneliness of a generation raised in empty houses." Bernstein criticized both those who fought for comprehensive sex education and those who insisted upon abstinence-only curriculums, insisting that "with our relentless focus on disease and pregnancy, we leave our children without much explicit guidance when it comes to high-risk activities of the heart."[67]

Of course, most teens writing in for advice from experts such as Susie Shellenberger, an employee of Focus on the Family, were more concerned with the immediate, physical consequences, such as the potential for pregnancy or the prevalence of sexually transmitted diseases (STDs). The advice Christian authors provided was simple and reminiscent of the federal government's 1980s anti-drug campaign: just don't do it. No advice was given on how to have safe sex. To one 14-year-old girl who was determined to have sex before marriage, Shellenberger, rather than offering advice on safety, replied, "You obviously wrote a Christian woman so she would tell you not to have sex."[68] Advice from conservative parents seems to have been generally the same, often being simply, "Do not have sex."[69]

Conservative parents, pastors, and youth ministers may have focused their attention on abstinence and felt that this was sufficient for sexual education, but STDs were one of the toughest issues that teens faced in the 1990s, and many Americans believed that trusting teens to abstain from sex was naive. AIDS was considered the primary threat, fueling existing parental anxieties, and even secular guidebooks for parents or teens included chapters on alternatives to sex, such as abstinence.[70] For Christian families specifically and conservatives in general, the emphasis on abstinence was a two-pronged attack, meant to discourage premarital sex but also to encourage heterosexuality. Some conservative politicians, such as Jesse Helms, argued that AIDS education was tantamount to promoting homosexuality among teens and therefore should not be included in school curriculums.[71] Instead, abstinence-only sex education was billed as a solution to all the problems, and federal funding for AIDS education was often rejected by conservative states such as Texas.[72] Teens were urged to avoid sexual activity outside marriage and were made to fear both AIDS and other STDs. Christian writers blamed comprehensive sex education for the prevalence of STDs, arguing, "Young men and women who have their whole lives ahead of them will have it snuffed out in their prime because they believed everything their health class taught them about condoms and safe sex."[73]

Criticism of the government for pushing condom usage—for "giving up" on the youth of the nation—is also common in these advice columns and books and was part of a larger backlash against federal efforts to promote condom usage among teens and to provide students with comprehensive sex education in order to combat AIDS. In 1991, high schools in some of America's largest cities were toying with the idea of distributing condoms to students. They were met with vociferous opposition from some of the nation's leading conservative religious authorities. Monsignor John Woolsey, of the Catholic Church's New York diocese, argued that it was a "ratification of sexual promiscuity." Rabbi Abraham Hecht, president of the Rabbinical Alliance of America, agreed: "This gives a stamp of approval to something we feel is immoral and unhealthy."[74] Protestant Christian writers agreed with their Catholic and Jewish counterparts and argued that handing out condoms to teens would simply encourage more sexual activity among them. They explained that by pointing out the "tremendous" failure rate of condoms, they wanted "to appeal to those who are toying with the idea of risking their lives for a few moments of sexual pleasure."[75]

The frequency of questions on the issue to authors and advice columnists like Susie Shellenberger indicates that Christian girls were also very concerned about abortion in the 1990s, which is unsurprising given the intense political debate surrounding the issue. In the 1980s, abortion became the primary moral battleground for conservative politicians, much as civil rights had provided a moral impetus for liberal politicians in the 1960s. Thus, young women of the eighties and nineties were undeniably shaped by the conservative political agenda, spread to their parents' generation through the media, Christian publishers, and church leaders. Politically active female crusaders such as Beverly LaHaye fueled the fire against abortion throughout the 1980s, making it one of the central issues of the profamily movement in conservative politics. In one of her books, LaHaye compared abortion in the United States to the Holocaust. She wrote: "I believe Almighty God is going to pour out His wrath on this nation if we do not, once again, protect the right of the unborn."[76]

A lack of education on contraceptives, fears of pregnancy, and the overall tension surrounding the issue of female sexuality left young women of the 1990s extremely concerned about abortion as they sought to develop their own political opinions on a variety of topics. Many wrote letters asking for lists of companies that were prochoice so they could boycott their products. Others wrote in asking for details about the procedure and expressing concern that everyone would assume they were prolife just because they were Christians. At least one girl, age 13, wrote in asking whether she should get an abortion; she was advised against it.[77] Much of the advice given to these teens centered on how to defend one's prolife beliefs when confronted in school or by peers. One "fact" given to use as support for a prolife, antiabortion stance was that "prior to its legalization, 90 percent of abortions were done by physicians in their offices, not in back alleys." This fact was obviously flawed, since so-called back-alley abortions or those done at home would not have been reported and therefore could not have been included in any statistics from the era prior to legalization. Planned Parenthood was also repeatedly referred to as "the leading abortion provider in the nation."[78]

TRUE LOVE WAITS

Teenage sexuality, premarital sex, a lack of morally acceptable options for pregnant teens, and the fear that AIDS was spreading beyond the homosexual community meant that for parents, sex in the 1990s generated the same level of anxiety that drugs had generated in the 1980s.[79] In addition to offering up advice for young women, these books published by Christian presses in the mid- to late 1990s sought to draw attention to a fast-growing campaign to promote abstinence among Southern Baptist youth. Books, articles, and advice columns published after 1993 refer repeatedly to the abstinence-only sex-education programs as an answer to the many perceived threats of premarital sex. Within this climate of fear, the Sunday School Board, an organizational committee within the Southern Baptist Convention, the larger of the two branches of the Baptist denomination, which has been divided since prior to the Civil War, and one of the two largest Christian denominations in the United States, second only to the Catholic Church, took on the task of educating young Christians about the dangers of premarital sex. In 1993 the Sunday School Board set out a plan to market several book series and educational materials to both parents and church youth groups. These materials were meant to take away some of the awkwardness associated with sex education and to enable Southern Baptists to "positively influence a growing movement in the United States advocating abstinence and chastity."[80] This marketing campaign swiftly took on a life of its own in the form of True Love Waits. Intended to back the new Christian Sex Education resources, True Love Waits and one of its founders, Richard Ross, stressed that abstinence was okay despite what society and peer pressure told young people and that the only safe sex was abstinence. Ross spent fifteen years ministering to Southern Baptist youth in many cities in Texas and Tennessee before going to work as a youth-ministry consultant for LifeWay Christian Resources, a Christian publishing house in Nashville, where he became the spokesperson for True Love Waits in 1993.

The True Love Waits program spread quickly throughout the Southern Baptist community and beyond, crossing both the denominational boundaries separating American churches and the Atlantic Ocean. It began in Tennessee, in the Southern Baptist churches of Nashville. Teens in these congregations were encouraged to stand up, take the pledge, and sign commitment cards. These cards stated, "Believing that true love waits, I make a commitment to God, myself, my family, those I date, my future mate, and my future children to be sexually pure until the day I enter a covenant marriage relationship." Ross anticipated that within a year more than one hundred thousand teens would have taken the pledge. This turned out to be a conservative estimate. By May 1993 True Love Waits was receiving national attention in mainstream publications such as *Time* magazine and on NBC's *The Today Show,* only adding to its popularity.[81] In 2004, the True Love Waits program reported that 2.5 million teens had signed a virginity pledge since 1993.[82]

Though it began as a Southern Baptist program, True Love Waits spread to other conservative denominations very quickly. Many of those interviewed for this project came from a variety of denominations, including Churches of Christ, Southern Baptist, Presbyterian, and nondenominational congregations. With the participation of the Catholic Church, True Love Waits became a presence in the two largest denominational bodies in the United States. Within a year it had also spread across international boundaries, into Canada and eventually into Europe and Africa. One of the coordinators of the campaign said, "When we started out, we were just hoping Southern Baptists would get involved. But then other religious groups became interested and it began to spread across denominational lines in the United States. Now, with the Canadians' involvement, we have the potential to impact the entire North American continent."[83]

The rapid adoption of the program was a result of the national debate surrounding teenage sexuality and the popularity of True Love Waits, not as a marketing campaign but as a lifestyle choice. True Love Waits was able to cross both race and class boundaries in a way that other programs and organizations could not, primarily because of its focus on preventing both pregnancy and disease. Black urban teens embraced the program in strong numbers. A youth minister in Houston, Texas, explained, "These kids are hungry. They are starving for someone to tell them the truth."[84] Youth leaders worried that the pledge would be difficult for urban youth to take and live up to given the pressures that they faced daily, including the messages within rap music, peer pressure, and what was presented in movies and music videos. Many African students also completed the program and turned out in great numbers to take the pledge and sign their promise cards, largely as a result of its focus on preventing the spread of AIDS.[85]

In all the media frenzy that surrounded the campaign, the fact that True Love Waits was originally intended to be a marketing campaign was lost. It was meant to help the Sunday School Board sell a book series devoted to teaching the value of sexual abstinence, and while it was extremely successful in this regard, it also managed to spur growth in numerous other areas of Christian popular culture. Christian bookstores and organizations such as Focus on the Family profited from the sale of True Love Waits–inspired music, Bibles, advice books, magazines, and jewelry. For example, by the end of 1993, a CCM album to support the program was in the works, garnering True Love Waits and abstinence-only sex education a mention in *Billboard* magazine.[86] Many popular groups and individuals in the 1990s recorded new songs for the album, including Michael W. Smith, DC Talk, Petra, and the Newsboys. The music was meant to uplift those who had taken the pledge and to serve as a reminder of that promise. At the same time, it was intended to be an alternative to the supposedly dangerous mainstream secular music, which was presenting "a message that is in direct conflict with the biblical view of sexuality."[87] Rebecca St. James, who took the True Love Waits pledge at the age of 16 while performing at a park in Illinois, recorded a song, "Wait for Me," about sexual purity for her album *Transform*. "Wait for Me" focuses on the romantic notion that you need to save yourself for your future spouse, who is waiting for you. The lyrics read:

> Darling, did you know that I dream about you
> Waiting for the look in your eyes when we meet the first time
> Darling, did you know that I pray about you
> Praying that you will hold on, keep your loving eyes only for me[88]

Perhaps the most obvious commercial aspect of True Love Waits was the marketing of promise rings and other jewelry meant to remind teens of their promises to both God and themselves. Jewelry was marketed almost solely to young women through popular teen magazines such as *Brio,* published by Focus on the Family. The majority of young women who wrote in asking for advice about sex were given the same advice: stay abstinent and purchase a "love pendant," a promise ring, or some other piece of jewelry to wear as a reminder of your promise to God.[89] Many advice books included order forms for jewelry or tear-out pledge cards within their pages. *Brio* magazine devoted an entire issue in 1993 to True Love Waits and the campaign for abstinence that was filled with references to True Love Waits jewelry. In *258 Great Dates While You Wait,* readers are reminded, "Your promise to God is the most important factor. But if you DO want a physical reminder, there are other things besides a ring that you can use."[90] The authors suggested that teens laminate their pledge card (there was one located in the back of the book for convenience), purchase a "love pendant" for only twenty dollars from Focus on the Family, or get their parents to buy something for them as a special gift. These tokens were meant to provoke a sense of guilt if teens found themselves in a tricky situation. But guilt is hardly a strong motivating factor. Morgan, a young woman who became pregnant in high school, explained that she simply removed her promise ring before she had sex with her boyfriend, putting it back on afterward. She also admitted that she was not worried about disappointing God but very concerned about disappointing her mother, who had always insisted that she remain abstinent.[91]

According to the *Baptist Press,* teens who took the pledge felt as though they were rebelling against dominant trends in society. Many of them were proud of their decision and spoke openly about the effect that True Love Waits had on their lives. Paul Ballenger, 19, stated, "I'm proud to be a virgin and I'm willing to tell that to the world." Both Paul and his 18-year-old girlfriend, Susan Fitzgerald, vowed to remain abstinent until marriage, and both saw a need to discuss that vow and their beliefs before committing to a serious courtship. Susan narrated their story: "After we had dated about two months, I asked him what he thought about sex before marriage. I think it sort of shocked him." Paul admitted that the decision was not always an easy one. "I come home every weekend from school, and it is a constant struggle. But I've made a commitment to more than just myself. I've made it to God, and I've made it to others. I think true love can wait."[92] Young people's involvement in the program also put many parents at ease. Bo Hague, a teen from Oklahoma, stated, "The parents of the girls I date don't ask questions because they know I've made a commitment." These teens emphasized that they had made a promise not only to themselves but also to their future husband or wife. Traci Bixler proudly proclaimed that she had even written a sealed letter to her future spouse explaining her commitment to waiting for him, one that she would give to him on her wedding night.[93]

Journalists, much like the young people who took the pledge, compared True Love Waits to rebellious youth movements of the past.[94] In 1993, the *Washington Post* ran a story entitled "Virginity is New Counterculture Among Some Teens," which reported on the growing tendency among teenagers to refer to themselves as "vocal virgins" who had taken on the idea of chastity with a sense of pride and accomplishment. In one article from 1993, a *Baptist Press* columnist referred to the *True Love Waits* campaign as the "flames" that would become a "bonfire" of virginity and purity. This fire would make chastity the new popular fad among young people, he argued, pointing out that Madonna's "Like a Virgin" would take on an entirely different meaning.[95]

Much like other countercultural youth movements and many conservative Christian organizations, True Love Waits ended its first year of recruitment with a celebratory demonstration in Washington, DC. Referred to as DC '94, the event drew more than twenty-five thousand teens in July 1994. The National Mall was filled with two hundred thousand signed sexual-abstinence pledge cards sent in by teens across the country. There were similar displays in other parts of the world. Gatherings were held in Uganda and in parts of Canada, where teens marched in parades to show their support of the campaign or simply joined together to watch the festivities in Washington, which were broadcast on television.[96]

While True Love Waits gained a strong following among conservative Christian churches, it was not without its critics. The program, which received attention primarily for its emphasis on preventing teenage pregnancy, did not teach birth-control methods or educate those who did choose to have sex about protecting themselves so they would not end up with an STD. Richard Ross admitted that not all young people would abstain from sex before marriage, but he insisted that it was absolutely essential to say to young people, "Don't have sex. It kills people. It hurts people's lives," promoting the idea that sex was innately wrong.[97] The journalist Nell Bernstein harshly criticized abstinence-only sex education and the teachings of leaders such as Richard Ross, writing: "Young people are learning in school that sex can hurt or kill them without learning that it can also give them a connection to another person."[98] Not surprisingly, the strongest criticism centered on the rejection of sex education that included information on any form of contraception other than abstinence. One young woman recalled, "My mom taught me all the time that abstinence was the most important thing. She never really taught me the option of condoms and other forms of birth control."[99]

True Love Waits was not the only program that taught abstinence as the only option for safe sex. *Time* magazine reported that there were more than a dozen such programs in 1993, thanks to Reagan-era funding for the development of classroom materials to teach teens to "just say no" to sex.[100] Sex Respect, developed by Project Respect, out of Golf, Illinois, and used in the curriculums of a few thousand schools, did not include any information on contraceptives and was criticized for failing to offer any follow-up programs or guidance for teens who did not abstain from sex and found themselves with an unwanted pregnancy or with an STD.[101] Other programs were created, some with a religious background and some not, to counteract the seemingly destructive message presented by True Love Waits that sex was bad and no amount of education about it would make it safe. Girls, Inc. targeted its pregnancy-prevention curriculum to lower-income teens. These girls were encouraged to delay sexual activity: "While we're focusing on postponement, we're not doing it in a context of fear and scare tactics."[102] Opponents of True Love Waits and abstinence-only sex education in general argued that it was "erotophobic" and that this fear could prevent young teens from learning what they needed to know to protect themselves. Pam Smallwood, education director of Planned Parenthood of Central Texas, insisted that "if all kids learn about sex is that if you touch it you'll die, how can you ever expect them to develop healthy relationships?"[103]

While many teens found empowerment by participating in these programs and resisting peer pressure, others saw them as detrimental, particularly for young women. When asked about her own experience with abstinence-only sex education in Missouri, Sarah argued that because girls are held to such a high standard with regard to morality, they are more likely to experience paranoia and stress due to lack of sexual education. "You can't just teach kids abstinence," she said. "It's not practical, it's detrimental to women's sense of self."[104] Of young men, it was often expected that they would have premarital sex, but if young women gave into peer pressure, they were deemed sluts. Kira, who grew up in conservative western Texas, explained that even though everyone stressed waiting, very few actually did, and many of the church leaders, parents, and adult advisers had not followed their own advice. It was generally understood that you could "do it, but just don't get caught."[105] Those who did not keep their promises were left to deal with the consequences of their lack of education, such as unplanned pregnancies or STDs. After getting pregnant during her senior year of high school, Morgan, also from western Texas, was rejected by her friends and her church, her mother demanded that she get married, and her boyfriend's mother told her to get an abortion.[106]

In recent years, abstinence-only sex education has come under fire for its inability to prevent teenage sexual activity, primarily because many of those who took the pledge did not keep it. In a study led by Dr. Peter Bearman, researchers found that of approximately twelve thousand teens who took the pledge, 88 percent reported that they had engaged in sexual intercourse before marriage. Rates for STDs among those who took the pledge were nearly identical to rates for those who did not; however, because those who took the pledge tended to have less education on the topic, they were less likely to know that they were infected and therefore more likely to spread the disease to others. The pressure to maintain technical virginity also led many to participate in riskier behavior, such as experimenting with anal and oral sex without the use of a condom. Deborah Roffman, an educator and author, was quoted in the study as saying, "Kids who are engaging in oral sex or anal sex will tell you they are still practicing abstinence because they haven't had 'real sex' yet."[107] On the other hand, the pledge did tend to delay the start of sexual intercourse by approximately eighteen months. Teens who took the pledge also married earlier and had fewer sexual partners.[108]

Medical professionals were not the only ones who criticized True Love Waits and programs like it. In 2005, a young woman named Shelby Knox offered viewers a glimpse into the lives of Christian teens when she starred in the documentary *The Education of Shelby Knox*. Knox grew up as part of a Christian family in conservative Lubbock, Texas, which as of 2005 had teenage-pregnancy and STD rates that were among the highest in the country. The documentary highlighted the fact that Lubbock's sex-education program focused solely on abstinence, offering no information on contraception and condom use, and followed Knox's efforts to change the policy. Knox's involvement in the campaign to promote sex education in public schools, despite her conservative upbringing, and the testimonies of many other young women from western Texas who were interviewed for this project lend support to the notion that young women were not simply indoctrinated by their conservative religious faith but actively shaped their own lives as Christians while struggling with the contradictions and double standards associated with being a young woman.[109]

While the motivation behind advice guides and abstinence-only sex education was certainly a noble one, programs such as True Love Waits were ultimately disappointing for young people and counterproductive for the Christian Right in a variety of ways. Those who kept their promises often ended up with intense feelings of anxiety and paranoia about sex as a result of the fear tactics readily used by many youth pastors, leading them to seek answers from organizations such as Planned Parenthood, a service for young women that is often demonized by the Christian Right.[110] Those who did not keep their promises found themselves at greater risk of pregnancy or STDs and were alienated from or rejected by their Christian peers. Regardless of the group of teens analyzed, it is clear that the beliefs and rules of their parents' generation did not always transmit to the children. These young men and women shaped their own ideas about living as Christians in the United States. Morgan put it best: "What my mom told me is different from what I'll tell my daughters."[111]

CONCLUSION

Young women who came of age in the 1990s and the mothers who raised them combined elements of conservative Christian culture with notions of feminism and women's equality to reshape the way women related to both the secular world and their own faith. Not all of the lessons they learned from their parents' generation took root in these young women, but they were able to maintain their faith while interacting with and shaping mainstream society. Mothers worked hard to raise their daughters in an environment that stressed a balance between being a strong woman and taking on the roles God had given women. Anamarie explained, "My mom was great about letting me know I can do all those things outside the home, but within the home and the church there are different roles for men and women, and that is okay." Laughing about the challenge her mom faced in raising her in a house full of boys, Anamarie said, "She still laughs about the fact that she tried so hard to make me a lady, but never really succeeded! But I have always been pretty girly anyway, so she didn't have to try too hard."[112] In spite of the anxieties and challenges inherent in raising children, mothers who stressed conservative Christian values and incorporated notions of feminist equality in society succeeded in raising a generation of young women who are strong in their faith but willing to adjust to and accept societal changes as well.

NOTES

1. Chip Alford, "Chastity Making a Comeback," *Baptist Press,* 18 March 1994. The main title of this essay, "A Bonfire of Chastity," is taken from Alford's article.

2. Phyllis Schlafly, *The Power of the Positive Woman* (New York: Arlington House, 1977), 139–66.

3. Keira V. Williams, *Gendered Politics in the Modern South: The Susan Smith Case and the Rise of a New Sexism* (Baton Rouge: Louisiana State University Press, 2012), 5.

4. Sue Lees, *Sugar and Spice: Sexuality and Adolescent Girls* (New York: Penguin Books, 1993), 15–16.

5. Joyce Landorf, *The Fragrance of Beauty* (Wheaton, IL: Victor Books, 1973); Viola Walden, *Woman to Woman: Questions and Answers to Today's Home Problems* (Murfreesboro, TN: Sword of the Lord, 1987).

6. Gene A. Getz, *The Measure of a Woman* (Ventura, CA: Regal Books, 1977), 16–20.

7. Robert Wolcott Smith, *Love Story: The Real Thing* (Waco, TX: Word Books, 1975), 75.

8. Landorf, *Fragrance of Beauty,* 19. Phyllis Diller was a comedienne in the 1960s with wild, out-of-control hair. "Mama" Cass Elliot, of the musical group The Mamas and the Papas, was known for being overweight. One of the group's hit songs from 1967 proclaimed, "And no one's getting fat except Mama Cass."

9. Ibid.

10. Ibid., 76.

11. Ibid., 13–24.

12. Kathy Peiss, *Hope in a Jar: The Making of America's Beauty Culture* (New York: Metropolitan Books, 1998).

13. Beverly Hyles, quoted in Walden, *Woman to Woman,* 96.

14. Joy Martin, quoted in ibid., 98.

15. R. Marie Griffith, *Born Again Bodies: Flesh and Spirit in American Christianity* (Berkeley: University of California Press, 2004), 165.

16. Ibid., 217.

17. Walden, *Woman to Woman,* 129.

18. Lauren Winner, "The Weigh and the Truth," *Christianity Today* 44, no. 10 (September 2000), www.christianitytoday.com/ct/2000/september4/1.50.html.

19. Betty Malz, *Making Your Husband Feel Loved* (Lake Mary, FL: Creation House, 1990), 7, 118, 9.

20. *The Eyes of Tammy Faye,* dir. Fenton Bailey and Randy Barbato (Universal Pictures, 2000).

21. Ibid.

22. Ibid.

23. Barry Alfonso, *Billboard Guide to Contemporary Christian Music* (New York: Billboard Books, 2002), 168–72.

24. Amy Grant, "Find a Way," *Unguarded,* A&M Records, 1985, compact disc.

25. Williams, *Gendered Politics in the Modern South,* 5.

26. "About Amy," accessed 20 March 2013, www.amygrant.com.

27. Andrew Beaujon, *Body Piercing Saved My Life: Inside the Phenomenon of Christian Rock* (New York: Da Capo, 2006), 33–34.

28. Steve Rabey, "A Chastened Singer Returns to Christian Basics," *New York Times,* 11 May 2002, www.nytimes.com/2002/05/11/us/religion-journal-a-chastened-singer-returns-to-christian-basics .html.

29. Ibid.

30. Mark Powell, "Children of the Day," in *Encyclopedia of Contemporary Christian Music* (Peabody, MA: Hendrickson, 2002).

31. Beaujon, *Body Piercing Saved My Life,* 23.

32. Marsha Stevens-Pino, BALM Ministries, accessed 13 October 2011, www.balmministries.net /fr_home.cfm.

33. Alice Echols, *Hot Stuff: Disco and the Remaking of American Culture* (New York: Norton, 2010), 39–70.

34. Bill Carmichael and Nancie Carmichael, *Answers to the Questions Christian Women are Asking* (Eugene, OR: Harvest House, 1984), 125.

35. Ibid., 129.

36. Nancy Gibbs, "How Should We Teach Our Kids About Sex?," *Time,* 24 May 1993, 62.

37. Susie Shellenberger, *Guys and a Whole Lot More: Advice for Teen Girls on Almost Everything* (Grand Rapids, MI: Fleming H. Revell, 1994), 154–57.

38. Ibid., 135.

39. Greg Johnson and Susie Shellenberger, *What Hollywood Won't Tell You About Sex, Love, and Dating* (Ventura, CA: Regal Books, 1994), 225.

40. Ibid., 226.

41. Morgan, interview by author, 17 May 2012.

42. Ken Camp, "Youth leaders urged to take stand on sexual purity, homosexuality," *Baptist Press,* 2 August 1993.

43. Anamarie, interview by author, 1 June 2012.

44. Kira, interview by author, 25 May 2012.

45. Williams, *Gendered Politics in the Modern South.*

46. Shellenberger and Johnson, *What Hollywood Won't Tell You,* 152.

47. Darien Cooper, *You Can Be the Wife of a Happy Husband* (Wheaton, IL: Victor Books, 1974), 39.

48. Johnson and Shellenberger, *What Hollywood Won't Tell You,* 86.

49. Susie Shellenberger and Greg Johnson, *258 Great Dates While You Wait* (Nashville: Broadman & Holman, 1995), 19; Johnson and Shellenberger, *What Hollywood Won't Tell You,* 66.

50. Joshua Harris, *I Kissed Dating Goodbye* (Sisters, OR: Multnomah, 1997), 99–100.

51. Rebecca St. James, *Wait for Me: Rediscovering the Joy of Purity in Romance* (Nashville: Thomas Nelson, 2002), 31.

52. Morgan interview.

53. The quotation is a reference to 2 Corinthians 6:14.

54. Sarah, interview by author, 10 May 2012.

55. Johnson and Shellenberger, *What Hollywood Won't Tell You,* 49–50.

56. Ibid., 136.

57. Whitney Strub, *Perversion for Profit: The Politics of Pornography and the Rise of the New Right* (New York: Columbia University Press, 2011), 179; Kristin Luker, *When Sex Goes to School: Warring Views on Sex—and Sex Education—Since the Sixties* (New York: Norton, 2006), 91–118.

58. Nell Bernstein, "Learning to Love," *Mother Jones* 20, no. 1 (January–February 1995): 47.

59. Ibid., 44–54.

60. Ron Stodghill II, Julie Grace, Richard Woodbury, Charlotte Faltermayer, and Timothy Roche, "Where'd You Learn That?," *Time,* 15 June 1998, 52.

61. Luker, *When Sex Goes to School,* 231.

62. St. James, *Wait for Me,* 40.

63. Kira interview.

64. Johnson and Shellenberger, *What Hollywood Won't Tell You.*

65. "The Man Who Ignited the Debate: An Interview with Joshua Harris," *Christianity Today,* 11 June 2001, www.christianitytoday.com/ct/2001/june11/5.42.html.

66. Harris, *I Kissed Dating Goodbye.*

67. Bernstein, "Learning to Love," 49.

68. Shellenberger, *Guys and a Whole Lot More,* 145–46.

69. Morgan interview.

70. Loren E. Acker, Bram C. Goldwater, and William H. Dyson, *AIDS-Proofing Your Kids: A Step-by-Step Guide* (Hillsboro, OR: Beyond Words, 1992), 103.

71. William Link, *Righteous Warrior: Jesse Helms and the Rise of Modern Conservatism* (New York: St. Martin's, 2008), 348–49.

72. John Gallagher, "No Thanks," *Advocate,* 26 December 1995, 23.

73. Johnson and Shellenberger, *What Hollywood Won't Tell You,* 200.

74. S. Tifft and K. L. Mihok, "Better Safe Than Sorry," *Time,* 21 January 1991, 66.

75. Johnson and Shellenberger, *What Hollywood Won't Tell You,* 200; Philip Elmer-Dewitt and Lisa H. Towle, "Making the Case for Abstinence," *Time,* 24 May 1993, 64.

76. Beverly LaHaye, *I Am a Woman by God's Design* (Westwood, NJ: Fleming H. Revell, 1980), 117; LaHaye, *Who But a Woman?* (Nashville: Thomas Nelson, 1984), 116.

77. Shellenberger, *Guys and a Whole Lot More,* 110, 103, 159.

78. Johnson and Shellenberger, *What Hollywood Won't Tell You,* 219, 200.

79. Bernstein, "Learning to Love," 47.

80. Johnson and Shellenberger, *What Hollywood Won't Tell You,* 200.

81. Jeff Schapiro, "'True Love Waits' Cofounder to Retire from LifeWay," *Christian Post,* 28 September 2011, www.christianpost.com/news/true-love-waits-cofounder-to-retire-from-lifeway-56687/.

82. Lawrence K. Altman, "Study Finds That Teenage Virginity Pledges are Rarely Kept," *New York Times,* 10 March 2004, www.nytimes.com/2004/03/10/us/study-finds-that-teenage-virginity-pledges-are-rarely-kept.html?_r=0.

83. Chip Alford, "Canadian churches to embrace True Love Waits campaign," *Baptist Press,* 1 October 1993.

84. Ken Camp, "Black urban youth hungry for stand on sexual purity," ibid., 14 September 1993.

85. Craig Bird, "Kenyan Students take True Love Waits pledge," ibid., 18 November 1993.

86. See *Billboard,* 16 July 1994, 46, and 5 July 1997, 13.

87. Chip Alford, "Christian musicians endorse True Love Waits campaign," *Baptist Press,* 8 September 1993.

88. St. James, *Wait for Me.*

89. Shellenberger, *Guys and a Whole Lot More,* 15.

90. Shellenberger and Johnson, *258 Great Dates While You Wait,* 38.

91. Morgan interview.

92. Terri Lackey, "Baptist teens' no-sex pledge catching national attention," *Baptist Press,* 22 April 1993.

93. Art Toalston, "His date's parents aren't suspicious," *Baptist Press,* 18 August 1993.

94. Alford, "Chastity Making a Comeback."

95. Ibid.

96. Charles Willis, "U.S. Celebration caps year of True Love Waits," *Baptist Press,* 29 July 1994.

97. Camp, "Youth leaders urged to take a stand."

98. Bernstein, "Learning to Love," 49.

99. Chip Alford, "True Love Waits hits NBC's Today Show," *Baptist Press,* 1 October 1993.

100. Gibbs, "How Should We Teach Our Kids About Sex?"; Elmer-Dewitt and Towle, "Making the Case for Abstinence."

101. Elmer-Dewitt and Towle, "Making the Case for Abstinence."

102. Gibbs, "How Should We Teach Our Kids About Sex?"

103. Jodie Morse and Hillary Hylton, "Preaching Chastity in the Classroom," *Time,* 18 October 1999, 79.

104. Sarah interview.

105. Kira interview.

106. Morgan interview.

107. Ceci Connolly, "Teen Pledges Barely Cut STD Rates, Study Says," accessed 3 May 2012, www.washingtonpost.com/wp-dyn/articles/A48509-2005Mar18.html.

108. Ibid.; Altman, "Teenage Virginity Pledges are Rarely Kept."
109. *The Education of Shelby Knox,* dir. Marion Lipschutz and Rose Rosenblatt, PBS, 2005.
110. Sarah interview.
111. Morgan interview.
112. Anamarie interview.

12

"A Little Bit Too Much Africa for Me"

Steve Harvey, Black Sexuality, and the Global South in Still Trippin'

RICHÉ RICHARDSON

A sanctuary unlike any other in South Africa, this charming and unspoiled region is a nature lover's wonderland. Dappled shadows from the lush vegetation and cool breezes from the Indian Ocean, the area's beauty will leave its mark on your soul. Here, endless beaches and clear skies invite you to relax and dream in our Zimbali resort. Within this subtropical paradise, set within the serene confines of a coastal forest reserve, you will find the highest expression of exclusive hospitality: Fairmont Zimbali Lodge in Durban, South Africa. Whether visiting for business or leisure, guests will enjoy five-star service, including on-call butler service, ensuring an unforgettable African experience at our Durban resort.

—FROM THE WEBSITE of the Fairmont Zimbali Lodge in South Africa

Since the 1990s, the comedian Steve Harvey has been a force to be reckoned with in the world of entertainment. His routines as a stand-up comedian and his appearances on *Showtime at the Apollo,* along with his television series *The Steve Harvey Show* (1996–2002) on WBTV, were foundational in establishing him as one of the most prominent black comedians in the contemporary era. His performances build upon legacies established by legends in the field such as Richard Pryor and Eddie Murphy.[1] Over the years, through his projects in a range of media—television, radio, film, publishing—Harvey, a native of Welch, West Virginia, has built an entertainment empire. While his comedy career and popular syndicated daily radio show, *The Steve Harvey Morning Show,* have drawn a primarily African American audience and have helped build his media enterprise, his nationally syndicated talk show on daytime television, *Steve Harvey,* which premiered in 2012, has exponentially broadened his audience in the popular arena and boosted his fame at the national level.

Harvey's national audience expanded measurably when he became the host of the legendary daytime television game show *Family Feud* in 2010, a role that signaled his growing popularity in the American mainstream. His media visibility has further increased as a result of his hosting *Little Big Shots,* showcasing the talent of children, which debuted in 2016, and the Miss Universe Pageant (though Harvey had to issue an apology for mixing up the contestants and incorrectly naming the first runner-up as the pageant winner in 2016). Harvey's comment on his talk show in 2015 that "I don't give a damn about slavery" called into question his politics of race, and his view of blackness in particular, though he is known for his ongoing commitment to black community outreach and his support of education, including the historically black colleges and universities (HBCUs), such as Morehouse College, which his son attended. Significantly, in 2016 Harvey served as the commencement speaker at Alabama State University, in Montgomery, Alabama, which awarded him an honorary doctorate. In his speech, Harvey, who had attended Kent State for two years but never completed his degree, mentioned his lack of a formal education. According to the *Montgomery Advertiser,* Harvey "got emotional as he described the adversities he has faced: flunking out of school, losing everything he owned twice, and showering at gas stations while living out of his car in his 20s."[2]

In the 14 October 2013 issue of *People* magazine, a story entitled "Steve Harvey: His Incredible Journey" highlights the entertainer's career achievements and also acknowledges his past struggles, including being homeless for three years and living in a car. In the article, Harvey is quoted as saying that "when I'd land a gig, they'd put me up in a hotel, but after, I'd have nowhere to go. I'd lost everything."[3] That Harvey has risen above such challenging experiences and gone on to have a phenomenal career makes him all the more fascinating and inspiring for many of his fans. A 2010 article in the *New York Times* links his book on relationships to his increasing popularity:

> It's not going out on a limb to say that Mr. Harvey has never been more popular—and he is not exactly a stranger to the spotlight. He has appeared on television before, in his own sitcom and as host of a variety show, and he was for years a successful stand-up comedian. But it is the books that have landed him on "The Oprah Winfrey Show," "Ellen," and "Good Morning America." His turn as a relationship adviser is not a complete career reinvention, it is definitively a dramatic redefinition.[4]

Harvey's bestselling 2009 relationship book *Act Like a Lady, Think Like a Man,* on which the 2012 comedy film *Think Like a Man* is based, has been widely popular within the self-help genre. In this book, it is intriguing, for example, that Harvey refers to sex as "the cookie" and describes the masculine need for it as insatiable, sanctioning myths of black masculine hypersexuality, in light of the primarily black and feminine audience to which this book is pitched and his own raced and gendered subject position.[5] He drew on his own experiences in marriage, including two divorces, and parenting to develop this book and its 2010 sequel, *Straight Talk, No Chaser.*[6] Harvey's bestselling self-help books related to male-female relationships, primarily pitched toward an audience of single black women, encourage women to get into the minds of men to turn the dynamic of dating and relationships to their advantage. Most significantly, these books have grounded his enterprise within discourses related to gender, masculinity, and sexuality.

Harvey, like the film director Tyler Perry, who originated in New Orleans, Louisiana, stands at the vanguard among southern black men who have emerged as veritable media moguls in the entertainment arena in the twenty-first century. Perry's film enterprises, which have been largely defined by the issues they address—race, gender, and sexuality—have often been associated with controversy because of the strategies they have sometimes deployed in addressing these subjects. He has garnered fame primarily for his body of films, which boldly address topics such as the sexual abuse of women and girls in African American contexts and foreground the matriarchal character Madea, whom he portrays in drag. However, Harvey's import as a southern black masculine subject in shaping discourses of race, masculinity, and sexuality in contemporary black popular culture has not been as obvious or recognizable as Perry's.

I want to suggest that Harvey's routines, such as his live stand-up performance in his 2008 comedy show *Still Trippin',* importantly make up his discourses on blackness as well as masculinity and sexuality. The politics of constructing African and African American identities, along with black masculinity and sexuality, beg notice and analysis. Such politics model unsettling rhetoric related to African and African American subjectivity in dialogues about the racialist implications of the actor Michael Clark Duncan's appearance as a character in *Planet of the Apes* (2001) and in Harvey's primitivist, exaggerated descriptions of the Zimbali Lodge in South Africa. It is important to study *Still Trippin'* closely for the implications it holds for discourses on the "global South" as constituted in and through the African American context. This provocative popular production suggests the transnational impact of celebrities such as Harvey in constructing and disseminating images of blackness in the realm of popular culture and speaks to the importance of thinking about black and southern subjects in a global context. It both registers and reflects the intensification of cultural flows and exchanges in the global arena in the new millennium, including the global impact of African American culture.

It is important to recognize the levels on which *Still Trippin'*, even without incorporating explicitly antigay invective, reinforces politics of heterosexism and homophobia in black comedy and cites this linguistic economy through its xenophobic construction of Africa. This discussion of the aforesaid construction of Africa seems important, too, given the ways in which earlier comedians, such as Eddie Murphy, constructed and commodified Africa through a primitivist narrative and linked it to hypersexuality and exoticism, in effect reinforcing familiar narratives of the continent within colonialism and imperialism. Significantly, *Still Trippin'*, which endorsed the candidacy of Barack Obama for president in 2008, provided one of the most salient models in black popular culture of constructions of Africa at a time when Obama, because of his Kenyan ancestry, was according increasing prominence to Africa in the nation's public sphere.

A MONKEY IN A MOVIE

Still Trippin', produced by James Tripp-Haith and directed by Leslie Small, was taped live in Newark, New Jersey, in the months before Barack Obama's historic election in 2008. In this performance, Harvey returned to the roots of his long career in stand-up comedy. The performance marked his fifth stand-up tour and the twenty-third year of his epic comedy career. As this landmark live stand-up performance begins, Harvey acknowledges his indebtedness and thanks to God, reminds his audience that "this ain't the radio show," and underscores that he will be a bit more frank than he typically has been in that forum, that is, that he will incorporate the kind of talk, including the use of profanity, that the radio prohibits and censors. However, the initial dialogue segment draws on the radio show and reconstructs a dialogue with one of the show's past guests, the Academy Award–nominated actor Michael Clark Duncan, who had been acclaimed for his compelling performance as the character John Coffey in the 1999 film *The Green Mile*, directed by Frank Darabont.[7] In introducing the dialogue to his primarily black middle-class audience and to make sure they know who Duncan is, Harvey describes the actor as "big, dark, Michael Clark Duncan" and mentions the actor's connection to this film. At the outset, Harvey underscores that he didn't know Duncan very well at the time of the interview.

Harvey emphasizes his shock and concern over Duncan's revelation that he was scheduled to appear in a remake of the film *Planet of the Apes:* "Now, you've seen Michael. Now, I'm looking at Michael and I'm thinking to myself Michael know good and hell well he ain't got no business playing no monkey in no damn movie! This ain't gone be good for nobody involved! So I didn't know what to do I was so put back. Let me tell you, why is his big ass gone play a monkey in a damn movie?"[8] Harvey's implication is that Duncan, because of physical characteristics such as his dark skin, large build, and Africanist features, looks too close for comfort like the black stereotypes that are typically linked to the monkey in the American cultural imaginary.

Planet of the Apes, the science-fiction film that premiered in 1968, focuses on the experience of an astronaut who returns to Earth to find a world dominated by talking, bipedal apes who have evolved to a point where they wear clothing, dominate civilization, and have subdued and enslaved Earth's human population. The ape population has a hierarchy, with the darkest and most subordinate ones positioned at the very bottom and the fairest ones, who resemble Europeans, at the top, recasting the disparities in the United States premised on race and class. The film links the decline and destruction of human civilization to warmongering among men. One of the most famous scenes depicts the captive blond, blue-eyed astronaut portrayed by the actor Charlton Heston being brutalized. "Take your hand off me, you filthy ape," he asserts, when touched by a member of the species. The film, which was followed up with several sequels, launched several television series and became a popular-culture phenomenon, to the point of emerging as a merchandising brand. In recent years, it has undergone revival through several films, including the remake in which Duncan appeared, which was released in 2001.

Dumbfounded and perplexed by Duncan's revelation, Harvey turns to his show's phone line, where multiple callers, unsettled by Duncan's announcement of his upcoming movie role, urge Harvey to intervene and discourage the actor from performing in what they perceive to be a demeaning role that "will set us [black people] back 200 years." The callers' personal and public anxieties that Harvey describes are implicitly shaped by the longstanding stereotypes of

African Americans in the Western imaginary, including the litany of images of blacks in American popular and material culture that stereotype blacks and dehumanize them by associating them with animals, particularly monkeys. The racialist ideologies that frequently have been related to black identity are tacitly referenced in Harvey's and the callers' panic about Duncan's role. They demonstrate awareness of the longer history of disparaging black bodies through scientific racism, which intensified exponentially in the nineteenth century in the wake of Charles Darwin's publication of *On the Origin of Species* in 1859, which constituted blacks as a missing link between the ape and human beings on the Great Chain of Being, ranking them as inferior and subhuman. In cinema, movies from *Tarzan the Ape Man* (1932) to *King Kong* (1933), as well as their various sequels and adaptations, have also dehumanized blacks implicitly and explicitly and constituted them as inferior. At the same time, the comments of the callers described by Harvey are steeped in conventional black uplift ideologies, primarily linked to upward mobility and black middle-class and elite respectability, which stressed the importance of African Americans' putting their best foot forward.[9] Significantly, Harvey refers to his audience as "bourgie," or primarily black and middle class, a term he also uses in his references to his wife.

Harvey recalls lambasting callers who urged him to challenge Duncan's role choice with the retort, "That's easy for *you* to say. Your ass on the phone. You ain't in here with this big black bastard." In referring to him thus, Harvey constructs Duncan, who weighed 315 pounds and stood six feet five inches tall, as an intimidating figure. Although Duncan was reputed to be personable and was typically stereotyped as a "gentle giant," an image established in relation to his character in *The Green Mile,* Harvey's narrative, evoking Duncan's appearance and potential power in light of Duncan's strength and physical advantage and constructing him as menacing and bestial, alludes to conventional stereotypes of black masculinity as violent, dangerous, and threatening. Moreover, Harvey draws on hyperbole and the grotesque in describing an image of Duncan attacking him: "I go over there and say something crazy to his big, black ass, he get me in a headlock and start squeezing, now my little asshole just shoot out 'cross the room." Harvey's imaging of himself as helpless and at the mercy of a violent and angry Duncan registers their encounter as a symbolic rape and in effect links the actor to the myth of the black rapist. Harvey, who is notably lighter skinned by comparison, encodes the color black as menacing and links this quality, as he does physicality, to his fear of Duncan. Furthermore, Harvey's dialogue draws on black masculine heterosexist homophobia in the bestial, rapacious image of Duncan that it evokes.

Harvey's tone shifts measurably, however, when Duncan tells him that he is being paid $10 million to play the role of a monkey, a substantial sum for an appearance in one film given the typical marginality and struggles of black actors in Hollywood, a sum that rivals the typical salaries of award-winning white actors. As Harvey declares, "For $4,000,000, I'll be the best damn monkey you ever saw." He says that he would willingly shame blacks, come to work with a bunch of bananas, and swing on cables. He then proceeds to imitate the motion of swinging on stage.[10] Harvey further underscores his willingness to perform in this capacity by mentioning that he would eat banana pudding, answer exclusively to the name Cheetah, and "paint my whole ass pink"—here he has his back to the audience and motions as if he is painting and incidentally draws attention to the pink lining of his suit jacket as he continues to imitate monkey behavior on stage. Harvey's explicit verbal references to monkeys in this segment of the show continue and become more emphatic, to the point that the monkey emerges as the primary motif discussed in the final segment of the show (see the next section). In some cases, such references are reinforced by Harvey's imitation of monkeys in gyrations and movements on stage, including mimicry of simian sounds and mannerisms, which seem designed to add animation and dynamism to Harvey's performance and to intensify its humor.

Harvey performs the show in a black vernacular voice, a typical feature of black comedy. He draws on purportedly personal recollections and memories related to letters, e-mails, interviews, and phone conversations in developing the narrative content of the show's segments. Harvey mentions the need to improvise and talk about his family to fill up the daily four-hour time slot of his radio show, a point he complements toward the end of the show by mentioning his reminder to his wife that "somebody's got to write these jokes" to pay the bills, stressing the importance of drawing on events in everyday life such as the experience at the Zimbali Lodge. These moments suggest the extent to which scenarios invoked throughout his performance are potentially contrived and exaggerated and reflect fantasy and invention more than his lived reality. It is necessary, then, to distinguish between Steve Harvey's stage persona and voice in performance sequence and his actual life experiences. Yet, at an interpretive level, the first-person voice used throughout the show leaves room for the audience to conflate and confuse these personas and in that sense reinforces the impact and believability of his various comedy vignettes.

Of course, it is useful to situate Harvey's frequent and profuse citations of monkeys in this popular comedy routine as a by-product of African American folk traditions, whose symbolic relation to this vernacular genre are classically elaborated by Henry Louis Gates Jr. in *The Signifying Monkey*.[11] Yet, such references, as Harvey's initial concern about Duncan's role in the film and the panic of his callers suggest, cannot easily be divorced from the monkey's linkages to racist and ideological scripts of blackness in the national imaginary. Such imagery has frequently been invoked in reactionary and racist propaganda in the political arena concerning President Barack Obama. For example, on 18 February 2009 the *New York Post* published the unconscionable fantasy of the president as a dead monkey in a cartoon by Sean Delonas.[12] This image poignantly illustrates how demeaning, ridiculing, and humiliating the black subject to the point of dehumanizing the black body, whether visually or verbally, frequently serves as a performative instrument—and weapon—in disputations with black subjects.

Similarly, in July 2009 a Boston police officer referred to the African American Harvard professor Henry Louis Gates Jr. as a "porch monkey" in an e-mail after Gates's arrest in his Cambridge home by the white police sergeant James Crowley and amid the controversy over racial profiling that was unfolding nationally.[13] This comment dramatized the persisting tendency to resort to images of animals such as monkeys in constituting scripts of the black body and demonstrates the accessibility of the black body to verbal and violent assault in a white-dominated national culture in which vestiges of white supremacist and fascist ideologies still linger in the cultural imaginary and inflect public opinion. That the term *monkey* and related images surfaced so toxically in the public sphere of politics after President Obama was elected as an instrument for pathologizing black masculinity suggests the persisting impact and influence of the term as a racial epithet. This phenomenon also in effect unsettles the contemporary rhetoric of the postracial and postblackness. What is at stake in such ideological images of monkeys was made patently clear in 2012 when Christian Head, an African American surgeon at the University of California, Los Angeles, brought a lawsuit against the university alleging that he had been compared to a gorilla at a public presentation that depicted him as a gorilla being sodomized by his white supervisor in an image projected onto a screen at the event.[14]

The verbal economy of *Still Trippin'* relies heavily on a vocabulary and stage performance techniques that were established and popularized within blackface tradition. In the segment on his opposition to his son's plan to get a tattoo, Harvey evokes this language in criticizing blacks who get tattoos in Chinese, because their unfamiliarity with the language could put them in a position to unwittingly accept tattoos that include racist epithets such as *jigaboo* or *black spook*. The repeated references to monkeys in *Still Trippin'*, along with Harvey's references to such terms, iterate epithets that were routinely related to black subjectivity in American minstrel performances and popular in the nation beginning in the nineteenth century, epithets that also inflected stereotypical references to blacks in American film during the twentieth century. Such stereotypes saturated American material culture in advertisements for a variety of goods and commodity items, from foods to tobacco, toys, and soap. *Still Trippin'* ironically recasts a litany of verbal sound bites and visual images that were routinely associated with American minstrel performances.

The residual impact of these stereotypes in shaping images of blacks in contemporary film and popular culture is compellingly critiqued in Spike Lee's 2000 film *Bamboozled,* which examines white film and television producers' insistence on stereotyping blacks, while also critiquing black executives in the entertainment industry who internalize such stereotypes and sanction and commoditize such scripts of blackness. In the film, the black television producer Pierre Delacroix produces a neominstrel show set on an Alabama plantation called the *Alabama Porch Monkeys,* which gains popularity by reviving blackface performance practices, invoking some of the most egregious racial stereotypes, which historically inflected popular representations of black identity in the United States.

Against this backdrop, it is provocative to ponder the extent to which Harvey's comedy show reinscribes and reproduces conventional stereotypes of the black body steeped in historical southern ideologies. While Harvey's stand-up show occurs in the northern state of New Jersey, he draws on a range of familiar southern stereotypes for its narrative content. I suggest that the explicit and recurrent use of terms such as *monkey,* along with repeated uses of the term *black* as a color epithet, draw to some extent on minstrel motifs in *Still Trippin.'* Harvey's mimicry of monkeys through pantomiming relies on the lingering presence of such images in cultural memory and recasts such ideological performance practices before a contemporary audience in the twenty-first century. His insistent reference to the monkey for purposes of comic relief and his relating them to black masculine bodies, beginning with his dialogue on

Duncan, underscore a limited vision for thinking about and imagining black subjectivity apart from conventional raced, classed, gendered, and sexual stereotypes of the black male body.

At the outset of *Still Trippin'*, Harvey suggests that he will present a more honest and genuine dialogue than that on the radio show. He implies that on the radio he must temper his opinions and words, being forced to wear the proverbial mask and to veil his views.[15] It is crucial to differentiate Harvey's private and personal identity from his comedy-stage and radio-talk-show-host personas and to recognize the public and performative aspects of the latter roles. This distinction makes clear that aspects of his dialogues on stage, including the language he uses, may serve distinct rhetorical and performative purposes and may not necessarily reflect his identity or thoroughly articulate his views. Yet, precisely because of his prominence and popularity in the world of entertainment, it is crucial to ask what is at stake in his rhetorical construction of Michael Clark Duncan in relation to conventional raced, sexed, and gendered stereotypes of black masculinity under the guise of critiquing them by questioning the actor's decision to portray what Harvey refers to in his routine as "a monkey in a damn movie." This segment of the show suggests that maintaining racial dignity and resisting racist images are not as important for African Americans as personally profiting from commoditizing racist images and making money.

Harvey mobilizes highly conventional ideologies of race, gender, sexuality, and class in constructing Duncan as a menacing, potentially threatening and violent black man in the skit, along with demonstrating, mocking and drawing comic relief from homosexual panic in his performance, notwithstanding the heterosexual identification of himself and Duncan. In his construction of Duncan, Harvey alludes to the historical stereotype of the black buck, valued primarily for his sexual prowess in the context of antebellum slavery for having physical strength and power. This segment invokes and reinforces conventional racial images of black masculinity as primitive and bestial, including the image of the black rapist, that were established in the postbellum South.[16] Harvey invokes sexuality in describing Duncan by drawing heavily on sexual imagery in casting himself as someone who is vulnerable to being attacked by Duncan. This segment in *Still Trippin'* demonstrates the continuing influence of southern-based ideologies of black masculinity in the millennial era and their currency in black popular culture, revealing levels on which they have been nationalized and globalized.

JUNGLE LOVE

The comedian and actor Eddie Murphy's 1987 stand-up comedy film *Raw* is notable for circulating a primitivist, animalistic, hypersexual narrative of African femininity. It is useful to consider that narrative as a backdrop for Harvey's representation of Africa in *Still Trippin'*. In the show's dialogue, which follows up Murphy's 1983 stand-up show *Delirious,* Murphy muses:

> If I ever get married, I have to go off
> to the woods of Africa
> and find me some crazy,
> naked, zebra bitch
> that knows nothing about money.
> She got to be butt naked on a zebra
> with a big bone in her nose
> and a big plate lip
> and a big, fucked-up Afro!

Murphy compares the hairstyle he envisions for his African bride to Angela Davis's iconic Afro hairstyle from the early 1970s, indicates a preference to find her "butt naked on the zebra," suggests that the marriage would be advertised in the media with headlines such as "Murphy Marries Bush Bitch," and underscores that keeping her away from the influence of American women would be a priority for him:

> I'm gonna bring her home
> and lock her up in the house.
> You go off to Africa
> and get you a bush woman,
> you can't let her mingle
> with American women.
> Because they'll change her shit up.
> American women stick together.
> Last thing they wanna see
> is you got some trained
> bush bitch in your house.

It is notable that Murphy, when speaking from the standpoint of his stage persona, imagines and idealizes African women as being subaltern and submissive. His logic in this skit reveals a fantasy of African women as being wild, primitive, and hypersexual and by extension links such scripts to Africa as a place. That such representations were propagated during the 1980s, when an African nation such as Ethiopia was mentioned often in national headlines in relation to the issues of hunger and famine, as South Africa was in relation to the issue of apartheid, suggests the irony of Murphy's caricatures of the continent in these popular productions. Aspects of films featuring Murphy, including *Trading Places* (1984) and *Coming to America* (1988), both romanticize Africa and reinscribe such primitivist narratives.[17] This logic about Africa that describes it as a jungle is in effect replicated in *Still Trippin'*, revealing levels on which African American entertainers have internalized, appropriated, and recast such colonialist and imperialist narratives of Africa as a "dark continent" and promoted such ideological representations of Africa in black popular culture.

If the opening dialogue of *Still Trippin'* is inflected by rhetoric that draws on conventional racialist scripts in the southern imaginary that construct black masculinity as being dark, dangerous, and bestial through its portrait of Duncan, the final dialogue relies on colonialist and imperialist narratives of Africa as a "dark" and primitive continent. Significantly, this narrative unfolds against the backdrop of Harvey's romanticizing description of Africa as a place where "when you get off the plane, you feel immediately at home," and "where the origin of mankind started," framing a trip to the continent for blacks in the diaspora as "spiritual" and "going back home." Harvey urges his audience members, "Save your money and go." As he puts it, "That's where we from. When you go there, you going back home."

While Harvey reconstructs an interview on his radio show in describing the dialogue with Duncan, he recollects a letter in discussing his trip to Africa, paralleling his emphasis on "the Strawberry Letter" and the "e-mail bag" on his radio show in earlier segments of the performance. The letter he describes is the letter sent to him by the Zimbali Lodge in Durban prior to his trip. He highlights the initial section, which underscores the need for visitors to Africa to be immunized. A primitivist narrative of Africa emerges, displacing his romantic description, as he cautions his audience members to be sure to get any immunizations and to take any medicines stipulated to protect themselves from contracting illnesses due to bites from insects: "Carry yo' ass to yo' doctor and take all the shots they got, and every pill they give you, 'cause when you get over there, they have stuff for you that you are not able to deal with. They got insects over there that when they bite you, yo' ass die." Moreover, he describes seeing mosquitos much larger than the ones typically seen in the United States. Other precautions that he summarizes in the letter from the Zimbali Lodge include leaving pets at home "because we have all the wildlife you need" and the importance of staying on "the lighted path" and going out with a partner when walking at night.

Emphasizing a passenger's dog, along with potentially deadly insects, contributes to Harvey's primitivist portrait of Africa that coalesces in this segment of the performance. In describing the content of the letter, Harvey notes that when you go to the jungle, "everything over there, in order to eat, they have to kill something. Ain't nobody over there setting out no bowls of milk or nothing. Here, Kitty Kitty, here, Kitty Kitty. . . . They see what they want, they go tear it apart, and they eat it, so don't bring your dogs." After talking about the content of the letter, Harvey begins the story of what happened at the Zimbali Lodge by describing a passenger who was on his flight boldly flouting and violating the pet policy. He begins this main portion of the narrative related to the Zimbali Lodge by noting having been shocked when he and his wife saw a "white lady" board the flight to Durban with a dog: "She get on the plane, and what does she have on her arm but that little bag, with the little damn dog in it." In mentioning this passenger openly violating the rules, implicitly on the basis of her social privilege, related to her racial identity as well as to her elite class background, Harvey creates a vivid, animated image of her toting the dog in its carrying case. He acknowledges that his wife dissuaded him from speaking up to remind the woman of the pet policy at the Zimbali Lodge and says that he was most concerned that the dog would bark on the flight and keep him awake.

Harvey describes the Zimbali Lodge conservatory as an "incredible place" located in the jungle, with "no fence, no gates." "This really a little bit too much Africa for me," he recalls. He goes on to describe its location as being "in the bush," a place that he had anticipated just driving out to see and then returning from to enjoy the comfort of a downtown hotel for room service, rather than actually waking up in the midst of the so-called bush, and admits finding the accommodations "very uncomfortable." While this urban setting represents the ideal accommodations that he would prefer to have in Africa, he expresses appreciation for the special suite to which he and his wife have been assigned at the Zimbali Lodge because he is regarded as "the king" of comedy.[18] It is notable that the description of the conservatory on the lodge's website, a section of which is quoted in the epigraph above, emphasizes its location in the "forest." The description also overviews the conservatory's wildlife: "Animal life within the forest reserve include bush buck, blue duiker, bushbaby, vervet monkey, banded mongoose and even wild pig."[19]

Harvey mentions his insistence on being escorted to the suite ahead of his wife, who had gone to the gift shop, because of his excitement about being in Africa for the first time. He explained to the perplexed desk clerk:

> Hey man, we going to Africa for the first time, I got to go get set up down here. 'Cause we gon', you know, gon' break the cottage in. First time in Africa loving. We fin' to do some jungle. I got to go set up for some jungle love down here. I'm fin' to have some wild stuff going on in here. You know, I got to get baby oil up on the walls and everything. We gon' be sliding on the walls on baby oil. I'm wild when I'm in there. You, know, I'm in Africa, let's do something we ain't never done before, you know. Let's get some banana peels, stuff like that, throw it in the water. I'm gon' go down here and get it set up real sexy so when she come down here, we can go ahead and get started.

This revelation led the clerk to describe him as "a player." The term *jungle love* echoes the title of the hit song by the Minneapolis-based group The Time, led by Morris Day, which was featured on the soundtrack of Prince's 1984 film *Purple Rain*. Moreover, it evokes the title song by Stevie Wonder from Spike Lee's 1991 film *Jungle Fever*, which describes the interracial desire between blacks and whites that is primarily driven by sexual stereotypes, with an emphasis on white women's attraction to black men, whom they perceive to be hypersexual. Both songs acknowledge the longstanding primitive view of black sexuality within the Western imaginary. Harvey's idea that Africa is a catalyst for a wild and free sexuality for him and his wife also very much reflects these impressions.

Harvey describes being left alone at his suite door by the clerk with his bags and a key card that he discovered was not working. "And then I look around and I realize just how dark it get in Africa. See, this ain't no regular night time. When it's dark in Africa, it don't be night it be blue-black. It be damn near burgundy out there. It's damn near burgundy. You ain't never seen no night like this. I turned around and realized, man, it's dark as hell out here!" Harvey then goes on to imitate the "jungle sounds" that one begins to hear in the dark. He leads his audience to imagine his fear, a fear they might experience in a similar situation, standing alone at night in such close proximity to a jungle in Africa. He describes the "lighted path" as being lit only every forty yards and being "pitch black" otherwise.

Significantly, the monkey motif from *Still Trippin'* resurfaces assertively in the performance at this juncture. Harvey muses: "I'm standing in this spot and then I think it was a monkey. A monkey went swinging by on a vine and its tail rubbed me 'cross my lips." He indicates that his fear escalated. "Another monkey came up behind me and took his little monkey hand and stuck it straight up in my ass." Harvey describes having a panic attack in which he exclaimed, "The monkey fin' to rape me. The monkeys is violating me!" He describes being upset when the clerk came to check on him and asked what was wrong and admits calling him a "black bastard" because the problem with leaving him alone with the monkeys should have been obvious to him. Hence, the performance's final segment echoes and repeats aspects of its opening segment by saliently mentioning the monkey as a motif while discussing Harvey's own endangered body, which is framed as being potentially at risk.

Whereas in the opening segment Duncan's dark black, masculine body serves as the potential menace, in the final segment Harvey presents the monkey in the dark jungle as being the primary threat to his body. His recourse to rape metaphors also provides continuity in these two segments that frame *Still Trippin'*. In his panic about rape by a monkey, Harvey also alludes, of course, to the myth that AIDS originated in Africa as a result of sex with a monkey.

The story Harvey narrates about the visit to the Zimbali Lodge decenters him, however, when he shifts to focus on the "white lady" with whom he and his wife boarded the flight to Durban, whom he has mentioned earlier. He notes that when he saw her again in the lobby at the lodge, the main difference he noted was that the carrying case was empty, and he inferred that something had happened to the dog. At this point the woman, having insisted that her dog be found and returned, became irate with the clerk and referred to him as an "asshole" and a "black bastard." Harvey describes intervening and taking charge of the situation after the clerk reminded the woman of the policy prohibiting household pets: "Listen to me. Let me help you. I picked the bag up and zipped it up. I said, listen here. Take the bag on back to your room. Your dog gone. Ain't no more damn dog. . . . Your damn dog is gone." Harvey says that he told the woman that her dog had been eaten when it went into the bushes.

While the dog is the second animal that Harvey references and draws on in what shapes up to be a primitivist narrative of Africa, Harvey concludes the segment by returning to the monkey, the animal he invokes most saliently throughout his entire stand-up show. While the complications related to checking into his hotel room and the loss of the woman's dog are the main topics that emerge as he reflects on the first evening at the lodge, he describes waking up the next morning feeling excited about having a golfing game in Africa and "to see what that's like." He recounts leaving for the Zimbali golf course, located uphill and a mile away, in a typical one-speed golf cart early in the morning, when it was still dark. He recalls his lingering fear and being "traumatized" about the monkeys he had seen the night before, noting that en route to the golf course "I see some monkeys, but it's a bunch of 'em. And on each side of the road was these two monkey troops. It was about 40 monkeys on each side and they ass was up there arguing. I mean they was having a full-blown argument. Look, I'm from the projects. I know a argument when I see one." Harvey mimics their movements, including their preparations to attack each other, by yelling out and jumping across the stage. "Now the monkeys is closing in." Harvey describes his increasing panic as he tried to drive his golf cart past the monkeys, panic that increased exponentially when they shifted their attention to him.

Describing a scene in which he was thoroughly embattled with the monkeys, he says: "The monkeys done got behind me. I'm fin' to cry. All of a sudden, a monkey ran 'cross my lap.... He did it so fast that it scared me." Out of fear, he urinated on himself, and he became even more afraid when another monkey jumped on the golf cart and stuck its tail in his ear. "And then this monkey jumped up on the golf cart and took his hand and slapped my ass so hard, pow!" He says that after he grabbed a golf club with the intention to kill a monkey to make an example of it, one took it from him and threw it into the bushes. He describes continuing to urinate as his panic increased and even defecating as the biggest monkey in the group jumped out to attack him. In invoking encounters with monkeys, Harvey draws on hyperbole and aspects of the grotesque. Such strategies are particularly useful in this final segment.

Harvey stages *Still Trippin'* in the United States, but the show's taping and circulation on cable television networks such as HBO and in DVD format has allowed it to reach a broader audience. Its mention of sites such as South Africa invokes geographies located in the global South and underscores all the more the importance of comparatively examining Harvey's reliance on conventional raced, sexed, and gendered southern stereotypes alongside primitivist narratives of Africa that recast colonialist discourses in his performance. That Harvey, one of contemporary entertainment's most popular southern and African American comedians, fails to offer a more subversive or visionary script of black identity, essentially mirroring and repeating the conventional stereotypes of black subjectivity, suggests a crisis in black representation in contemporary popular culture in the comedy genre. The continuity in representations of Africa as a primitive and hypersexual place that we see in Eddie Murphy's and Harvey's routines reveals that very little has changed in black comedy's representations of Africa over the past several decades. The strategies for representing Africa in stand-up comedy, including a reliance on terminology such as *the bush,* have largely remained intact. At the same time, Harvey's performance in *Still Trippin'* reveals that a profoundly ambivalent and reactionary portrait of Africa lingers in the African American consciousness.

NOTES

Epigraph: Information about the Zimbali Lodge can be found at the conservatory's website, www .fairmont.com/zimbali-lodge/.

1. For a comprehensive study of African Americans in comedy, see Mel Watkins's *On the Real Side: A History of African American in Comedy* (Chicago: Chicago Review Press, 1999). See also Watkins, *African American Humor: The Best of Black Comedy from Slavery to Today* (Chicago: Chicago Review Press, 2002).

2. Andrew J. Yawn, "ASU Graduation: Steve Harvey Awarded Doctorate," *Montgomery (AL) Advertiser,* 8 May 2016, www.montgomeryadvertiser.com/story/news/local/community/2016/05/07/asu-graduation-steve-harvey-awarded-doctorate/83991026/.

3. See Charlotte Triggs, "Steve Harvey: His Incredible Journey," *People,* 14 October 2013, 75–78.

4. See Steve Reddicliffe, "Multimedia King? Survey Says, Steve Harvey." *New York Times,* December 24, 2010. The article can be accessed at the link www.nytimes.com/2010/12/26/arts/television/26harvey.html?pagewanted=all&_r=0.

5. Steve Harvey, *Act Like a Lady, Think Like a Man: What Men Really Think About Love, Relationships, Intimacy, and Commitment* (New York: Amistad, 2009).

6. Steve Harvey, *Straight Talk, No Chaser: How to Find, Keep and Understand a Man* (New York: Amistad, 2011).

7. Duncan died in Los Angeles on 3 September 2012.

8. Steve Harvey, *Still Trippin',* dir. Leslie Small (Codeblack Entertainment, 2002). All quotations from the performance are from this DVD.

9. For a sustained dialogue on the black uplift movement, see Kevin K. Gaines, *Uplifting the Race: Black Leadership, Politics, and Culture in the Twentieth Century* (Chapel Hill: University of North Carolina Press, 1996).

10. This episode also recalls an episode in Charles Fuller's *A Soldier's Play* (New York: Hill & Wang, 1982) that the character Sergeant Vernon Waters describes. According to Waters, during World War I, while stationed in France, white soldiers paid a black southerner to parade around naked making monkey sounds, pinned a tail on him, and dubbed him "Moonshine, King of the Monkeys" to shame and humiliate him and his fellow black soldiers after they had won decorations. I discuss the implications of this scene in my book *Black Masculinity and the U.S. South: From Uncle Tom to Gangsta* (Athens: University of Georgia Press, 2007).

11. Henry Louis Gates Jr., *The Signifying Monkey: A Theory of African-American Literary Criticism* (New York: Oxford University Press, 1988).

12. See Philip Sherwell, "New York Post Apologizes over 'Racist' Barack Obama Cartoon," *Telegraph,* 20 February 2009, www.telegraph.co.uk/news/worldnews/barackobama/4724866/New-York -Post-apologises-over-racist-Barack-Obama-cartoon.html.

13. Crowley, a white police officer, went to Gates's home in response to a call from a woman in the neighborhood about a possible break-in. Gates, who had just returned from a long trip to China, had been trying, with the aid of his driver, to open his jammed front door. When the officer refused to accept the two forms of identification that Gates offered and asked him to step outside, Gates concluded that he was being targeted racially. The officer arrested him when he spoke up for himself and protested the situation. The charges were dropped, but the situation led to a national debate about racial profiling in the ensuing days and weeks. President Obama, during a national news conference, said that Crowley's arrest of Gates, a friend of Obama's, had been "stupid," which led to a firestorm of critique from law-enforcement officials around the nation. In an effort to resolve the situation, Obama famously invited both men to the White House for a "beer summit."

14. In July 2013, Head won the lawsuit, receiving a settlement of $4.5 million. See Stephen Caesar, "Black Surgeon to get $4.5 Million in Racial Bias Suit," *Los Angeles Times,* 18 July 2013, articles. latimes.com/2013/jul/18/local/la-me-ucla-settle-20130719.

15. Here I refer to motifs in African American literary history established in Paul Laurence Dunbar's poem "We Wear the Mask" (1896) and W. E. B. Du Bois's classic book *The Souls of Black Folk* (1903).

16. Angela Y. Davis, *Women, Race & Class* (New York: Vintage Books, 1983).

17. It is notable that Murphy presents a romantic narrative of Africa in the lyrics and video for his 1993 song "I Was a King."

18. This title comes from the 2000 film *The Original Kings of Comedy,* directed by Spike Lee, featuring Harvey alongside other popular stand-up comedians, including D. L. Hughley, Cedric the Entertainer, and Bernie Mac, which was filmed in Charlotte, North Carolina, over two nights.

19. See the Zimbali Lodge website, www.fairmont.com/zimbali-lodge/.

CONTRIBUTORS

TRENT BROWN is an associate professor of American studies at the Missouri University of Science and Technology. He is a coauthor, with Reverend Ed King, of *Ed King's Mississippi: Behind the Scenes of Freedom Summer* (University Press of Mississippi, 2014) and the editor of *White Masculinity in the Recent South*, also published by the Louisiana State University Press.

STEPHANIE M. CHALIFOUX is an assistant professor of history at the University of West Georgia. She teaches US women's history, women's labor history, and the history of sexuality. Her current work explores sex work, identity, and the US South in the post–World War II era.

FRANCESCA GAMBER has a BA in Afro-American studies from Harvard University and a PhD in historical studies from Southern Illinois University at Carbondale. She is the principal of Bard High School Early College in Baltimore, Maryland, and an adjunct faculty member at the University of Baltimore.

KATHERINE HENNINGER is associate professor of American literature at Louisiana State University, where she specializes in southern literature, visual culture, and women's and gender studies. She is the author of *Ordering the Façade: Photography and Contemporary Southern Women's Writing* (University of North Carolina Press, 2007) and numerous articles on photography, gender and sexuality, postcolonial theory, and southern literature and culture. She is currently at work on two monographs: *Southern Sexualities and the National Imagination* and *Made Strangely Beautiful: Southern Childhood in U.S. Literature and Film*.

RICHARD HOURIGAN is a teaching associate at Coastal Carolina University, where he teaches courses on African American history, South Carolina history, and southern politics. He holds a PhD in history from the University of Alabama. His current research explores the effect of tourism on a changing South during the modern civil rights movement.

KRYSTAL HUMPHREYS is an assistant professor at the New Mexico Military Institute in Roswell. She received her PhD in history from Texas Tech University in 2013. Her work centers on the intersections between youth culture, gender, religion, and conservatism in the United States.

MATT MILLER is a musician and an independent scholar of popular music, race, and the American South based in Atlanta. His PhD dissertation on rap music and local identity in New Orleans was revised and published by the University of Massachusetts Press in 2012.

ABIGAIL PARSONS is the founding director of the LGBTQIA Resource Center at the Georgia Institute of Technology in Atlanta, where she coordinates programs, develops policy, and provides direct services that impact the inclusion and well-being of LGBTQIA students and employees. A sought-after speaker and educator on issues of queer and trans inclusion strategy, she currently serves on the board of directors for the Equality Foundation of Georgia. She received her PhD in women's, gender, and sexuality studies from Emory University, where her research focused on race, gender, and sexuality in contemporary southern novels and films. Her current work examines narratives of queer death and survival.

RICHÉ RICHARDSON is currently an associate professor in the Africana Studies and Research Center at Cornell University. Her essays have appeared in a range of books and journals. Her first book, *Black Masculinity and the U.S. South: From Uncle Tom to Gangsta* (University of Georgia Press, 2007), was highlighted by *Choice* as one of the Outstanding Academic Titles of 2008. Since 2005, she has served as co-editor of the New Southern Studies book series at the University of Georgia Press.

CLAIRE STROM holds the Rapetti-Trunzo Chair of History and is director of general education at Rollins College. She served as editor for *Agricultural History* for thirteen years and has written extensively on American history during the Gilded Age and the Progressive Era.

WHITNEY STRUB is an associate professor of history and director of the Women's and Gender Studies Program at Rutgers University–Newark. He is the author of *Perversion for Profit: The Politics of Pornography and the Rise of the New Right* (Columbia University Press, 2011) and *Obscenity Rules:* Roth v. United States *and the Long Struggle over Sexual Expression* (University Press of Kansas, 2013), as well as coeditor of *Porno Chic and the Sex Wars: American Sexual Representation in the 1970s* (University of Massachusetts Press, 2016). His work has appeared in several scholarly journals, as well as at *Salon, Vice,* and *OutHistory.*

JERRY WATKINS holds degrees in history and American studies from Georgia State University and King's College London. He is currently a visiting assistant professor of history at the College of William & Mary, where his teaching focuses on sexuality, social justice, and the twentieth century. He continues to research and write about queer southerners and to work with local LGBTQ-history projects. His forthcoming book, *The Queer Redneck Riviera,* explores the relationship between sexuality, tourism, and community building in Florida's Panhandle.

INDEX

INDEX